Sondheim on Music

Minor Details
and Major Decisions

Mark Eden Horowitz

The Scarecrow Press, Inc.
Lanham, Maryland, and Oxford
In Association with
The Library of Congress
2003

SCARECROW PRESS, INC.

Published in the United States of America
by Scarecrow Press, Inc.
A Member of the Rowman & Littlefield Publishing Group
4501 Forbes Blvd., Suite 200, Lanham, Maryland 20706
www.scarecrowpress.com

PO Box 317
Oxford
OX2 9RU, UK

British Cataloging in Publication Information Available

Library of Congress Cataloging-in-Publication Data

Horowitz, Mark Eden
    Sondheim on music : minor details and major decisions / Mark Eden Horowitz.
    p. cm.
Includes discography (p.) and index.
    ISBN 0-8108-4437-0 (alk. paper)
    1. Sondheim, Stephen—Interviews. 2. Composers—United States—Interviews. 3.
Musicals—United States—Analysis, appreciation.
    4. Sondheim, Stephen—Criticism and interpretation. I. Horowitz, Mark Eden. II. Title.
    ML410.S6872 A5 2002
    782.1'4'092—dc21

                                                                        2002010564

∞™ The paper used in this publication meets the minimum requirements
of American National Standard for Information Sciences—Permanence of
Paper for Printed Library Materials, ANSI/NISO Z39.48-1992.
Manufactured in the United States of America.

Contents

Acknowledgments

There are many people to thank—people without whom this book either would not have happened, would have been less than it is, or would have been less gratifying to work on. They include:

My wife, Loie Gardiner Clark, for her constant love and encouragement, her extraordinary skills as a grammarian and editor, and her gracious relinquishment of the dining room table.

My parents, Judy and Terry Horowitz, for raising me with the arts, supporting me in my choices, loving me unconditionally, and exemplifying a good and meaningful life.

Steve Clar for his efficiency, hospitality, and insight.

Copyist, Chuck Gallagher, for his accuracy, ingenuity, and care.

My musician friends, who helped, explained, suggested, and understood: Rob Fisher, Jon Kalbfleisch, Michael Lavine, Bruce Pomahac, Larry Moore, Jeff Saver, and Russell Warner.

Many at the Library of Congress who in various ways made possible and supported this project: Abraham and Julienne Krasnoff, members of the James Madison Council, for the grant that made the initial interviews possible; James W. Billington, Winston Tabb, Diane Nester Kresh, Jon Newsom, Elizabeth H. Auman, and Vicky Risner for being far-sighted professionals who genuinely care about the work the Library does and believe in the importance of projects like this one; Iris Newsom for being both a careful and caring editor; my colleagues and friends Raymond White and

Loras Schissel who generously shared their knowledge and expertise; and Samuel Brylawski, a friend who has been my mentor at the Library and a touchstone in my life.

I thank—fundamentally—Stephen Sondheim, for his work and the many ways it has informed and enriched my personal and professional life; and the precious gift of his time.

Introduction

While Sondheim and James Lapine were creating *Sunday in the Park with George*, the two went to the Art Institute of Chicago and stood with three of the museum's curators before the miraculous canvas of Seurat's *A Sunday on La Grand Jatte*. "What is that object up there?" they asked, pointing to an indistinct object in the middle distance. Instantly and simultaneously, the curators gave three different responses: a stove, a waffle iron, a . . . whatever. Sondheim and Lapine would eventually reimagine this comic incident in their musical's second act.

Similarly, such disagreements are common among musical scholars in deciphering composers' manuscripts. What does *this* piece of marginalia mean? How should *that* symbol be interpreted? How was *that* chord supposed to function? Rarely do we have the composer's direct commentary on how he approached his work and what his notes—both musical and textual—literally mean. After Stephen Sondheim generously agreed to bequeath his manuscripts to the Library of Congress, a series of videotaped interviews with the composer was proposed with the intention of anticipating the questions of future scholars. As such, and unlike the many, many interviews Sondheim has granted to date, these were never intended for publication but rather to serve as a complementary crib to the manuscripts. On that basis the project went forward with Sondheim's cooperation and the support of a grant from the Library of Congress.

What makes these interviews unique is their exclusive focus on Sondheim's work as a composer. Even so, the interviews became far more wide-ranging than I had imagined, with Sondheim discussing not only the nitty-gritty of how to interpret his sketches and manuscripts, but how he goes about the process of writing and composing—in short, his thoughts and observations about the art and craft of the musical. It was only after the interviews were completed and I began transcribing them that I realized they would be of interest and use to a broader audience; hence, this volume. Using clarity as my guide and goal, I edited the verbatim transcripts—eliminating verbal tics, false starts, and some repetitions; completing sentences where their endings seemed obvious; occasionally reordering clauses within a sentence and adjusting grammar accordingly. I am grateful for Sondheim's willingness and care in going through this edition to clarify his meaning even further.

After many months of planning, preliminary examination of Sondheim's manuscripts, and consultation with scholars, musicians, and some of Sondheim's associates, the interviews were recorded over three days in October 1997 in Sondheim's Turtle Bay home—with his manuscripts close to hand. These manuscripts include sketches, drafts, and fair copies for individual numbers, and general sketches for each show where he experiments with thematic material, accompaniment figures, and other musical ideas. We began by looking at the manuscripts for *Passion*, at the time Sondheim's most recently completed score. Assuming there to be an evolution in his work as a composer, I wanted to make sure we captured where he was at that moment as opposed to where he began. I also assumed the details of the later works would be freshest in Sondheim's mind, and that many of the questions and answers would reflect backward on earlier shows.

As a result, we spent far more time on *Passion* than any other score, though this first long chapter includes many digressions about other shows. From there we worked backward through *Assassins, Into the Woods, Sunday in the Park with George, Sweeney Todd,* and *Pacific Overtures*—each show becoming a chapter here. *Merrily We Roll Along* was skipped because of limited time, but most of the questions raised by my examination of its manuscripts were effectively answered in the context of other shows. His earlier work, although often alluded to, was excluded by the constraints of tightly budgeted time and resources. However, the chapters "Interlude" and "Finale" cover a number of more general questions that I felt were important to ask but that did not easily fit into our discussions of the specific shows.

The fact that we paused every half hour for the cameraman to reload tape cartridges might explain some seemingly odd breaks or disjointed moments. Also, this is the record of a freely flowing conversation; therefore, it is not as structured as an entirely scholarly book would be. Early on I decided not to attempt to direct the conversation *too* much but to simply enable one thing to lead to another. If Sondheim had something he wanted to say, I wanted to hear it.

*   *   *

The following chapters tend to start with details about musical composition and become more general as they continue. One of the benefits of this book over the videotapes is that it includes excerpts from the musical scores and sketches under discussion. Some of you picking up this book might be discouraged by the fact that it begins talking about music on a fairly technical level. Be reassured that there is much that follows that requires no musical expertise at all. And to those pleased by the initial focus, it too reappears throughout.

For those unfamiliar with "figured bass" or "classical" musical notation who wish to understand more clearly those examples and portions of the discussion that deal with it, let me offer a few explanatory notes. Roman numerals are used to represent the various chords corresponding with each tone of a scale—I through VII. Thus, in the key of C, I is a chord based on C, II is a chord based on D, III is a chord based on E, et cetera. This allows progressions to be rooted in any key. While some composers who use this method differentiate the notation of major and minor by using upper case Roman numerals for major chords and lower case for minor, Sondheim does not. What he does do, which is more rare, is to precede most Roman numeral chords with an upper case or lower case letter indicating on which key (or temporary "tonicization," as he puts it) the chord is based. Sondheim's "gII_7" indicates a 7th chord based on the second step of a G-minor scale, or A-C-E♭-G. Subscript numbers 6, 7, 9, 11, and 13 indicate the color or type of chord, whereas numbers that begin in the superscript indicate the inversion. Thus, in the key of C, a I_6 indicates a C-major chord with a 6th: C-E-G-A. And a I^6 indicates a C-major triad in 1st inversion: E-G-C. A $^6_4$ is a triad in 2nd inversion, $^6_3$ is a 7th chord in first inversion, $^6_4$ is a 7th chord in 2nd inversion, and $^6_2$ is a 7th chord in 3rd inversion. These numbers indicate the intervals between the top notes to the lowest note in descending order. Thus, an E-major 7th chord in second inversion reads down: G♯-E-D♯-B, B to G♯ being a 6th, B to E being a 4th, and B to D♯ being a third. All notes of a chord are not necessarily to be sounded, though that usually cannot be determined in the sketches.

As Sondheim states clearly in these interviews, he views himself as a very tonal composer. The notations in his sketches are basically a shorthand for spelling chords quickly during the compositional process and do not necessarily reflect how he *thinks* of the chords functioning. The sketches often include alternate harmonizations that he wishes to consider, either with alternatives written below or in parentheses.

Sondheim is a rare, if not unique, composer in the world of musical theater and song writing. He creates a discrete musical language and vocabulary for every one of his musicals. He invests enormous intellect and effort into each melody, harmony, and rhythm; each spelling of a chord; the accompaniment figures and in which registers they are placed; and every dynamic. He plans how extended numbers will develop and evolve so that they hold together and are satisfying without becoming relentless or boring. As his own lyricist and as a dramatist who collaborates with librettists and directors, he writes music that is true to his characters and their situations. He is impeccable in his prosody, matching music and lyric in intent, inflection, and stress. Yet as individual as each score is, the unmistakable Sondheim voice sings through even his cleverest pastiches.

One of the pleasant surprises of these interviews was Sondheim's reflections on the work of some of the musical theater composers who came before him. No other composer has been more fortunate in his personal connections to the tradition. Sondheim's mentor was Oscar Hammerstein II, and his musical collaborators included Leonard Bernstein, Jule Styne, and Richard Rodgers. Dorothy Fields was a family friend, and we know he admired and communicated with talents as diverse as Bernard Herrmann, Cole Porter, and Frank Loesser. Stepping back another generation, among Hammerstein's collaborators were Vincent Youmans, Rudolf Friml, Jerome Kern, and Sigmund Romberg—*his* mentor, in turn, having been Otto Harbach. Sondheim is connected as directly as possible to the entire history of the musical—in far fewer than "six degrees of separation." That unbroken chain makes his insights and perceptions all the more valuable and rare.

During breaks in the interviews, Sondheim made two comments to me of which I am particularly proud. As these were not taped, I cannot swear to his exact words, but their sense resonates in my memory. First: "A lot of the questions you're asking, no one's ever asked me before." And later: "I'm saying things in these interviews I didn't know I thought, until you asked the question and I had to ask myself: What *do* I think about that?" I am grateful to Sondheim for the thought he put into these interviews and his permission to share them with you.

Part I

THE INTERVIEWS

Chapter One

Passion

MH: I'd like to start with your sketches for the opening number of *Passion*, "Clara/Giorgio I," which in the published score is "Happiness (Part I)." You wrote "Big X" above this sketch and it reminded me of Gershwin writing "GT" for "good tune" on his sketches. Is there any similarity in meaning?

Example 1.1

SS: No, that mark usually means that I want that idea to go with an accompaniment. This is from a sheet of vocal ideas for Clara and Giorgio, and probably the "X" means that it corresponds with an "X" someplace else in an accompaniment figure, or a few bars of accompaniment. So that I know that I want *this* to go with that accompaniment figure as opposed to another. The "Big" means it's to be the big statement. Each of the lines is a separate vocal idea. I separate them, as one does, between staves, with little parallel lines. And I sketch in little words that come from the lyric sheet to remind myself that this theme is for that particular set of lyrics.

MH: If you're working on the same section, why would you have alternate sketches in different keys?

SS: I probably have outlined a harmonic scheme someplace else. And sometimes I change because I realize that it's going out of a vocal register or that it's something that's awkward. For example, suddenly the melody will get too low, and yet if it's still within an octave-and-six or an-octave-and-five—something that a singer can do—I'll leave it in that key. But if the tessitura gets too low or too high I'll switch the keys around before I get the key that I'm working in locked in my head. So, if I'm writing something in E-flat, and I realize the melody's getting too low, before it gets too entrenched in an E-flatness in my head, I'll take it up to a G major and rewrite the accompaniment in G major (or sketch out the accompaniment in G major) and then start the melodic flow going in G major.

MH: Once you've completed a song, and it's in a show, and the key has been changed to suit the performer, do you still think of it in the original key?

SS: Yes, if I'm asked to play it at the piano, I'll play it in the key I wrote it. Often, I will write in a key that I can sing. You'll notice in the manuscripts over the years the keys get lower. I used to be able to sing up to an E, even on a full stomach, and now I cannot get up above a C and my voice has darkened. I can sing lower now, but I'm essentially a bass-baritone. So, for demonstration purposes, I have to write in something that I can play and sing—to play to producers, directors, collaborators, et cetera.

MH: Do you think of different keys as having different feelings?

SS: There are a number of things I feel about keys. Flat keys are easier to read and play in; I don't know why, but that's generally true—you'll find most musicians will say that. I switch keys from song to song—I try to, unless I'm deliberately making a large scheme of key relationships which I did in some of the longer pieces in *Passion*. If I'm just doing a score of songs, I will deliberately write in a key that I haven't written in for a while. I write partly at the piano and partly away from the piano. In the early days, particularly my first six or eight shows, I would write mostly at the piano, and my fingers would fall—my muscle memory getting too habituated—I found myself writing the same chords. I'm not very good at keyboard harmony. I never took keyboard harmony, I only took theoretical harmony. That serves me well, because if I have to make a modulation from C to E-flat, I have to find my way, and in finding my way, it gets some kind of personal statement, some freshness, in it. It may not be the way that other people would do it, and sometimes its very clumsiness will become part of that. Somebody who's got keyboard harmony can just glibly (that's both good and bad) get from one to the other in sixty-four different ways. But, if I want to get from C to E-flat, in the key of E-flat, and I write another song in E-flat and I want to get from C to E-flat, then my fingers are likely to go in the same places. So I deliberately will write it in E major. When I feel I'm getting stale I go into sharp keys because they're so foreign and scary.

MH: When you were writing these sketches for *Passion*, would you have been at the piano, or could you have been either at the piano or away?

SS: Generally I feel my way into an accompaniment figure at the piano. I know in this case (this is the opening of *Passion*) I wanted to use bugle calls throughout the show because it takes place mostly in a military post, and a bugle, as you know, is just the triad. So I wanted to start with that. Since it starts with Giorgio, who's an army man, in bed with his mistress, it also has to be a romantic piece—a post-coital piece. In order to do that and not make it just sound military, I put in a dissonant accompaniment in the left hand, but I kept the bugle idea in the right hand. So you get this, which

Example 1.2

doesn't sound like a bugle exactly, but it becomes a major motif during the whole show. But I had to find with my fingers, as opposed to my head, the dissonant pattern in the accompaniment in the bass in the left hand. Once I found that, I could then proceed to write melodically about it and against it. What's very interesting here is I see it's in A-flat (it's deceptive because it sort of starts with an E-flat tonality, but it's in A-flat), so that once the accompaniment gets going I will then start working out the melodic idea. That's generally the pattern. Sometimes a song will start with a melodic idea; particularly the more pretentiously composed pieces start with an accompaniment.

MH: What do you mean by "pretentiously composed"?

SS: What I mean is ambitious. "Pretentious" has a pejorative flavor to it, though not in my head. What I mean is extended—extended writing. *Passion* is composed not so much of songs, but of arioso passages that sometimes take song form. The opening is sort of a song form, but it's fairly extended, and it's fairly loose. The idea of *Passion*, for those who don't know, is that nothing comes to a conclusion.

MH: Musically?

SS: Musically. Musically the idea is to make it one long rhapsody so the audience will never applaud. There are some perfect cadences in it, but not very many. The audience is never encouraged to think that something is over, because I didn't want the mood broken and the audience being made conscious it was in a theater.

MH: In retrospect do you wish you had?

SS: No, I'm glad. It's right for the piece. Applause would be entirely wrong for it. The piece is a rhapsody; a rhapsody is what it is. It's just wrong to break the flow with applause; it was always conceived as a long song.

MH: On this sketch, you have "penult." and a natural above with the question mark. What did you mean?

Example 1.3

SS: I'd want to do this at the piano, but this is the climax before the end—that's what "penult." means—and this is the harmony I wanted to reach. And I think, although this is written in five flats, I didn't know whether I wanted an A-flat on top or an A-natural, because there's a B-double-flat in the bass. Obviously, I wanted a clash between what looks like a B-major triad over what looks like an A-major tonality in the bass.

MH: And things in parentheses indicate an alternate?

SS: Everything in parentheses indicates an alternate. For example, in this first chord, I didn't know whether I wanted the C-flat in or not, so I put two D-flats in as an alternate, which makes essentially the same sound, but makes it much more of an F-sharp minor chord. Because— look at that—it's a first inversion of an F-sharp minor chord if you read these notes from the top as C-sharp, F-sharp, C-sharp, A, C-sharp, A. And I suspect I found that . . . because obviously I didn't want it to end (that's why it says penultimate), I didn't want it to feel as if it really reached a cadence, but I suspect I settled for that. I'd have to compare this sketch with the final manuscript, but I suspect I did not settle for something quite so bare.

MH: If you were working on this away from the piano, would you then take it to the piano to make the decision?

SS: You got it exactly. Usually I'll check it at the piano and say, ugh, no, that's not what I meant. But most chordal stuff I work out at the piano. If I have a chord, and a chord, and a chord, and I want to work out some contrapuntal passage, I might work on the couch and then take it to the piano and check it. But if I'm looking for the chordal structures, I'll generally do that with my fingers at the piano.

MH: What do the red arrows throughout your sketches mean?

SS: That means what I like. As you'll see, there are a lot of pages of accompaniment figures, and after I've written down as many ideas as I can, and I feel as though I'm ready to give birth, I'll go back over it and decide what it is that I really want to remember and try to preserve. When something is the basis of the piece, I don't need a red arrow for that, and it may be surrounded by variations on it. But where I had another idea, I wanted to be sure that I considered it.

MH: Do you mean another idea for the same moment?

SS: Well, for the same piece, though perhaps another place in it.

MH: After you've done all the sketching, is that when you play everything through and decide what to arrow?

SS: Yes, when I think I've exhausted the possibilities—at least for that moment. I'll have a set of ideas, and I don't want to bore the listener. Then I will look through and see, because all of these are related to each other, either harmonically, or in terms of melodic outline, or in terms of rhythm. So it isn't like it's an idea for another song—it comes out of the same network of ideas, but it does offer contrast and variety. The trick always—well, in any art, I guess, but particularly in any art that takes place over a period of time—is how to give it variety yet make it hold together. How do you prevent it from becoming an add-a-pearl necklace? At the same time you don't want to just repeat ideas. It's the whole business of long-line development.

MH: Has it become any easier?

SS: I recognize the dangers of boredom more now than I did at the beginning.

MH: With an audience?

SS: No, I can't judge. The reason a lot of people complain the music is difficult is because it does tend to change. It's something I picked up partly from Cole Porter and partly from Leonard Bernstein. One of the things about Lenny's music that I like is he keeps surprising you—particularly rhythmically. Just when you think something is going to be a 3/4 bar, it turns out to be a 4/4 bar, or when you think it's going to be a four-measure phrase, it turns out to be a three-measure phrase. So you rarely get a chance to get ahead of the music, and that keeps the music fresh—because it's full of surprises. He used to say—it's not his phrase, but he's the first person I heard it from—that music should be inevitable but fresh. And when you listen to Jerome Kern, you know exactly what he meant. Anybody who studies a Cole Porter song is due for a lot of surprises, because what looks like a simple AABA form, turns out to really be A-A prime-B-A double prime—he does not repeat the A section. It's almost repeated, but not quite. And the result is the ear is constantly freshened, and that's what keeps music alive over a period of time. People who like my music and say they discover new things in it the more they listen to it, it's because there are these little surprises scattered throughout. So that what is jolting on first hearing, on the second hearing you start to see more how it's part of the pattern—even if it's not a conscious process.

MH: But Porter wouldn't do it through the rhythmic changes that Lenny would?

SS: No, Porter did it melodically and harmonically. You look at "Just One of Those Things" and see the tiny variations, and yet, it's so close to the standard form that it could become popular. He's the great experimenter from that point of view. Kern is the great harmonic experimenter. With Porter, it's really in terms of melodic line and how he keeps spinning it out in little tiny variations and, of course, the harmonic sophistication. And Lenny has a lot of harmonic surprise, but primarily the thing that surprises you is rhythmic structures, I think.

MH: Did you ever talk to him about that, or do you just know?

SS: No, I just know.

MH: And you actually did write "long-line" in this example.

Example 1.4

SS: Ah, well. These two chords represent the entire progression of this passage, so it's the spinning out of these two—they're written as whole notes, but that means nothing. I write long-line stuff in either whole notes or half notes; a whole note could represent four bars, eight bars, twelve bars, sixteen bars. And the half note underneath means: say you have a C on the top—there's the "C-ness" of it. (I'm beginning to sound like Lenny—Oy.) There's the C-ness on top, but then there's a G and an F, which means that for the first couple of bars it will have G as a tonal center, next F as a tonal center. And to be able to visualize that is of great help when you're writing extended pieces—as opposed to a song form, which, as I say, is either AABA or ABAB. I rarely use long-line stuff when I'm just writing a thirty-two-bar song, although there is an aspect of that. I know in "Too Many Mornings" I did that, but that's a longish song. Usually I don't bother, but if I'm writing extended passages like this—most of the stuff in Passion is extended—then to hold it together, the glue has to be harmonic and has to be spinning out the triad and spinning out the harmony.

MH: But the reason you would actually write "long-line" there?

SS: Is to remind myself where I'm going. One of the things I loved when I went to the Library of Congress and saw the Gershwin sketch for the trio at the end of *Porgy and Bess* was he knew where he was going. He would just put little thumbtacks all along the way to remind himself: Okay, I gotta reach the C-major chord over here. And he's spinning out the melodic line and then he thinks: I'll fill in the harmony later, I won't worry about how I get from here to here, I just want to be sure that I get *there*. That's, in a sense, what these are—these are bedposts. Oscar Hammerstein used to talk about "thumbtacks" in terms of lyric writing—laying out the carpet, and then putting in the other tacks along here: Here's point A, here's point B, here's point C. You can see it in his lyrics, they develop like little plays because of that. It's not just repetition, there's development. He gets from point A to B to C. I'm not talking about it in terms of dramatic action, I'm talking about it in terms of idea. I thought: Well why not do that musically too? And then when I studied with Milton Babbitt, I found out there's a nice tradition dating back at least to Mozart that spins things out that way.

MH: When you start "spinning out the melody," do you ever get to a point where you realize, because of what the melody's done, that you want to go back and change a "thumbtack"?

SS: Usually what happens is that I've worked on it so much that the unconscious takes over, and I arrive where I want to arrive. I'm sure there are times when, of course, I bend it. I'm not rigid about it, and I realize that the melody itself will imply something. But since I'm somebody who believes that the heart of music is harmony, as opposed to melody, it's very important for me to have the sense of where the harmonies are going. And the harmonies imply the melody. And quite often the long-line will turn out to be of melodic value. I'm sure at a certain point I took this opening business and the lower voice, and used that, because what's implied here is you have here an E-flat tonality in the left hand and a C-major tonality in the right hand. I'm sure I used that juxtaposition throughout. Even if it's not C major and E-flat, but that relationship. And the E-flat isn't entirely resolved because it's got an unresolved fourth in it. So again, it will hold the piece together.

MH: What also interested me in this sketch, is that it looks like you divided what was originally one measure into two measures—15A and 15B. How do you decide the amount of breath or time that a moment needs? Is it for the actor?

SS: I have an instinct, and it may not be accurate, but it's true, that when Lapine heard this he said to me: I would like to have a little more time

Example 1.5

there. Not necessarily for staging, but emotional time, because this looks to me like it was squeezed in later. However, it may be that I just decided that I didn't want to get to what would have been bar 16 so quickly. It just may be that. There's this whole thing: I wanted so much to get that post-coital sense of relaxation, and that means that there should be pauses. Everybody has a different way of dealing with that moment, but in this case, I wanted Clara to be both a little coy with him and at the same time she's relaxing—the balloon is deflating. And that meant that I put in little passages of rest that ordinarily I wouldn't do. If this was just a ballad I would try to keep it going, but being a post-sex ballad, I wanted to have places where she would just breathe. I do know there was some place in this opening number where Lapine asked for more time, but it's probably later on. This is only the sixteenth bar, and the music starts with an orgasm. She's only been singing four bars here, and I just didn't want it to go on so quickly. That's why that extra measure's there. And I think what happened was I played it over and I thought: No, no, she needs more breathing space here.

MH: There's so much thought behind your choices, do you ever wonder how the performances of actors in future productions might be affected by not having information about the intentions that were behind these decisions?

SS: I wish they would be. I had a nice experience with Alun Armstrong. He played Sweeney in the Declan Donnelan production we were doing of *Sweeney Todd* at the National Theater in London. I was rehearsing Alun and the quintet in the letter-writing scene in the second act. I worked out with him when he dipped the pen in the inkwell, and when he wrote and when he signed, when he grunted and when he giggled—all that to go with the quintet singing—because I work out everything in detail. He's an aggressive fellow, and he actually turned and he said: "You mean you thought these things out when you were writing this down?" He thought that that kind of stuff—when you dip a quill pen—is worked out during rehearsal. I said: "Yes, of course, every single dip." Now the director may change it, but I know exactly when I want him to dip the pen in and when I want him to cross out a word and repeat a word. There are moments during "The Letter" where he writes a word, and then he thinks, and he kind of slavers over the word because he likes it so much because it's going to draw the judge into his trap. That's all worked out. I don't know what a director who doesn't know this will tell an actor when he asks: "Why does he repeat that word?" I know why he repeats it.

MH: Do you write it down anywhere?

SS: There's no way to do that. Though, actually, I do write stage directions down. I think probably on that one I wrote something like "He muses." So the answer is: Yes, I work out all these things in detail. It's a knee-jerk reaction from an experience I had with Jerome Robbins when we were writing *West Side Story* and I played him "Maria." Lenny was off someplace, and I was the one who played it for him. And he asked me: "Well, what do you see happening on the stage?" I said: "Well, Tony is singing this love song. . . ." Jerry said: "Well, what's he doing?" I said: "He's singing . . . he's full of emotion." He said: "You stage it!" We started talking, and I learned then that it is of great value to a director to stage every song you write within an inch of its life. They can use it as a blueprint, or depart from it entirely, but they have something to go from. So I stage everything. And I tell my collaborating director what I intend, but he doesn't have to, and often won't, pay any attention to it. I worked out the whole opening to the second act of *Sweeney*—the beer garden scene, "God That's Good"—where Mrs. Lovett is serving twenty-seven people at once. I worked out what each customer was doing—the one that was underpaying, the one that was drunk, the one that was a glutton, et cetera—and I had them at different tables. And Hal Prince said: "I think it would be much better if they were all at one table." So Hal completely changed my basic scheme, but the details are still there for him to tell the actors. I had the guy who's sneaking away with trying not to pay at *that* table while Mrs. Lovett's back is turned over *here*, and I had him trying to sneak out and Tobias catches him. Hal had them all at one table, so he had to work out how someone could try to sneak out—because at a big table everybody sees everybody—it's not so easy to work out. But he wanted a big table because he wanted that sense of Dickensian stomping. When it was done in a revival at the Circle in the Square, there were different little tables, and that was the way I intended it. Hal's production had much more of a kind of vigor, but that production had much more detail in it.

MH: Did you have to change the score because of it? Did Hal need more or less time because of the changed staging?

SS: No. That sometimes does happen in revivals. That happened just recently for the concert of *Into the Woods*. Somebody said: "Could I get some more bars here?" And I said: "Absolutely." We needed more time to get people onto the stage so I allowed extra vamps.

MH: In some of your sketches and drafts for "Happiness (Part II)," you have it opening with the word "Christ" instead of "God." What was behind your decision to change it from one to the other?

Example 1.6

SS: I love the word "Christ." I love the sound of it. It seems to be more agonizing. "God, you are so beautiful" has a kind of sentimental feeling to it. "Christ, you are so beautiful" has a sense of shock. "Christ" is a shocking word. I prefer "Christ" and my guess is that Lapine persuaded me to change it, not to make him a villain or anything like that. It also has to do of course with the fact that "God" can be extended as a note, and "Christ" cannot. You can't go "Chr-i-i-ist"; it loses all its value. But you can go "G-aaahd." You can sing a love song with that single word. So I can't tell you definitely what the reason was, it may have been Lapine, or I may have heard this sung and I thought: It's a little too shocking. To say "God" on the stage forty years ago was a shock. Now it's not such a shock. To say "Christ" still is a shock. It really is, to quote, taking the Lord's name in vain. I'm not just talking about to the Christians in the audience, it just has that feeling—it' a real [loud clap].

MH: Would the fact that *Passion* takes place in Italy—a Catholic country—have anything to do with your choice?

SS: I didn't even think of that. Of course James and I talked a lot about that, so it's conceivable that character wouldn't have said "God." I don't know what the Italian word would be that would be an equivalent. When you say "God, it's hot outside," you're not really swearing. But if you say "Christ, it's hot outside," that's got real force. I just wanted one of those expletives that isn't an expletive.

MH: Would you elaborate on the erasures in your sketches?

SS: When I start writing a piece out in detail—making real copy—and then I turn against it, or I decide to change something, but it's not worth erasing most of a page, I'll rewrite the bars I want to keep on a fresh page. Then on the original I'll lightly erase the page and bar numbers, but not so thoroughly that I can't see them. Then I know that this was a discarded page, and I don't end up with two page twos with two bar eights, and say: "What . . .?" Because erasures don't mean anything, I erase all the time. And often, my so-called completed copy will have a lot of erasures in it. It's not a fair copy. I have the luxury of giving it to a copyist who will then write it out in neat form. She often gets a manuscript from me that's full of erasures. Incidentally, one of the small, practical problems of writing music today is that in the old days I used to have a messenger come to the house and pick up the manuscripts and take them to the copyist. Ever since the fax machine was invented, we send faxes. But if you send faxes of erased notes, you get a call from the copyist asking: "Is that an E-natural, or is that a D-natural?" You can read my manuscript okay in person, because I write very heavily with a pencil (and I write also with Blackwing pencils, which smudge very easily). I try to write very dark for the copyist to understand it, hoping that she won't have to call me.

MH: Do you always work with the same copyist? Do you request someone in particular?

SS: For many years I worked with a well-known copyist around town named Mathilde Pinchus. After she died I worked with her assistants for a while, and now I work with a woman named Peggy Serra. She's very quick and very smart. Because of the kind of harmony that I use, she doesn't make assumptions. She doesn't assume that just because I'm in F major, that a note's an A-natural.

MH: In this sketch, I'm struck by the layers of harmonies that you've indicated and the way that you use Figured-Bass—the fact that for almost every harmonic change, you also imply a key change. So, as I read it, it looks like you're starting with a II chord in the key of G minor, going to a I chord in the key of A-flat.

Example 1.7

SS: Well, if you have an A-flat chord, how are you going to notate the A-flat if you're in a G-minor tonality? You can't, because in G minor, the bass of the II chord's going to be an A-natural. So, if you're going to go to an A-flat chord you have to change the tonality first. If all the notes are going to be within the G-minor tonality then I'll just go: II-III-IV-V—whatever it is. But if you're going to change, how else would you notate it? There's no other way to do it. I was not brought up on Guitar Notation; I was brought up on so-called Figured-Bass, or Classical Notation. I find Guitar notation useless because you don't get enough information about the positions of the chords and the building of the notes. You get what the notes are, but not what the bass is and what the basis of the chord is. So I use this rather elaborate form of notation, but also to remind myself. Here I have an idea for an accompaniment, and now I want to carry it out harmonically, and I know I'm going to use this little passage in bar 10, which I've just sketched in. That's going to be the rhythm of the accompaniment. So, quickly, while I've got the harmonic scheme in mind, I will write out the harmonies. What's interesting here is these are all alternates for the passages.

MH: So you don't mean this to be read as chords superimposed on each other?

SS: No, not at all. Because you have so many choices. Particularly if you're using any kind of dissonant harmonies—in terms of musical theater, not Alban Berg. Since there are so many choices, and since, whether you use E-flat-G-B-flat and D, or E-flat-G-B-flat and C is an enormous difference. And those have entirely different notations, I have to have the alternates. There isn't an awful lot of difference between E-flat I_6 and E-flat I_7, but there is a difference. And I want to remind myself: Don't settle for one without examining the other very carefully. And then when you see them on a level—if it's going to be a G-minor I^6 it's going to go to an F-major I^6. If, however, it's an E-flat I_7 it's going to go to C-minor I^6_4. So that when they're on a horizontal line it means: If I choose *this* then that follows, if I choose this other one then that follows. Usually the top one is the one that's going to work, and I probably ended up using the E-flat, C-minor, et cetera. I was also screwing around with the melodic outline and deciding whether I wanted to use four sixteenths, or an eighth and two sixteenths, and sometimes that makes a huge difference.

MH: You asked: How else are you going to notate those chords? But in your mind are you also thinking of it as a modulation to that key?

SS: No, no, no, no. First of all, I never think in terms of modulation, particularly in this kind of music. It's constantly changing—within chord to chord—keys, so to speak. No, I know what the tonality is—I write very tonal music. But to go from chord to chord, where there are changes of the center of the tonality? No. This just means for these four notes, that's going to be an A-flat tonality. Even though one could notate it, if you wanted, as C minor. That could very well be a C-minor-VI^6, but it's an A-flat chord simply because in between I've gone to something else. So, it's much easier for me to refer to these and read each chord as a separate chord. Rather than think: All right, shall I write this in A-flat with a flatted fifth? No. I'd rather write it in whatever other notation I want to use—depending. An F-minor I^6 (if that's what I was doing), if it's going to be A-flat-C-D-F, as opposed to an A-flat chord with a sixth on top and a flatted fifth. That's all. It's just whatever's easier for me to read.

MH: The inversions that you chose here—what is it about them . . .?

SS: Well, I learned a long time ago, and I try and use it more and more, that—particularly in music that you want to keep moving—most composers of songs and in musical theater tend to use block harmonies. That is to say, everything's based on the root position—generally. And certainly that was the tradition, with the rare exception of Kern and sometimes Porter. Rodgers wrote mostly root positions. And yet, inversions are exactly what gives something variety while you're holding it together with glue. Assume you're in C major and you want to get to a I chord. You know a lot of stuff is written over a pedal point in musical theater; I write with a lot of pedal point, but it isn't just a matter of writing wrong notes in the right hand while you constantly have your ostinato bass; it's a question of how long do you want that bass to pound into your listener's ears? Musical harmony, as you know, moves by bass line. That is the motive that changes things. And it doesn't matter how you screw around with the notes on top; if the bass remains solidly consistent, it's going to sound that way throughout. So, if you want to stay in C major, and you want some variety, why not go to a C I^6? Now the instability of first inversions is something that's very hard to deal with when you're so used to block harmony. I get scared sometimes when I use a I^6 that it's all going to fall apart. Because, you know, it's so easy and satisfying to pound away at the I-V-I-V-I-V, as most songs do. But when you get to the I^6 chord, it becomes a little more interesting. Because the I^6 chord tends not to want to go back to the V, but to lead to a IV or even, sometimes, to a VI chord. So, if you're in C major, the E will pull toward an F in the bass or pull towards an A in the bass. I'm talking in the simplest possible chordal terms. But at least you're getting away from that C-G-C-G-C-G. So, that's why I try to give myself as many opportunities as I can. I see there are a lot of first inversions in this passage, and clearly I wanted the passage to move—I wanted it to be liquid—and one way of doing that is inversions. Look at that, for two bars you've had a pedal tone underneath, and it's about time to get off the pot, so to speak. That's why I try to use inversions.

MH: Do you go for a bass line that you think will give you melodic counterpoint?

SS: That's what long-line composition is: What's going on on the top, and what's going on in the bottom, and how they do that, and how do they then make the music stay within F major, before you get to the second movement, so to speak, which goes to the A-flat major. I often will make long-line with just two lines—the top and the bottom—because that's how you make music move. And sometimes, if I'm trying to be clever, the melodic line will be the inversion of the bass and vice versa. There are all those kinds of things. But they're more than being clever, they really hold the music together. I'm a firm believer that the ear hears things that the mind does not know, particularly in non-musicians, but even in a musician. That, if it's there, it's there. You look at a sidewalk, you don't see the grouting, but the grouting is there. If you've built sidewalks, you see the grouting. You say: Gee, that's bad grouting over there. (This is a terrible metaphor and I'm going to pound it into the ground.) The whole point is that what cements music is a musician's business, and the idea is *not* to make it effortful for the listener—to make it effortless for the listener. But that cement is what makes the piece hold together, and if you put too much cement in, it absolutely rigidifies it and it becomes boring. Actually, "grouting" is a very good metaphor now that I come to think of it, because it holds it together, but allows it to expand and contract and prevents it from breaking. That's exactly what should be going on with the business of an inversion: An inversion is to allow the music to expand a little bit—instead of just going I-IV, why not go I-I⁶-IV? I remember, there's an inversion in "Losing My Mind"—which is an absolutely traditional thirty-two-bar song—but I used an inversion, and when I got to it, I thought: Gee, that's good, that's something Kern would have done. It's very simple, the song's mostly based on root position harmonies, and then there's this one inversion—I think it's in the sixth bar of each eight—and it just

Example 1.8

gives real . . . air. It's a tiny thing, but it gives real air. You have this desert and a tiny little oasis in the middle. I think it pays off in terms of letting the listener off the hook, and giving the listener a breath—the ear a breath—to go on and not fall asleep. Unfortunately, in musical theater, particularly in the last forty years, audiences like to fall asleep—they like to know what's happening next, they don't want to be surprised. But I think what makes a song last—or music last, or art last—is surprise; particularly narrative art—music, in the sense of narrative art that exists in time.

MH: When you hear other people's work, can you hear those subtleties consciously?

SS: No. Absolutely not. All I know is that my ear is surprised. I've been around the block so many times that I tend to be ahead of the chordal structure of *most* music that I hear in the musical theater. So when it surprises, it really surprises. Sometimes, as in a score like Adam Guettel's *Floyd Collins*, which I think is a great score, I want to study the music when it's published. I really want to see how he did it. I've heard the recording three times. The music's not all that dissonant, it's just that he's got a fresh mind; he doesn't go where you expect him to and yet it sounds inevitable. You know that's what Lenny meant: It mustn't sound "dump-bump-be-um-pump, ump-*eem*" [sings "shave and a haircut" with a wrong final note]. It shouldn't be arbitrary, it should be inevitable. You get that in Kern, and you get that in Adam Guettel's work too. And that's the mark of a good composer, because he's surprising without going: Nyah nyah, nyah nyah; you thought I was going to G, Nyah nyah, I'm going to F-sharp. Anybody can do that, and they do it all the time. Lenny criticized the score of *Forum*. He said there was a lot of wrong-note music in it, and I bristled when he said that, but he was right. A song like "Pretty Little Picture" has absolutely unnecessary dissonances in it because I was so afraid of writing a triad. When you're young and you're trying to make a style for yourself (it's true of every composer I know) you decorate the music so that it doesn't sound like anybody else's. And, of course, the real point is, if you try to make it sound like everybody else's and it's yours, it'll come out your own. So, it's ironic, but every young composer has to go through that. I went through it with *Forum*. There's some stuff in *Forum* that is natural to me, but there are other things where I can just hear myself being ashamed of what I was writing.

MH: Ashamed at the time, or subsequently?

SS: It was unconscious. It was: How do I make this interesting? And one of the ways you don't make something interesting is adding a tritone on the top, and yet everybody does it—you write: C-E-G-*F-sharp*.

MH: Do you feel restricted writing for musical theater? Based on what you've been saying, do you wish you had pursued other types of music?

SS: That's a hard question. As you know—as *you* know—I don't like opera, but I have a feeling that I wish I did. Because, I'll tell you something, it's much more satisfying and easier to write something like *Passion* than it is to write something like *Merrily We Roll Along*. To write a thirty-two-bar song that has freshness and style to it and tells the story is really hard. And nobody does it anymore. Everybody writes so-called "sung-through" pieces, and it's because anybody can write sung-through pieces. It's all recitative, and they don't develop anything, and it just repeats and repeats and repeats. And that's what most shows are. I don't even go see the shows; it's so boring to me. But it's really hard to write a song, and nobody writes songs anymore in the musical theater—they write extended pieces. And I know from *Passion*, it's much easier to write extended arioso stuff than it is to write songs.

MH: Then do you have more pride in *Merrily* as a musical accomplishment?

SS: I don't want to compare, because I'm very proud of *Passion*, but, yeah, I'm very, very proud of *Merrily*. *Merrily* was the hardest score I ever had to write, and it was partly because I was trying to recapture what I was like when I was twenty-five without making a comment on it. It's about two young songwriters, and I wanted to convey what they would have written back in the late fifties, early sixties, without making it a takeoff or a parody. *And* they're supposed to be talented. Writing it was like pushing a pea up a hill with your nose. What I like about it is it sounds effortless to me now—it just sounds like a nice score—and I know what went into it. *And* it tells the story in thirty-two-bar songs. I mean some of the songs are 108 bars, but they're sections of thirty-two bars—and by thirty-two bars I mean the whole thing is based on modules of four-bar and eight-bar phrases. Whereas *Passion* is all: Oooh, I think, yes, she'll sing a little longer here, now . . . Aaah, I'll give her a little rest here . . . Now maybe I could bring that theme back in here. I see why opera composers had a good time: it's much easier.

MH: What about non-vocal music?

SS: I haven't written enough to have any wisdom on that.

MH: The desire?

SS: I would love to write ballet music. I'm square enough that I like the "Dance of the Hours." When I first played my music for Jerry Robbins, he said: "You ought to be writing ballet"—that I write dance music. It had never occurred to me, but he was right. If I wrote any concert music it would be ballet.

MH: We're looking at "Fosca's Entrance I, 2." I was just intrigued by these few notes here.

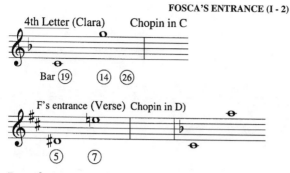

Example 1.9

SS: When I write—when I start—if I have an immediate idea, before I start a sketch sheet, I'll put down some kind of basic idea. Where it says "Chopin in C" alludes to how I was imitating Chopin for Fosca's piano piece. "Bar 19, bar 14, bar 26" looks to me like a later notation. But the point was the range was going to be from C to G.

MH: The vocal range for that character?

SS: Yes, exactly. And here I've written "verse" over the E-natural.

MH: Why would you think that? What would make you say her verse should be in E-natural?

SS: I have a feeling this is her actual entrance. And the numbers in circles mean bar numbers—in this case, bars 5 and 7. So, let's see if there's a D-sharp in bar 5 in some remarkable way . . . and of course there isn't. This is the Chopin thing. Clearly, what I'm doing is I'm trying to figure out how to have her sing against the Chopin. Because there are two things going on here: there's the piano piece and her vocal. That's what I obviously am trying to work out. Let's see, we're in the key of . . . we're sort of in the key of D, but not really.

MH: Usually, the audience thinks it's her playing piano upstairs.

SS: I've established that earlier, so I know that I want to use that. What goes on before the entrance is that we hear the music earlier. And now this is in the orchestra, and it's an echo of what we heard before. So this is the orchestral version of the piano, which I've done with sustained chords and with an occasional whiff of the accompaniment figure from

Example 1.10

the piano piece. What's interesting here is the flat signature above where it says "4th letter." I remember vaguely now, I was making a transition from Clara's song—you know she has this sort of waltz ". . . our little room. . ." et cetera—and against it, in comes dissonant music which is Fosca. Clearly what I was doing was making a relationship between F major and D major. D major being what Fosca's going to get into here. This may be the long-line of it, because look, it returns to F major.

MH: Fosca's keys became lower in the actual show, so how do you deal with key relationships for different sections with different singers when the keys change with the casting?

SS: Unfortunately, unlike opera, in musicals you cast for the people. In opera you force: it's a five-hundred-pound soprano and she's forty years old and she's playing Juliet—that's what you do. Because the suspension of disbelief that audiences bring to opera is so much greater than what they bring to so-called musical theater. I've rarely had to change musical structure to suit voices. Fosca's entrance, for example, is a solo; Giorgio's is speech, so it doesn't matter what key it's in. There is no over-arching design to the score of *Passion*—it is not one long piece like *Wozzeck* or *Lulu*.

Sections are done that way, but I'm too practical to force people into some kind of scheme that. . . .

MH: There's no score like that of yours?

SS: No, none. There are sections, there are sections. But where the individual sections are set is arbitrary in the sense that you accommodate the singer. So I never think in terms of an over-arching musical structure. One of the reasons I don't like opera is it's so full of *longueurs* and recitative; in musical theater what you want is the ability to cut things. If you've built an entire structure, and you suddenly decide that the center, the capstone, which happens to be this beautiful aria in E major and it's what everything has accumulated to is E major, and then you decide it's boring and you want to cut it out, there goes your structure. I argue: You know operas have intermissions, so what the hell's the point of writing one—unless it's a one-act opera like *Wozzeck*. Would *Tosca* really suffer if the entire second act were a half-tone lower? Would the design go out the window? Would we be bored to death? Would we feel a thing wasn't working? I don't think so.

MH: In an ideal world, say, fifty years from now, somebody's doing a production of any of your scores, as opposed to going to the published piano-vocal scores, would it be preferable if they went back to your original manuscripts and used the keys that pieces were composed in?

SS: That would be fine. I don't think it would make any difference. It's all in the color of the voice. As long as they don't change anything within the piece I don't think it matters, I really don't. I once had to change the structure within a piece. It was Mrs. Lovett's first song in *Sweeney Todd*—"The Worst Pies in London." I had it quite worked out in terms of its own harmonic design and the long-line, and Angie couldn't handle it. Because, though she can sing in head, it has an entirely different effect—it's a comic effect particularly—and so I had to take the whole second half of it and switch things around to accommodate her voice. I think the song turned out fine anyway, but ideally it would have been the other way, because I had a specific harmonic plan.

MH: So when New York City Opera did their production of *Sweeney Todd*, did you think of going back to the original version?

SS: It never occurred to me to go back. Also, that would mean to re-orchestrate. All those practical considerations.

MH: This is a moment that's just impressed me a lot because of how quickly yet subtly it changes the mood.

Example 1.11

SS: It's probably by chance.

MH: It's the end of the first section, where Fosca has the breakdown, and then very quickly the transition to the "have you explored the town" section. What do you try to do musically to create a transition like that—for both the audience and the actor—and to give them something to play?

SS: It's an hysterical woman who has realized that she's talked too much, and she may be chasing away the man of her dreams whom she theoretically just met, but whom she's been spying on, and she suddenly decides to become charming. But Fosca's idea of charming is our idea of hysterical. And so that's what's behind the change in music. So what I want to do is find something that's chattery and chirpy and slightly annoying. That is the intention musically. Now, if you say: Why did I choose chords like that? That's all it's doing—to echo the moment.

MH: Do you do things musically to help the actor make emotional transitions?

SS: No, make the character. When Donna Murphy auditioned for us we gave her this piece. Her audition performance could have gone on stage that night. She's intelligent. There's something in her that identified with the character right away, and I write careful scenes. I say this with no modesty at all: When I'm writing dramatic stuff, I'm a playwright. This is a worked-out scene, and I can instruct the actress how to play this scene, and the music is part of the dialogue. I can tell her why the music gets quick *here*, why it gets slow *here*, why there's a ritard *there*, why there's a so-called key change *here*, why it suddenly goes up and down—all of that—because I have reasons. Now the actress may choose to ignore them, but Donna, who was just auditioning, did not have a chance to ask me, but she understood it. And this piece is psychologically very well laid out, and all it takes is a good actress to understand it exactly. It's one of the reasons why actors like to sing my stuff—because I'm essentially a playwright in song, and I'm not asking them to sing songs, I'm asking them to play scenes. It doesn't matter whether they're in thirty-two bars, or thirty-three bars, or a hundred-and-nine bars, or six minutes. One of the reasons it convinces you is because psychologically it's true. If I were writing this as a play—as a monologue—I would do the same thing: She would get grinding, grinding, and suddenly start stirring her coffee and get chirpy without any music at all. That's all. And notice there's only one bar where she gets to breathe before she changes tone.

MH: Why would making it one bar be noteworthy?

SS: Because ordinarily when you go into a new rhythmic section you give the audience a chance to hear the rhythm for a couple of bars. Not in opera obviously, but in a musical.

MH: Why didn't you give her the chance here?

SS: Because I think she's too hysterical. I think everything's got to be off-beat. I think Fosca's one of those people who, when you think she's going to be quiet, she screams; and when you think she's going to scream, she's quiet; and when you think she's going to cry, she laughs. She's completely out of control—she's a loose cannon. What I wanted this opening number to do was to make the audience really frightened of her—to say: *Oy, there's a bundle.* And I think it does. I think at the end of this song they're ready. Because, you know what happens right after this song: she has this screaming, hysterical fit, which is one inch away from making the audience laugh, but because of the song that precedes it, they don't laugh. There was a tendency to giggle a little bit—to have a woman watching a funeral procession and suddenly scream and have an epileptic fit—because they're not prepared for it. But they are prepared for it because of this—because of that transition.

MH: My assumption is that this is one of your "long-line" sketches.

Example 1.12

SS: It sure is. I have to refresh my memory on this. Obviously I wanted to start with a nice B-flat. I must have had an idea, because this is odd—going to an A and an E there (or a B-double-flat and F-flat as I wrote it.) When I do a long-line sketch, I divide things into sections. The first section is clearly the "intro" before she enters. And obviously this B-flat either comes from the Clara section or from the Chopin music, but the point is this is where she comes in. Now I had devised a 7/4 arpeggio [see m. 12, Ex. 1.13]—and from what that implied, I started to work out the harmonic structure. The second section leads up to the lyric about the flower—"There is a flower . . ."—where there is a change of music both in texture and in register: it goes up into the upper octave, and also has a light waltz flavor which I wanted to use later at some point. So the second section of the sketch is really the first section of the song. Now,

Example 1.13

Example 1.13 (continued)

where you see the half-notes, it doesn't really mean a half-note, it's just for notation purposes—half-note, C-sharp-half-note, D-half-note, F-sharp, and then to G-natural—and means that these sections are functioning as an outline.

MH: Is that melodically, or harmonically?

SS: Harmonically. Because you notice all the thirds. And what interests me here is why I put the B minor at the bottom, because it doesn't really . . . with the A-natural above, it doesn't really sound, but that's what that means. I wanted the Bs to be here. Obviously the scheme is to go from B-flat to B-natural to B-flat. So it has some kind of arc effect that way. And then, you think: What do those notes have in common? You see it leads to a G—it's G minor, but in fact G minor/major—and G minor has B-flat and G major has B-natural. So, that the whole passage is built on the alteration of B-flats and G. The "recap" I put in G minor for some reason, and went from G minor to B minor. Half-notes represent the inner motion of the harmonies. Quarter-notes are sections within that. Let's compare this to the later manuscript and see if I've written it in a key where we can make some sense of what I intended. Oh dear, the later manuscript is in D minor. Obviously what I did was I worked this out and then I transposed it. I must have done that for range or register purposes. So, unfortunately, what we have is D minor. The way the sketch went from B-flat to B minor—the full copy goes from D major to D minor, I mean B-flat to B-flat minor, but . . .

MH: I thought it was a B-natural minor.

SS: B-natural minor. Sorry, in the sketch it is B minor. But the progression in this later version is from D major to D minor. D major being the verse. Now why did I change it? Let's see: it clearly opens with the Chopin—it starts out with a nice triad. And then it goes into D minor, but look, it's got a G-C-E [see m. 10 of Ex. 1.13]. And in the sketch it's B minor, but it's got an E-A-C-sharp. It's the same thing, it's just transposed. In other words, the first three notes in the arpeggio outline D minor, but on top of it I'm laying in another chord. If you hold your foot on the sustaining pedal down and play those first six notes you'll get that chord. It'll be transposed, but you'll get that chord. So clearly what I want to do is relate the major chord in the Chopin to this minor version of it. It softens it by bringing in the flatted seventh. I'm sorry it's transposed, because otherwise we could watch how the thirds move in the accompaniment figure. . . . I'm moving those thirds up and down, and the C and the E become a D and an F. The C-sharp and A become a D and B. They're parallel. The whole idea is to build it on thirds.

MH: To relate back to the military figure?

SS: No, I don't think so. I think it's because it's my favorite chord.

MH: What is?

SS: The kind of chord in which you take a triad and lay on top of it another triad and it's all within the same key. It's sort of a jazz chord is really what it is. And it's unresolved which is what's nice about it. Ordinarily, in D minor, that would be a C-sharp, but by making it a C-natural it has a softer more fluid sound. And it's just something I like a lot.

MH: Do each of those subtleties—whether it's a C or a C-sharp—do they mean something to you intellectually, or is it emotional feel?

SS: It depends. Sometimes it's because of the way I've worked out the longline, and sometimes it's just I like that sound better. A lot of music's chosen, I think—at least by me—just because I like it better. Because it fits the emotion better. And when you talk about: If you're writing the character, and I'm writing the character, a chord that suits you might not suit me and vice versa. A chord that conveys to you the essence of her character, might not convey it to me. It's Rachmaninoff melancholy; this is a chord you find all the way through his music. It's that kind of Russian melancholy that has an "Oy . . . oy . . . oy" kind of feeling. And Fosca's feeling sorry for herself. As a matter of fact, I remember, I was worried about this becoming sentimental, because I wanted her to feel sorry for herself, but to be fierce. And that is why (if you want to talk about intellectual) I chose the melodic line to start with sixteenth notes instead of something slower. And this is against the eighth-note accompaniment. Ordinarily, one would match the melodic idea to the rhythm of the accompaniment. But here, I deliberately did not, because I wanted her to have these stuttering phrases over this melancholy Russian music. Now I didn't mean it to be Russian of course, but that's my idea of melancholy. So, that's the reason for the choice of that kind of stuttering melody as opposed to a flowing melody. Because she's sorry for herself, but she's pretending to be angry—not pretending, but she's sharp-tongued and short, and she's being contemptuous of him. And she says: "I do not read to think" because it's the only way she knows how to behave. She doesn't want to get soppy, I think. And she's fierce. But as the song goes on and she becomes more and more passionate about what she's saying, you'll notice the melodies change from sixteenth notes to eighth notes . . . as it gets: "search for truth, I know the truth" as opposed to "I do not read to think," which is the way it starts. And then, when she gets to "I read to dream. I read to live," she starts to become kind of Puccini-esque, expansive, because she's getting passionate. And it's precisely by falling into that that she realizes what she's doing. That's why she does that second part in that chattery attempt at charm. So what the long-line sketch is is a scheme of how I'm going to get from point A to point B—these transitions in her. Because when you make an emotional transition, it probably—I don't want to say that this is dogma—it should probably be accompanied, I think, by a harmonic transition of some kind—whether it's a transition from major to minor, or to a whole other key; what you call a modulation. It's interesting, Milton Babbitt never uses the word "modulation," he uses the word "toniciza-tion." It means: We're going to make a new tonal center. And it's a much bet-ter word than modulation. There's something transitional or temporary about modulation. And maybe that's the way to use the word. For instance: We're going to modulate to E major before we go back to C major. But if you tonicize E major, you're really making a whole new statement in E major. I know this kind of harmony, which I've used before for a kind of melancholy, is something I like a lot. It's very pleasant and it's still sad.

MH: What would be behind the specific choice of the B-flat to the B-minor-natural to the B-flat to the G?

SS: It's because, if you look at the whole passage, all those bass notes are in a key and one passage even has an F in the bass. Some things I put in parentheses because I don't know if I'm going to state the note. But the point is it's a B-flat-V chord, and what I'm doing is alternating between B-flat and B, B-flat and B. The G is an attempt to find an accumulation which encompasses both those notes. Now, if I wanted to end the piece earlier—if I didn't want it to go on—I would have ended up with the B-flat. But I didn't. At the same time, I just don't want to go to another key in an arbi-trary way—to go to A major or something like that. So the G is an attempt to sum up the statements in B-flat and B-natural. It's related—it's in-evitable (well, I like to think of it as inevitable), but fresh. The point is, it is related, but it's new. It's not arbitrary. The fact that it goes into G minor is also not arbitrary. It somehow relates to the scheme—at least that's the intention. It may not work, but that's the intention.

MH: So, for instance, to go to C-sharp would not be related?

SS: No, of course not. Because C-sharp doesn't relate to both B-flat and B-natural. If I say: Include B-flat and B-natural. What do they have in common?'

MH: But it could have been a D.

SS: It might have been, but a third is so much more powerful a statement than . . . well a fifth would be okay, but then it would have to be . . . and then if you have D and D-flat you would have had a tritone in there—im-plicit. So that it wouldn't make the G quite as satisfying, I think.

MH: But if it's B minor and B-flat major, they share the same D.

SS: Oh, I see, you're suggesting that the D be the bass that it goes *to*. I suppose you could make a case for that. Sure, I see what you're saying. The trouble is the key of D minor has both an F and an A in it. The key of G minor has the B-flat. The key of G major has the B-natural. So the bass has both those notes in it. I hasten to add, it's only in extended pieces like this where I work things out in such detail.

MH: This is a sketch for "Scene III, Part III—Fosca," and what intrigued me here was the rhythmic notation above.

Scene 3 - Fosca

Example 1.14

SS: That's an alternate for whatever I was writing there lyrically—it's not a basic rhythm, it's a melodic rhythm.

MH: So it's just an alternate way of writing that same moment?

SS: That's an echo of Fosca's entrance theme—what leads into "to feel a woman's touch." What I'm doing here is trying to develop the melody and deciding whether I want it to be one way or the other. In other words, do I want a melodic grouping of notes to be at the end of one bar or the other? I think it comes out to the same number of notes so that whatever lyric I was writing would fit either of these schemes. The rhythm above is merely an alternate for me to consider. Obviously, whatever the lyric is, if I want it to be more pushed, I would use the rhythm which is a beat less. If I want it to have more breathing space, not for the singer, but for the emotion, I would use the other. But, you'll notice, they're really the same rhythm—rhythmic groups—it's just that one has been shoved over.

MH: How would you would make the final decision?

SS: I would have to see what the lyric was, and it would be based on: Does the thought really push itself ahead, or does the thought need a little air?

MH: So these are not primarily musical decisions?

SS: But based on the emotion of the lyric.

MH: Do you ever want to do one thing musically, but something else for the lyric?

SS: Yes. If that happens, then I change the lyric. But here, because this is a very arioso, very free passage, it's just as satisfying musically, I think—whether it comes in a beat earlier or not. It's still the same downbeat feeling—I mean when the downbeat occurs, I don't mean downbeat as an adjective. Whenever the downbeat occurs, it's still the same feeling. And also, sometimes it has to do with the emphasis on a word, because if it comes in on the second beat of the bar, it's a much weaker beat. So, if I don't want to emphasize that word, I would use one; if I do want to emphasize that word, I would use the other. So, sometimes it's determined by emphasis. Bear in mind, this is always in terms of arioso writing, it is not in terms of song writing. Because song writing has many more rigid rules—or it doesn't feel like a song. You can't just keep changing rhythms in a song and expect it to maintain its shape, because it is only thirty-two bars.

MH: Increasingly, I've noticed that you tend to change meters more frequently within a song than you used to.

SS: But that's because most of the shows I've written recently aren't song shows. The last song show I wrote, really, was *Merrily. Sunday in the Park with George* and *Into the Woods* have songs in them, but they're not primarily song scores. *Into the Woods* is full of fragments that drift off. *Sunday in the Park* has extended sections. *Assassins* has a lot of songs in it.

MH: The "Ballad of Booth" includes a lot of meter changes.

SS: Really? I wouldn't say there are a lot of meter changes. Are you talking about the sentimental section, or the Balladeer's section?

MH: Where the Balladeer sings "Johnny Booth was a happy fella . . ."

SS: I guess there are. But the feeling of that is square. Even though there are some meter changes, the feeling is fairly square. I know it changes occasionally from four to three, and maybe even five. But the feeling is square, because it has that steady rhythm in the accompaniment.

MH: Next is your sketch called "Scene IV," which is "I Wish I Could Forget You."

SS: When you said "Scene IV" it confused me, because ultimately this became "Scene VII"— which is how I think of it.

MH: What interested me here was the evolution of the melody, and I've
done a chart that tracks your various sketches through to the final version.

"I Wish I Could Forget You" Scene 7 (Part II)

Example 1.15

SS: As you know, this melodic idea is the basis of the show. That includes: "I do not read to think"; and that whole thing, rhythmically of
[sings] or [sings] exists all the way—"to feel a woman's touch"; and in
the opening lyric with [sings] "I'd die right here in your arms." I use
this melodic motif, this germ, this cell, as they say, throughout the
show, in many, many guises. Both rhythmically and in terms of the outline of the melody. Sometimes the note goes up and sometimes the note
goes down, but, essentially, it's stepwise motion with a third at the end
[sings] or [sings]—"To feel a woman's touch." Essentially, these opening notes are the same all the way through the show. Much of the score
is a study in variations on those six notes. And it was conscious on my
part to do that so that there would be some sense of repetition without
its being repetitious—some sense of development, some sense of holding it together so it wouldn't just be a tapeworm—because I loathe
recitative—so there would be some sense of melodic cement, or glue,
holding the thing together. So much of what Fosca sings, and much of
what Clara sings when they are in their love moods, is based on that
motif. And Giorgio too. There are significant differences in harmony,
but not in melodic outline.

MH: Going through the sketches, I was interested to note that the first three versions were in 6/4, which changed, alternating between quarter notes and half notes, before you got to the final version, which is all eighth notes. I assume that final decision relates to the kind of thing you were just talking about.

SS: I think I decided to relate it more closely to the opening and to "I do not read to think."

MH: And it wasn't until the third sketch that you got the F-sharp on "my."

SS: Oh, that's interesting. . . .

MH: Do you remember how you found that note?

SS: Sometimes one does that just because a melody sounds boring.

MH: But that's not the "wrong-note" thing?

SS: No. I just think it makes it a better tune. The whole idea of melodic writing—for me—is similar to what I was talking about earlier regarding harmony, which is: How do you keep it inevitable but fresh? How do you say you think this is going to be the next note, but at the same time it isn't arbitrarily out of the ballpark?

MH: How *do* you do that?

SS: I don't know. It's a matter of personal decision, and there would be other composers who would solve it differently. One composer who would say: Gee, I think that's a very boring way to end that little tune. And another composer would say: Gee, I think that's perverse. But for me, it's the right combination of perverse and non-perverse. But it requires trying out all these versions—the reason for all these sketches is precisely that. It's also: How do words sit on the music? Let's not ignore lyrics here. If you take this line: "I wish I could forget you," and sing it in that rhythm: [sings] "I wish I could forget you." It doesn't work quite as well as: [sings] "I wish I could forget you." Also, look at the difference in tone, even if I keep the rhythm exactly the same, just by taking the "you" down instead of up: [sings] "I wish I could forget you." It has a finality to it, as opposed to: [sings] "I wish I could forget *you*," which prompts us that something further is going on. At least to my ear. A lot of it has to do with being very careful not to end your melody before you want it to, or not to darken a tone of a lyric, because just the direction of one note can

completely change the tone of a sentence, (although this is not a particularly vivid example). Even when the lyrics fit, even when they sit on
the notes the way they should—and inflection is all-important to me,
all-important—so it really is what the emotion's about. It's another reason
actors like to sing my stuff; I inflect for them very well. Inflection's everything. Stress is another aspect: It's very hard to make things so they're not
misstressed. I'm hardly impeccable on this, but I try to be. Most lyric writers, except for the very best, don't even bother—it doesn't bother them, it
doesn't bother the audience—but it bothers me terribly when things are
misstressed. You don't sing "night*mare*" you sing "*night*mare," and if the
accent's on the *mare* it just bothers me dreadfully. But inflection is a subtler matter and very much a choice of course, because, again, there would
be another composer who would say: Gee, I think this is exactly the
wrong way to set "I wish I could forget you." I think that last note should
not be a stepwise motion; I think it should be "I wish I could forget *you*"
[sings a leap up]. The minute you go off stepwise—even if it's on an off-
beat—you give a distinct emphasis to the word. If I go up a third: [sings]
"I wish I could forget *you*," right away there's more accent on the "you"
than [sings] "I wish I could forget you" is different than [sings alternate
melody] if you set those words to it. It delays the rhythm by making those
quarter notes. I think the reason I changed the meter from 6/4 to 4/4 was
to echo more the sixteenth notes when she sang: "I do not read to think."
And by making them eighth notes—instead of a quarter, two eighths, and
two quarters—it relates the themes. And, I think, it's more conversational.
It did mean that there was much more space between because the illusion
of space in between those two bars is greater than just holding a note—
even though this may be the same number of beats—when the tune is
stretched out that waaaaaayyyy, and then the next phrase comes in there,
it's much closer than [sings phrase], even if you hold the note [continues
singing]. There's more air there, so you have to be sure that the lyric is going to accommodate that. In other words, you don't want a run-on sentence. Actually, each one of those phrases, ideally, should have almost a
period; each one should be a separate sentence. But these clauses, "I wish
I could forget you, Erase you from my mind" for me, tremble on the brink
of too much space between a subordinate clause and a main clause. But I
wasn't able to get two sentences. It fits the music much better if you come
up with something like: "I wish I could forget you. I wish you'd go away,"
as opposed to "I wish I could forget you, Erase you from my mind."
Where's the subject of the second one? Gone with the wind. So suddenly
it's songwriting, as opposed to conversation. And for this show, particularly, I want it to seem conversational. It's a subtle thing, but it's things
like that that lose kingdoms.

MH: How do you approach the whole process? If you're writing a song or an extended piece, you have your script pages, you know what's supposed to happen there. Do you then start with your harmonic long-line outline before the lyric, or does something else come first?

SS: It depends. I would say two-thirds of the time, maybe three-quarters, I will sit with a lyric pad first and just jot down notions that could, but not necessarily, be refrain lines but are central thoughts or things I want to say. Then I will often take the dialogue—because I usually write after the librettist has written the scene—and I will often set the dialogue on the piano and "let my fingers wander idly over the organ keys." [Note: Sondheim is referring to a poem by Adelaide Ann Procter (1825–1864)—'Legends and Lyrics: A Lost Chord': "Seated one day at the organ,/I was weary and ill at ease,/And my fingers wandered idly/Over the noisy keys."] More often I will get a melodic shape in my mind from what I'm writing lyrically, and that will often be the first musical notes on that piece. It will often not end up to be the actual tune that I use, but it has a set of stresses and inflections which echo or support what I'm trying to do. I am very helped if I can find either a harmonic accompaniment or a rhythmic accompaniment that will evoke what I'm trying to say. That's the reason to sit at the piano. And sometimes it's harmonic and sometimes it's rhythmic. The long-line is really about the harmonic progression. I don't really use that unless I have a long piece and I want to hold it together—something like the opening of the second act of *Sweeney Todd* or the opening of this.

MH: But the final melody comes from the lyric? And to get to that point, do you speak a line of lyric to get the inflection that you know you want, and do you use that to determine whether you want your melody to go up or down or whatever?

SS: Absolutely. Quite often, if you listen to the musicality of the language—the melody: "If you listen to this sentence. If you listen to this sentence. If you listen to this sentence," right away there's a melody. [Sings] "Badadadadadadadum." You don't go: "Badadadadadadadum." [Sings with downward inflection] "If you listen to this sentence?" It's: "If you listen to this sentence." Right away that phrase suggests a melodic outline and it suggests a rhythm. And if I were trying to set that—if I decide that that's an important line: "If you listen to this sentence"—I've got "Badadadadadadadum," and I try to work out something from that. It's the musicality of the language itself that suggests the music—for me. The land of opera is filled with the reverse, in which you take: [sings with wide leaps] "If you listen to this sentence." But that's not for me.

MH: There are the various "Soldier's Scenes"—numbers 2, 4, 8, 10, and 11. . . .

SS: The idea was to use one tune over and over and over again.

MH: But I was intrigued by this one sketch for "Scene 10 for Soldiers."

Scene 10 (Soldiers)

Example 1.16

SS: "Scene 10" was my attempt to give some variety to this repetitive joke. This is where the soldiers are gossiping about what happened on the cliff when Fosca and Giorgio were caught in the rain. (Incidentally, the bugle calls I used throughout the show are authentic. I got the music for some Italian Army music bugle calls, and I also stole one from the movie because I figured that was authentic too.) This sketch shows a series of sixths, and a seventh and a fifth. What is that? This does not look like long-line to me. What this does look like is a series of chords over a pedal point. Let's see what I did here. I don't think I ended up really using this. This scene leads into the nightmare and I think what I did was, knowing from previous soldier scenes that they included these sustained whole-note chords, I wanted somehow to break them up so that we could fragment them and suddenly get into the nightmare which follows. This segues immediately into the nightmare music. So instead of going [he sings] "dum-baum-baum," it's "dau, dau, bau, dau." By holding the half notes over the whole notes you get dissonances, so that you know we're going to something dissonant. It starts off fairly consonant with sixths, and suddenly there's a seventh there, and then the fifth which is very dissonant with what's around it. So this is merely a sketch for an idea I had.

MH: To become more and more dissonant over the pedal point?

SS: Absolutely, yes. It starts with a sixth, goes to a seventh . . . And notice how quickly it goes out of the key—we're in G major, and there's an E-flat minor in the middle of it.

MH: You raise two points. First, authenticity: When you're doing period pieces, how much research do you do?

SS: What do I know about Italian bugle calls? Nothing. And granted the audience wouldn't know the difference either, but why should I invent them when they're in public domain? When they're authentic, why make one up? I listened to a lot of bugle calls—a lot, three dozen. I got a recording of military bugle calls by the Italian Army. Don't ask me how; I think Paul Gemignani, the show's conductor, might have gotten them for me. And there are four or five different bugle calls in the movie, and I figured if anybody knew what the bugle call for retreat and the bugle call for reveille would be, it would be Ettore Scola who directed the movie. So I assumed that he had done research and gotten some military advisor to say, "This is what you want." So I figured why not use them? And they became valuable because I utilized them, I didn't just use them as decoration. I took little rhythmic ideas from them and little melodic skips from them. Granted, it's always 1, 3, 5, and 1—I mean it's just triadic—but it's very useful. [Sings] "Bump-ad-y-ump-ump-ad-y-ad-y-ump." I wouldn't think that up, but that becomes useful. It suggests things. Not necessarily that I echoed that in a melody, but to use that *against* a melody. To know that that's the rhythm: "bump-ad-y-ump-ump-ad-y-ad-y-ump" is important, or useful. So authenticity not for the sake of authenticity, but because it gives me something that I can steal from that is part and parcel of what I'm trying to do. I wouldn't take a Sousa bugle call; I would take an Italian bugle call.

MH: When you have a show that's set in a certain time and place, do you worry that certain chords or harmonies wouldn't have been done then?

SS: It depends. *Pacific Overtures* is a perfect example. I went and I studied for two weeks in Japan. I also got some records of the various Japanese instruments that I knew nothing about. From that I decided that we'd use the *shakuhachi*, the *sho*, and the *samisen*. And I listened to them, and listened to the Japanese scales which are essentially pentatonic minor scales—as opposed to the Chinese which are major. And then I tried to devise music that essentially used those elements, but was, of course, tonal music—Western tonal music. You can't imitate Japanese music, because the intonation is everything in Japanese music—it has nothing to do with the notes. So in the first act of *Pacific Overtures*—when the music is, for the most part, Eastern—it *feels* like the music belongs in that show, in that milieu, in that country, as opposed to a show set in New York in 1960. That's my idea of the uses of authenticity. I think authenticity is useless otherwise. If I were writing a novel, that would be a whole other thing. In preparing for *Pacific Overtures*, I got a sort of daybook of various Japanese customs, traditions, and superstitions from John Weidman, some of which I used in the lyrics. They are authentic, such as a spider on the wall being a sign of success. At least it's authentic according to this daybook which was printed in the early twentieth century, or maybe even later, by some-body who lived there, and so I have to assume it's authentic. And that's useful. It doesn't matter whether it's true or not, it suggests something ex-otic—in the real sense of the word. I think that's how authenticity can be useful. When I'm dealing with the old tunes from the Ziegfeld era, as I did in *Follies*, you listen to authentic Victor Herbert and Jerome Kern and uti-lize what they were doing. The same thing is true with language. One of the things we did with *Sunday in the Park with George* was that James La-pine very carefully wrote it so it sounds like a translation from the French. There are very few contractions in it—people usually say "cannot." It's slightly clumsy, and it's slightly stilted, and it seems to me just right. It prevents it from being colloquial in the wrong way.

MH: Did you follow that through with your lyrics?

SS: I tried to. Again, if your ear is sensitive, and mine is, to the nuances in the language, you can tell when something sounds twentieth century and when it doesn't. And I'm not talking about "ain't," I'm talking about something subtler than that. There are aspects of the lyrics that are slightly stilted—and deliberately so.

MH: In the song "Johanna" in *Sweeney Todd* there's a surprising blue note. Was it a tough decision to use that sound?

Example 1.17

SS: Yes. And I'm not sure I made the right decision. Sometimes, you make a choice, because all the other choices seem less good. It may not be ideal; and maybe, if I'd searched longer, I would have found the right note there. I was aware of that blue note, but everything else sounded either repetitious or boring or expected—expected in the wrong way, meaning flat, meaning anti-climactic. That note sounded slightly startling, and you're not the first person to point it out. It may have been a mistake.

MH: It's my favorite moment.

SS: Maybe that's because you're perverse. Seriously, can you explain why it's your favorite?

MH: I remember sitting in the theater the first time I saw *Sweeney Todd* (the recording hadn't come out yet), and I literally got chills up my spine at that moment.

SS: That's great, but it's partly because you were startled. If you'd heard a saxophone in the middle of it, it might have done the same thing.

MH: But for that point in the show too, it made me nervous—it just played out with everything else that was going on on the stage.

SS: One of the things that blue note does is it makes the next phrase really telling: [sings] "da-da-da-da-da-da DAH-dah, da-da-da-da-da-da DAH DAAHH." Suddenly the sun comes up with the change from minor to major (or "major to minor" as Cole Porter said, better than I). Incidentally, that happens in lyric writing quite often: you know that you've got a really good third line, and you can't make the second line so good, but it isn't so bad, because the second line's being a little weak makes the third line stronger. There's a lyric of Cole Porter's in *Kiss Me Kate* in "Where's the Life That Late I Led?" where he says: "It's lucky I missed her gangster sister from Chicago." That line simply doesn't belong in any way, shape or form in that lyric, and I thought: I wonder if he deliberately did that to make the rest of the lyric brilliant? Which is by having one terrible line, all the other lines say: Wow! I don't know. I don't think he was that devious, but I wouldn't put it past him—that he might have written that and thought: Gee, that line doesn't belong in this song, but what the hell, it'll make the ones that are *really* elegant sound *more* elegant.

MH: When you write something that's intentionally startling, do you ever worry about the fact that over time, it won't be startling anymore?

SS: No, I never think about that. And incidentally, I didn't use the note to startle. It's because I was looking for something warm and something that wouldn't anticipate the B-natural. (I remember it was a B-flat.) [Note: The published version is a third lower.] I didn't want to use the B-natural in front of it. And at the same time, if I used an A it was too flat; and I wanted it to be below the note that was coming. You know you don't have a lot of choices. You've got a B there you want to get to. Well, you've got a B-flat and an A and then you've got an A-flat and a G. What else? Now you know Kern was notorious for finding exactly the right note. (Was it Flaubert or Stendhal who talked about *le mot juste*?) Oscar Hammerstein used to describe listening to Kern play the first eight notes of the chorus for "All the Things You Are" and trying each possibility for the ninth note. Kern would try every single note of the scale, and once he hit it, go on to the next phrase. And that's what I did, I tried every note and I couldn't find one. Kern might have found a way of starting the phrase differently so it could have a different resolution.

MH: Do you often do that?

SS: Oh, yeah! Absolutely. Every possibility. First I look at what the scheme is that I'm using and what belongs. Usually the scheme will dictate it. But sometimes it's just dramatically unsatisfying—it's the right note, but it's not fresh. It's inevitable, but it's not fresh.

MH: So in "Opening Doors," in *Merrily*, when you have the character of the composer trying out the thirty-two different harmonizations of his theme, is that really how you approach it?

SS: You got it. That's what I do. That's my big autobiographical number; everything in that number is me. That's exactly what he's doing—he's try-ing everything out until he gets it. I don't know how many other com-posers work that way (I've never talked about it to any other composer of my own generation, and I haven't read enough about composers in the past), but I'm sure that Kern was not the only one to do this. He can't have been. I remember Oscar describing how it would drive him crazy, being in the next room, trying to write lyrics, and he just kept hearing this thing go over and over again, day after day after day, until it sounded fresh. Which is what's so great; you hear "All the Things You Are," and you can't imagine that he worked on it at all!

MH: Getting back to the "Soldier's number," there's one other thing I want to bring up: It seems that as your work evolves, your textures seem to be becoming thinner and thinner. Obviously not all the time, but this is a good example of a number where the textures are very thin. I know "less is more" is one of your favorite quotes, and I wonder if that idea is behind it?

SS: I think the older you get, the fussier you get about "less is more." I think that's why so many classical composers end up writing string quartets. It's called: I don't need the oboes and I don't need the trumpets; let's just do the music. Let's do a piece and limit the colors to black, white, and blue—no reds and no greens and no oranges. I found it happening to me. In the score I'm writing now for *Wise Guys*, I've got my usual five- and six-note chords in there, and I'm thinking: Do I *really* need five notes? How about four? How about a triad—just D, F-sharp, and A—no C-sharp, no inner voice—just D, F-sharp, and A? I'm not the first person to use it, but it doesn't matter. How about a little less? And it's hard, because (I have to speak for myself) the older I get, the less confident I get in what I do. And yet, I think: Don't cover it up with either wrong or extra notes. What's necessary? Don't have so many wrong notes. What's wrong with a straight V chord? It doesn't have to be a V_7. I just made a third revision on a song to make it simpler—simpler in this sense of taking out the underbrush, or the overgrowth, whatever you want to call it. I think that happens in a big way over a period of time. At least it has to me.

MH: How does it affect how you think of your old scores?

SS: I like the old scores fine. It seems right to me that *Sweeney Todd* is thick, whereas *Sunday in the Park with George* is very spare. And that seems right, because look what Seurat did—the score echoes the subject.

MH: When, because of the dictates of character and script, it calls for you to write music that doesn't call for 7th chords, is it as satisfying to write without them?

SS: In a way not. I like 7th chords—I live on 7th chords. (Ravel gave us that gift.) And when a piece doesn't call for them I try not to use them, but it's hard. If you're writing something like *Passion*, you can afford to have all these big dissonances and these big 9th chords and 11th chords and 13th chords, because it's all about huge stuff. But if you're trying to write lean. . . .

MH: Of all the numbers I've looked at, at least for *Passion*, I saw more alternate versions of that very simple melody—what you called "Train

Song, scene 11" in this sketch, but is what we now think of as "Loving You." [Note: The following examples were selected from eleven pages of sketches, ending with 8 measures from the final version.]

Example 1.18

Example 1.18 (continued)

SS: This was written late in the show. The older I get, guess what takes the most effort in the world? Simplicity. It's what we were just talking about. This is really simple, and it cost me an arm and a leg to get this simple. The problem with simplicity is it's really hard to do. There's this awful term "simplistic," and I'm not sure I even know what it means. There's simple-minded, and there's simple, and there's a big difference. Most pop music is simple-minded, and most show music is simple-minded—when it's not pretentious and over-complicated, or long-winded. "Simple" is really hard to do. That's what makes me admire the best of Kern so much—how "simple," it is. The best of Rodgers, how "simple" it is. Cole Porter's never simple, and when he tries to get simple, like "True Love" or something like that, it embarrasses me. I think it's terrible. He needs to be fussy, because his lyrics are fussy. But with the simple composers like Harold Arlen, it's really so admirable when a song is simple but still has character, like "Sleepin' Bee"—when it's not bloodless, when it's not *just* simple. And that's very hard to do. It took me a long time to accept this song because of that. With "Loving You" I thought: Oh, come on, there's so little going on in this song. But I was really encouraged because Lapine loved it, and Scott Rudin, who produced the piece, loved it. And I thought: All right, we'll put it on the stage if you like it that much. I thought: Oh gee, they like it because they can hum it. But what they liked was that Fosca was making a simple statement simply. And I tend, like many composers, not to be simple. Because, it's hard—it's much easier to hide behind a lot of chocolate sauce—and I kept thinking: I'm trying to please people instead of do the right thing for the character. And I realized that's what she's doing—it's right for her. This is not right for anybody earlier in the show. This is right for her at this point, because she's been reduced to this. And it is the simplicity of what she says that starts to change Giorgio's heart. This is the key moment in the show. I used to think it was "I Wish I Could Forget You." And it isn't. It's this moment. It's this moment where Giorgio first starts to hear her and hear what she's *really* saying to him. And as such, it's very moving. And I thought: Well, that calls for simplicity. It doesn't call for an aria, and it doesn't call for 9th chords (although it does have plenty of them in it, but you know what I mean); it doesn't call for decoration. But it's really hard to write. Not all moments call for this kind of thing, but when they do. . . .

MH: Did you always know there was going to be *this* song there?

SS: No, originally it was a song for Giorgio, as I remember it. I don't remember exactly, but there's a history to this song. I may have written something else—for her, or something for Giorgio, or a duet—and then James (as I remember it) kind of pushed me to write something simple for her. Ah, here in my notes, here's what was cut. This is Fosca explaining herself with a repeat of that "They hear drums . . ." melody, but against it the little musical theme from the garden. And here she is explaining herself: "You were right, I was wrong, I must learn to wait. You were right all along. Now I know, and I shall be there waiting, day and night. . . ." That's not simple. That's called "explaining yourself," instead of just saying what's in your heart. Now I'm talking about the lyrics, but that echoes

TRAIN (Sc. 11) - PART I (4/7/94)
(FOSCA)

Example 1.19

itself musically. Ah, and here's Giorgio, he sang in the train: "Do you know what I feel?" This was a whole duet between them—a discursive duet—and it never got into rehearsal. I don't even think this got copied. As you can see, it's a fair copy, but I don't think it ever got to the copyist. I think that this is what the song evolved from. I don't know if James used the word "simpler," or if he said, "I would just like something for her to sing to him at this point in the scene." But that's what it was.

MH: It sounds like the story about the inspiration for "Send in the Clowns."

SS: Exactly. It came out of the scene. It came directly out of the scene instead of being discursive. That's really what "less is more" is about—it's about being less discursive both musically and lyrically.

MH: When you were talking about other composers, such as Arlen, I was reminded that you've done a lot of pastiche work in some of your shows. Do you study their scores first, or is it just that you know them so well?

SS: I listen to the records to refresh my memory. On *Follies*, I just listened again. I had, as a kid, of course, played all their songs. They each have a distinct harmonic style, and that's what you imitate—the harmonic style. Arlen's harmonic style is immediately recognizable, so is Gershwin's, so is Kern's, so is Porter's, so is Rodgers'. If you play me a song that I've never heard from their mature years, I'll tell you who wrote it. Not from their early years, because in their early years everybody sounds like everybody else. But if you give me middle period Arlen, or middle period Rodgers, I'll tell you which is which.

MH: In *Follies*, how did you decide which composers to emulate?

SS: I just wanted the gamut—just everybody I liked.

MH: "Losing My Mind" is obviously Gershwin . . .

SS: "The Man I Love."

MH: But why wasn't it based on Arlen's "The Man That Got Away," which would seem to have made as much, if not more, sense there?

SS: First, "The Man That Got Away" I wouldn't believe in a *Ziegfeld Follies*—that's too sophisticated a song.

MH: And in *Pacific Overtures*, as part of "Please Hello," you wrote your own version of a Gilbert and Sullivan song and a Sousa number, but in *Assassins*, instead of doing *your* version of Sousa, you decided to use an actual Sousa piece?

SS: Because that's what they were playing when the assassination attempt on Roosevelt took place. That's authentic—that's exactly what they were playing.

MH: Also in "Please Hello," what's the Dutch Admiral's music based on?

SS: It's just a clog. I did thought association. What do you think of when you think Dutch? You think: the boy with his finger in the dike with the clog shoes and the little hat and the tulips. And you think clogs, and that's what you think of. That's all, so I was doing a clog dance.

MH: In the liner notes you wrote for Paul Weston's Jerome Kern album, you wrote one-sentence descriptions of the music of Rodgers, Kern, and Porter: "In Rodgers' music, deceptive simplicity is the trademark. Sudden surprising shifts of spare block harmonies under essentially diatonic, often repeated note, melodies with occasional unexpected chromatic leaps. The impressive feature of Porter's songs is their sophistication, the frequent use of Latin-American rhythms, the lush chromatic harmony and the lengthy extensions of standard chorus forms." How you would describe your . . . style isn't exactly the right word. . .?

SS: I don't know how I would describe myself because I'm so eclectic. People say they hear my style. I'm not sure I would recognize something I'd written. I'm not sure—musically. I know there are certain chords I use over and over and over again, but I'm not sure I would recognize something I'd written. Because I write in a lot of styles, because often I'm imitating a milieu or something like that. And yet, people I respect say they can tell something of mine; and people I don't respect say it. But I'm not sure I would recognize it. I do recognize when people are imitating me, but usually it's an imitation of my lyric style. And I recognize when they're doing a takeoff on my music by using lots of wrong notes, and thick chords, and that sort of thing—I recognize what they're parodying. But I'm not sure that I would recognize a piece of mine that I hadn't heard before.

MH: Certainly, in the same way you described Porter's lengthy forms, I can't think of anyone else who's done such extended musicalized scenes as you have.

SS: Ah, but you're talking about form now, I thought you were talking about musical style.

MH: But that's one of the things that you mentioned.

SS: Okay, fair enough. I think I could tell that—as a musical-dramatist, I think I could tell my style. But as a composer, I'm not sure I could. I'm not sure.

MH: What do you look for in other peoples' work? How do you judge it?

SS: Surprise.

MH: That's it?

SS: Surprise. Just don't tell me something I already know. And I'm not talking about lyrically, I'm talking about musically too. Let me hear a voice, and let me be surprised. (As well as, of course, because I'm interested in theater music, somebody who knows how to dramatize things.) Very few people know how to make people laugh, but that I always admire—when somebody makes me laugh. Freshness and an individual voice. Somebody you haven't heard before. That's rare.

MH: Is there anything you can suggest for people of how they can get to that point—how they study, what they look at?

SS: Oh sure, of course: keep writing. How do you tell somebody to become a grown-up person? That's all. You develop. If you don't develop, you don't become a grown-up person. The same thing is true of an artist. You find your voice. One of the most startling and thrilling things I ever saw in a museum was a Mondrian exhibit at the Museum of Modern Art. In his early days, like everybody else, he was imitating others and that sort of thing. He was drawing representative things, and then, you turn the corner, and there was a painting of a cow, and a second painting of a cow, and it started to break apart, and a third painting of a cow, and by the time of the fifth painting, he was almost at *Broadway Boogie Woogie*. He had found his voice. And the same thing happened in a Matisse exhibition a few years ago. You turned the corner, and you saw where and with what painting he found his voice. But prior to that he imitated other people. And you could see all the influences coming in. He found his voice. It was always very clear in Lenny's music where his influences are. The one influence in Lenny's music that nobody ever acknowledges, including Lenny, is Paul Bowles. That's really who he was influenced by. But you can hear the Copland. But you can hear Lenny! It's Lenny. I don't care if you can hear strains of the other people. He had a voice. And that's what you listen for in music, is a voice. Even if you hear where it comes from. I'm eclectic the way Lenny was eclectic. But I've a voice, I've a voice.

MH: Was there a score where you found your "cow"?

SS: Curiously enough, you can hear it as early as *Saturday Night*. (You know, that's finally going to be done.) It's just little peeps through the marshland, but you can hear the voice starting to sound. And then in *Forum* you can start to hear it develop more. *Company* is the first full-blown score I wrote that's really me and nobody else. When I say "nobody else," it's everybody's influence, but it's me.

MH: Have you ever solicited musical help? Did you ever go to Lenny and say: I don't know how to get from here to here.

SS: No, not in terms of composition. I did that when I wrote the background music for a play called *Invitation to a March*, because I was orchestrating for the first time in my life, and I had never studied instrumentation, and he helped me with that. And he helped me make transitions from instrument to instrument. But I don't ever remember going to him with a specific piece of music and saying: What do I do here? I don't remember that.

MH: In your sketches for the "Flashback Sequence," I was struck by a musical quotation from the "Emperor Waltz" you wrote at the bottom of one of the pages. I assume for some reason that piece resonated with you at that point in the score. Do you remember why?

Example 1.20

SS: No, there must have been a specific reason. Obviously it was meant to be source music of some sort. Originally, Jim Lapine wanted this whole flashback sequence to be done as a mini-operetta. He wanted somehow to encapsulate and perhaps make it of a different style. When he used the word *operetta*, it must have had something to do with that. I don't know why I picked the actual "Emperor Waltz," except there is the little sequence in the flashback where Fosca dances with the Count. And it may have been that, thinking of it as a mini-operetta, I wanted to use a waltz that would suggest the period. I don't think I chose it for its melodic value, but for something that would immediately suggest a costume operetta. That's the only thing I can think of. I had no intention of utilizing it as music, but merely as source music. I was brought up on movies, and what do you associate with when you see costume dramas that take place in the late-ish nineteenth century? First of all, it seemed to me that what she would be doing would be waltzing with him, because that suggests the period—whether it's Italy or France or England or in America. But particularly in Italy and France—I don't mean that they waltzed in Italy, but just that feeling of costume.

MH: I'm curious about your musical memory. How you store other music and are able to write it out from having heard it?

SS: Well in this case the tune is so well known that it is in my head. This is obviously some free association; that's why it's written at the bottom of the page. I usually start writing at the top of the page when I'm collecting thematic ideas, and I usually put at the bottom, either something that need not be stated—except that I want to write it down—or a quotation from something.

MH: I came upon this letter with your manuscripts—a letter to Jeremy Sams in 1996, presumably as he was preparing to direct the London production. You wrote: "J is under the impression that you intend to cut the echo chorus of 'to feel a woman's touch' after the train sequence. If so, I hope you'll reconsider. It may not be necessary to make the scene change in your version of the staging, but I like the sonic texture of it in the place." I found the concept of *sonic texture* fascinating. What did you mean by it? [See example 1.21 "Transition (Scenes 10–11)"; note: It is clear that Sondheim's letter is referring to "Transition (Scenes 10–11)" as published in the piano-vocal score, although this precedes rather than follows the train sequence. According to Sondheim, this discrepancy is because the placement and order of some of the transitions changed over time.]

SS: It feels like a lonely solo. It feels a capella (even though there is, in fact, orchestra going on) and it feels distant, and there's an ineffable sadness about it when it's sung that way. And I didn't want to lose that color. So perhaps I meant *color* rather than *texture*. But the texture is about a very vehement beautiful solo voice against a simple vocal chorus—vocal set of chords. It's a color and texture—it's a texture really, that's not used elsewhere in the show. I think, as a matter of fact, that was not my invention, I think that was the invention of Lapine and Paul Gemignani, the music director in New York, when James was looking for a scene change. I think he conceived that, because I don't ever remember utilizing that.

Example 1.21

MH: But there are a fair amount of them through the show.

SS: Yes, but that's very often the director and, particularly, Gemignani, who has a first-rate theatrical imagination for the use of music. Much of the connecting material in shows I've written, meaning scene-change stuff, has been devised by Gemignani and either Hal Prince or Lapine. Then I go over it and maybe make emendations. But the feeling is something that arises during rehearsals. Lapine will say: "I'd love to have something very kind of distant and mysterious here." And Paul will come up with something. Or, for some of the percussion used in *Pacific Overtures*, Hal would say: "I'd love to have something harsh here." And Paul, who had a massive array of percussion instruments, would devise something on a percussion instrument. That's quite often how it happens, because directors don't really like to have writers around while they're *making*. Lapine is less self-conscious about that than most, but Hal is quite fierce about it. And I can't blame him; he doesn't want someone looking over his shoulder while he's making, and Lapine's the same way. So I stay away until they're ready "to show me something"—which is usually one act. In order to make the act hold together, they have to devise some kind of what film composers call a scratch track. Gemignani's instincts are so much like mine, and also so sharp, and he works so well with his directors, that I rarely change things—except, maybe, picking a different piece of music. But the texture of this, I think, was devised by them.

MH: As long as you've brought up the role of musical directors, for future generations of musical directors, are there general points that you'd want to make about how your work should be conducted, and how it should be taught to performers and musicians?

SS: No. The older I get, the more meticulous I am about notation, in terms of things like metronome markings and dynamics. In the first few shows I wrote, I would just put *mezzo forte* and just leave it alone. But when I started working with Jonathan Tunick, who orchestrates most of my shows, he always wants me to play the score, no matter how meticulously notated it is, because he says he gets so much, both dynamically and in terms of tempo and rubato and all that, from the way I play it. And quite often it's different than what I've written, because I don't realize that I'm getting louder or softer. When I'm preparing the manuscript for re-hearsals, I'm quite meticulous. Once we're in rehearsals I don't do anything until the show is open; and then, when I'm ready to get the score published, I add further details that arose out of the performance. I will realize that the singer slowed down, because I told her to, but I hadn't no-tated it in the score. So, by the time it goes to the publisher, it's fairly meticulously notated, and I would like people to follow those notations as much as possible.

MH: Do you use a metronome when you're composing?

SS: Yes, absolutely. And sometimes it's off because, when I'm playing at home and singing to myself, it often is faster—sometimes it's slower, but usually faster—than the metronome marking I meant. In other words, I make the metronome marking, and then, when they get it into rehearsal, it's too fast or too slow.

MH: Do you find that once something is orchestrated, the tempos need to be changed because of differences between the orchestra and the piano?

SS: No. It happens during rehearsal. You know, orchestrations in musical theater are done during the rehearsal period, so if Jonathan hears some-thing that's too fast for a certain texture of instruments, he'll adjust. In other words, the cast doesn't adjust to the orchestra, the orchestra adjusts to the cast.

MH: When your work is orchestrated outside the original production of the show, or when—as with the recording *Symphonic Sondheim*—people do things with the music. What are your wishes regarding what they should or shouldn't change?

SS: When they're going for free interpretation, let them do whatever they want. I remember when I was working with Dick Rodgers on *Do I Hear a Waltz?*, and he heard a recording of "Lover" that was played in four, and, of course, it's a waltz, he was berserk. And I could understand it, but that was an interpretation—everybody knew what the song was. When a song is first heard, I want it done exactly the way I intended it. When it's heard a second time, in another arrangement, another singer, something like that, fine, let them do anything they wish with it. You can't ask performers not to interpret. I don't like them changing lyrics, and I don't like them changing notes. But if they want to change tempi, if they want to even sometimes change from three to four, that's . . .

MH: When you say "notes" you mean melody, but what about harmony?

SS: I don't want them to change the harmonies either. But they do, they do.

MH: And you never find their changes intriguing, or interesting?

SS: No, it's awful. "Send in the Clowns" was made popular by two singers: Judy Collins, for whom Jonathan Tunick orchestrated it, so the chords are correct, and Frank Sinatra, for whom Gordon Jenkins* orchestrated it and who made one chord change. It was unwitting, but, of course, Sinatra's recording has been copied by everyone. People who make records, I fear, do not look at the sheet music, they listen to other recordings. And the result is, that chord has been copied—it's in the middle of the release, where he dropped a suspension—and it just kills it for me, it just kills it. But because that was such a popular record, most people do that, and it's awful. You know, you spend hours choosing a chord, or working something out contrapuntally. And to have it dismissed like *that*, because somebody has a tin ear, is awful.

*After the first printing of the text, it was determined that the actual arranger for the Sinatra recording of "Send in the Clowns" was Gordon Jenkins.

Chapter Two

Assassins

MH: Moving on to *Assassins*.

SS: Or moving back.

MH: Or moving back. I guess this is the *Merrily* version of *This Is Your Life*.

SS: Right—*This Was Your Life*.

MH: We've discussed your long-line plans a bit already, but there are a couple of them for *Assassins*, and I'd like to start by talking about them a little more.

SS: *Assassins* is very much a collection of songs. Some motifs are used over and over again, particularly "Hail to the Chief" and a couple of others, I think. This is really, in the old-fashioned sense, a musical comedy—whether people think it's a comedy or not, it's a collection of songs. There's no attempt here to make a "score" except insofar as it relates to the characters. It's eclectic—different kinds of styles, reflecting the periods and reflecting the characters. So if there's any kind of long-line stuff, it's within some of the pieces themselves.

MH: I only meant for individual numbers. In particular, these sketches for the "Ballad of Booth" are intriguing for the kind of work you were doing.

Example 2.1

SS: Wow! One of the things about the "Ballad of Booth" is, I have a feeling it didn't end up this long. But my guess is that these are two different versions (mostly because one is in B-flat, and one is in G), but it may have been—you know, what he sings is in two sections. As I remember it, the "Ballad" itself is in B-flat, and I'm surprised that I made a longline out of the Balladeer's version, but apparently I did. The problem with this number, or the task I set myself, was that I wanted to combine two entirely different songs and yet make them feel as if the Balladeer's version—which is supposedly a kind of banjo song—would act as a framework for a very romantic middle section and that they should

BOOTH BALLAD
Interlude & Booth

Example 2.1 (continued)

somehow be related. And my guess is that's why I worked out these various long-line things, but it would take me a while to go back over this and figure out exactly what I was doing. I notice, however, that there's a great deal of interplay between the fifth note of the scale and the sixth note of the scale, and I see that's both in the harmony and in the melody. And I see that it's reflected in the bass line in G major—the D-E-D-E—so, it looks like I was hovering around the relationship between five and six. You'll notice that, at least in the first part of this,

there are very few accidentals, which means this must be the Balladeer's section, because he didn't deal much in accidentals. The reason
there's so much work on this is that I knew that I had to somehow keep
these two songs separate but glue them together in some way. I suspect
the long-line of the Balladeer's section both reflects and is reflected by
the long-line of Booth's section. And yet Booth's section is rubato and
free-flowing, and the Balladeer's is rhythmic and steady.

MH: Most of your manuscripts are for piano accompaniments, but this
one was obviously conceived for a ukulele or banjo.

SS: I know. Once we invented the character of the Balladeer, we figured he
would have a guitar or banjo slung over his shoulder—sort of Woody
Guthrie style. When I say banjo, "Oh Susannah" was what I was thinking
of. Those repeated chords at the beginning are much more banjo chords,

Example 2.2

or banjo-style, than guitar-style. I rarely think instrumentally, but in this case it seemed important that the Balladeer always have some sort of guitar or banjo accompaniment.

MH: So when you write those chords, what are you thinking?

SS: I'm thinking of three notes that can be strummed on the banjo. That's all.

MH: This is your only show I can think of that didn't have a full orchestration until the recording session.

SS: Yes, this show was done with three instruments originally.

MH: What was that process like—since you didn't get to work out the orchestration in rehearsal?

SS: I just trusted Michael Starobin by then because he'd done such a sensational job on *Sunday in the Park with George*. When it came time for the orchestra rehearsals, I went there and went over some stuff with him—whatever objections I had. It was taking a big chance, but I didn't mind taking it with Michael at all. You always want to hear the orchestrations in advance in case there are any egregious, I won't say errors, but choices that you disagree with.

MH: For the Hinckley/Fromme number, "Unworthy of Your Love," there are a lot of fairly significant differences among your sketches. For instance, in this version it has a much higher tessitura.

"Unworthy of Your Love"

I am nothing you are devil + God, Charlie, take my body and blood for your Love

Example 2.3

SS: I don't know why I wrote it so high up. I have learned over a period of time not to take singers over a D or D-sharp, even if they're sopranos. The soprano sound is not my favorite sound anyway, and you get up around an F. . . . When I'm singing, I'm singing an octave below and it doesn't matter, but boy, when you start to hear them up there it gets hard to understand the lyrics and, for my money, it's not a pleasant sound. There are, of course, exceptions—if you have Barbara Cook singing an F, that's a different matter. My guess is here I started to work out everything, and I thought: Oh dear, it's all too high. You'll notice I wrote "transpose as needed." Instead of putting it into another key, I'm sure I said to Paul Gemignani: Tell me what key you want it in, and if there's any problem with the relationship of the two voices, I'll fix it. That's my guess, because ordinarily I would never give this to a copyist without a specific transposition saying, "take this down," before handing it to the singer.

MH: This song is an example of what Stephen Banfield calls, "diegetic music"—meaning in the show, the character of Hinckley is actually writing and performing it as a song. And it's my understanding that you did some things musically in this song to indicate a naive composer.

SS: There's one place in the opening vamp—in the accompaniment—that is like he's making an error while he's playing. That should be another F-sharp in bar 6.

Example 2.4

MH: Is that hard for you to do?

SS: No, I thought it was fun. I was wondering if anybody would catch it. It's for me. As I told you before, I think that an audience's ear, no matter how uneducated it is, I think they sense it—I think they sense that something's out of the pattern there. It's as if he made a mistake playing the guitar.

MH: Would this be a rare example of, if somebody does do a pop record- ing of the song, you would actually prefer the F-sharp be used?

SS: I probably would, but it doesn't matter because it's merely an eleventh in the chord instead of a third. I never think about pop record- ings. If I published it as a separate number I suppose I would prefer it with the F-sharp. Something else that I notice is that I had an earlier percussive accompaniment that would have had the orchestra come in more heavily.

MH: Do you remember why you changed it?

SS: My guess is that either it happened before the notion that he actually was writing the song, or I didn't think of his actually playing and writing on the guitar until the second thought. That's all I can think of, because there's a complete piano copy that I wrote with the percussive, orchestral accompaniment, so there must have been a real reason to change it. I must have thought better of it. I know it never went into rehearsal—it was al- ways guitar in rehearsal.

MH: In your sketches for "Another National Anthem," you've written out these series of chords that are labeled "cadences." The piece begins with that choral sequence; am I right in assuming that's what these sketches were for?

Example 2.5a

SS: That's what these are. I'm trying out different cadences, because that whole lament idea is two chords, but I also knew that this was going to be a dissonant piece. Originally, I must have intended for the song to end, as opposed to fade out, because usually when I write cadences I really am talking about stopping points—usually at the end, or sometimes in the middle if there's a demarked section. But since this is one continuous piece, interrupted by the Balladeer, my guess is those cadences are the choral sections. On the other hand, those vocals were set fairly early, so

Example 2.5b

it's possible that these were cadences that I wanted to use to end, let's say,
a section of "Another National Anthem," and then to transition into the
Balladeer's section. That's another possibility.

MH: And where you've written "final cadence"?

SS: That means, obviously, I really meant the piece to end. But now that I
look at it, that's not really a very consonant chord, so maybe by that time
what I meant was: That's the last chord I wanted to hear before the fade-
out as people wander off the stage. But certainly that's the last chord I
wanted to have.

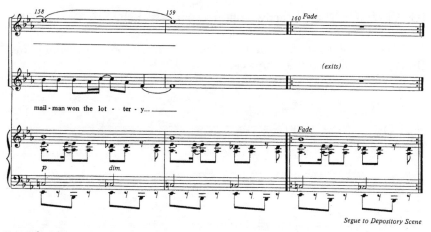

Example 2.5c

MH: So when you refer to cadences, in some cases it's literally the end of the song, but sometimes there are internal cadences that you're talking about.

SS: Yes, usually to end a section. And it's sometimes to avoid a straight V-I, but without, again, being "wrong note"—something that's built into the harmony, or a variation. If I've used another cadence before, then I want to use that.

MH: Why did you think the vocals at the beginning should be pre-recorded?

SS: Just to give that distant effect. I wanted it disembodied—I wanted that disembodied lament.

MH: A number of twentieth-century composers have worked extensively with using pre-recorded sounds, and I'm curious if that's something you've explored, or thought much about.

SS: No, not at all. These are usually practical matters. The cast in *Assassins* is made up of the Assassins plus the group that play the bystanders—five people. The five people are the ones who did that choral part, but it was taped, so it became part of the orchestra. But that was to keep it regular; I wanted to be sure that it was absolutely regular.

MH: Is it mourning?

SS: Absolutely. That's exactly what it's supposed to be.

MH: The added number for the London production, "Something Just Broke," also utilized that choral effect.

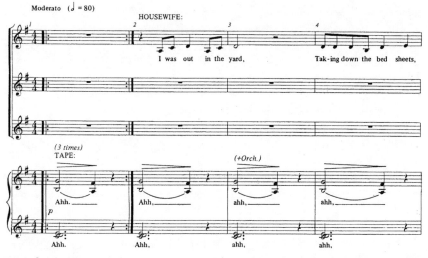

Example 2.6

SS: In fact, that's why I had written it originally. I'd always intended to write "Something Just Broke," and there just wasn't time. We opened the show off-Broadway, and we thought we would have it transfer. I assumed by the time it transferred I'd be able to write this extra number, but then it never transferred, so I wrote it for London. It was always intended that there would be a moment in *Assassins* about what happens to the country when a president gets assassinated. Most people don't know, but the country went into just as deep mourning for McKinley and Garfield as they did for Lincoln. Kennedy was different because, by that time, the communications revolution had happened, and everybody knew it all at once. But in Lincoln's case, McKinley's case, and Garfield's case, it took a while for the news to get across the country. But the trains carrying the bodies of the presidents were greeted with just as much weeping and wailing in the case of two minor presidents as in the case of Lincoln. It's a constant when the country goes into a convulsion like that, and that's what that number's about—the country's convulsion. "Something Just Broke" deals with the deaths of all four presidents. It starts with one, but then you gradually realize you're hearing from a farmer in 1893, and then somebody's talking about Dallas, Texas, in 1963.

MH: It seems one of the through lines of your work has been history through the eyes of the bystander. Such as the numbers "How I Saved Roosevelt," "Someone in a Tree," and "Four Black Dragons."

SS: It's more than a coincidence, those are shows with John Weidman. The socio-political shows I've written are all—all: *Pacific Overtures, Assassins,* and the one I'm writing now with him, *Wise Guys*—they all involve that double facet of the observer and the observed. I don't think any of the other shows do.

MH: Is it a technique that intrigues you musically?

SS: No, it's John's doing. "Someone in a Tree" is his invention. He gets full credit for that notion of history as prisms through different time zones. That's absolutely his. And "Something Just Broke" is something we discussed. I thought: How do I get the whole country onto the stage? "How I Saved Roosevelt" is a good example of one of the things that's nice about *Assassins*: Everything in it is actually true and happened—not when people meet across a hundred years, that didn't happen—there were five bystanders, each of whom claimed that they had saved Roosevelt's life.

MH: Of all of your shows, *Assassins* is the only one I can think of where there are not only characters who really lived, but who are alive today. How did that affect your writing for them?

SS: Well, the only one who's alive is Gerald Ford, isn't it?

MH: Well, Squeaky Fromme and Hinckley and Moore.

SS: Gosh, you're absolutely right. No, it didn't occur to us. I ran into a lady who was a great-niece of Czolgosz, and unfortunately told me that the family pronounced the name "Solegosh," and we'd gone through the whole show pronouncing it Czolgosz. I told John, and we just cocked our eyebrows and left it as it was. As a matter of fact, it was even farther away than "Solegosh," it was "Solegoak," or something like that, but really a different pronunciation. And we didn't know whether it was Bick or Bike—B-Y-C-K—and we had no way of finding it out. I still don't know.

MH: Do you have any sense that, from now on, the history of how these things are viewed will be affected by the show?

SS: No, the show wasn't that popular.

MH: In the MTI piece that you did on *Assassins* you say that you "chose to emulate Stephen Foster for his poignancy," and you described Booth's section of the "Gun Song" as "seductive, almost evil." Can you talk about what it is in music that makes it emotional—that makes a piece of music poignant or evil?

SS: It's impossible. That's like talking about programmatic music and saying: Oh, that's the sea. And then you say: No it isn't, it's the sky. You can't use literary terms about music—that's the whole point of music. The whole idea of the MTI piece is to give an indication to people who are going to put on the show. (I think that whoever is listening or looking at this should know that MTI is the firm that leases these shows to groups that want to perform them, whether they're amateur or professional. And in order to give an indication of how the pieces should be approached from the author's standpoint, Freddie Gershon of MTI had the bright idea— and a very bright idea—of having the authors videotaped talking about the works.) So I'm on that tape demonstrating things at the piano in terms of tempi and approach, but also trying and give them a color that they can relate to. To say "Stephen Foster" immediately sets up some kind of algorithm in the head, and they'll go ahead and at least try to approximate it. If I said "Cole Porter," they would do it a whole different way. "Poignant" is a word I would ordinarily never use, because it has to do with reaction, not with the piece itself. What strikes you as poignant might strike me as laughable, so I don't think you can give affect to music. If I say a piece is poignant, all I mean is, it's poignant to me. In this case I was saying: The notion behind this has the plaintive quality of Stephen Foster. But it's strictly "music appreciation" guidelines—it's to be taken seriously, but not too seriously.

MH: Are there certain obvious things that you do when you want to generate certain emotional reactions in an audience or character? Things like: tritones mean this. . . .

SS: No. There are people who associate keys with emotions—the way Seurat associated colors with certain emotions. I don't. There is a tendency— and I don't know whether it's because of the relation of the fingers to the eye to the brain to the piano—to think of sharp keys as bright and flat keys as romantic or, I don't want to say sad, but soft. Whereas there's a kind of bright (no pun intended) sharpness about sharp keys—at least in my mind. If I were writing a lament it would occur to me to write it in a flat key or a white key; it would not occur to me to write it in a sharp key.

MH: What about major keys, minor keys, or the modes?

SS: Well, you see, it took a long time for me to write in minor. I happen to love minor modes, but for some reason I wrote show after show after show without writing a song in a minor mode. I can't really remember the first time I did it consciously, but I do know that *Pacific Overtures* was full of minor modes because the Japanese pentatonic scale is a kind of minor pentatonic. But prior to that, you'd be hard put to find a lot of minor stuff in my work. It's hard for me to think of any. I mean I'm sure I did write something in *Forum* or *Follies* or *Company* or *Whistle* in a minor mode, but offhand I can't think of them. I do know that the verse of "Miller's Son" I remember as one of the very first times I thought: Oh look, I'm writing in a minor mode.

MH: So it wasn't a conscious decision to write it in the minor?

SS: No, it wasn't. I don't know why that is, because as a kid I used to play "Aase's Death," and lots of things in minor keys. For some reason I didn't write in them for some time. Most people associate minor with sad, and I think there's a reason probably; I don't know what it is, but one generally does. But "Losing My Mind" is a sad song, and it's in a major key.

MH: Looking through the *Assassins* manuscripts, I was surprised—particularly given the smaller scale of the show—how many song ideas you worked through. There were eight pages just listing possible titles and ideas for songs.

SS: Well, there were also many other scenes. The show first started with the idea of assassination through the ages, starting with Julius Caesar. Then we realized that was unwieldy, so we decided to restrict it to American assassinations, but we included ones like Harvey Milk. John wrote a whole Harvey Milk scene. Then we decided *that* was unwieldy and we would restrict it entirely to presidents, which was a wise choice. Because the incubation period was a long time, many of those ideas were for other versions of the show. I'm reminded of one idea that John had—a wonderful idea and I'm sorry we never did it. It was a trio for three of the vice presidents—Lincoln's vice-president, Garfield's vice-president, and McKinley's vice-president—when they get the phone call (we took the liberty of having phone calls): "Excuse me sir." "What! Me?!" You know, three people totally unprepared for what's been thrust on them. It would have been very funny. But there were a lot of ideas.

MH: Tell me about the process of making those choices and decisions. I know you work very much from what the librettist gives you . . .

SS: Very much.

MH: . . . but do you subtly pressure them, and say: "I'd really love to write *this* number"?

SS: It's not what they give me, it's what we work out together—what we decide would be effective musically. Obviously, in talking about the scenes I get lots of ideas and I jot them all down. Sometimes I will try an idea and I can't make it work, so I'll go on to another idea. That happens frequently, where, given a situation, I will have four or five central ideas, and if I can combine them and make them one piece without packing the trunk too tightly, I will use them and just find a refrain line that is the central idea. But if it comes to: Shall we have a song for the three vice-presidents, or shall we have a song for the three presidents' widows? Then I have to decide, do I want a comic song or do I want a serious song? (Because I don't think you can make a comic song out of the widows.) That would be one way of making the decision. And then I would probably think to myself: Well, maybe I could use the same music and have the three widows at the beginning of the show, and then, two-thirds of the way through the show, the three vice-presidents with the same music with a comic lyric. All those ideas, you start to juggle them. Ideas are fun to think of, the execution is: *Oy, Got in himmel!* But getting the ideas is always fun.

MH: It raises the question of plotting the score.

SS: "Routining."

MH: How does that process happen—where the up tempos, the ballads, the . . .?

SS: I don't think as much about up tempos and ballads as I do about—a word we used earlier—textures. That is, I don't mind having three ballads in a row, but I don't want three ballads sung by a male voice in a row. Because by the time of the third song, the male voice has outstayed its welcome. So if I were writing a show, for example, that only had men in it, I would just see to it that one number was a solo, one was a trio, and one was an ensemble, or something like that, to give it variety. There used to be an old rule that you don't put ballads back-to-back, but that dates back to the Rodgers and Hammerstein era. Nowadays you can do anything. It's a question of how the dramatic arc of the show progresses and where the music is required. And it's a matter of where is music necessary to the show? The really hard part about routining a musical is where is music necessary. You can sing about anything. We could sing this conversation, but does music enhance it? Is music necessary to it? Or is music merely a decorative way of our talking to each other? And you have to decide if decoration—I mean generally I'm against decoration, but every now and then. . . . In *Forum*, for example, I had a terrible time writing that score (Next to *Merrily*, it was the hardest score I ever had to write.) because I had been brought up by Oscar Hammerstein to think of songs as being little scenes and necessary to telling the story. And Burt Shevelove said: "But there's a whole other way to write songs—the way the Greeks did it, and the way Romans did it, and the way Shakespeare did it— which is, to savor the moment." And that, in fact—up until Rodgers and Hammerstein—was precisely the way all songs in the musical theater were written, except for Oscar's. Take, for example, "Let's Do It"— it's taking an idea and playing with it for four minutes. It doesn't move from A to B, it's certainly not necessary, even to the light texture of the show—to that kind of story. But, the point is, songs had a different function in those days. I like to say Rodgers and Hammerstein spoiled it for all of us, because you can't write those frivolous songs anymore. But *Forum* was one of the last gasp attempts to do this. You can take the songs, most of them, if not all, out of *Forum*, and you haven't hurt the story at all. I used to complain to Burt and grumble that: "The script is so brilliant, these songs are just going to hold things up." He said: "No, this script will be relentless without the relief and respite of songs that just take little moments and play with them and give them air." And so I gradually got to accept that. But, with that exception, in all the shows I write, the songs are plotted based on where they are necessary to tell the story and where the story can be told better by song. There's an old cliché that when a character reaches a peak of emotion, and it's too great for speech, he has to sing. There's some truth to that, but not a lot, because characters don't often reach that peak of emotion. Yes, for "Everything's Coming Up Roses" the character reaches a peak of emotion where she can't contain herself anymore. But for most of the songs in most shows, it's not the peak of emotion, it's where does music explode the emotion? Where does the music enlarge, or even sometimes, I suppose, diminish and make crystalline, whatever the notion is, at the same time it carries the story forward?

MH: You've been using more and more underscoring in your shows. How is that music used?

SS: It's interesting you say that, because the person who's fondest of underscoring is James Lapine, and if you trace it back, the underscoring plague started with *Sunday in the Park with George*.

MH: I thought that in *Sweeney* you consciously used continuous underscoring.

SS: Ah, but that was for a different reason, which is that I wanted to write a horror movie, and the way a horror movie gets written is that you keep the music going all the time. John Williams is responsible for *Jaws*, not Steven Spielberg. That's not to put down Spielberg, just that I remember sitting in that theater, and the screen lit up, and there was this underwater shot, and those double-basses started, and I was terrified. I didn't even know what I was looking at. Music can do that. Music doesn't have any particular literary context, but it does have the ability to stir a certain kind of emotion. Also we associate things with music—we've been exposed so much to instrumental colors defining things, particularly in movies. You always hear a bassoon accompanying a drunk coming home in the movies of the thirties, forties, and, I suppose, into the fifties too. And growling double-basses do suggest a beast of some sort. We have those thought associations that I don't think a nineteenth-century audience would respond to in the same way— they wouldn't hear a bassoon and associate it with a drunk. You hear a saxophone, it's usually a sexy girl. It's from years of inculcation through the movies. So there are connotations that come with music, but it's usually instrumental colors. All I know is that John Williams frightened me to death with that. Horror movies and suspense movies are very much co-created. Bernard Herrmann *is* Alfred Hitchcock; that's why Hitchcock used him all the time. What happens in *Psycho* in the orchestra is just as frightening as what happens on the screen. And not just the shrieking birds, but those unresolved chords that keep going on so that nothing ever reaches a cadence, and so you're constantly upset, because it's all a kind of—"irresolution" is the best I can say. But it promises something else: You're not through yet . . . you're not through yet . . . something else is going to happen . . . it's not over yet. Herrmann was the master of that, but many composers do it. I tried to do it in *Sweeney. Sweeney* is an homage to Bernard Herrmann. I even used a chord in the show that's what I call my Bernard Herrmann chord, and that is one of the basic building blocks of the whole piece. But I realized that as soon as the music stopped, I didn't want to give the audience too much of a chance to remember where they were—which is watching a lot of stage blood, and a lot of over-acting—that's not a criticism of the actors—but larger than life. What makes *Sweeney* effective—if it's effective—is that everybody is over the top, because if they're not, it's really silly. But *if* they're over the top, it's silly unless you can keep the tension going, so I wanted to keep the music going, so I wrote a lot of underscoring. And that's a case where all the underscoring is mine—that was not devised by anybody else but me.

MH: And underscoring that you've done subsequent to *Sweeney*?

SS: I did a lot of underscoring for Lapine consciously, and a lot of underscoring for *Into the Woods*.

MH: How do you approach it as a composer?

SS: Usually you're developing themes and vamps—rhythmic ideas—that are associated with either that character. . . . I'm very much a leitmotif man—I really like the notion that an audience will register certain tunes, or rhythmic ideas, or even harmonies, with given characters. And you can build on that. It's very convenient. I don't know why more people don't do it. If I have a theme for you, and a theme for her, then when the two of you get together, I don't have to wonder about what I should write: I'll take your music and her music and combine them. So you're building up a bank for yourself. I made motifs for Sweeney, and for Mrs. Lovett, and for the Beggar Woman; and when everything starts to collide towards the end, I have all the material to build on. If you set those things up, it's effective for the audience. That's what dictates the underscoring. When Sweeney comes on we get the Sweeney motif. I try to keep it a little less obvious than that, but I've got the motif to work with. Also, again from Bernard Herrmann, I picked up how to create suspense. I don't know that I can really articulate it, because it's more of a feeling than anything else—when you use skittering music to create nervousness and that sort of thing. It's fairly literal stuff, it's not very subtle, but then in a melodrama, subtlety is not what you're after. Incidentally, underscoring is easy and fun to write, and if I were not in musical theater, I would enjoy writing movie music. The trouble with movie music is you're not in charge of it—eventually the director or the producer throws half of it out, or changes something. But given autonomy, I think it would be really fun to write movie music.

MH: How was writing the *Stavisky* score?

SS: Alain Resnais, who directed it, really respected it, but half of it is not in the movie, because he decided to take everything that had to do with Trotsky out.

MH: How did it open you up musically—the fact that you weren't limited by the range of the voice?

SS: It's great. That's why I talked before about how I'd like to write ballet music if I ever wrote so-called concert music. Lyric writing is, for me, hell. It's genuinely unpleasant, even though I often end up proud of what I've done. But it's really, really, really hard. Particularly with *this* language, which is a great language, but there are certain aspects of it that are hard to sing— as opposed to Italian, where virtually every word is singable. And when I don't have to write lyrics, I feel it's really fun; it's a picnic. Now working out music involves a lot of hard work, and choosing and trying to make things fresh and trying to be inventive. That's true of lyrics too, but you're free, you're not restricted by a language; you're only restricted by the fact that there are only twelve notes in the scale, that's all you're restricted by.

MH: When you were talking about having motives for different characters before, I started thinking about the score for *Anyone Can Whistle.*

You've discussed before that the score is about the real music as opposed to the show business music—that is, the music for Fay versus the music for Cora. So when you then write a duet for those two characters—"There's Always a Woman"—how do you approach the music?

SS: That was just musical comedy. I didn't take it that seriously, I didn't think that deeply. The thing was to distinguish between the two styles, that was all. I think when it came to the duet—well it's show-biz duet, in the sense that there are punch lines.

MH: And it was cut.

SS: It was cut. It was cut because it wasn't very good.

MH: There's one last long-line sketch from *Assassins*—it's the "Opening Shooting Gallery." [Note: When asked about this example later, Sondheim explained: "The lines under the whole notes are the equivalent of double whole notes in printed music—that is, they indicate demarcation points more important than the plain whole notes."]

Opening
(Shooting Gallery)

Example 2.7

SS: Unfortunately, this is undiscussable because this is the original version of the number. The original "Shooting Gallery" number was a good deal longer than the Mahler *Resurrection*, and complicated, and, oh my God, the counterpoint, and. . . . Anyway, this is the sketch for that, and it's literally now a third of what it was, and much better, and it's still pretty long. But I like it very much now; I think it's the right proportion. "Less is more" is a hard lesson to learn. You know, I've discovered recently—to my horror (and I think I'm going to have to do it on *Wise Guys* too)—that my opening numbers tend to be much too long. Now I know that it's because I'm setting all the ground rules up—for the rest of the show, for myself—and so it's harder for me to be economical. And I wish I could say I'm just letting myself go and intended to draw back, but it's unconscious. I'm surprised when I end up with a twelve-minute number that should have been four minutes long. I'm surprised, and they're not only long, but they generally tend to be overly complex at the beginning, which is, of course, exactly the wrong message to send to an audience. *Wise Guys* opens with four songs—four vaudeville songs—that then start colliding with each other. At the moment, I suspect that it's about a quarter too long. It may not be, but I may have to reconceive it for three vaudeville songs. This is something that recently occurred because we had a reading two weeks ago. I finished the number a couple of years ago, and we had a reading of the whole show in March, but with only two of the numbers. But now that almost half the score is written, and now that I really heard it at the recent reading, it didn't stand up. Because the second number is also quite long. So it just sounded like a show with a lot of long numbers. But it shouldn't be. And even though it's a medley of four numbers, it just started to feel a little overweight and overlong. And I realized: Oh my God, I do this all the time. You know the opening number of *Sunday*—Dot's number—is also quite long. I set up almost all the music in the show in it, but it holds together okay, and I don't think I cut much of that from its original. It is long, but I don't think it's *too* long. But *this* was much too long, much too long.

MH: Do you tend to think it's important to compose a score chronologically?

SS: Absolutely. For me it is. I almost always do it. There are exceptions in the composing, but it's hard for me at the moment to think of a score since *Forum* that I haven't composed from the beginning to the end. *Company* is an exception, and I remember the last song I wrote was "You Could Drive a Person Crazy," because I couldn't figure out how to make a song work in that scene. And I remember that I wrote "It's Hot Up Here" almost right off—I think it the was the first number I wrote, maybe the second, for *Sunday*—because I just thought it was such a good idea, and I couldn't wait to write it. But otherwise, *Sunday* was composed chronologically. I know *Sweeney* was, and I know *Into the Woods* was, and I know *Assassins* was.

MH: I have the impression that *Follies* was composed by the chronology of the musical styles of the pastiche numbers, rather than the chronology of the show—that you started with "One More Kiss."

SS: No, you have to remember, *Follies'* gestation period was over a period of five years, so there were a lot of things that were replaced, and the characters changed, so there's no way to tell. When I started to write *Follies*, I wrote it from the beginning, but then it got interrupted by other things—another show, and then Hal came in, and we decided to change from realism to surrealism. That meant some songs had to be thrown out—so the whole process was screwed up. Luckily it doesn't matter so much in *Follies*, because there are the two styles, as you say. The first song I ever wrote for *Follies* was "One More Kiss," but that was because I was feeling my way around pastiche, because I wasn't sure I could do it. Certainly with a real plotted show, absolutely. *Follies* is a sort of revue, and so is *Company*. But *Company* was pretty chronological. *Follies* was less so as it turned out. But the story-telling shows from *A Little Night Music* and *Pacific Overtures* on, all were composed chronologically.

MH: We won't discuss your sketch for "Opening Shooting Gallery" in detail, but could you tell me what the A, B, and C mean?

SS: Those are sections. Remember this number is introducing various people. The A is probably the proprietor. It's preceded by "Hail to the Chief." The B is introducing Czolgosz. The second A is the proprietor again. I knew that I wanted to hold the number together by having the proprietor keep coming back in the scene to sing the refrain.

MH: Do you remember what the "Coll." stands for?

SS: It might be one of the characters, but it also might have been a bit of business. I don't know what that is for sure, but if what it is is something to remind myself of what that section deals with, it may have been "collecting money"—it may stand for "collection." It probably indicates an action, and I wanted to remind myself that that action occurred during that section. [Note: A later examination of the manuscript led me to believe the abbreviation is actually "call.," standing for "calliope."]

MH: When I was looking at the MTI videotapes for *Assassins* and *Into the Woods*, I noted that in both of them you ended up talking about the importance of getting the audience's attention right away in the opening number. In *Into the Woods* you do it musically with the "I Wish" on the offbeat, and in *Assassins* it's with the lyric, "Come here and shoot a President." How do you think of an audience and how do you write for them?

SS: To get their attention, the thing is to surprise them—not to let them get ahead of you. "Once upon a time—BOOM!" takes the wind out of them. Because an audience hears "Once upon a time" and by the time you're on the third word, already they're starting to relax—"Once upon a time there was a little girl." But give them "Once upon a time—SMASH!"—with a chord, and it's "Uh, oh," and then they know not to expect anything—that their expectations are going to be upended. They'll never know when music's going to come in, and they'll never know when it's not going to come in. Whereas with *Assassins*, I was trying to shock them with the lyric idea. "C'mere and kill a President"—for an audience who doesn't know what the show is about—is a shocker. And then they know. It's, again, setting up ground rules—what Oscar taught me—set up the ground rules. It tells them: This is going to be a shocking show.

Example 2.8

MH: When you're working, you've spent so much preparation time thinking about the show and talking with your librettist, how do you back out of the process when you go to write and think: What does the audience know at this point? What don't they know? And how am I trying to tell them?

SS: That's an unanswerable question. And more shows have foundered on the shoals of that, and I'll give you one: *Anyone Can Whistle*. One of the reasons for its failure—if not the major reason—is that we never made clear to the audience in the first fifteen minutes what we were talking about. Are these loonies? They're called "Cookies," but, in fact, they're non-conformists. But they're in an asylum. What is going on here? Now, I think, it wasn't clear to us. We could talk about it, but that's not the same thing as being clear. And the result is the audience never felt settled. Now granted, they might not have liked the show anyway because there are aspects of archness in the show and things like that, but I do know that we didn't have a chance, and it's because of that opening. It's hard to gauge. One of the major things one does during what they call previews or out-of-town tryouts is you sit with the audience. If you're real smart, you pay no attention to applause, you pay no attention to coughing. You pay attention to concentration. Are they getting what you're saying? If they don't like it, there's nothing you can do about that, because you can't, at least, I don't believe in pandering (you don't just go up a half-tone and make a bigger second chorus; some people do, but I don't). But are they getting it? And are they understanding, not only what you're about, but what the story is? Do they know that: He's her father? Do they know that: She is this? You've got to be very careful about exposition. Now you don't want to just lay it out dully, but you want to make absolutely clear to an audience what the ground rules are—what kind of a show it's going to be—and who these people are. The opening of *West Side Story* is wonderfully effective because you see six juvenile delinquents standing around and then they start to dance, and you say: Oh, I see, it's about ballet delinquents! You've got to know that. Really. There's an anecdote I like to tell, so I'll tell it here for posterity. *West Side Story* was my first Broadway show and, even though I got slammed in the reviews, I was very pleased to have a show on. It was the second night, and I was standing in the back, and the curtain went up and you saw the guys standing there, and they start snapping their fingers, and you hear "Da dadada da, da dadadada da-da" and suddenly they went into what Jerry called "the sailing step," where they spread their arms out to show they own the turf (which is about a minute into the number). Three rows from the back a man got up in the middle of the row, put his coat over his arm, and said: "Excuse me, excuse me, excuse me, excuse me." And he made his way out of the row, came up the aisle and, of course, I was standing there, aghast. And he could tell from the fact that I was standing at the back, and I was slack-jawed, that I was connected with the show, and he just looked at me balefully and said: "Don't ask." And I got the whole picture: This is a guy who's had a hard day at the office, he's on his way home, he thinks: Maybe I'll stop and see a musical, there's this new musical that just opened. So he sits there. He thinks it's going to be a *musical*—there going to be a lot of pretty girls, and there's going to be lots of lively music—and he sees six ballet dancers being juvenile delinquents to dissonant music, and he thought: Oh, no, no, no. I suspect he went to the nearest bar and poured himself three Martinis. But this was not what he wanted. And I thought: That makes the opening—we told him what it was going to be like, and he knew he would hate it. And he would have hated it. And that's why I know that's a good opening—he knew he would hate it.

MH: Today, after we leave, presumably you're going to go work on a number for *Wise Guys*.

SS: I hope.

MH: Do you try and see it from a fresh perspective? Do you imagine it from the audience's eye?

SS: I've discovered over a period of years that essentially I'm a playwright who writes with song, and that playwrights are actors. And what I do is I act. So what I'll do is, I'll go upstairs, and I'll get back into the character of Wilson Mizner, and I'll start singing to myself. It'll take me a while to make that transition, because it's been a couple of days since I've been Wilson, but I'll get upstairs, and I'll be Wilson.

Chapter Three

Into the Woods

MH: I'd like to start with this series of motives that you had sketched out. [Note: See Examples 3.1 and 3.1 (continued).]

SS: Right, these are absolutely traditional leitmotifs. Before you even ask your question, let me tell you: Originally I was going to have each character personified by an instrument and by a theme. So this is literally my master sheet. You'll notice how neatly this is written, even though it's got some erasures; that's because this is a compilation of things I'd worked out on other sheets. And this is my master list, with each character notated at the left hand, or over each motif. So that "B & BW" means Baker and Baker's Wife. ("BW" were also my initials for "Beggar Woman," so every now and then I look at that and think: Wait a minute!) But that's what these things are, and "W" is Witch, "CM" is Cinderella's Mother, et cetera. So I determined I was going to have a whole series of themes and then utilize them, so that's what this sheet is.

MH: Aside from the bean theme, which we'll talk about a little later, what surprised me when I looked through all of your motifs, I realized that virtually all of them started with an interval of a major second or, in a few cases, a minor second. It struck me as rather extraordinary.

SS: It all came out of "I wish." I just decided that okay, you've got ten characters here—I'm making it up, there may be eleven, there may be nine—and each one's going to have a theme. And then there's the bean theme, and so how do you utilize these—in tandem—and why bother to write themes unless they're going to somehow relate to each other? So, just as most of the

Motifs

Example 3.1

themes in *Passion* relate to those first five notes, or the bugle call, in this case, again, it seemed to me that I could relate the themes by beginning them each with the same motif. It makes it easier to write if you have a character come on and a theme that you've heard starts and then goes into another direction—it holds it together. So, if Cinderella goes "da-dum," and the next character goes "da-dum, da dah," and the next character goes "dadadada-dum," you can then interweave them so much more easily—as opposed to having to change the opening interval. Because the opening of a theme is like the opening of a show—it's the identifying moment. It's: How do the notes start? In Shostakovich's Fifth Symphony, the octave leap in the slow movement says everything, and then everything comes out of that.

Motifs

Example 3.1 (continued)

MH: So, rather than restricting you, it opens you up in a way.

SS: Yes. It also makes it easier. It gives you a bank to draw on when you get stuck.

MH: Why did you chose a second—why not a fourth, why not a fifth?

SS: How would you set "I wish"?

MH: "I *wish*." [said with an inflection and a shrug]

SS: Ah, well, that's the Jewish version. Yes, and for the Jewish Cinderella it would actually be a minor second—"I *wish*." Or it would actually go down—"I *wish*." But it is about inflection. I mean, if you want to get pretentious about it, I suppose I picked a second because she's a repressed girl. She's too repressed to sing a third, or a fourth, or a fifth. That's one way to look at it, isn't it? "I *wish*." Cinderella would never raise her voice, she would never go "I *wish*"—that's raising. . . .

MH: But in a way then, Cinderella's the key character, not the Baker.

SS: The show begins and ends with. . . . Ah, no. Everybody in the show has a wish—*wishing* is the key character. Of course the Baker's the key character, but *wishing* is the key character. James didn't want me to end with "I wish." James wanted to end with "Children Will Listen" and have me build it up into a large kind of vocal ode. I thought that was too sentimental and I said this is a show about wishing—whether it's wishing for a child, or wishing for freedom, or wishing for the world to be better. So, that's why. At any rate, it was my choice to have this inflection—a step up. And once you do that, it dictates a lot. And I found the most useful motive, although it's used mostly in accompaniment, to be the one that Jack's mother sings: "ba dum, ba dum, ba dum, ba dum. . . ." [see motif labeled "JM"], which relates, of course, to the title tune: "dadada dum da dum da dum da dum." [see motif labeled "Woods"] They all have little echoes of each other. This turned out to be a very valuable decision, because Lapine really wanted many of the songs not to end, but to drift into dialogue. So to prevent a truly frustrated feeling of coitus interruptus, when you hear something you've heard before there's a certain satisfaction, even if it doesn't end. At least that was the rationale I had.

MH: So it was a rationale, but not from the beginning?

SS: No it wasn't, but that's what I mean. This was a valuable choice, because when it turned out he wanted to truncate numbers and to keep them fragmentary, the fact that they all were related meant that you weren't listening to a new tune truncated, you were listening to a variation of an old tune truncated. And that made it less unpalatable.

MH: On the subject of the "bean theme": You said on one of the MTI videotapes, "The story is in a sense about the bean theme." You go on to explain that the story is, to some degree, about how the bean theme evolves through the course of the show, and that in "No One Is Alone" the bean theme finally becomes calm.

SS: Again, this is for the MTI thing. Talking about intervals of a second is not going to be of much help to somebody doing the show, but to indicate to people: Look below the surface and see how this theme is twined into the show throughout, and how it's reflected in so many ways. That will help not only the musical director, but the director, I hope, and maybe even the actors, to understand the process of the composition of the show. So what I said is an exaggeration, although not entirely untrue, because the bean theme is the most prominent theme, except for the title theme which evolves out of these others, and is, in fact, utilized as a theme in different disguises. These things we were just talking about are all variations of one idea, but the bean theme remains the bean theme whether it's in an inversion or not, or whether it's an augmentation, or not. It remains the bean theme. Whether it's used in the accompaniment, or in a melody, or as a piece of underscoring, it's always: Yump, bump, bumbum, bump. Obviously, anybody who's in any way sophisticated musically is going to understand this and hear it, but the MTI videotapes are for people who are not musically sophisticated. But once they understand some of these things, their eyes open, and they say: *Oh!*, and they start to become aware that everything is related. And just that awareness will affect how they approach the show, even if they don't utilize it in any way. I mean, how are you going to utilize that knowledge if you're an actor, or whatever? But to know it is very important. They then know that things are not arbitrary in the show, and I'm going to guess that it helps them unify the show in terms of acting styles, in terms of scenic approach, whatever. If they know the music is conceived, not "bitsy-piecy," but that it has some kind of over-arching notion—or set of notions—maybe that will reflect itself in the work they do. I really believe that. Now I may be full of it, that may not happen at all—but it can't hurt, as they used to say in the old Jewish joke.

MH: You mentioned just now inversions of the theme, and I know there's one in "No One Is Alone" during the lyric "People make mistakes."

from "No One Is Alone (Part II)"

Peo-ple make mis-takes.

Bean Theme

Example 3.2

SS: That's the big one.

MH: What was behind the decision that *that's* a place to hear an inversion of the bean theme? What does that say?

SS: Nothing. Thanks to Hammerstein, I had a nice moment with Richard Rodgers—this was in my late teens before I worked with him, maybe it was later. I went up to his office and I said: "One of the things I admire so much is how the release of `People Will Say We're in Love' is the inversion of the main theme." He looked at me as if I were crazy. He had no idea that it was—it had been instinctive on his part. It was something Milton Babbitt taught me when he analyzed "All the Things You Are" and went through all the subtleties of what Kern had done. And I said: "You mean he thought all these things up?" Babbitt said: "Some of it was conscious, but some of it was unconscious, like when you learn to drive a stick-shift car—eventually all that coordination becomes unconscious." Or riding a bicycle, which is my version of it. It becomes unconscious— all that coordination. In Rodgers' case, he instinctively went for the inversion. In this case, I just went for it because I was looking for a release—it was conscious—and I knew that I was using the bean theme constantly in this song, and I thought it would be fun to invert it here, and it makes for a nice chordal effect—that kind of Ravel chord there—that's very nice.

MH: But too much shouldn't be read intellectually into that decision?

SS: Intellectually? No. But certainly the utilization of the bean theme in that song, even when it's not an inversion, is certainly deliberate.

MH: Have you discovered later that you've done things unwittingly that you had no idea you had done?

SS: Only during the writing. Not later, but during the writing I will make sudden discoveries. I believe that the unconscious is what writes and that the way to write a song—or anything, I suppose—is to live, eat, and breathe it all the time, and that when you go to sleep the work is done for you. For me, if I interrupt it too much with social life, with distraction, or with other work, it dissipates and I have to get back into it. That's why I work on one thing at a time. I believe if you inundate yourself with what you're working on, the brain starts to put all these things together. So I find it not just a coincidence that the next day I will write a new passage of music and say: Hey, that has the same relationship harmonically that the first section has; isn't that interesting? It's because of what's going on in the back of your brain unconsciously. Now sometimes it's a conscious decision, but often it's unconscious, and I have these little moments of delight where I realize that I'm still holding the piece together, that something is not irrelevant, that the idea—whatever musical idea came—was not by chance. You know, the fact that I took the melody from E to C, instead of C to E, means it's an inversion of something in the first section, and I didn't even know what I was doing, but the mind is doing that sort of stuff. Often, if you're stuck on something—everybody who ever writes and, I'm sure, paints or anything else creative, knows this—when you go to bed, in the morning, you suddenly have "fresh" ideas. It's what happened overnight that makes those fresh ideas. And if you're working on one piece, those fresh ideas are germane to that piece. I do not get a late idea for *Follies* while I'm writing *Passion*. No, the ideas all belong in the *Passion* score—they belong in that style, and they belong with those characters. I'm a firm believer in that.

MH: When you do go back to revise *Follies*, or something like that, how hard is it to get back into that world?

SS: Very, very hard. I wrote "Country House" for the 1988 *Follies* in London, but it belongs in *Company*. It's not a bad song, but it's the wrong style. I knew what I wanted to say, but I couldn't get back into the *Follies* style. The other three new songs for that production were pastiches, and they were easy to get back into, because you can say: All right, instead of *this* composer, I'll pastiche *that* composer. But "Country House" was a book song, and I couldn't get back into the style. I just couldn't do it.

MH: How did you try to do it? Did you go back and look at your sketches?

SS: I listened to the score again, and I tried to inculcate myself into it. I couldn't do it. It's very hard. But it's partly because I'm one of those people who writes an entirely different show each time—as opposed to a Rodgers and Hammerstein who, if they wanted to, could recycle stuff. Lenny recycled stuff all the time, and a lot of stuff from *Candide* went into *West Side Story*, and a lot of *West Side Story* went into *Candide*. It fools the eye and fools the ear, but I can't do that; I just can't. The shows are too different in my own head. What is useful in one show, is not in another. And therefore, it means, that if I'm working for a year on *Passion*, and then I suddenly have to do a revival of *Follies*, I can't do that—I can't get back into it, it's going to come out like *Passion*.

MH: In looking at your sketches for *Into the Woods*, I noticed that some of your thematic material was, not just melodic but harmonic; you even have chords that are themes.

SS: Absolutely. And they generally relate to the title song, because, again, I wanted a kind of "Follow the Yellow Brick Road" to go through the show. Because *Into the Woods* presents the problem of three or four major plots going on at the same time, and eight or nine major characters going on at the same time, you have to be careful. How do you carpet tack it—how do you keep the score from just riding madly off in all directions, like a Stephen Leacock character? And one of the ways to do it is to keep reminding the audience through chords. Again, because the characters have different themes, you can't use reprises very much, so I reprised chords. But most of those chords show up in the title tune.

MH: There are some chordal sketches that are labeled "bean theme." What does that mean?

"Bean Theme" [with sketches for "Witches Lament"]

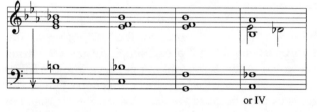

or IV

Example 3.3

SS: I'd have to see the sketches, and my guess is that if you take those five notes—which can be harmonized in many, many ways, at least as many ways as a Bach chorale theme—and so my guess is I was trying out different harmonizations. You can take that and it can go into at least three keys that I can think of offhand. So right away you've got three entirely different territories. And within those territories, you've got a I chord, and a I_6 chord, and all that sort of stuff. There are a lot of variations you can do there. I wanted a theme that was versatile, that's why I picked it.

MH: I think my favorite song from *Into the Woods* is "On the Steps of the Palace." It may be a little obvious to comment on, but it seems to me that the constant back-and-forth between two notes in the bass line reveals a lot about the character of Cinderella.

SS: Well, but it really comes out of "Very Nice Prince"—that's really what this accompaniment figure is from. So it's really for Cinderella and the Baker's Wife. I wanted something liquid and running—it's two

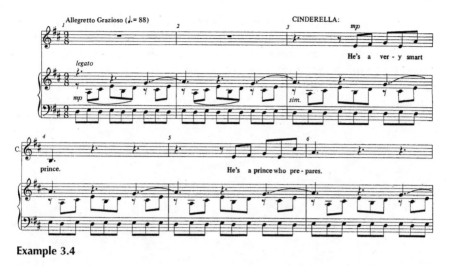

Example 3.4

girls getting together and dishing a ball. I wanted something that felt like conversation flowing. That's really what this sort of vamp is about. Also, that bass blurs the harmony, so you're never quite sure where you are. You don't know whether this is a tonic chord or a dominant chord, and the unsettled quality was what I was working for. I thought: All right, two ladies have differing reactions to the ball—one is jealous because she would love her life to be more tidy and glamorous, and she thinks the other one is a princess of some sort; and the princess has just had both a wonderful and terrible time and feels like a fraud. They're two very unsettled ladies. It's like "Lucy and Jessie"—each one wants the other one's life. One of them says: It must be wonderful to go home to a baker every night and know where you are. And the other one says: It must be wonderful to be a princess and go to a ball. And each one says: Yeah, but. . . . So that unsettled quality, I'm sure, is what suggests it. I don't even know if this was conscious, but it's my instinct as to why I chose that. So what you get is this blurred, not demarked, uncertain, harmonic flux. In "On the Steps of the Palace" I don't know if you ever know where you really are until bar twenty-three when it says: Oh, I see, we're in D major. In "Very Nice Prince" I don't think you ever know where you are.

MH: How do you compose a song where the harmony itself is so uncertain—if you can't be sure if you're in the dominant or the tonic. . . ?

SS: I just think it's up to the audience—let them worry about it. There was a nice phrase in my counterpoint book in college—it was a very conservative little book on counterpoint—and the author disapproved of a certain technique and said: "This is the refuge of the destitute." And I think this is the refuge of the destitute—it could be viewed that way. I don't think I felt that way, but. . . . Actually, it's easier not to make up your mind, isn't it?—as Cinderella points out. It reflects her state of mind.

Chapter Four

Sunday in the Park with George

MH: *Sunday in the Park* is an extraordinary score, and unlike anything else.

SS: It's an extraordinary show—it's a show that's unlike any other.

MH: I wanted to start with one page of your sketches that you've labeled "George Painting," but in its final form is known as "Color and Light, Part I." You've written yourself a little note at the top of the page. [See example 4.1.]

SS: "Pointillism is in the instrumentation and accompaniment." Originally, I had a schematic idea. I'm German by ancestry, and I have a Germanic neatness sense, and I make lists. So, just as it had occurred to me to assign a different instrument to each character in *Into the Woods*—an idea which I jettisoned fairly quickly—in the same way I thought: Isn't it interesting that Seurat had, on his palate, eleven colors and white. And I thought, eleven and one make twelve. And how many notes are there in the scale? Twelve. And I thought, ooh, isn't that interesting. So I thought I would utilize that in some way, shape, or form. You know the way he never mixed a color with a color that wasn't next to it on the color wheel—so he would never mix yellow with blue; he would mix yellow with yellow-orange, or he would mix blue with blue-violet, but he would never mix yellow and blue.

MH: When you say mix, do you mean literally, or next to each other?

SS: Literally. That is to say, if he was to make a dot, he would either use a color—augmented, or mixed with white—or a color mixed with the color

91

Example 4.1

next to it. But he would never mix the two colors, because the idea was to let the eye mix the colors. If the painter mixes the colors then the eye doesn't get a chance to, does it? If you take yellow and red and make your own orange out of it, it's not going to be the same thing as putting a yellow dot next to a red dot then letting the eye mix it. So I thought, wouldn't it be nice to do the musical equivalent, and then I realized it would make all the score minor seconds. This is not a good thing, because I would never be able to mix C with E; I'd have to mix C with D-flat, or C with B. I realized this was a dead end fairly soon, so I didn't do it. But this is clearly early on, and this is the first painting song from George. So then I thought, what I would do is use pointillism—and that's what this is about—in the rhythm. I looked at the painting; you know everybody thinks that Seurat painted in dots—he didn't, they're dabs. And there's a big difference. If you look at the strokes closely in the painting, he could only have applied them fairly slowly and meticulously. Well, that's fairly boring on a stage. People think of it as dots, so I thought: I will take the liberty of having him do it like that—stipple. You know he never used lines: all the outlines in all the pointillist paintings that he did are the result of putting a line of yellow dots next to a line of blue dots, and the eye mixes them and makes its own illusion. You get up close to it, there are no lines! It's a series of dabs next to a series of dabs. It's a complete illusion. And that was his point—no pun intended. But I thought, on the stage you can convey that—this is called taking liberties—by having him applying dots fairly rapidly and rhythmically. And I thought: Okay, if I'm going to do that, then I'm going to have a rhythm in the accompaniment that's going to echo that, so it's [sings "Color and Light" accompaniment]. You know he had a square palette, not the usual free-flowing palette, because he was very organized and every color had to be next to every color with a little white or not. And if you listen to the alternation—which becomes very important in the score—between the major and the minor [sings phrase], it's because I was holding on to that notion of the minor second. The alternation between a major third and a minor third, if you juxtapose them, is exactly like juxtaposing yellow with yellow-orange, or red with red-orange. It's exactly the same thing. And that juxtaposition is the point of this score. The opening arpeggio is two major chords, one juxtaposed with the other. In the same way, this is the juxtaposition of major and minor. And it pays off in "Move On." You know "Move On" is a compilation of all the themes in the show in one song. You hear that alternation of major and minor in the accompaniment there; it's an echo of this. And it comes from that notion that I had and threw out—of two notes right next to each other and the ear would blend them into one note. And you want to know something? I really believe that in "Move On" when that alternation occurs—[sings phrase] that little major/minor alternation—that the ear blends those two things and it comes out to be this unsettled, but very poignant chord. At least it does to me. I really hear it that way. Not here, but in "Move On."

MH: Why not here?

SS: In "Move On," because it's legato. Here it's staccato, so you hear very distinctly the separations. But when you're hearing " . . . you have to move on," under the "on," after the cadence there, you hear the major and the minor and they alternate. And what you get is a sense of *moire*. And I think it tells. I think it makes it satisfying. Because, ordinarily, that kind of uncertainty between major and minor would unsettle the audience. In

Example 4.2

"Move On," I think it feels like a cadence. And I think it's because it's been set up here.

MH: Did you think of that at this point, before you started to write "Move On"?

SS: Oh, no. When I got to "Move On," I thought: Okay, here's the culmination, what'll I do? I know, I'll take all the themes and put them together. And that's what I did. No, I had not planned it. When I started to write "Move On," I thought: Hey, how about using that opening arpeggio as your accompaniment arpeggio? And the minute I thought of that, the doors flew open. Once I knew that [sings arpeggio phrase] would become [sings accompaniment phrase]—that it would become the whole pillar, and all the building blocks of the accompaniment. Once I knew that, it started. Everything feeds in. This is what I mean by the unconscious—all these things coming in, all those themes, all those rhythmic themes, the moving thirds that she does with George and his painting in her solo, and it becomes the moving thirds accompaniment of "Finishing the Hat." That all plays into it. Everything. It's because for a year I'd been in this one country, and I'd spoken this one language. When it came time to write "Move On," I used my entire vocabulary. I hadn't quite finished it when we had our first reading for the Shuberts. I remember they were sitting there, and I thought: Oh, I've got to play an unfinished song, but I've got to let them know there's gonna be this big love song at the end of the show. I still had a couple of songs to write, but I wanted to get the climactic song done. My memory is that it was not hard to write—nothing's easy to write, but not hard compared to uphill struggles I've had before. And it was because of all of this. I tell you, if you prepare your table, the meal is easy to cook.

MH: I'm embarrassed to say that it wasn't until you were talking a few moments ago that I realized the lyric is "red, red-orange," I'd always thought it was "red . . . red . . . orange."

SS: Have you ever seen the painting?

MH: No.

SS: Go! First of all, it's the most magical experience. I can't talk about it without crying. It has such stillness in it. All the colors are faded now. He got bad advice from his good friend Pissarro. The only nice one in that entire group of Impressionists was Pissarro—as you probably know, they were all awful people, particularly to Seurat—but Pissarro supported him. Pissarro, in fact, did some pointillist painting. Pissarro said: "Listen, there's this new kind of paint and it has a real shimmer to it." And that's what Seurat was always after—shimmer. What he didn't know was it was the kind of paint that fades. By 1891 when Seurat died, the painting was only eight years old, and the colors had already started to fade. It's now behind glass at the Art Institute of Chicago so that no sunlight's hitting it and all that sort of stuff. It's still pretty vivid, but when you go up close and see what this man did, it's thrilling. Each one of those is a choice. Three million choices—however many dabs there are. It's a transitional painting; it's not pointillism entirely. He started to paint it with the kind of short strokes that he'd used on *Bathing at Asnières*, and then halfway through somebody—I think it was Pissarro—said to him: "Why don't you use this technique you've been trying these seascapes with—the little dotting techniques?" And he said: "All right."

MH: Getting back to "Move On," I'd like to talk about my favorite, remarkable page from the score.

SS: As you can see, all this stuff you've heard before in the score. The big harmonic change—which I suspect is what you like—the big, rhapsodic, harmonic change has no intellectuality behind it at all. It wasn't thought out, it sort of came to me, and it's because of my admiration for Rachmaninoff.

Example 4.3

It's a Rachmaninoff change. I don't mean it comes from anything specific, but if I heard this passage, and didn't know I'd written it, I'd say: I know who wrote that. It seems to me to be his harmonic style. I guess my favorite piece of his is the "Rhapsody on a Theme of Paganini." His rhapsodic style and his rhapsodic harmonies are . . . Though I'm not a Russian, I feel like a Russian when I listen to him. All the figuration is from other places in the score. There's nothing on this page that you haven't heard before, in terms of the way the notes [sings a phrase] . . . you've heard all that before. This is a case of where an inversion counts for a million bucks—at bar 119 at the lyric "and the care"—the fact that that's an inversion makes that whole chord work. If you put the root position under that, it lands like a wet washcloth, and I thought: I'm actually using an inversion—great! And because of the inversion—which is a first inversion of a B-flat chord, so you've got a D in the bass—what it does is lead to a dominant G. It's a fake dominant which leads eventually—because that's really a five of C—leads eventually to a huge C-major climax in bar 127, and it just feels like you've entered a new kingdom—which you have. And I did something smart: When I entered the new key, I reinstated the [sings alto line from m. 127]—because that's a very sweeping theme when it's arpeggiated legato that way. And, of course, "life" is a great word to sing. I'll tell you another thing, you're asking a singer to leap up to a high G there, when he's been singing fairly low: Mandy Patinkin's voice helps that a lot, too. But I must say, when I sang it to myself, I thought: Hey, that's good. I remember thinking: I hope I don't have to compromise on this because of whoever sings it. No, I take it back, Mandy had been cast already. I initially wrote George as a bass-baritone and I wrote Dot as a soprano. And, of course, it turns out we cast Bernadette Peters, who has got a bass-baritone, and Mandy, who's a soprano, and the duets didn't quite work. You'll notice, throughout the score, there are very few times when their voices actually go together, because their ranges are quite different. Though there are many notes that overlap, their tessitura's are so different that where you're hitting one person's strong voice, you're hitting the other person's weak voice, and that makes for very bad duet writing. If you're asking both of them to give a real zest, and only the man can do it because she's in her wrong register or vice versa, you're in trouble. There are notes in the scale where the two of them have equal power—because they both have strong voices—but not all the way through the register. Mandy is a little wider than Bernadette, but Bernadette is really powerful in the low notes.

MH: So would you have written "Move On" as it is, if you hadn't cast Mandy?

SS: No. It's just that in writing it I thought: Well if anybody can handle this, Mandy can. Actually, the range for George is not *that* great. It's a wide range, but this G-natural is the top note, and he may go as low as B-natural. An octave-and-six is not a lot to ask of somebody singing a semi-operettaish score. But there aren't an awful lot of singers on Broadway who have enough strength so that the low notes sound like something more than a pickup. Anybody can have a two-octave range if the low notes are just pickups.

MH: Would this song have been as exciting written down a fourth?

SS: Gosh, I can't tell you. I think what makes it exciting is what happens with the harmony, I don't think it's about the register—I don't think it's about the highness of it. It's just when Mandy does that it's so thrilling, because when he takes his baritone and puts it in the tenor range it's really terrific. I love this page too. But it's because of that Rachmaninoff change, and that's not analyzable, that was merely I got the idea, and I just did it.

MH: And your use of thematic material—because you've prepared your palette, you have the option of so many choices.

SS: Absolutely. It's just that that particular chordal progression is something that's not used elsewhere in the show; that just happened that Thursday, that's all.

MH: One of the things about the score of *Sunday* that hasn't received much comment is the set of parallels between the first act and the second act. I've tried to plot them out, and according to my eyes and ears, "Sunday in the

Example 4.4

Park with George" in the first act is closely related to "It's Hot Up Here" in the second.

SS: Absolutely. And they also both deal with the same subject, which is posing.

MH: "Color and Light" and "Chromolume #7."

SS: Absolutely.

MH: "Finishing the Hat" and "Putting It Together."

SS: Are the same tune. You'll be happy to know that Mandy had been in the show about a year-and-a-half, and we were having a farewell party. I don't know what it was that I said, but he replied: "What do you mean they're the same tune?" I said: "Mandy, you've been singing it for a year and a half. You didn't know that 'Finishing the Hat' and 'Putting It Together' are the same tune?" And he looked at me as if I had taken his Christmas away. He had no idea that for a year and a half he'd been singing the same tune in both acts.

MH: I must confess, it took me a while to realize it.

Example 4.5

SS: It's vaguely disguised. And also, as we say, the tone is different. In fairness to Mandy, he sings other stuff in between. It isn't like one song follows the other. On the other hand, the entire "Day Off" sequence is mirrored in the entire art gallery sequence.

MH: It looked to me like "The Day Off" and "Children and Art" share similarities.

SS: No, really? Well, yes, there's a little thing. "Children and Art" really is a sui generis. There may be parallels. Again, when you're thinking in one language, it comes out there are going to be similarities. I usually have one Arlen song in every show, and "Children and Art" is my Arlen song in *Sunday*. And there's a reason for it; George's grandmother is talking about how she was brought to America into the deep South, and that's where she grew up as a child. So I wanted to echo that, and when I think of the deep South, I think of Arlen. It's unfair since he comes from Buffalo or some place in New York State and was the son of a cantor, but still, he wrote those bluesy songs. You listen to "Blues in the Night" and you think: Gee, that guy must have been born in Georgia. But he wasn't. So because she is brought over from France as an infant and is brought to Carolina, or somewhere in the deep South, I decided to use this sort of blues structure. I know you're talking about the actual tune of "The Day Off," and there is a relationship there, but I think of the whole "Day Off" section with all the little vignettes in it; and the art gallery section with all the little vignettes in it are more related to each other. "Finishing the Hat" comes at the end of the "Day Off" section, and "Putting It Together" operates through the entire art gallery section, so the parallel is not absolutely rigid. But then I've learned not to make rigid parallels, but to suggest them. I think it would have been a mistake to just have "Putting It Together" at the end, the way "Finishing the Hat" is.

MH: When you were working with Lapine on the score in general, was there some plotting out that there would be certain parallels between the two acts?

SS: No, because the second act was entirely different. The second act was originally supposed to be what happened to the painting and how it affected people's lives after it left France. There's a mystery about what happened to that painting for about twenty years. It was rolled up in Seurat's studio, and you can tell it when you look at *Les Poseuses*, because he's got the canvas leaning in the corner. Then, according to what I know, it ended up rolled up in a room over a café in Paris. Somehow—I think it was a rich American woman—she found it there, or it got into her hands, and it didn't cost that much, but she brought it to America and presented it to the Art Institute of Chicago in, I think, 1924. I had thought it would be fun to do a contemporary "Sunday in the Park" by going to Central Park and having a replica, so to speak, of "The Day Off" at the opening of the second act—only today it's Sunday in Central Park, with kids skating and baseball players and people strolling and Joe Papp's theater, and all of that—a parallel of the whole "Day Off" section. I think we started the second act with that, as opposed to "It's Hot Up Here"—although we may have started with "It's Hot Up Here"—and James kept shifting back-and-forth in time. The central section in the second act was the painting hanging in the museum and people coming up, and how it affected their lives. And James had couples, and single people, et cetera, to parallel the whole "Day Off" section—a flirting couple, a married couple. We spent two days in Chicago looking at the painting and sitting and listening to people saying such things as, and I quote exactly: "Why, it's all made up of little dots." Another woman came in and said: "It looked so much better in the other gallery." All kinds of reactions. And we just stood there looking. We also had a nice moment when we went to the curators—there were three of them—and asked them to tell us whatever they knew. And we asked: "What is that object up there?" This is in the show. And the three of them had different answers, and they all looked at each other as if they'd been betrayed. Nobody knows what that object is. Is it a stove? Is it a waffle iron? Nobody knew what it was, but it was hilarious to have three scholars all saying completely different answers at the same time. And James echoed that. And then he had a really interesting idea; the penultimate climax of the second act was a flashback: Dot came up to George's studio to say good-bye, and he was painting. He had persuaded the two Celestes to pose for him—they were thrilled—and then they discovered they had to pose nude, and they wouldn't do it. So he got Dot to pose nude, and he used three visions of her—which is, of course, what *Les Poseuses* is. It's the same model from three angles, with the painting of *Sunday* rolled up in the back. That was the farewell scene. I remember James offered the script to Bernadette when we did it at Playwrights Horizons and she read it and she wanted to do it. I met her over the phone; she called me, saying she was thrilled. She said, "But I have to tell you one thing, I don't do nude." She thought she was going to be asked to pose naked on the stage. Which, of course, she wouldn't have had to do. The whole thing was more surreal and almost documentary-like. So there was no musical plan for the second act. I just wrote the first act, and then we changed it and made the act the way it is now. And I thought, okay, these two acts are so different, and I know people are going to be discombobulated by the fact that the first act seems like the end of a play; and then we've got this whole other show to give them. And I thought one way to tie the two acts together would be to make—this is a word I learned from Milton Babbitt, and I loved it—architectonic similarities. And that's what it is. So that's the reason for this—to make two disparate acts hold together. In *Into the Woods*, which has a similar structure, there's a story—there's a real plot that goes on—which is a result of the first act. So the two acts string together because the second act depends on the first act. But in *Sunday*, the second act is an entirely separate entity—it's another ship—so the way to link them together, it seemed to me, was to make it some kind of parallel structure. So "It's Hot Up Here," even though it may relate to Dot's opening number in the fact that it's posing, and she's also central to it, is essentially a prologue to a reiteration of the structure.

MH: There were a lot of things I noticed in the show that I've never seen referred to in the reviews. For instance, the fact the Boatman wears an eye patch, and in the painting you never see that side of his face. There are a lot of cute, fun things like that. And there's the man with the horn or trumpet, and I always assumed that the sixth of "Sunday"—the bugle call—absolutely grew out of you seeing that character in that painting.

Example 4.6

SS: Absolutely correct. And, in fact, in the Playwrights Horizons production it was a trumpet. We had only three instruments: we had rhythm, keyboard, and trumpet in the original. And that trumpet was used for just that purpose. You're absolutely right, that's where it came from.

MH: And the Celestes?

SS: The two Celestes? That's James's whim. I'll tell you another one that's really interesting is the lady who we have as the mother—the lady sitting next to the nurse. If you look closely, you don't know whether it's a lady or a man. It could be an old man. In fact, Randall Jarrell wrote a whole poem about this man who's sitting under the tree. To Randall Jarrell that was a man, to James it was a woman. And he made her George's mother. I remember vividly when we first got the notion. James went home, and he took a piece of tracing paper, and he made little outlines of the seven main characters—the ones in the foreground. And he drew an arrow—George's mother, question mark; George's mistress, question mark; painter, question mark; and boatman, and all that. Some critics—critics, meaning commentators—have thought that the boatman is a jockey. Nobody knows, nobody knows. What interested Seurat is in that painting, and apart from the technique and the geometry of it, it's the social commentary. He was also a social satirist. You know, he's almost like a Daumier. And he was very interested in how costume delineated character. There are many clues in the costumes—the fact that a monkey was often the symbol of a whore; so it tells you that a gentleman has a whore with him, that sort of thing.

MH: I heard Lapine give a talk in which he said that he found out after the show that the fishing rods associated with the women meant that they were prostitutes; and if he'd known before the show it probably would have changed the characters of the Celestes.

SS: Absolutely. But who in the audience knows that? But you think about "fishing," and what that means. Which brings up the Mizners, as a matter of fact, because Addison Mizner always referred to his evening clothes as his fishing costume, because he wore them when he was fishing for dowagers and money. So it persisted in the twentieth century. But everything in that picture is completely calculated: the colors are calculated, the geometry is calculated, the costumes are calculated. There's not a single spontaneous thing in that picture; that's called: "I'm working something out," and also, "I'm making a comment, and this is what this means." It's full of codes, some of which I'm sure we don't understand.

MH: As a composer, how much did you identify with Seurat? Did you want to try and emulate that intellectualism?

SS: No. In the design of the show, and the design of the music, sure. But you know the point is music—whether it's frozen architecture, or architecture is frozen music, it doesn't matter—it's about structure. And, of course, this is the perfect painting for somebody like me to musicalize because it is all about design, and it's all about echo, and it's all about the effect of this next to that, or this apart from that. It's so musical. The more I got to know the painting, the more musical I felt. Anyway, you must go to Chicago to see the painting. You'll just die. It's great.

MH: Back to your sketches for "Color and Light." On this one you wrote a note "alternate pointillism"; what does it mean?

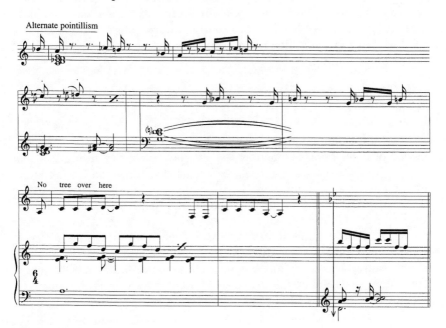

Example 4.7

SS: This looks like something I never used. These little fragments of two sixteenth notes next to each other separated by space [sings phrase]. And what I'm doing is: George is deciding [sings phrases, mimes painting]. These are all echoes of what he's doing with his hand. The whole number is about what he did with his hand. When I say "pointillism," I'm talking about his hand motions exclusively.

MH: Did you actually plot out where on the painting each stroke was supposed to be—so when George sings "red, red-orange" you knew where on the painting that was? And, if so, did you tell Mandy?

SS: Every single one. When the lyric says "diagonal," I really mean he's doing a diagonal. Because I looked at the painting and I saw these demarcations that are made entirely by complimentary colors. I mean, you look at that painting—I could not believe it—there is no line. That's a painting without a single line in it! And yet you see everything—there are fifty people in that painting. Fifty people! The other thing Lapine pointed out is, nobody's looking at anybody else. Nobody! Fifty people are *not* looking at each other. Why? They're very clearly people, and yet there's not a line in it. I was clearly trying to find a rhythm here. This is obviously one of the early sketches. Before this I thought: All right, if this gets too boring, or [sings phrase], then maybe I'll use that. In other words, let's say the first section will be [sings phrase]. And then George thinks: Gee, maybe that's not right. So he goes [sings phrase]. And I tried to think: How did he do it? Well, I'm sorry to say, unfortunately, because they're not dots, he did it more deliberately and slowly, which doesn't have a lot of rhythmic vitality to it.

MH: This fascinated me, where you have a note that says the "colors are talking." [See example 4.8.]

SS: The "colors are talking" may have been a lyric I wrote. The little "x"s instead of notes relates somehow to—I've never done anything like that before—it looks to me like those are chordal structures and I don't know what the notes are going to be. Usually when I do that I put stems on the "x"s. This may be a time when I didn't put stems on the "x"s. It says "strokes"; this is entirely about painting strokes. So clearly what I'm doing is relating these as chordal structures. Or, conceivably, these are different rhythmic ideas. Maybe I wanted to go [sings rhythm]. I ended up going: [sings phrase]. This is obviously what I chose to do. And here's "Sunday" [sings phrase]. One line here is clearly what I ended up with, but in between I'm suggesting alternates. These may be accompaniment rhythms, in other words I'm going [sings phrase]: but I'm going [sings phrase while

Example 4.8

knocking in a different rhythm]. Those could very well be rhythmic ideas, and, why I didn't put stems above them, I don't know. Usually when I do that kind of sketching, and I put an "x" with a stem above it, it means: I don't know what the notes are, but I do know what the rhythms are.

MH: I showed a copy of this sketch to a musicologist, and his assumption was that you were working out possible patterns. That, if you have a melodic theme, you would then select the different notes that correspond with the rhythms above as a way of evolving your thematic material.

SS: No, it's more likely simpler than that. I'm sure it's about rhythmic emphasis. If I was doing what you suggested—which, curiously enough, I have done—I wouldn't notate it that way. I'd write an alternate line; I'd actually write the notes out. I'd write: "G-B-G." I wouldn't go: "X, X, X"—that's what I think I would do. No, I know what I'd do. I'd write stems down—I'd write a quarter stem there, two eighth stems there. So I'd say it's gonna go [sings phrase]. And I do that quite often—when I don't know whether I want all the beats spoken or not—I'll do an alternate with the same notes with a stem down. If it's a different tune, I'll write it on a different line.

MH: Can you think of an example?

SS: You'll find it throughout. You'll find many sketches where there are stems down as well as stems up. They might not be here, because in *Sunday*—you can see how clean these pages are—I pretty well knew where I was going and what I was doing, so there wasn't an awful lot of alternate stuff. But that's how I do alternate stuff: I put stems up and stems down. Another thing I might do is put parentheses around notes. Here we have G-C-B-G, and if I didn't know whether I wanted all four, and just the first, third, and fourth, I would put parentheses around the C. That's what I usually do.

MH: In the song "Sunday," what you did chorally is unlike any other choral writing that I'm aware of that you've done, and I can't think of a work by another composer in which the vocal lines build with the accompaniment. What brought you to that point—how did you find that? [See examples 4.9a and 4.9b.]

SS: I don't know. Of course, the notion of dropping the orchestra out for that one bar is a steal from the end of *Candide*, because I think that is one of Lenny's greatest moments when the chorus takes over and the orchestra drops out. But, as for the build, it's just a build. With the possible exception of "Our Time," I think "Sunday" is the only anthem I've written. By anthem I mean one of those choral things. Usually when I have a chorus they're all treated differently, because I don't like that kind of convention. I love the sound of a chorus, but it's hard for me to justify eighty people singing the same thought. Here, because they're all figments of George's imagination, I can justify the fact they're all singing the same thing. So this is one of the few anthems I've written, which may be what's causing your comment, but maybe I'm not understanding your question.

MH: For instance, on the word "trees," the way the voices fill in the chord over time.

SS: My guess is that Paul Gemignani did that.

Example 4.9a

MH: Really?

SS: Yes. Because my guess is I just wrote "trees" as the melody. I'm not sure, because, of course, that descending line is very important. Often I will write choral stuff and then Paul will call me and say: "Listen, we're a little low on sopranos, a little heavy on basses, so do you mind if I invert . . .?" I say, "No," because his ear is very good. This particular bar I don't remember whether I wrote that or not. My guess is that Paul did that, but I'm not sure. I hate to take your Christmas away, but I'm always honest.

Example 4.9b

MH: How do you approach choral writing?

SS: I approach it with great trepidation because I know nothing about it. For somebody who's been around the block as long as I have and who has made a living out of it, I know less about the human voice and how singers produce the sounds they produce than I should. I could have joined the choir in college, and I should have, because Jonathan Tunick once told me that the way you learn orchestration is to sit in an orchestra. I could have learned something about the human voice by sitting in a choir. But I don't sing particularly well, though I sing vaguely on pitch. And I had no interest in being in a choir, and now I'm sorry, because I thought song writing was: You wrote a melodic line you sang, and you had an accompaniment. It never occurred to me that one day I would be writing choral stuff. The first choral stuff I ever wrote was the opening of *Company*. I was terrified, and I said to the conductor, Hal Hastings: "Here's this, do anything you want with it; this may sound ghastly." Because, you know, I had canonic entrances and it had choral bits. To my surprise, he said: "No, most of it works very well." He did say: "Here's a passage where I think there's too much spread in the voices," et cetera. So I got a little more confidence as a result of what he did with *Company*. So now I write my choral stuff, but I always tell Paul: "Do anything you want." This, what you call the "spread" there, that is unusual, but he knew what I was going for. But it may be mine, I would have to take a look. I do not have enough confidence in choral writing, so I write very simple choral music. I thought, if I just gave Paul the tune at the climax of *Sunday*, that it would end with the orchestral accompaniment spreading—which I had written—and that would work. And Paul devised a line that goes down, that follows the harmony, for the lower voices, that gives the chorus the feeling of spread, and that's the thing you love so much. That's his doing, not mine. What I do chorally that has some sophistication to it is the contrapuntal stuff—like the opening of *Company*. I remember, for example, writing the barbershop chorus in "The Gun Song," and I literally got a book of barbershop songs to see how they created that kind of close harmony. My only instrument is the piano, and the spread on a piano and the spread of four voices are entirely different; and you have to understand how a baritone and a tenor interact vocally. I had no experience doing that, because I've never sung in a group. As I said before, Jonathan Tunick said you learn orchestration, not just through books, but by sitting in an orchestra. That's how he got to be what he is—he played the clarinet in an orchestra. In the same way, if I'd sung in the choir at college, I would know more about how Gustav Holst creates *his* effects. I did listen to choral music, but until you've done it. . . . I now know more than I used to, just the way I know more about registers than I used to. I wrote this elaborate chorus for *The Frogs*, and it sounded squeaky and thin, and yet there were like twenty-five voices; and I said to Jonathan Tunick: "There's no point. . . ." And he said: "No. First of all, the key was a little too high, *and* you're doing it in the swimming pool at Yale, *and* the reverberation's muddied all the harmony. It's not your fault as much as you think it is." But I should have known: if you're writing for a chorus in a swimming pool, you've got to thin out the harmonies. It didn't occur to me. I thought, if the notes are there, they'll come out. Wrong. The same thing here. I thought if I just have a crescendo on this line—holding up before the orchestra drops out—it would work. And Paul just enriched it by taking the harmony, and taking the lower voice down, and that's exactly what thrilled you.

MH: You write a lot of numbers for large groups of people. They're not always singing chorally, but how do you plot out the structure of a number like, in *Sweeney*, where Tobias is singing "Ladies and gentlemen . . ." and then Todd and Mrs. Lovett are interjecting comments and asides?

SS: That's crossword-puzzle work. That's the kind of thing I *can* do. That's what I mean by contrapuntal writing—I can look at a page and I can work out lines so you can see the patterns on the page. It's texture. What Paul did was, he took a texture, and he spread the texture of the voices. That's what I don't know how to do. I can make a choral piece for all the people in this room with everybody having a different line. I can do that, because that's *working things out*. But I can't tell whether it will be a full sound, or a thin sound. I mean, I can tell, but I may be wrong. I don't have enough . . . the way someone who's experienced can say: "No, you've got to get them all together on this moment, and then you've got to have the basses go *this* way and the sopranos go *that* way." That's where it would be guesswork for me. I just don't know.

MH: When you have different things happen vocally on top of each other, like the layered sections of "Opening Doors," how do you decide: These are the key things I want the audience to hear and pick up on, and the rest of it is just texture?

SS: It's problematical. Generally, if you want things heard by an audience, it has to be solo or tutti—all together. Audiences cannot distinguish between two tunes, two melodic lines, or two different lyrics going together—unless they've heard each one before.

MH: So why do you do it? What's the point of those moments?

SS: Well, it's usually a mistake, but sometimes it is a case of: They don't have to understand the *details* of what's going on, all they have to understand is *what's* going on. So, if we decided to have a riot in this room, it's not necessary that they hear every individual line, all they have to hear is all the different kinds of anger and the different kinds of hysteria.

MH: Do you try and make sure that certain words are the ones that get telegraphed through?

SS: Sometimes you clear the undergrowth and somebody comes through specifically. But when all the people are singing at the climax of "Opening Doors," and they're excited because they're going to put on the show, the audience doesn't have to understanding anything, because the number has built up to that. By that time, we know what it's about, so no, details are not important. But generally, I'm getting cleaner about that, because it does tend to unsettle an audience if they can't distinguish what's going on. Even if they know what the general idea is, it's not quite as comfortable as if they really understood. That's, again, justification. It's a lot easier to just put all the lines together and say it'll work.

MH: Knowing that there are those people who will get the recordings and the scores and follow the lyrics they couldn't catch in the theater, and they will get some gratification at finding that out, does that play at all into what you do?

SS: I suppose. But I'm afraid it's all justification. And I think sometimes it is justified. Sometimes they don't have to understand what's going on, but I think you have to be careful about that. It's very hard for me, because I really hate the "peasants on the green" form of operetta and opera writing, where suddenly *everybody* is singing the same thought. But, no, they're not. Unless it's revolution, of course—if it's "up the Democrats, down the Republicans"—yes, you can do that.

MH: "Wintergreen for President"?

SS: "Wintergreen for President." That makes sense doesn't it, because it's supposed to be the entire country. But if, as the case with "Opening Doors," everybody has a different agenda and they're all singing at once, I don't know how to make them all sing the same thing.

MH: "Please Hello"?

SS: No. Because each one has a different agenda. But also, in "Please Hello," by the time all the voices go together, you have just heard the individual things. In other words, you hear an individual admiral, and then a second individual admiral overlapped by the first individual admiral, who, even though the words are different, you know what he's doing. It's just important to know the two people are arguing—just to know that the two are each asking for a specific kind of treaty. And then the third Admiral comes in, and he gets an entire solo, and then he asks for a treaty, and we know. . . . It probably would have been more comfortable for the audience if, each time there's an overlap, I'd repeated the same lyric, but I get bored doing that. It's wrong, because that is a convention. But I think: Why would anybody repeat themself? It's foolish thinking—it's realistic thinking in an artificial form, and, even as I'm speaking, I think: Well, what's the point? But, it's what I do.

MH: On this sketch for "Sunday," below the D-I$_6$ chord, you've written "progression up." What does that mean?

Example 4.10

SS: I want to keep the progression going that way. I had an alternate—see above where it goes from I⁶ to B-flat V? Here it goes to an entirely different harmonization. So, obviously I wanted to keep a rising line going, because that's an A-natural—so G, A-natural. Then there's the I⁶₄, which would be, again, an A-natural in the bass. I think what that means is a rising line in the bass, but I'd have to look at it again. I use dotted lines when I have alternates, but I notice there's a double line, and I'm not sure what that's about. A double line usually means the end of. . . . I think this G didn't go anywhere, I think that's the end of whatever I wanted to do.

MH: One of the most fascinating set of sketches for *Sunday*, were the ones marked "Miscellaneous Notes." I'd like to start with what you wrote on the cover.

SS: This "long-line" is the opening. It's a juxtaposition of two triads, and those are the two triads—in this case, an A-major triad and a D-major

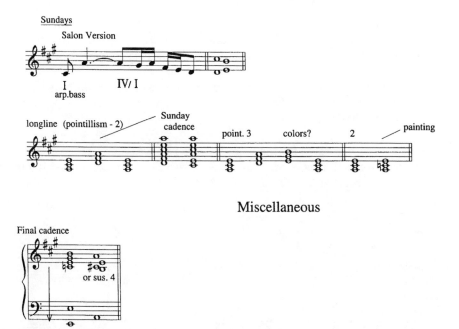

Example 4.11

triad, all in the same key. But if you look: [sings] "dah-dah-dah-dah, dum; yah-dah-dah-dah, dum, ya-da, dum." If you look at it, it's always A major and D major juxtaposed together. That became the basic idea—to go from A to D to A, but juxtapose them.

MH: Speaking of the figures that begin the show, it surprised me that there wasn't a different figure associated with of each the words: "order, design, composition, balance, light, and harmony." Is that too obvious?

SS: No, it just didn't occur to me. There's no particular pictorial idea of this juxtaposition; it really has to do with the notion of what he did—which is juxtapose one color next to another. So I'm juxtaposing one major triad next to another, and here, these are what the results are—those are the "baskets." That is to say, you take these six notes and then you put them together, and that's what you get. And those are distillations of the opening arpeggios. The trick in the opening arpeggios of *Sunday* is that the bass is never stated. The first chord goes C-sharp-B-E-A-E; the bass A is never stated. The second one goes C-sharp-E-D-A (that's where the D major comes in). Again, it's either the third of A major, or the seventh of D major that's in the bass. So that none of the chords feels like a cadence until we get to "harmony." And then—

boom!—an A comes in in the bass. So the idea again is to keep putting the colors together and juxtapose them until finally they lock in on the word "harmony" and it becomes very clear what they are. [See example 4.12.]

MH: Were those Seurat's real words or was that a creation of yours?

SS: Oh, no. That's all James.

MH: In the little sketch for the "Sunday" theme, when you get to the second measure, is that a chord, or are those possible alternate notes of where the melody might go? [See example 4.11.]

Example 4.12

Example 4.12 (continued)

SS: Possible alternates—and it's not that I "got there." The double line means the first idea is over. I wanted to use this and this and this; probably to juxtapose them together, I'm not sure.

MH: D and C, against E and B?

SS: Exactly—D and C-sharp.

MH: Right. Sorry.

SS: Well, that's important, because the seventh is what counts. The fact they're in between these double lines means that's the end of one idea; here's another idea. It's possible—and there's no way of knowing—that I meant this as an alternate. I usually put parentheses around an alternate, but I might not have. The fact that they're all whole notes, and they're not close together, implies that it is an alternate, but I'm not sure. I probably would have put a stem if I meant them to sound together.

MH: On this page of the sketches, it looks to me like you're trying to come up with a tone row.

Example 4.13

SS: Yes it does, doesn't it? This is probably for the Chromolume.

MH: But it also surprised me that you had two E-flats in it.

SS: That is odd, isn't it? Also, there are only eight notes there, so clearly something happened. I have no idea what I was doing there.

MH: This brings up the subject of different musical techniques and theories: atonalism, twelve-tone music, Schenker, et cetera. What musical theories have you looked at, thought of, studied?

SS: I haven't studied atonal music. When I studied with Milton Babbitt I asked him if I could study atonalality, and he said: "You haven't exhausted tonal resources for yourself yet, so I'm not going to teach you atonal." And he was absolutely right; I'm still in tonal.

MH: Do you listen to atonal music?

SS: Oh, I listen—the same way I listen to all kinds of music—but I'm not particularly fond of atonal music. I'm very tonally oriented. I'm very old-fashioned—I'm about 1890. I'm still early Ravel—that's my idea of terrific. I know something about these things, but I rarely use them. I have no idea why I would use the tone row this early, because I don't think the Chromolume thing was ready. I can't tell where this is, but the fact that this says "4th Sunday" implies that I was thinking of the second act. I'm not sure what all these notations mean.

MH: Well, that was my next question. Obviously the initials are the different characters—"G, D" is George and Dot, and "G, OL" is George and Old Lady. But how do the initials relate to the music to the left of them?

SS: These are various variations of the arpeggio, and I guess I wanted to.
. . . What's interesting is—I've checked off the two Celestes twice and George and Dot once. You know, what I may have been doing is taking variations on that opening arpeggio—four sixteenths and a dotted half note—and utilizing different ones for different characters. It may have been that I was trying to make leitmotifs for each of the characters based on the same rhythmic figure. That's what it looks like to me, but I have no memory of this.

MH: Did you ever have the idea—we sort of touched on it earlier—that during a number like "Color and Light," the twelve tones and the twelve colors on a palette would be linked? So, for instance, when George says "blue," there's a note that's blue; when he says "green" there's a note that's green.

SS: Exactly. Absolutely right.

MH: But it didn't end up working?

SS: I realized that I would straitjacket myself.

MH: Not necessarily through the score, but in one moment.

SS: In that moment—in that number. I think it's for that number where that notion occurred to me. I may be wrong—it may have occurred to me early on—but, absolutely.

MH: On the next page, it looks a lot like you were taking thematic material, and working a lot with inversions and rows.

Example 4.14

SS: Clearly, what's above are in diatonic moments. Below, however, is some kind of attempt at a row. I think this is exactly what you just asked me—which is—I was experimenting with using tone rows to respond to the colors. These are early sketches where I'm feeling my way into the score. I think I'm doing exactly what you just asked about—I'm trying to find a way of utilizing twelve colors equals twelve notes.

Chapter Five

Interlude

MH: Since we're of running out of time today, I just had some generic questions I'd like to get in; first, the dating of your manuscripts as they come from your copyist. I notice that there are a lot of dates throughout a work.

SS: It means revision. Each page that has a date has been revised. There is the date at the top of the manuscript, or, if there's no date, it means this is the first version that the copyist has copied. Then, if you turn to page three and there's a date on it, it means this page was revised on this date. I do that, because I do revisions all the time as I'm writing—even before rehearsal, or sometimes during rehearsals, but mostly before rehearsals. I make my fair copy, and I give it to the copyist to copy, and it comes back, and it's printed; it has a whole different *thing* to it—it's like a writer when a piece comes out of the typewriter. And I prop it up on the piano, and I go over it to proof it, and in the proofing I think: Geeze, did I really write that? I'll check my original manuscript and say: I really wrote that; it sounds awful. Or: That sounds flat; I'm going to change that to a D-flat. But it's already been copied! So I'll tell her: Change the D-natural in bar thirteen to a D-flat; and take the quarter note . . . change this rhythm. . . . Sometimes I'll dictate whole bars over the phone; I just did a lot of this last week to a song in *Wise Guys*. So, when she prints it out again, it's going to have a different date. Then, as in the case with *Wise Guys*, I'm on my third revision of some pages. I played it over again after a two-week hiatus and I thought: That's not good, that's not right. So each page tells when. If you went through my—what they call rehearsal copies—you would find the original versions, but you'll also find the April 3rd version of page thirteen, and the April 9th version of page thirteen. And each one has some red pencil—and I always do it in red pencil—because that's the only way you can tell, from the ink marks. And the reason I save each of these is, I may say after the fourth revision: You know, the first one was better; what was it? And I can then go back and see what the earliest version of that passage, or that chord, or even that note was, because I may have forgotten. It's a diary.

MH: To me, who's not a singer, your music is hard to sing. In terms of writing for voices, how does that affect your choices—knowing that it's hard for somebody to come in on the "and" of the fourth beat or to sing the major seventh in a chord?

SS: I've had mixed reactions about that. Some singers say: I don't know why people say your stuff is so hard, because for me, anyway, it's very logical. I'll have others say the opposite—particularly when melodic lines skip, particularly when they go down a seventh, or something like that. That's quite hard for people to get. Also, throughout everything I've written, I have too often—and I think the key word is *too* often—utilized something in the accompaniment that directly clashes with the voice. And part of the reason for that is I work at the piano. And at the piano, that hidden C-sharp sounds okay when you're singing a D. But when it's exposed in the orchestra, and that C-sharp is played by a clarinet, and the singer's supposed to sing a D, they get really upset, because they tend to sing the C-sharp if their ear hears that particular instrument. On the piano—particularly when you put your foot on the sustaining pedal— God forgives you everything. Anything works—anything. You can sing any note and, no matter how dissonant, it's fine against the piano. But I've learned. And that's why I say: I'm taking out the wrong notes in *Wise Guys*. I catch myself. A passing tone will go: F-E-flat-D-flat, but the singer is being asked to sing an E-flat when the F sounds. Now I hear the E-flat in the passing tone, but the singer hears the F, and I thought: No, don't do that, have the E-flat in the accompaniment occur when the singer sings E-flat. Well, it completely screws up my figuration, so I have to rewrite the figuration. It can no longer be [sings one version]. I've got to start on the second note [sings second version]. And that's a whole other thing. I have to rewrite the passage so that the E-flat in the accompaniment will fit the E-flat in the melody. That's what I've been doing lately. I'm trying to learn to do that. The older I get, the more I try to do it, and the harder it gets, because you're screwing things that really struck you. When you write at the piano, and just to go [sings figure], and somebody has to come in, it's different than when you sing it yourself. Because: I don't have to sing on pitch, and nobody's listening to me, and it's a piano, and I have a sustaining pedal. *You* have to get on the stage, sing it, sing it accurately, and the clarinet is playing an F while you're singing an E-flat. On the other hand, I remember Larry Kert telling me, "Someone Is Waiting" from *Company* was the hardest song he'd ever had to sing—and he'd sung many difficult songs. Now, on the surface of it, "Someone Is Waiting" uses stepwise motion—there are very few leaps in it—and I didn't know why it was so hard to sing; and he couldn't tell me why either. There's something about the movement in that song, because there are no open dissonances like I've been talking about. It's a mystery. But I know, when he told me it was difficult, that it must have been difficult to sing. And of all the songs in *Company* that people sing, that's the one they never sing. There's got to be something hard about that song, but when you look at it on paper, there are almost no dissonances, and there are virtually no accidentals. I don't know what it is, and neither did he, but *something* is wrong. But I've had mixed reactions from singers, so I don't know. I think there are times when my melodic lines have leaps in them that are hard for people, and perhaps they could be written better. Maybe the melodies shouldn't leap the way they do.

MH: I don't think of it as being melodic difficulties, I think of it as being either the clashing or rhythmically knowing when to enter.

SS: Well, generally when there are rhythmic tricks—if I'm not writing a kind of standard thirty-two-bar song say, where I want the melodic line to be fairly even and strike the mind as a melodic line—I will use my rhythms according to the rhythm in the inflection of the speech. And when I say the rhythm and the inflection [sings]: "Rhythm and the inflection of the speech." It's that. It's to echo the rhythm of how we talk. And that sometimes means that you have a dotted eighth note, and then a sixteenth rest, and then you come in on the downbeat. It's all about the rhythm of the lyric. I try, when I'm writing, to make those rhythms as easy to read as possible, but I will always be pulled toward the rhythm of the speech. And that makes for some very peculiar notation.

MH: Quote: "I also hear registers; I spend a lot of time at the piano choosing registers."

SS: That has to do mostly with accompaniments. I find it very difficult. (Milton Babbitt claimed that I think orchestrally, but *I* think I think pianistically.) And it's a question of where do you put the register? Do you have the accompaniment figure in the middle octave, or the octave above, or two octaves above? For somebody who writes orchestrally, those choices become much more clear-cut, because—if you choose a flute, that means a flute; if you choose a bassoon, that means a bassoon. But it's hard for me because if you're on the piano, you can go anywhere. And it's also variety, because I have a tendency, again, to choose piano registers that are in the middle and are compromised—just the way I tend to write mezzo forte instead of really taking a stand and saying either forte or piano. There's nothing like mezzo forte to cover *all* territories. Similarly, if you put all the accompaniment in the middle two octaves, who can throw stones at you? But it's not always the best. And over a period of time it becomes oatmeal—it blands out. So, I think registers are very important for accompaniments. When it comes to registers for voices, of course, that's just a matter of choosing a voice.

MH: To what degree can people, looking at your manuscripts, use cut material to inform their characters?

SS: Fine, if they want to study it. Just don't put it in the show. There's a very good reason we've cut everything. Every time I've ever cut anything from a show there's a good reason. I can't stand when people restore stuff and want to restore stuff. There's a very good song in *Night Music* called "Silly People," sung by Frid, the servant. It says what the show's about—and I like the song a lot—but the reason we cut it is because it's a character you don't care about at that point in the show. And, of course, I get requests quite often from companies asking to restore this song—partly because it gives the actor who plays this tiny part a chance to sing, and partly because it's a pretty song and it seems relevant. But, *no*—one of the reasons that George Furth and I have never—until last year—allowed the script for *Merrily We Roll Along* to be published was that we were not satisfied with it. Then, because of Jim Lapine's production in 1985 and then our subsequent changes—not very many, because that was the big change—we finally combined two scenes in one. We did it in Leicester in England; we looked at each other and said: Okay, that's the best we can do now; this is good now; this is what we want it to be. And then we allowed it to be published. When I publish a vocal score, it means: All right, I'm willing to let this go for posterity, which is why I insisted that the Judge's song be in the vocal score of *Sweeney Todd*—because I wanted it for the future. It's in the appendix, where it becomes optional, but I wanted it printed. Meaning: If you want to do this song, here it is. I think I may have put the tooth-pulling sequence in too, but, again, it says, "optional."

MH: "Marry Me a Little" is back in recent productions of *Company*.

SS: Right. And so we've been talking about the reprinting of the vocal score.

MH: So you feel good about that?

SS: Yes. I think *Company* is better with "Marry Me a Little" at the end of the first act, and no "Tick-Tock" dance in the second act. I think it's better. So I would love to republish that.

MH: The two *Follies*?

SS: Oh, I prefer the first one. And there's going to be a big production out at Paper Mill Playhouse this spring, and it's the original. There are some changes in the script, but it's the original score.

MH: How would you feel about the original, except for "Ah, But Underneath" instead of "Lucy and Jessie"?

SS: Leave it the way it was meant to be. All that stuff was compromised. Musicals—this will sound terribly kind of self-serving and modest, but—you write a show with your collaborators. I didn't want to change *Follies*. I always liked *Follies*. I liked the book of *Follies* better than Jim Goldman did, and so did Hal. Jim Goldman and Cameron Mackintosh wanted to change it for London, and make it more real and less surreal, and have all kind of changes. I didn't want to do it, but I think it's unfair to stamp your foot when somebody offers you another production and say: No, no, I won't let you try something new. Who knew? It might have turned out better. It didn't. And when it didn't, I said: I don't want this show ever shown in America, and I made it legally certain that the London version can never be shown here. I don't want it shown again in England either, but Cameron has the right to do it. But Cameron's given in now too, and there was just a production in Leicester last year, and it's the original.

MH: And in the new *Night Music*, they've put in the "Glamorous Life" from the film and inserted portions of "My Husband the Pig."

SS: Yes. That's for England. I don't want to change that. It was perfectly okay, but I prefer the original.

Chapter Six

Sweeney Todd

MH: As we've been talking, you've occasionally mentioned how you've started pursuing an idea but then couldn't figure out how to get it done. I've also read quotes from you discussing *Sweeney Todd*—that there were eight scenes that originally you couldn't figure out how to musicalize, and then later you figured out how to musicalize five of them. What is it you figured out? Does that reflect your growth as a composer? Have you figured out any of the other three yet?

SS: No. I sort of figured out the five, but I've never gotten around to doing them. I thought I would do them for the National Theatre production in London, but Julia McKenzie said: "Oh, please don't give me anything new to learn. *Please* don't give me anything new to learn." That was all the incentive I needed not to work, so I didn't do it. One of the scenes involved the trio in the second act, which I'd always wanted to do, where Mrs. Lovett tries to poison the Beadle. It's the scene, in the original, that Hugh Wheeler avoided. But I think it's a wonderful scene and would be very singable: she gets a packet of rat poison with a great big skull and crossbones, and you see her pouring it into the beer, and then she puts the poison away; and while she's doing it, he switches the beer unknowingly, so we know she's going to drink the poison. Meanwhile, he's singing the parlor songs, and she's coming on with him and *shmeicheling* him. It's a really funny trio scene. I'm sure Rossini would have loved it. The dialogue passages in *Sweeney*, for the most part, are fine, but there are aspects of them I would change—the whole scene in which she sings the song I like least in *Sweeney*, which is "Wait." It doesn't work the way I intended it to, and I don't think it's the actor's fault; I think it's mine. I would like to have another go at musicalizing that whole scene, because there are things Sweeney could sing that echo things he's sung before; and then she could have a moment in the middle where he goes crazy, and she calms him down, and it would work very nicely.

MH: But your mastery of techniques—do you see an evolution in what you're able to accomplish because you've done it so much and tackled different things?

SS: No. I think each show is equally hard and equally easy. It's easy, when you're not writing thirty-two-bar songs, and you're just pouring the sauce all over the place, and just having people go in to a kind of semi-recitative; as I say, I loathe recitative. But a semi-recitative like the "There's a hole in the world" section of *Sweeney Todd*—that kind of thing.

MH: It's never been clear to me whether the final version of the "Prelude" for the organ is yours—the recording and the score are different.

SS: I wrote different kinds, but they're all mine. And they're all clumsy, and they're all academic. It's funny, because I was trained on the organ when I was ten years old and went to New York Military Academy. I just loved the gadgetry of it. It was a four-manual organ, and a very large one. In fact, I think at the time it was the second largest organ in New York State—second only to Radio City Music Hall's, and bigger than the Roxy's. I was so small, my feet could hardly touch the pedals. But I loved the whole thing. I took one year of organ when I was there, so I thought I'd be able to manage this, but, in fact, I really don't know the organ—what makes the textures, and what makes effectiveness. So it's quite an academic overture, no pun intended to Mr. Brahms. I was really sorry that I didn't study the instrument more before writing the piece. It just doesn't have . . . all I wanted was mystery. What I intended was that the theater should be covered entirely in black—like the inside of a coffin—and that all the seats and all the upholstery should be in black; and that on the stage you would see, with his back to the audience, this sort of *Phantom of the Opera* organist playing. And at various points in the story he would pound away with all stops open—something I used to do to scare people at military school and at college also, where there was a chapel and you could make it dark and scare people. Then Hal Prince had the idea of the steam whistle—which turned out, I think, to be a much better idea. The grating sound of the whistle is much more unnerving and upsetting than just big, loud, sting chords. So the organ idea eventually was scrapped as a presence on the stage, and, of course, the theater was never covered in black. But we wanted some kind of non-overture music, the way, again, a horror film would have—just to get the audience into the mood. Unfortunately, what I wrote is about as scary as an academic exercise—it doesn't have any atmosphere. I just failed. The sketches are attempts at utilizing themes from the show to make a prelude that would get an audience in the mood. It's no good; I prefer the show just starting dry.

MH: So for future productions, you'd prefer no organ prelude?

SS: It's not that. If people feel they can do it, fine. If not, not. Maybe there's a way that utilizes certain stops so that it would sound better. It's too thick-textured; it's too contrapuntal; it doesn't have enough sustained chords in it. I don't know.

MH: Do you think the fact that you played the organ when you were younger affected you as a composer? For instance, do you use more pedal points than you might do otherwise?

SS: No, not at all. I don't think that had any lasting effect at all.

MH: In this set of sketches, you've labeled a chord as the "Sweeney chord," but it's not what I think of as the "Sweeney chord"—among other things, I don't see the minor third.

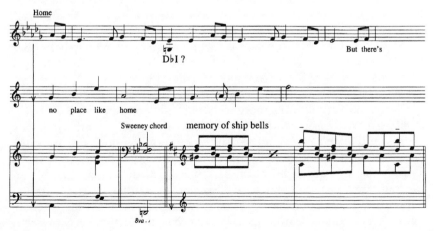

Example 6.1

SS: No, it's a slightly different one. What now says F-flat would ordinarily be a G-flat—that's what I mean by the "Sweeney chord." However, this is the Bernard Herrmann chord, and I used this elsewhere in the piece, but I don't remember where.

MH: The chord that I think of as being the chord that's wedded through *Sweeney* is a minor chord with a major seventh, in an inversion.

SS: That's right, with the seventh in the bass. That's why I say, if you change that F-flat to a G-flat you'll have exactly that. You'll have the D-natural, and then E-flat, G-flat, B-flat.

MH: But it also appears in other inversions, at times.

SS: Absolutely, but I don't want to make too much out of it. I didn't use it as consciously as I have said. It's just that the sound of it underlay the music, and so it *informed* the music. I mean, if you look at the "Ballad of Sweeney Todd" and the way the harmony moves in there, that chord—not this one—occurs in many variations. As I said earlier about how something lodges in your head while you're working on a given show, it just kept turning up. But you're absolutely right. It's fascinating to me that I changed that F-flat to a G-flat.

MH: Still looking at one page of your sketches for "Opening I-I," which begins with Anthony's "I have sailed the world . . .," there's a note that reads "memory of ship bells." [See example 6.1.]

SS: Oh, yeah. I was going to use that. I didn't, eventually. Look, there's that "Sweeney chord" again—I was obsessed with it. And that doesn't look very bell-like to me—that's what I call my "Stravinsky motif"—so I think what that must have meant is that I was going to overlay bells on it.

MH: When you say "Stravinsky motif," what do you mean?

SS: The kind of eighth-note motion that usually occurs when Sweeney is about to murder somebody. It's a series of seconds alternating with fourths, fifths, and sixths, all steady eighth-note motion, and it's chromatic. In fact, it arises out of the opening vamp of the "Ballad of Sweeney Todd"—*that* sets up all the stuff. But then I had developed that, in the opening, into thirds. It presages Sweeney's madness. And I call it "Stravinsky" because it has a Stravinsky texture—it has a high, woodwind, dry, dissonant texture to it. It's not that it's taken from Stravinsky or has any kind of Stravinskian particularities—either motivic or har-

Example 6.2

monic. But it feels like Stravinsky to me. I associate a lot of Stravinsky with dry, woodwind chromaticism.

MH: When you gave the score to Tunick to orchestrate, did you say: I want a dry, woodwind, Stravinsky sound?

SS: No, I rarely say anything—particularly to Jonathan. But here is an example of where register counts. The reason it's up there is precisely because I hear it in my head as woodwinds. When Milton Babbitt said I hear orchestrally, he wasn't entirely wrong. I think I hear pianistically, but I knew that the color of this had to do with that skittering thing—I knew that this was not a string sound. And when Jonathan says that he likes to hear me play, I can assure you that when I play that, I don't play it legato. I don't play staccato, but I play non-legato. And that tells him, without my saying it, that I don't hear it as a string sound. So if you heard me play this, you'd know it wasn't strings; and yet it's up in the string register, and it seems like strings.

MH: Another thing I noticed in the sketch was that the lyric reads "But there's no place like home," as opposed to "But there's no place like London," which is the final lyric. Why did that change?

SS: I think it's because "no place like home" is so American—that's the old sampler song. I think that's why I did it. I like "London" a lot better.

MH: It also gives you two syllables. Does that play into it?

SS: That's interesting, because, yes, it makes it less square. With "there's no place like home," there's a finale to something like that. But not, "no place like London." Also, one of my favorite things about British music is where you hit the downbeat and then follow it with an eighth note; I don't know if you'd call it an appogiatura on the downbeat. That, to me, is characteristic of British music, and it shows up a lot in Walton and in Britten. So when I heard "London," I thought: Yeah, that's very British.

MH: We touched on this a little earlier; this is your original manuscript for "The Worst Pies in London," and the interesting thing is the difference in the modulation and the melody here, as opposed to the final version.

Example 6.3

SS: Well, you see, the original version would take her up to an E-flat. And when Angie gets up there, she has to change into her head voice. You'll notice in *Anyone Can Whistle*, there's a place in the "Miracle Song" where she uses it for comic effect. But here, I really wanted her to say: "These are probably the worst pies . . ." in the same chest sound. That's why I changed it. This song, as originally written, would be within Angie's range. It's just that she would have to switch, because her chest range is really only about an octave-and-two; and I'd rather have her cheat on the low notes than cheat on the big ones. If this were written as an opera for opera singers, I wouldn't bother, because opera singers know how to negotiate that sort of thing, but this is going to be sung mostly by musical theater people.

MH: When it was done at New York City Opera, do you remember which version they used?

SS: The compromised version is the published version; that's the one that's orchestrated.

MH: And it's because of the orchestration?

SS: Yes. Two things occur to me. One is the climax of *Sweeney* when Mrs. Lovett sings "I love you," just before he kills her. Angie could not hit that in chest, and when you hear it, her voice thins out. Dorothy Loudon, who took over for Angie, virtually has no head voice, but she has a large chest voice that goes up high enough. And when she belted "I love you," it was *horrifying*. When Angie did it, it thinned out and it made Mrs. Lovett less desperate, and less crazy, and less—I want to say menacing, except she isn't being menacing at the moment—less, well anyway, *less*. So it's nice if it can be all a mezzo sound up to there. Another mistake I made, or a mistake I made, was in *A Little Night Music*. I wrote the part of Anne for an octave-and-six. But Anne has to be beautiful, young, and be able to play a selfish girl without being a bitch, as well as have an octave-and-six. Victoria Mallory, who played the part originally, could handle all of it. Her voice is light, but she could handle all of it, and she was beautiful. So I used her low register and I used her upper register. Ever since then, there's never been a girl who could do all that, until the girl who just did it in London, Joanna Riding. But all these years: either they can act, and they're not pretty, and they can negotiate it; or, they can act, and they're pretty, but they can't negotiate all the octave-and-six throughout the show. She's got to go real high in "A Weekend in the Country," and she's got to go real low elsewhere. I really utilized the versatility of Vicky's voice, and screwed myself by doing that, because it meant that I strait-jacketed all subsequent singers into this rare combination.

MH: But did you really screw yourself? That was what you wanted, and that was the premiere production.

SS: Yes, but for that one production. That's the advantage of writing an opera for opera singers. Unless, of course, operas do the same thing. I'm sure there are operas where the coloratura can only be handled by the Joan Sutherlands of the world—one every generation. And I think those operas probably suffer as a result. Because they're either done with people who

are inadequate, or aren't done at all, because they can't find a soprano—
she'll say: "I'm not going to sing five high E-flats in a row."

MH: On to "My Friends," and your sketch with the arrows and "strum"
written above. Obviously, those are where the accompaniment chords are
to be struck. What was the decision-making process behind that?

Example 6.4

SS: If you look, it's periodicised every seventh beat—after every seven
beats it occurs. What I did was, I wanted to take the squareness out of it.
I didn't want a regular emphasis on the downbeat, so it would keep a little surprise going in the bass.

MH: Why seven, as opposed to, say, five?

SS: Well, I don't know. But if you take five, you're doing it on a sustained
note. In that sense, it's an arbitrary choice. There's no mystique to the
number seven in this; nor does it come in seven-note phrases, or anything
like that. It's just, that's what I chose. Nor is it consistently seven, but
that's the way it starts. The point is to keep it off the beat. I utilize this
technique *all* the time—it's all the way through *Sunday*—because I'm so
self-conscious about being square. I will deliberately do that sort of thing
in the bass, and deliberately do syncopations in the accompaniment figure, even though I'm writing in four-bar phrases. I don't change meters
that much, and this is my way of keeping things fluid and liquid. And this
is a perfect example of that.

MH: With "Green Finch and Linnet Bird," the first question is about the
bird calls and where they came from. Did you research them?

SS: I listened to birds up in Connecticut and jotted them down. I sat there
and I listened. I thought: Where am I going to hear birds?—I know. Where
I live in Connecticut, there are a number of songbirds. Not too many, and
they don't screech a lot, and they're the same birds—because they have
little homes around there—and they call to each other, and they really are
doing it. Hugh Wheeler was a birder, and he once came up there to visit,
and he'd listen and he'd say: "That's a wren, or a starling"—whatever.

You could hear one calling to another, so the motifs are quite consistent. And there aren't that many of them, so I was able to discern one from another. So these are all mostly authentic; not all of them.

MH: Do you know if they're authentic for Britain, or that didn't matter—it's too pretentious?

SS: Oh, Mark, no! There's a limit to research. Although, I'll tell you something about this show and Britain. I wanted the Beggar Woman to have a lot of dirty Cockney slang. I have a couple of books on language that involve Cockney and slang, but I couldn't find what I wanted, because, unfortunately, they're dictionaries, and it's hard to look it up and find things. So I made things up—this is in New York—and I gave it to my friend, the playwright Peter Shaffer, and I said sort of smugly: "Listen to this, and tell me what you think is authentic and what's inauthentic." And he picked every single inauthentic out! And I said: "Please don't tell anybody." And that's the way it was on Broadway. When I got to London for the London production, I spoke to somebody there who was brought up Cockney, and he gave me phrases out of his own experience—although he's now a big music publisher—and I was able to incorporate those. Because the score was not printed until later, the stuff that's now in the score is the authentic Cockney.

MH: The accompaniment to "Green Finch" has always intrigued me—the last eighth note of most measures is always where the change happens—does that relate to the bird calls?

SS: No.

MH: Do you know how that figure evolved?

SS: I have a feeling that's a little trademark of mine. This may have been the first time I've used it, but I have a feeling that has occurred a lot in subsequent things. But maybe not. If anything, it echoes the opening. At the moment, you know my stuff better than I do. The whole idea of the "Ballad of Sweeney Todd" is: [sings accompaniment figure]—it's that leaning. You know there are stress notes, and you lean into the piece and come back [sings]. So everything has this little yearning, wavelike feeling. And I think this is an echo of that [sings]—so there's a little dying fall at the end of each of these things—so the phrases have a little yearning and a little leaning. If you don't change the chord, you're not yearning for anything, because you're not looking for resolution. Incidentally, this is the kind of thing I was talking about that's—it's probably unconscious—but it's knowing that this

Example 6.5

is a girl who's yearning for something. So this is characterizing by music. It's very hard to talk about how you musicalize character. When people talk about characterization in song, they're really talking about lyrics most of the time. It's rare—I mean, we could sit down with a Puccini score, and I swear he knows how to characterize musically—but there are not many composers who know how to characterize musically. The characterization usually comes from the lyric. This kind of thing is musical characterization. This would not be the right accompaniment for the Beggar Woman; this would not be the right accompaniment for Mrs. Lovett—even at one of her most balladic passages. It's wrong for her, because it *haaas* a kind of *ooohhh, ooohhh, oohhh* feeling. And that's why I chose it.

MH: When you do write for character, do you find that you write more complex textures in the accompaniment, the more complex the character is—somebody like Ben or Giorgio, as opposed to a Petra or Anne?

SS: No, it's just that the moods vary according to what the scene is. In the case of Ben: there's the glib Ben; and then there's the heartbroken Ben; and then there's the regretful Ben; and then there's the bitter Ben. When you have scenes that have that color, you can put that color in the music. So you don't use a light-hearted waltz when he's bitter—unless you're—

MH: —doing "Could I Leave You?"

SS: Yes, which is not his song. I just said "light-hearted waltz," out of the blue. Obviously, one of the reasons he sings "The Road You Didn't Take" the way he does, is that he's trying to be charming. But he's actually falling into the pattern. As opposed to singing it contemplatively, he *could* sing it contemplatively: "Oh, it's interesting, you grow older, and these things pass you by." You could write that kind of song, but the kind of feverishness that's in that song is, it seems to me, very important for the character of Ben. That's something I'm good at and that I'm sensitive to—musical dramatization, musical playwriting.

MH: You've commented that the Witch in *Into the Woods* is the one character in that show who doesn't lie. Would you do anything musically to reflect that?

SS: No, that's all in the lyric; I wouldn't know how to do that. What I wanted was to make her always either very fierce or very tender.

MH: Here's what I assume is a long-line sketch for "Green Finch and Linnet Bird," but it struck me that this long-line is virtually the melody of the song, which is unlike other sketches of yours I've seen. [Note: When later asked about the meaning of the fermatas in this example, Sondheim said that "they signify echoes, not the main note." See example 6.6.]

SS: Wow, right. Well, the other long-lines haven't been worked out in such detail. Look how many notes there are in this line. Nothing you've shown me so far has this many. But you see, that is exactly what Milton Babbitt and I did with the Mozart 39th. He was showing me the long-line structures of the 39th and how it reflected itself in the shorter sections, and even in the little melodic motifs. That's what holds the piece together. That's exactly what happened here: in working out the long-line, and working out the melody, they came together, so that they reflect each other. So, in fact, the melody is the long-line. This is a very good synthesis. And my guess is, if you really took apart the other long-lines I had—the ones we've been going over, which are sort of shorthand—if you really examined the melodic structure, you would find that they do echo what's going on; it's just that I haven't put the details into the long-line sketch. Here, I was putting in the details.

MH: What surprises me is that this is a fairly standard song, as opposed to one of your more complex musical scenes.

SS: Yes, I know. It may be—I'd have to really analyze this and go over it—but maybe this was too long, and it turned out to be shorter. But as I look

[from sketches for "Green Finch and Linnet Bird"]

Example 6.6

at it, it is a standard song, but it's fairly long. It's hard to remember the creative process.

MH: Judge Turpin's "Johanna."

SS: This song is often cut.

MH: Yes—which, I understand, is something that upsets you. You feel strongly that it should be kept in the show.

SS: Yes—he's the only character who's not musicalized. If this song isn't in the show, he doesn't have anything to sing that is his alone. All he sings is the duet of "Pretty Women," and it seemed to me very important. Hal Prince was extremely offended by this song—or he thought the audience would be, anyway—because of what seemed to be a kind of masochistic self-flagellation. But in Victorian terms, and considering the Judge, and his guilt about his lechery, it's far from it. And I tried to incorporate a certain comic aspect into it, in the fact that he couldn't take his eye off the keyhole, looking at Johanna on his knees. I think it works very well. And when we did it at City Opera, I persuaded Hal to reinstate it, because by that time the show had reached its shape. There's another reason, too. When we started previews, I thought the show was in very good shape—Hal says to me that it wasn't in as good shape as I think it was, but I thought it was in fine shape—but there was a sense of *longeur* in the middle of the first act. It was because we had just gotten interested in Sweeney and Mrs. Lovett, and *then* we went to "Green Finch and Linnet Bird" where we got involved with Johanna and Anthony and the Judge, and *then* we went into the town square—which is really about Pirelli and Tobias, although Sweeney and Mrs. Lovett are on the outside—and *then* we went to the Judge's chambers, and it was the Judge and Johanna, *then* we got back to the pie shop. In other words, there were about fifteen to twenty minutes there where we were separated from our main characters, and then picked up the thread of the story. And the story *is* about Sweeney and Mrs. Lovett—it's not about Johanna and Anthony; that's the subplot. So we felt we should cut something. The first thing I cut was half of the challenge song between Pirelli and Sweeney—well, it's Pirelli's song—"The Contest." I took out all the tooth-pulling stuff. And, I think, with the same fell swoop, we took out the Judge's song. Hal, I think, was very relieved to take out the Judge's song, but there was a dramatic reason to take it out. Once the show had found its shape—it seems like a paradox—reinserting the Judge's song after all this time didn't interrupt it as much. I don't know why that is, but somehow, the globule that held it together still held it together, even with the insertion of the Judge's song. So in future productions, I hope the Judge's song is included, because I don't think it breaks the tension. When we did it in London, the guy playing Pirelli thought he would be singing both parts of "The Contest." When we decided to cut the second half—because, again, we thought, maybe now it would work and the shape would be okay—it still seemed we were spending too much time with Pirelli. The actor wanted to quit, but Hal persuaded him to stay in the show. There's a BBC documentary that shows it.

MH: I'm curious, were you making any parallels between the Judge and Sweeney, with "My Friends" and the Judge's "Johanna," in that they're both ritualistic, self-hypnotic numbers?

SS: No. I see what you're saying, but no. This is merely a musicalization of the Judge. Every character in the show gets a moment when you get to know that person. So this is the equivalent of "My Friends," the equivalent of "Green Finch and Linnet Bird," the equivalent of "Ah, Miss" or "There's No Place Like London," the equivalent of "The Worst Pies in London"—those are all solo numbers. I determined that in a piece like this, because it's so much about plot, I better give each one a solo.

Ordinarily, I wouldn't put so many solos in a row, just because I would worry about texture. But if you really look at the first twenty-five minutes of this show, it's a series of solos. Even though Johanna and Anthony are on the stage at the same time, she sings a solo, then he sings a solo. In the square, there are a lot of people, but Tobias has a song—with a lot of people—then, essentially, Pirelli sings a solo. Mrs. Lovett sings a solo. And even "My Friends" is *mostly* Sweeney. And then, "Poor Thing"— solo! And I thought: Oh god, this is going to be a series of—you might as well have people come out in "one" with a microphone and do a concert. But I determined that it was much more important, for the audience's sake, that everybody should be very clearly characterized.

MH: I found this sketch for the Judge's "Johanna" confusing—with the Ds in parentheses, and the lines between them, and then the dots on top.

[from sketches for "Judge's Johanna"]

Example 6.7

SS: Well, the dots at the top just mean staccato. The lines are a repeat of the chord; that's just my shorthand. I write a four-note chord and I repeat it three times. Instead of writing the four notes every single time, I write out the four notes and then I draw vertical lines. The D that's in parentheses, I would have expected that to be D-natural or something—in other words, I would have thought it would be an alternate choice. But I think, maybe, I was deciding whether it should be quarter-note rhythm or eighth-note rhythm. Except that I ordinarily would have put little eighth stems there. I don't know. The other thing it may be is: Maybe I want the D on top—maybe I don't want the F. The point is, it's an alternate. In the second measure, the first quarter-note D is in parentheses, and then there are only three beats left, so it looks like I was considering having a rest there.

MH: Just below it, where your sketch has "(augment?)," what does that mean?

SS: That just means: take each rhythmic duration and double it. In other words, it's an alternate accompaniment that, instead of going: [sings], I might go [sings alternate].

MH: In your sketches for "Todd's breakdown"—"Epiphany"—there were a number of things in just these four measures that intrigued me. First, where you've written "(or D-flat V for exaltation)."

[from sketches for "Epiphany"]

Example 6.8

SS: We're in the key of D-flat, and in the second measure what I have is a II chord. The II chord is like a mild version of a V—the II chord doesn't have that immediate need to be resolved into a I; it usually goes to a V. But a II chord, particularly as it's used in a lot of songwriting, is really a V on the second inversion. So, in this case, instead of being an A-flat bass for a V sound, it's an E-flat bass, but it's the same chord. I've got some dissonances there, but essentially, the bassline, if it's the II, then it's not as strong a pull as it is to the A-flat. Usually, for exaltation, they use 6/4 chords, but, over the years, I've used 6/4s less and less and less, because there's something slightly corny about hitting a climax on a 6/4. So I tend to hit it on a V now—going straight to the V—instead of going 6/4-V. When I plot a piece like this, which requires a certain emotional journey for the character and the performer, I like to know where I'm going to end—not just lyrically, but musically. Will it be a big statement of the theme at the beginning? Will it be a chordal hold? That sort of thing. You'll notice that at the top I've written: "The work The work!," because I thought his insanity would be wonderful if I could somehow make it so that Sweeney thought that he now knew what he should do in the world—which is to kill everybody—and that, in his mind, it was work. Like Michelangelo painting the Sistine Chapel, it was his calling. And the word "work" is great—if it's a speech—but sing the word "work," and you are in serious trouble, which is why there are rests there. It doesn't have a feeling of climax. If it was "The wooork!" you could do it, but holding that "e-r" sound in "work" is not a good thing. So, obviously, I opted not to do that. But clearly what I'm trying to do here is to arrive at the climax of the piece. I had this little counter theme [sings], and I could feel that, because that's the kind of motif that you can build and build and build, and think of how you can get [sings]. It's like Ravel—it's like "Dawn" in *Daphnis and Chloe*. Obviously, I try to find what kind of chord I wanted to reach for the big statement of his *yearning* for his dead wife that would lead into "The work, the work, the work!" All for naught.

MH: And "(urgent)/March theme"?

SS: The whole point of this piece at this time, is that you're dealing with a schizophrenic personality: He alternates between his fury at the world and his yearning for his dead wife, and his frustration at just having been cheated of his revenge. And since the show is about revenge, it's the *major* thing. It's like Othello discovering the handkerchief—it's the same thing. So I thought: What I have to do is find a way of holding a piece together where a guy is going to go through the *Three Faces of Eve*. He's got to keep switching personalities, and yet somehow it's got to hold together and not just be a tapeworm. And this theme turned out to be extremely useful throughout; I'm not sure whether this arises from an earlier theme or not. I thought: All right, what is the climax? It's his determining that he's going to kill everybody. And it should be a passionate declaration—like *Love* or something like that. But for the anger, I wanted to use a chugging sound. And that's what the second idea is— an attempt to find a chug. And then I got the idea of utilizing the Dies Irae here, so that you get the Dies Irae in the accompaniment [sings again]. And once I got that, I didn't need this. But this is an attempt to find it. I just thought of the urgency as a march. It's not really a march— I mean you can't march to it—but it's a chug theme. It's a steady four, and every beat has the same emphasis so that it's locomotive, or something like that. "March" is not really the word for it, but I'm doing shorthand here to get the ideas on paper. But that's the idea; and what that became is the Dies Irae statement. [See example 6.9.]

MH: In a case like this, is the music internal or external? Does the music help drive him mad, or is it a reflection of his madness—as if he's hearing voices or something?

SS: Reflection. It never has occurred to me that music affects the character. I'll think about that now. But to me, always, I'm characterizing mood. I'm characterizing urgency, then I'm characterizing tenderness, then I'm characterizing anger, then I'm . . . it's playwriting. In a scene, the character does not get affected by the words, the words get affected by the character.

Example 6.9

MH: One of your sketches for "Ladies in Their Sensitivities," at the top has "V-G/Ch-D," et cetera. I assume that means: "Verse in G, Chorus in D."

SS: Absolutely correct.

MH: But do you remember your reasoning behind the plotting of that?

SS: No, I don't really know why I want to go from G to D, because that sounds to me like one of my reductions—where I'm reflecting something in the theme and vice versa. In other words, the tonicization of G, and then the tonicization of D, and then each one of those going up a tone, has some kind of significance. "Ladies in Their Sensitivities" doesn't have a very tonal feeling to it.

MH: Do you remember how you came up with the 5/8 meter for this song?

SS: No, I don't. I don't write a lot of fives and sevens. Probably what happened was the score was starting to feel square to me—that's a guess—and starting to feel like it was compounded too much of twos, fours, and threes. This is instinctive reaching for variety. It certainly has no dramatic significance. I'm very concerned, always, with writing conversational songs. And conversation tends not to be as square as two, three, and four. Conversation tends to divide itself up into units of two and three and four and five and six and seven. And since this is a very conversational song—as opposed to a statement song—I think that may have led me to that. That's the best I can offer.

MH: I understand dramatically the point of the song is to get the Judge to go see Sweeney, but I've often wondered why this particular song, "Ladies in Their Sensitivities." Why not, for instance, have the Judge have a toothache and have Beadle say: "Oh, I know this great guy to pull teeth." What was it about the idea of "Ladies in Their Sensitivities" that made that the topic of the song?

SS: Oh no, no, no, no, no. The Judge is trying to make himself attractive to his ward—he's trying to be sexy. It's all about: "You don't look delicious enough, sir." The whole thing starts with the Judge announcing that he intends to ask his ward to marry him, and the Beadle says: "Oh, but sir, you look a little slovenly and you need a shave." A toothache wouldn't have anything to do with that.

MH: So, it's more than just plot for getting the Judge to Sweeney?

SS: Well, there's more to it than that. The real plot is that Anthony and Johanna are making love—or *about* to make love—in the Judge's house. Unfortunately, because of the abstract nature of the set, there was no suspense. I wanted to put the audience in suspense and watch him going home, and be about to enter his house when they're making love— or about to make love—and then be diverted by the Beadle—to go *that* way and go to the barbershop. If this were a movie (and I hope it will be), I would try to convince the director to make this a suspense sequence in which you have the young couple about to be discovered by the villain and killed, and, at the last moment, diverted because of vanity. The Beadle is harping on the Judge's vanity, and the Judge has that opening speech that Hugh Wheeler wrote: I've decided to offer my ward marriage and I'm going to bring her a little gift, and strange. . . . He intends to marry her, he's already proposed to her, and she's been horrified. So the whole aspect of the Judge's attractiveness to a young girl—this middle-aged lech's attractiveness—is the key, so that's why it's there.

MH: Along the same line, the Parlor Songs—"Sweet Polly Plunkett" and the "Tower of Bray"—why those songs?

SS: That's the scene in Chris Bond's script that I wanted to transform into a trio—into a duet—where she's trying to poison him, and she's going to poison herself. The point is, the plot calls for him to come into the place when she isn't there, and then she discovers him and gets completely panicky. So I thought: All right, what's he going to do? And, of course, he would go into the room and sit around, or yell for her, or something like that. But it's a *musical*, and there's the harmonium there. Also, there wasn't anything for the Beadle to sing in the second act, and that's an important character. And, I thought: Here's a chance to get him to sing. At the time, I didn't know we were going to get a countertenor like Jack Eric Williams—it was just going to be a high voice, but not a countertenor. I'd already written the songs, but particularly after we'd hired Jack, I was glad, because I wanted to give him a chance to show off.

MH: My question is not so much the fact of the songs, but why *those* songs? For instance, did you choose the "Tower of Bray," because there's a sort of bell motif that goes through the score, and you wanted to echo that?

SS: No, I went through a book of English folk songs and tried to figure out: All right, do one about a maiden; and then do one about something that has many choruses—like "Oranges and Lemons, say the Bells of St. Clemens." That's really what that is. I thought the fun of it is, it's got to be a song where he gets her to agree to sing with him, and then there turn out to be endless verses, and she doesn't know how to get rid of him— that's all. Also, there was to be much more of a scene. When I said trio earlier, if I'd written that she poisons him, the idea was that it would also be a trio with Toby in the basement, so that we would have the three voices going at once. I still wanted to use Toby in the basement. I thought: All right, the way to make this more functional is to have them sing a song that Toby knows. So Toby starts to sing from the basement, and in the distance the Beadle hears this other voice joining in and says: "What was that?" "Oh, it was just the wind." You know, one of those scenes. It's got to be a classic melodrama scene. I wanted something that sounded like the kind of song that you sit around singing, and you go to verse after verse after verse after verse after verse. That's why it called for two songs: the Beadle comes in; he sits and sings something for himself; then, he says: "Why don't you join in?" And she says: "Oh, all right," because she's trapped. And, of course, it's now a song that Toby knows. So the second song is the danger song, in which she's panicky because he's going to hear the voice in the cellar and then go down and discover and blah blah blah. And then they get interrupted by Sweeney just in time.

MH: You mentioned the idea of a film of *Sweeney* . . .?

SS: Apparently, Tim Burton fell in love with the show when he was in London in 1981 and saw it ten times. And so he wants to do it. At the moment, it's been optioned by, I think, Columbia, and Burton still wants to do it. Although I now hear he's doing *Superman Twelve*, so. . . .

MH: You stated before that you think film musicals usually don't work, unless they're the Astaire/Rogers style, or something like that.

SS: Absolutely.

MH: Do you conceive of *Sweeney* as being something that could work?

SS: I don't think it's going to work for two seconds. (This is not to be shown until 2099.) No, I don't know. The only time a musical on the screen's ever been sung through, because it's a whole opera, is *The Medium*. No, there's the *Umbrellas of Cherbourg*, which I don't think works for a second. It's just Burton's enthusiasm; and I thought: Well, why not try it, what's to lose? I used to think that if you put out a bad movie of a show, it'll hurt the show, but it doesn't. I won't mention chapter and verse, but there have been many, many bad movies of musicals, and the musicals still keep playing in summer stock, and it doesn't hurt. I can mention one, because all the people are dead and it won't hurt anybody: *Guys and Dolls*. It's a terrible movie musical. It hasn't hurt the show one ounce. So, if this works, then I'm wrong; I'll eat my words—*happily*. And if it doesn't work, I'll say: You see—well, I told you so. So I can't lose.

MH: The "Final Scene." You've discussed before that part of the point of the score is Mrs. Lovett and Sweeney's themes clashing, which happens in this number. On your fair copy for this number, there's a note.

SS: This is to the copyist who was a sweet lady, but very square. Her name was Mattie. I wrote: "Mattie, I know this looks weird, but it's the clearest layout I can think of." The idea was to have two songs that have nothing to do with each other going together. One is one meter, and the other is in another, and, in order to make it clear to the singer, I arbitrarily divided things into 5/8 and 6/8, so I could draw lines down so the singers would know where to come in. Actually, it did not take Angie very long to learn this. Angie is very musical, but she's not really an experienced singer of stuff like this. I thought: Oh my God, it's going to be so hard for her to learn. Not at all. And it's partly because, if each singer sticks to his or her part, it's very clear. You have to turn your ear off to what the other person is singing—that's the trick. So, actually, this is not a very complex passage; it's the rhythmic equivalent of polytonality—it's Milhaud putting the right hand in E-flat and the left hand in E—each one is simple in itself; it's just, when they clash, it makes for dissonance. So this is very simple-minded business. It's just, on paper, Mattie, having copied so many scores in which, if the vocal is in 4/4 then the accompaniment is in 4/4, I just thought: If I do it the way I would ordinarily do it—which is dotted lines

[from "Final Scene"]

Example 6.10

(well, there is a dotted line here; that's to show where the downbeat is)—
she'll go crazy. So I devised this method.

MH: A friend of mine conducted the show and told me it was a nightmare
to conduct this section.

SS: I don't know why it should be, because the accompaniment is fairly
square.

MH: I think it was trying to cue in the singers for their entrances.

SS: Aaahh! That's the point. If the singer is insecure, of course there's a
problem. I don't think Paul Gemignani ever had to cue Angie—once she
started, once she got the downbeat, she went. I don't think he had trouble. First of all, he would have told me. He would have come to me and
said: "Look, can we simplify . . .," or something like that, because you
would always defer to the performer in something like that. Not that he
would distort the music, but, as he does with registers, he would come to

me and say: "Look, this is difficult for her; is there anything you can do—
have you considered *this*?" or something like that. And, of course, you're
writing for performers—I almost always defer, which, incidentally, is not
true of Lenny. For example, when we wrote *West Side Story*, he was bound
and determined that Tony should sing a high C in the obligato section of
"Maria." The only people we could find to play Tony and could sing a
high C were fat tenors, who were forty years old and from operetta and
opera. Lenny actually tried to push one of them on us; it was just ridicu-
lous. We ended up with Larry Kert, whose top note, when he started to
sing the show, was an F. He was primarily a lyric baritone, not a tenor, and
Tony had been conceived as a tenor. We could not find any. Tenors tend to
speak on the stage like capons; it's difficult to find one, particularly if
you're going to ask him to be a gang leader. So we ended up with a lyric
baritone. And Larry, when he entered the show, sang up to an F, and when
he finished, he sang up to an A. The high C is still written as an alternate
in the score, but Lenny agreed to relax and let Tony just go up to an F or
an A. He did not do the same thing in "A Boy Like That," and Carol
Lawrence was forced to sing higher than her voice because he wouldn't
make that compromise. You can hear on the record, she goes into a squeak
at the top of "I Have a Love." Now granted, in subsequent performances,
in subsequent productions, they find ladies who can do that, which is
great, so maybe Lenny was correct in doing it. The same thing is true here.
I could have simplified this, but I thought, if Angie can handle it, then she
can handle it. How much do you demand of a performer? If Angie
couldn't have handled this, I would have simplified it; I would, because
you've got to defer to the performer.

MH: Since you write chronologically, and this is the very end of the show,
did you know from the very beginning that this moment was going to be
about the clash of those themes and meters?

SS: No, I just knew that I was going to have a clash. Actually, I think I conceived of it as a sort of duet. And I decided: You know something, if it's a
duet, then they're together—just the fact the two voices are together implies that they're *together*. But the whole idea is she's thinking one thing,
and he's thinking another, and they have different agendas. He's intending to kill her, and she's intending to marry him, and those are called . . .
in some instances, the same, but not in this one. Also, I wanted to echo her
nervousness. She knows something's wrong. She knows she's made a
slight mistake by not telling him that the woman that he killed was his
wife. She knows she's made a slight error, so she's a little nervous. And he
is focused and rigid. Well, if you have a guy who's like *that*, and a lady
who's nervous, how do you put the two things together? Answer: you

don't! You just have them *occur* simultaneously. This was so easy to write, because I didn't have to do any work! It's just: You sing your part, darling; you sing your part, darling. I don't care whether you're together or not. The whole point is, don't be together. It was hard to notate; it was not hard to write.

MH: And worked like a . . .?

SS: Oh, it worked like a dream! Incidentally, it worked like a dream because of the two hours that preceded it.

MH: I'd like to discuss "City on Fire" and the "Asylum Song," because your sketches include a fairly lengthy section here that's been cut.

SS: Yes, this is part of a whole chase sequence I had going. It actually comes from something else—Hal got worried that the audience had nobody to "root for" in *Sweeney Todd,* so he wanted to make Johanna and Anthony the people the audience would identify with. So I devised a chase through the cellars when Sweeney is after them with a razor. And I said to him: "You know, if people aren't rooting for Sweeney, then there's no show." But I wrote this extended chase anyway for "City on Fire." And Hal did stage it. This was actually in, at least, the first preview, where they ran across the bridge. So that's what this is, but I haven't seen it since.

MH: It makes Johanna less of a heroine. It makes her more ditzy and crazy.

[from early version of] **CITY ON FIRE PART II**
(INMATES, JOHANNA, ANTONY)

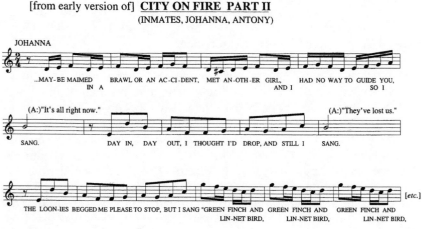

Example 6.11

SS: I still have that one line where she says: "You said you'd marry me Sunday, that was last August"—I still got that. The interesting thing to me about the plotting that Christopher Bond did is that *she's* the one who shoots Jonas Fogg. Anthony's too tenderhearted, so she said: "Oh, come on, let's get out of here, enough of this." And she takes the gun and she shoots him. I love that idea of a heroine—that she's ditzy, but she's capable of killing people. That struck me as a really swell idea. This is also an echo of Johanna's "Kiss Me."

MH: There's a cut section of "By the Sea" where Todd has various counterlines, such as: "God the woman's mad/This is very bad/Anything you say." Obviously, you cut it because you didn't want it there, and that's fine, but an actor playing Todd who looked at that would say: At this point in the show, Todd is just agreeing to agree, but he really thinks this woman is mad.

SS: Right.

MH: Can he look at your sketches and think that?

SS: He can, but you know, that's in the stage directions. It's very clear that Todd is completely distracted. The whole point of the song is Mrs. Lovett is trying to wake him up, so to speak. It's very clear that's what she's doing. And he's a guy who's got to be distracted. There are still shards of that left in, where he sings: "Anything you say, anything you say." And that's enough, that's all. Originally, I was going to make that a full-blooded duet, and I thought: No, the idea is, when you are brooding, you don't talk; you think, and you brood, and you're sullen, and you're glum, and you're glowering. And she's trying to make you cheerful. And you don't want to rock the boat, and say: "Yeah, yeah, it's fine." And that's the way the scene should be—it calls for silence.

MH: I have a couple of general questions about *Sweeney*. One of the things that surprised me is, it's such a huge score, and yet there is much less sketch material proportionally than there is for the other shows.

SS: It was such an easy show to write, I can't tell you. It just wrote—as Barbra Streisand would say—"like buttah." The first twenty minutes, the first seven songs—right up to Pirelli—I just had a good time, because I was writing a horror movie and that's one of the things I love. Then the Pirelli sequence was a little more difficult. I was afraid that the show was going to get too long. When I started it, there was no Hugh Wheeler; there was just me and the Christopher Bond text. Then I realized, Christopher Bond's entire play was thirty-five pages long in acting form, and I was only up to page three—or something like that—and the show was twenty minutes long. The point was, it was going to turn out to be the *Ring* if I didn't cut it down. And I got panicky. I wish I hadn't—I wish I'd stuck to my guns and just done it myself, but I couldn't. And Hugh had written murder mysteries under a pseudonym for a long time; and we'd worked together very happily; and he was British—he knew what Sweeney Todd was as a legend and all that. And I'm very glad, because he made some changes that are very important and very good for the show. But it was at that point that the show became not quite so easy to write because I got worried about length. Then, with Hugh aboard, I felt confident again, and it was fine until I got to the "Epiphany"—or to that moment. In Bond's script, it's the one weak moment: I never believed why Sweeney would turn from frustration at an individual killing, to wanting to kill the human race. In Bond's script, he literally just says: "I have tasted blood." I may be paraphrasing, but it's about tasting blood and wanting more—that's all it said. And I thought: Boy, in something as operatically melodramatic as this, that's not enough. Hugh wanted to make it a religious turn—he wanted to bring in the whole religious thing. And I said: No, let me think about it. And so, it took me a month to write the "Epiphany," and ordinarily a song of that length takes me—if I'm writing at my top speed—about two weeks. But the real problem was to find: What is it that turns him—exactly what is it? Working that out was difficult. Hal always used to complain—and, I think, with justification—that I wrote so much at the last minute. I have this reputation for incomplete scores. They're not that incomplete—*Night Music* excepted, and there are reasons for that—but the fact is that I do tend, as the deadline approaches, to write more and more. So the director and the choreographer don't get a chance to digest the material. And Hal had never really made it clear that, by shoving him three songs in the last two weeks, I was hobbling him, because he doesn't get a chance to think about what he wants to do with them. Hal recognized my rhythm on this, so, even though we went into rehearsal without the final scene—without, really, the last fifteen minutes—I said: "I'm sorry, but. . . ." He said: "I'm not worried; it's fine. I know where I'm going. I know where you're going; it's no problem." The show wrote that easily. So the answer is: This was an easy show to write.

MH: I noticed musical similarities between "Not While I'm Around" and "No One Is Alone"—the use of seconds and things like that. They're also similar in that they're lullabies and used by one character to calm another. Any reactions or thoughts about that?

[from "Not While I'm Around"]

[from "No One Is Alone"]

Example 6.12

SS: No. The thing that makes them different is what's going on in the bass. In "No One Is Alone," the bass goes [sings bass line], as opposed to [sings other bass line] in "Not While I'm Around." Otherwise, they are similar. One of the things I notice here is that the melodic line is four eighths and then a half note, and four eighths and then two quarters, although one is on the downbeat and one is on the third beat, but still. . . . Actually, when you come to think about it, you just said it: the function dramatically is similar, isn't it? It's an older person calming a younger person.

MH: But the use of seconds, for instance; do you think of that as being a calming sound?

SS: No. I'm a fan of suspensions and, rather than use thirds, I'll always use a second and *theenn* resolve it.

MH: Among your manuscripts, I found a copy of a letter you wrote to Declan Donellan for a London production of *Sweeney*. You wrote, in part: "I'm working on an accompaniment to 'Wait' that will be a little less Sergio Mendes." And here's a copy of your revised version.

[portions of rewritten version of "Wait"]

"Wait" (rev. 1993)

Example 6.13

SS: I always fall into South-American rhythms. I don't know why. In every show, and quite often, whether the songs are relevant or not. Here, I just thought: *What* are South-American rhythms doing in the middle of Victorian England? So I made something with less [sings rhythm]. Actually, there's an influence in "Wait"; the chord structure is influenced by a South-American lullaby—Montsalvatge's "Lullaby to a Negro Baby." I stole those chords from him, and first used those chords for "Don't Look at Me" in *Follies*. And then I used them here, and I'm afraid that the rhythmic idea crept in while I was asleep, while I wasn't noticing. It's always bothered me. This is the song that's the least satisfactory in *Sweeney* (and it's not because of me and Montsalvatge), it's because I wasn't able to find the proper expression of . . . again, you talk about lullabies; this is Mrs. Lovett trying to calm a completely berserk person. He's not younger, but it's a lullaby. It's: How do you calm somebody down who's having a hysterical fit? Well, his hysterical fit is he's jumping up every time the doorbell rings and grabbing his razor. And she doesn't want him going berserk *waiting* for this guy to come so he can kill him. It's not the right song; and if the movie goes ahead, I'm going to find something else for this. This will be on tape, and the movie will go ahead, and it'll be the same damn song, but. . . . I would *like* to find something else. I would like to find a way of expressing it. This was another scene that I intended to rewrite. Maybe it should be a duet—maybe it's: He says something rash, and then she calms him down, then he says something rash. Of course, that's going to be the same rhythm as the "Epiphany," which is coming up—where it's rash and then calm, and then rash and then calm. Maybe I can make capital out of that—it didn't occur to me until just this minute. Maybe there's a way of echoing that—that the changes he goes through in the "Epiphany" are the changes he goes through—or that *they* go through—in this song. But something's got to be done. At any rate, this is an attempt to take out the South Americaness of it. Although, I notice I've still got the dotted rhythm in the bass.

MH: If one does do this song, is this new accompaniment the one you'd prefer them using?

SS: I'd have to hear it again. Probably, but I don't know how I would do that now—with the score published the way it is. Also, this was reorchestrated for London; in this version, it's for a nine-piece band, so it's impractical.

MH: One of my favorite memories, from the original production, was when Angela sang the line: "Now goes quickly. See, now it's past!" Never had I seen time so concretely expressed. I *saw* that moment. It was breathtaking.

SS: Mark, you're the only person who got it. That moment justified the song for me, and I don't think anybody but you ever got that moment. You're the first person. And when I realized that nobody was getting it, I thought, it doesn't work.

MH: Well, for me, thank you.

SS: Thanks for noticing, because I thought that was a terrific moment.

MH: You're quoted as saying: "'A Little Priest' is going to be too fast forever and ever, and it's my fault for not slowing it down." I believe you were talking about the road company production with Angela Lansbury and George Hearn that was videotaped and shown on PBS.

SS: It is conducted too fast. There are aspects of the conducting that I didn't pay enough attention to when we were out there taping the show.

We didn't have an awful lot of time, because the budget constraints were terrible. So I let this too fast version go by. On records, it's different. On records, Goddard Lieberson—the father of the show album—said: "Generally, on records, you have to speed things up because there's no eye interest as there is on the stage." I remember, I was in charge of the *West Side Story* recording, because Lenny was away conducting, and when he came back he was shocked at the tempi, because many of the songs were much faster than they were on the stage. But they're exactly right for the listener.

MH: How much work do you do on the recordings? How do you prepare for them?

SS: A lot. When you have a record producer, you sit around with the record producer and determine: What are you going to cut? What transitional material are you going to cut? Are you going to include any dialogue, et cetera? And the most important thing to do is to determine what is the shape of the recording.

MH: Do you determine specific new timings? Do you sit with a metronome and say: "Okay, for the recording we'll do this number at . . ."?

SS: No, the producer will come to me and say: "Okay, here the total score is eighty-four minutes; we've got to cut seven."

Chapter Seven

Pacific Overtures

MH: *Pacific Overtures.*

SS: Same period. Different country.

MH: In your lyric sketches for the opening number, "The Advantages of Being Set in the Middle of the Sea," in the upper right hand corner of the first page you wrote a little note to yourself which fascinated me: "Hymn to order/(nature)." Did you mean that as a continuum? As opposites?

SS: No, as a continuum. Japanese haiku so often deal with things like plum blossoms and moon through the willows, and stuff like that. They're almost Oscar Hammerstein poems, now that I come to think of it. The order of nature is *basic* to Japanese philosophy. Nature tells you what to do, and nature is the overriding spirit of everything—it's what is *natural.* It isn't just pretty flowers, it's order. The whole Japanese structure—just until the last forty years—has been all about order. And it's the orderliness that they get from nature. The passing of the seasons is *key* to the way they think. And I tried to cover that in the lyric of the opening number.

MH: How would this note help you in the writing of that number?

SS: When I start a lyric sketch—as you can tell from all these little sketches here—you get the philosophy of the number. In this case, it's the philosophy of the country, because that's what I'm trying to set up in the opening number. I often start my lyrics with just making a list—free association—of what the song is about. Not necessarily the point of it, but the atmosphere of it, and what it's dealing with. Here I'm trying to, in one song, establish an entire culture—for an audience that's completely unfamiliar with that culture. Not just the culture that they may know from anti-Japanese movies of the war, but the culture that existed in 1852 when *things were in order*—before chaos arrived in 1853.

MH: The West.

SS: Right. So the idea here is to paint the picture—like a Japanese screen—that is completely calming. Or a Japanese rock garden. If I were doing a movie, I would show a Japanese rock garden first, because that's the ultimate of simplicity and order in nature—but then how man adapts that and makes a kind of tranquil art out of it. It's also a way of living—a way of life. I happen to admire it, too.

MH: Before you started this show, were you aware of Japanese culture?

SS: No, not really. I was brought up on movies, so I thought the Japanese were a lot of little people with buck teeth and glasses who tortured Americans. It was Weidman—being a sinophile, and having written this play—who introduced me, in that sense, to Japanese culture. Although, I think, he's really more interested in the socio-political aspect of it. It wasn't until I went over to Japan with Hal for a couple of weeks and that I saw it for myself. Not that it was in any way an epiphany, but just to be there, and see the ladies with obis in the department stores, and see the contrast between what was and what is now. To see a Japanese woman in an obi buying Chanel in a department store is something very weird. And you think: Oh, I see, this is a show about discombobulation. We tried to do that with an image at the end, during "Next"— the big contemporary number where the vaguely rock music occurs— and in the middle of it comes, from a hundred years ago, the samurai and his wife. That is what I was trying to capture. The whole point of an opening number is to not only lay out the ground rules for the audience, but to *tell them where they are*. Just like *Oklahoma!* did—famously, "the shot that was heard 'round the world"—when Curly comes on, singing that solo, and you see a woman with a butter churn, and a cyclorama with a windmill on it, and a prairie, and nothing else. You know where you are. You know you're not in New York. The same thing is true here. So it seemed to me that the thing to emphasize . . . actually, I was probably thinking of singing a hymn. When I put something on a yellow sheet, up in the right hand corner, that is usually the key idea. Following that are lists of ways to carry it out. I just start filling stuff out on the yellow pad that way. I always write on lined paper.

Up in the upper right-hand corner—if I'm writing a song particularly—
is: Keep this in mind; this is what the song's about.

MH: And it never changes?

SS: Well, sometimes it does, of course, but we're talking about the initial
impulse. This is probably the first yellow sheet I wrote for *Pacific Overtures*.

MH: Actually, this is the second version of the opening number.

SS: "The Advantages" is essentially the same number with a different
lyric. For some reason, Hal didn't like the original. I happen to love the
line: "The advantages of being set in the middle of the sea/Some advantages of being set in the middle of the sea: Kings are burning somewhere
. . ."—but he missed the sentence structure. I mean those as paragraph
headings: "Some advantages of being set in the middle of the sea:" *Colon*!
And he couldn't accept that, so I had to change it. And I changed it to: "In
the middle of the world we float/In the middle of the sea . . ." And so it
now has a statement to make. It's the same song. It's interesting that I see
I was going to make something of the "four"—there are four islands and
four floating cherry blossoms. "Floating" was always in this. That's what
happened. I still prefer "Advantages," but that's one of those compro-
mises. [Note: The first draft of the lyric begins with "Four islands, four
floating cherry blossoms/Let us paint a picture for you. . ."]

MH: Regarding "Someone in a Tree"—there's very little that happens harmonically in that number.

SS: Until the so-called chorus.

MH: So, how do you sustain interest in the listener with that kind of relentless music?

SS: What I discovered about Japanese art, what I finally cottoned on to, is
they're the ultimate culture in "Less is more." They are *the* minimalist culture—look at a Japanese screen . . . You know, fortuitously, I went to an exhibition of Japanese art at the Met. And I remember stepping out of the el-
evator, and there was a three-panel screen. And I couldn't believe it! The
first panel was absolutely blank; the second panel was absolutely blank
except for the end of a bird's tail; and the third panel had the rest of the
bird and a tree. And I thought: I can't believe it—two blank panels, and a
third, and it's a three-panel screen! Click. I thought: Ohhhhh, it's all about
less is more. So I wanted to echo musically the whole cultural idea of less

is more. Meaning, we're just going to take this one chord and, by making tiny little variations on it, we're going to gradually build it up and sustain it so that the audience never gets bored. But it's sixty bars of one chord. But the rhythm keeps changing, and the texture keeps changing, and *where* the chord keeps getting placed just changes a little bit at a time— maybe every four bars, or every eight bars. It is not insignificant that, when I met Steve Reich, he told me how much he loved this show—not just because he had a lot of training. It's similar to his own music, because so much of it is influenced by oriental music, which is influenced by oriental art. It's all part of the same cycle, isn't it? And that's what the verse of "Someone in a Tree" is—it's minimalist music. Nothing's going on, but everything's going on. It's phase music—in a very, very, very simplified form, of course. His version is far more sophisticated, but it is the same thing. And it works very well, because when you finally settle down to the chorus, and it finally hits the tonic chord, there's that sense of, *pheeeww!* I think it's terrific. So that's what that is: It's an attempt musically to echo the visual—and the literal—of Japanese art. What do you think haiku are about? It's called: *How simple can you make a poem?* Simple. Simple, meaning less. Less is more. Think of shoji screens. Think of tatami. There's only one size for a tatami mat. Only one size! You just gotta make your floor out of that size. You can make any kind of domino setup you want. One size! But within that, infinite variation—depending on how you place them. But six-by-three is six-by-three.

MH: Talking about "Someone in a Tree" and the harmonic speed of it, it occurs to me that a lot of your work is very language-based and idea-based—there's a lot of lyric there—and that must have an impact on your music. By necessity, your harmonic changes have to take place over a longer period of time—more subtly—because you have so much lyric to get through, your chord changes are more subtle over time.

SS: It's true that when a lyric hits a different tone, or I want to bisect something or demark something, that I will change the harmonic structure. But I write a lot over pedal tones—the way a lot of people do in the musical theater—and have ever since time immemorial. But it's less reflective of the lyric than it is of, maybe, lack of invention. Or, maybe the fact that there's a wonderful tension that occurs, both in ostinato rhythms and in pedal points—the waiting for the release. (No pun intended, but that is, incidentally, why the middle parts of songs are called releases.) "Someone in a Tree" is an extreme example of that—where the ear is held in a certain amount of suspense for sixty bars, as opposed to four, before it's released into the resolution. In the same way, for example, I use pedal tones in "Send in the Clowns." Almost all of it is over this tonic drone, but there are, as you say, subtle chord changes, but it's to keep the kaleidoscope going while you're anchored. Because a pedal tone is like an anchor—you're always there, tethered, like a goat tethered to a pole. The goat can wander around, but always, in the center, is this immovable tonic chord. I was experimenting with it, deliberately, in *Pacific Overtures*—in which I made the chord smaller, so there was less territory to go away from the center. In the same way, I use that often, and I'm afraid that it's a *reducto ad absurdum* that, if you studied most music—certainly most music since the fifties. . . . I'm not sure that this would be true of the composers in musical theater in the thirties and twenties and forties; I think their harmonies were more fluid and richer in terms of where the harmonies moved. The business of pedal tones came very much into vogue in the fifties, I think. I haven't actually articulated this before, but it occurs to me—and I bet I'm right—that if you look at the scores of the fifties and the sixties, the scores of my peers and contemporaries, you'll find there's much more pedal tone than there was in the thirties and forties, and twenties before that. I can think of specifics about Kern's stuff. You know, often a song will start with I-V-I-V-II-V-II-V-I. And Kern went: I-V-I-V-VII-V-VII-V. You don't find that in me or my contemporaries—we always go to II. And that tiny little variation makes for a big difference. Now, again—I shouldn't speak for my contemporaries, so I'll speak for myself—I tend to go I-V-I-V-I-V-I-V, but *over it* things are changing. Things are becoming liquid and there are little dissonances. You can get away with a lot of murder when you're over a pedal tone. You can put in a lot of dissonance because the audience's ear—the listener's ear—is firmly anchored in that basic first step of the scale, so they don't feel lost—they don't feel Schoenberged into anything. They just feel set in cement. It makes for more static, less interesting music, but it also makes for tenser music. And, as I'm spouting on now, it occurs to me that, because of the Rodgers and Hammerstein revolution—when songs had to tell more of a story—that that tension becomes dramatic. In other words, it may be more poverty-stricken to utilize a pedal tone over and over and over again, but it makes for more drama—or helps to make more drama. I think I could make a case for that, but I better not this afternoon, because I may be skating on thin ice; but I have an instinct that I'm right.

MH: "Prayer."

SS: "Prayer" was the first thing I wrote for this show, to find a Japanese. . . . I've told the story before, but I'll tell it for posterity if you like. I discovered a style. This is like the "Enigma Variations." This is the tune on which the show was based, and I threw it out. But it's also a technique. I had my little revelation on this show. I was up at Lenny's for dinner. It

PRAYER
(KAYAMA)
(I - 2)

Example 7.1

was just the two of us, and he was called to the phone. While he was on the phone, I had nothing to do, so I started to fiddle with the harpsichord he had there. I don't know how I got into it, but there were two manuals to the harpsichord, and I folded my arms across one another, and I started—because of the plucking thing—I started very, very, very gently to lean on the manual. And I heard this oddly rhythmed series of "plink, plink, plink, plink-plink-plink, plink, plink." Perhaps because I was working on *Pacific Overtures* at the time, I thought: Gee that sounds oriental. Wow, there's a texture here, now I'm getting—it may be Hollywoodized— but I'm getting an oriental feeling here. So I decided to write a song with a prepared piano—à la John Cage. And I wrote this song called "Prayer."

When I played it for Hal, I put paper and thumbtacks into the harp of the piano, and then proceeded to play these kind of vaguely pentatonic things, although there's a good deal of dissonance in this song. And, sure enough, it sounded right. Then, it turned out, at least for me, that dramatically "Prayer" would hold up the action. That what we wanted was an opening number, which said: This is the milieu, this is the territory, and now we're going to go to Kayama and Tamate—the samurai and his wife—and we'd better get into the action. "Prayer" held up the action. So that's what happened, and this is what started it all. I was able to utilize, however, some of this for the sequence in "Chrysanthemum Tea," where they try to pray the Americans out of the harbor.

MH: But musically, the score grows, to some degree, out of that number?

SS: Right.

MH: This page of your manuscript is labeled "Miscellaneous Ideas, Numbers and Notions," and it struck me that this page is probably the heart of your working out the score. [See example 7.2.]

SS: I bet I wrote this the day after I got back from Japan. I bought some records in Japan—a three-LP set which illustrated all of the Japanese court music, particularly gagaku. Within the album was a booklet which was, unfortunately, all in Japanese, but I had it translated. It explained everything about Japanese scales and Japanese intonation—all the specific technical stuff about how Japanese music is produced. And the scale turned out to be this *minor* pentatonic. Usually, when one thinks of oriental scales—when you do your sort of Charlie Chan/"Chopstick" music—you just play on the black notes. It's 1, 2, 3, 5, and 6, and it's [sings clichéd Chinese-sounding phrase]—you know, that sort of thing. That's *major* pentatonic. But I discovered that the Japanese seem to be about minor pentatonic. In this case, it's C, D, E-*flat*, G, and A-*flat*—as opposed to C, D, E, G, and A, which it would be if it was Chinese. I thought, whether this is authentic or not, it makes a *big* difference. So I made a list here of various ways to utilize that. Here, for example, these are chords that you can play on the *sho*. The *sho* is the little instrument that looks like a gourd with little pipes. It's like a little mouth organ, except the base of it is round and it has little pipes coming out of it; it looks like a planter. You blow into it, and it makes these various sounds with these five-note, six-note, seven-note chords, all of which are chord clusters. I *love* chord clusters, because, again, as with pedal tones, you can get away with anything with a chord cluster. It doesn't matter what the notes are and it sounds great. This is *clearly* out of this booklet, because here's stuff about Japanese drumming—rhythms

[from "Miscellaneous Sketches"]

Example 7.2

that the Japanese use. Here are the *biwa* tunings. I never used a *biwa*, which is a plucked instrument. I ended up with a *shakuhachi*, which is a flute; a *shamisen*, which is plucked; and the *sho*, which is blown. Clearly these rhythms and the patterns are from this booklet, because it literally says "patterns." I wouldn't write "patterns" unless it was out of some particular scholarly or analytical text. This says "dom" for dominant, I guess.

These are all patterns and scales. And here are tonal systems that obviously I came across. Because, as in Greek modes, the Japanese have tonal systems—different ones for different court purposes, for different times of the day, for different emotions—just the way the Greek modes worked, but they're Japanese modes.

MH: I love this at the top: "Noise + music."

SS: Exactly. I'm not sure what I meant by that, but there is that whole thing of whistles and bells and the fact that the intonations are not Western intonations—you don't hit a note exactly. In fact, part of the art of playing instruments and singing in Japan is how the performer hits the notes. It also says "Noh"—meaning Noh theater—"prolonged beats." So clearly I was listening to some Noh underscoring. Ah yes, look, it says even here "first, confero, side 3," so that means side three of the record. That's what this is; this is my distillation of what I learned from the pamphlet.

MH: Have you ever wanted to go back and write an Asian score?

SS: No. A large Asian conglomerate tried to get John and me to do that last year. But, no.

MH: I noticed in the lyric sketches for the Admiral's number—"Please Hello"—that the word "extraterritoriality" was originally part of the British Admiral's section. Do you remember how it got changed to the Russian? [Note: The lyric sketch for the British Admiral began "Extraterritoriality/I think that we can guarantee/Your territoriality/You mustn't think it sinister/If we should send a minister . . ."]

SS: No, I don't. Clearly, it's such a British word. One of the things I like very much about the Admiral's number is that it's accurate historically. That is *exactly* how things happened—the order in which the countries came and what they demanded. And it has, I am proud to say, been used as a history lesson in schools. And the notion of extraterritoriality, I think, was a Russian idea. But it's such a Gilbert and Sullivan word, that is probably why I was thinking of using it there, although I don't think the British demanded extraterritoriality. They may have; maybe every country that ever goes into another country demands that, because it's a subset of diplomacy—of diplomatic immunity. I don't remember now, having read the history, why it was so heavily emphasized in the Russian section.

MH: In Banfield's book he says, and I quote: "Sondheim's masterly way with repetitive accompaniment figures and the 'Hymnos' from *Frogs* is tremendous in its cumulative effect—an achievement without which the still greater achievement of *Pacific Overtures*, written the following year, would probably not have been possible."

SS: I have no idea what he's talking about. I really don't know. Do you know what he's talking about?

MH: I think it's something we touched on earlier, which is, how you grow as a composer and your ability, by tackling something once, enables you to go further the next time.

SS: I see. It's certainly possible, but that's an overview, and, as you know, overviews are anathema to me.

MH: Here's a quote from you. . . .

SS: Uh, oh. I've changed my mind, whatever. . . .

MH: "But if people can't hear the romance and passion of say *Pacific Overtures*, they're not listening. There's a lot of anger there too. There's a great deal of lyrical music in that score." What particularly interested me is the use of the word "anger," which is something that I wouldn't have associated with that score.

SS: No, I'm surprised, it doesn't sound relevant to me. I wonder what I was referring to. I think of a number like "Four Black Dragons." . . . You know what it is? I think I know what it is; it's the anger of the reciter. The reciter is outraged at what happened to the country, and particularly as played by Mako who is such a fierce personality. I think it's less in the score than in the attitude of the show. This is a man who is telling us without ever saying it: "We were raped." And they were, though it was highly controlled and ritualized. When Meiji becomes the emperor, at the penultimate moment—you know, when the puppet grows, becomes a person and breaks the sticks—and he becomes a real emperor and he says: "We will do to the West what they have done to us." That's anger. And they did it. And they were right. They were *wrong*, but they were right.

Chapter Eight

Finale

MH: I'd like to end with some general, quick questions. In *Forum*, there's really no "Free" song at the end.

SS: Oh my God, it never occurred to me till now. Why didn't you tell me in 1960? Jesus, you're absolutely right. No, he just comes out and sings a happy ending. That's interesting. Incidentally, he does have: "Free, Free, Free," and so it did occur to me. . . . But it wouldn't have occurred to me—no, you can't stop the action at that point. You know, when all the plot elements are tied together neatly at the end—with the brother, and the sister, and the marriages, and all that sort of thing—you just want to get out of the thing, just get out.

MH: Overtures. Very few of your shows have them, but for the few that do, did you actually arrange them, or make the decisions about what would be used?

SS: Let me think. No, I think I consulted with the orchestrator. Certainly, I consulted with Jonathan on *Merrily*. I'm trying to think, which ones have overtures? *Follies* doesn't. *Company* doesn't. *Night Music* has a vocal overture, which was Hal's idea—the idea of a sung overture.

MH: But you wrote the vocals?

SS: Yes, but the notion. . . . Usually, overtures, in the standard and traditional musical comedy sense, are put together by the arranger. The most famous—*Gypsy*—was put together by Red Ginzler. That's what they do.

MH: Did you look at Schillinger at all—did you ever study him?

SS: No, but I bought the books when I was seventeen. I was so fascinated by the idea of the systematic composition.

MH: Did you read them?

SS: Oh, yeah. I still have them.

MH: Did you understand them?

SS: No, I didn't understand them. And I didn't read them all the way through. I just looked at them and I thought: Gee, the idea of graphing music—what a great idea.

MH: Another quote from you—this one is about the interrogation scene in *Whistle*: "It holds up very well. It has one severe, and not quite fatal, flaw in it, which is the tune isn't good enough . . ."

SS: It's terrible! It will haunt me forever. It's a real jerry-built tune. It's just a functional tune, that's all. I still feel the same way, if that's what you're going to ask. Or, that's not what you were going to ask?

MH: I guess, I'm asking about inspiration, or, the idea of a "good tune," and what that means.

SS: Ah. For me, a good tune is a tune I like to listen to. You might not consider it so. A tune that I like, you might not like it. And that tune is a tune I don't like and I just couldn't find a better one—one that I liked more. So much of this now blurs in that territory about not what is good, but what one likes. And music is full of that. I don't like it.

MH: So much of what we've talked about here is "craft."

SS: Yes, exactly.

MH: But to what degree does inspiration play a part? You've mentioned before, the concept of the "muse sitting on the shoulder"—that it doesn't happen that way. But every once in a while, does a tune, does a phrase . . .?

SS: Oh sure, absolutely. That page that you love from "Move On": that's exactly the "muse sitting on the shoulder." I don't know where that came from. It just is right and terrific, and I knew it when I wrote it.

MH: "Windows." I may be crazy, but it's the one recurring image in your scores where that word not only recurs, but every time it recurs, it's a musically significant moment, which makes me want to read something into it as it relates to you.

SS: I don't know. It is about observation, isn't it? The first time I used it was in a song that I never put into *Forum*, called "The Window Across the Way." Now, of course, that was literal, because Hero is looking at Philia through his window to the house next door, but no. . . . The word I use most in my lyrics is "little" because it's a great. . . .

MH: But that's functional.

SS: Yeah, that's functional. No, I understand what you're saying. No, I don't think it has any specific thing. In the case of *Sweeney*, again, it's a literal window; in the case of *Sunday in the Park with George*, it is a metaphorical window.

MH: In *Passion*, it's a literal window.

SS: Yeah. They tend to be. It's also a great word. It's one of the great words of the language. The sound of it is so terrific—it's romantic, and it's sad. No, that's for archaeologists.

MH: Okay. I wanted to give you a few moments to respond to a couple of quotes of yours. "You can sweat a lot over music, but it's very fulfilling. I was trained and started out as a composer, and I fell into lyric writing, so to speak. I wanted to do both, but music was my joy." And then: "Oh gosh, the privilege of being able to write music is just—that's a gift from God."

SS: I still feel it. No, I can't go beyond that, that's just it. Every musician knows what I'm talking about—anybody, even non-musicians. Music . . . it's a magical art. I don't know how the human mind ever got to it, because everything else is somehow representational and literal, including painting. But not music. How did that happen? Is it from the birds? What is that from? How did we learn—how did we *make* music? I can understand, vaguely, how man learned to speak because he had to communicate things; but what is this? How did man learn to whistle, and where does the twelve-tone scale come from, and blah, blah, blah. I'm ill-educated this way, so you could probably answer, but it seems to me miraculous. To me it's as mysterious as astrology but, unlike astrology, completely believable. I don't know, I don't get it.

MH: Does it surprise you that you're a composer?

SS: Yes, because it really isn't in my family. My father was musical in that he played the piano by ear and he loved music. But I think what he really loved was musicals, because there was no music in my house—there were musicals. He was in the dress business and came from a world of entertaining buyers and taking them to shows. But there was no classical music or anything like that. My mother wasn't musical at all. And I never knew my grandparents, but I asked my dad, and he didn't seem to think so. So I don't know where it comes from. I do think it's genetic. I think it's not a coincidence that Mary Rodgers is a composer and Adam Guettel, her son, is a composer—Mary Rodgers being Dick Rodgers' daughter. I don't think that's a coincidence. I don't think it's because they were brought up with the sounds in the house; I think it's a genetic matter.

MH: Is there anything you want to say to posterity about your music—listening to your music?

SS: No, no, of course not. It's just, like all art—it's to be discovered by sampling, by listening. No, there isn't anything, except this: The way for writers who want to write is just listen to a lot of music and figure out how people wrote what they wrote. There is a lot of craft, and it's underestimated, even in a frivolous—I shouldn't downgrade it by saying frivolous—but even in a *commercial* profession, like musical theater, there's a great deal to be learned. To analyze a Kern tune or to analyze an Arlen tune is not more than a rung below analyzing the Mozart 39th; it's the same process. And without craft, I think art is nonsense—it's a sort of masturbation. Whereas, with craft, it's a form of teaching, which, I have said innumerable times, is the noblest profession on earth. What's nice about these interviews is it's about the craft, instead of about: How did you get to be a composer, and what was your education? But it's noble stuff. And the great thing about music is, if you're a musician and you're a composer, it's just fun—particularly if you're a piano player. It's just fun to sit and make sounds and say: "Ooh, that's good." And, if you have a purpose, to write them down, it's really fun.

MH: Thank you for teaching us.

SS: Thanks, Mark; my pleasure.

Part II

SONGS I WISH I'D WRITTEN
(AT LEAST IN PART)

On May 22, 2000, the Library of Congress produced a concert in honor of Sondheim's 70th birthday. The concert, conducted by Paul Gemignani and directed by Kathleen Marshall, opened with the songs from Sondheim's 1974 *The Frogs*, with new orchestrations by Jonathan Tunick. This rarity was followed by a number of Sondheim's favorite songs by other composers and lyricists. Sondheim spoke briefly, introducing these; a transcription of his comments follows. Also reprinted here from that evening's program are the introduction and complete list of "Songs I Wish I'd Written (At Least in Part)," and the birthday messages from Sondheim's fellow composers and lyricists as well as colleagues Gemignani and Tunick. Sondheim's comments:

To say why I picked each of these songs would take much too long. The fact is, when Mark Horowitz of the Music Division of the Library of Congress suggested this notion, he said: Just make a list of songs that you like. I made a list of fifty; I could have made a list of 150. But out of those fifty we selected about fifteen or sixteen to be performed this evening. Part of the reason behind them is that, as you all know, it's such a pleasure to share your enthusiasms with people. I wanted to include a lot of songs that most of you wouldn't know. I actually listed reasons for each, but for now will just give you some of them. I wanted to make an eclectic group. There are some, for example, that I find emotionally moving, like Adam Guettel's "Riddle Song" from *Floyd Collins*. Some songs I chose because they have enormous freshness and invention, for example, "Silverware," which I suspect most of you don't know, but which is one of the most extraordinarily unusual songs ever written. Some I chose because of their sheer skill and delight, like the song "Better," by Ed Kleban, and "When in Rome," by

Carolyn Leigh and Cy Coleman, which I suspect some of you know. For its tenderness, I chose Maury Yeston's "New Words." Some I selected because they contain favorite lyric lines in them: "When Did I Fall in Love?" and "The Eagle and Me." Some because they tell wonderful stories, like "The Golden Willow Tree." "Bambalelê," which is a South American folk song, because of its joy. I chose a couple that are very familiar. One, "You Can't Get a Man with a Gun," because most people, I think, don't appreciate how brilliant Irving Berlin was as a comic lyric writer. People think of him as sort of four-square and very simple, but he was right up there with Cole Porter, or any of the rest of them. There are, I think, sixteen jokes in "You Can't Get a Man with a Gun," all on the same subject, and every single one is a surprise, and every single one has a fresh rhyme that you don't see coming. It's remarkable. Finally, I included "My Man's Gone Now," I guess because it's the best song I ever heard, and it moves me. It's got a lyric by DuBose Heyward, whose lyrics for *Porgy and Bess* are, I think, the best lyrics in the musical theater. [Sondheim was visibly moved at this point] So, having emotionally destroyed myself: "But first. . . ."

From the Program:

Songs I Wish I'd Written (At Least in Part)

As various ideas for this evening's concert were discussed with Sondheim, he latched on to one which we had titled "Sondheim's Desert Island." It was Sondheim who suggested the title "Songs I Wish I'd Written" and then later insisted on the addition of "(At Least in Part)." It should come as no surprise that "At Least in Part" has many meanings: foremost among them is that this is not intended to be a complete list. Rather, these are the songs that "first occurred" to Sondheim as being, not only songs he wishes he'd written, but also songs that (again, for the most part) he thought in danger of being forgotten or dismissed. He also included songs by composers that he felt people, *wrongly*, supposed that he did not like or respect. From the 55 songs which he requested to be printed in this program (again, he wishes to emphasize, only a partial list), he selected the ones to be performed this evening.

STEPHEN SONDHEIM:
SONGS I WISH I'D WRITTEN (AT LEAST IN PART)

Music by Milton Ager; Lyrics by Jack Yellen, Bob Bigelow, and Charles Bates
  "Hard Hearted Hannah, the Vamp of Savannah" (1924)

Music by Harold Arlen; Lyrics by Johnny Mercer
  "Blues in the Night" from the film *Blues in the Night* (1941)
  "I Had Myself a True Love" from *St. Louis Woman* (1946)
  "I Wonder What Became of Me" from *St. Louis Woman* (1946)

Lyrics by E.Y. Harburg
"Buds Won't Bud" from *Hooray for What* (1937)
"The Eagle and Me" from *Bloomer Girl* (1944)

Music and Lyrics by Irving Berlin
"I Got Lost in His Arms" from *Annie Get Your Gun* (1946)
"Let's Face the Music and Dance" from the film *Follow the Fleet* (1936)
"You Can't Get a Man with a Gun" from *Annie Get Your Gun* (1946)

Music by Leonard Bernstein; Lyrics by Richard Wilbur
"Glitter and Be Gay" from *Candide* (1956)

Music by Jerry Bock; Lyrics by Sheldon Harnick
"Ice Cream" from *She Loves Me* (1963)
"Tell Me I Look Nice" cut from *She Loves Me* (1963)
"When Did I Fall in Love?" from *Fiorello!* (1959)

Music and Lyrics by Johnny Burke
"Sad Was the Day" from *Donnybrook!* (1961)

Music by Moose Charlap; Lyrics by Eddie Lawrence
"I'll Never Go There Anymore" from *Kelly* (1965)

Music by Cy Coleman; Lyrics by Carolyn Leigh
"The Best Is Yet to Come" (1959)
"The Other Side of the Tracks" from *Little Me* (1962)
"Real Live Girl" from *Little Me* (1962)
"The Rules of the Road" (1961)
"When in Rome (I Do as the Romans Do)" (1964)

Music adapted by Aaron Copland
"Golden Willow Tree" from *Old American Songs II* (1954)

Music arranged by Luciano Gallet
"Bambalelê (Brazilian Song of the Northern Interior)"

Music by George Gershwin; Lyrics by DuBose Heyward
"My Man's Gone Now" from *Porgy and Bess* (1935)

Music and Lyrics by Adam Guettel
"Riddle Song" from *Floyd Collins* (1994)

Music by Ray Henderson; Lyrics by B. G. De Sylva and Lew Brown
"Birth of the Blues" from *George White's Scandals of 1926*

Music and Lyrics by Peter E. Jones
"Bluellow" from *Peyton Place* (1994)

Music by Walter Jurmann and Bronislau Kaper; Lyrics by Gus Kahn
"San Francisco" from the film *San Francisco* (1936)

Music by John Kander; Lyrics by Fred Ebb
"Home" from *70, Girls, 70* (1971)

Music by Harold Karr; Lyrics by Matt Dubey
"Silverware" from *We Take the Town* (1962)

Music by Jerome Kern; Lyrics by Oscar Hammerstein II
"I Am So Eager" from *Music in the Air* (1932)
"The Song Is You" from *Music in the Air* (1932)

Music and Lyrics by Edward Kleban
"Better" (1973)

Music by Michael Leonard; Lyrics by Herbert Martin
"I'm All Smiles" from *The Yearling* (1965)

Music and Lyrics by Frank Loesser
"Make a Miracle" from *Where's Charley?* (1948)

Music and Lyrics by Hugh Martin (*with Ralph Blane)
"Ev'ry Time" from *Best Foot Forward* (1941)*
"Gotta Dance" from *Look, Ma, I'm Dancin'!* (1948)
"I Wanna Be Good 'n' Bad" from *Make a Wish!* (1951)
"The Trolley Song" from the film *Meet Me in St. Louis* (1944)*

Music and Lyrics by Bob Merrill
"On the Farm" from *New Girl in Town* (1957)

Music by Xavier Montsalvatge; Text by Ildefonso Pereda Valdés
"Canción de Cuna Para Dormir a un Negrito" from *Cinco Canciónes Negras*
(1958)

Music by Lewis F. Muir; Lyrics by L. Wolfe Gilbert
"Waiting for the Robert E. Lee" (1912)

Music and Lyrics by Cole Porter
"Every Time We Say Goodbye" from *Seven Lively Arts* (1944)
"Let's Be Buddies" from *Panama Hattie* (1940)
"Let's Not Talk about Love" from *Let's Face It* (1941)

Music by Richard Rodgers
"What's the Use of Wond'rin'?" from *Carousel* (1945); Lyrics by Oscar Ham-
merstein II
"Why Can't I" from *Spring Is Here* (1929); Lyrics by Lorenz Hart

Music and Lyrics by William Roy
"Charm" from *Maggie* (1953)
"What Every Woman Knows" from *Maggie* (1953)

Music by Arthur Schwartz
"By Myself" from *Between the Devil* (1937); Lyrics by Howard Dietz
"He Had Refinement" from *A Tree Grows in Brooklyn* (1951); Lyrics by Dorothy Fields
"There's No Holding Me" from *Park Avenue* (1946); Lyrics by Ira Gershwin

Music by David Shire; Lyrics by Richard Malby, Jr.
"Travel" from *Starting Here, Starting Now* (1977); originally written for the unproduced musical *The River* (1960)

Music by Charles Strouse; Lyrics by Lee Adams
"You've Got Possibilities" from *It's a Bird, It's a Plane, It's Superman* (1966)

Music by Jule Styne; Lyrics by Betty Comden and Adolph Green
"When the Weather's Better" from *Hallelujah, Baby!* (1967)

Music and Lyrics by Maury Yeston
"New Words" from *History Loves Company* (1989)

The following comments were solicited by the Library from the living composers and lyricists whose works were included in Stephen Sondheim's "Songs I Wish I'd Written" list. On hearing about this, Messrs. Gemignani and Tunick requested the opportunity to include comments of their own.

There are dozens of Stephen's songs I wish I had written. His work is an inspiration and a challenge to us all.

Lee Adams

Dear Steve,
After reading your insightful, intimate and ultimately moving profile in *The New York Times*, allow me to rewrite (as all musicals are) the caption under your shtetl-like photo on the cover, to whit:

YOU DON'T STOP WRITING BECAUSE IT'S GONE
IT'S GONE BECAUSE YOU STOP WRITING

Don't stop!

Jerry Bock

In a very gracious act of generosity, Stephen Sondheim has chosen fifty five songs he wished he had written to be performed at a concert celebrating his 70th birthday. Imagine that, it's his birthday and I'm getting a present because among the songs he chose are five written by Carolyn Leigh and myself.

Stephen Sondheim is a towering figure in the theatre and musical worlds who has put his personal imprint on a few generations of writers. He has legions of devoted fans and as many imitators.

Happy Birthday Stephen. Congratulations on your seventy years of creative accomplishments and wishing you many more.

Cy Coleman

Working with Stephen Sondheim over the years, I have learned so much. He challenges one, both musically and intellectually. He never takes the easy way out and does not expect you to, while all of the time allowing you your creative freedom. Working with Steve has always made me thankful and proud to be a musician.

Regards,

Paul Gemignani

Twenty years ago I sat down at Steve's piano and played what I hoped he would think was the best music he'd ever heard. My music. The next day, I must have written him the world's most passive-aggressive thank you note, because this was his response, which I still have, framed in my studio.

Dear Adam,

Thanks for the letter, but I didn't mean to be "not very encouraging." In fact, I hoped I was being quite the reverse: for me, true encouragement consists not so much of burbling as of detailed attention.

And then:

Just keep writing as we all do—or should. With love, Steve

Two months ago, I played Steve several songs from my current project. It was "cut this, move that, too poetic, too prosaic, excellent, not so excellent, etc." It was wonderful. It was liberating. It was, above all, loving, because a real mentor never burbles, and a mentee learns if he's lucky, that the point is not to be good, but to improve. It doesn't matter that I've played for Steve only twice. The lesson will span my life. And of course, there is his own work, never ever burbling, unsurpassed.

Adam Guettel

I was delighted to be included in Stephen Sondheim's list of "Songs I Wish I'd Written." But I'm somewhat bewildered because I'm fairly certain that Mr. Sondheim actually *did* write some of the lyrics he attributed to me. I remember writing "When Did I Fall in Love?" but I'm not too sure of "Ice Cream." And I can say with absolute certainty that he wrote "Tell Me I Look Nice." At least, I think so. As to the lyrics I wrote which *he* claims to have written, I would be happy to discuss them but I'm rather pressed for time. I will say, however, that whoever wrote them they're lovely.

Sheldon Harnick

A recollection, apropos: 1991. A study, with ten thousand recordings dominating the west wall, save a nook, housing a hi-fi with a modest reel to reel deck. Included, are one god of the theatre, and one neophyte. Minds bubbling, hearts burgeoning. Wine pouring. I'm showing great interest in his collection of reel-to-reel tapes of obscure show demos.

P: "WE TAKE THE TOWN? I love HOW DOES THE WINE TASTE!" S: "HOW do you know that? You've gotta hear SILVERWARE. S: "Gee, I wish I'd written that! What else do I ha . . . OH! You've gotta hear this one from KELLY-it's seven minutes long!" P: "When was the last time you cleaned these heads?" "I'LL NEEEEEEEEEEEEVER GO THERE ANYMORE!", Moose Charlap screams from the most distorted recording I'd ever heard in my life. S: "Isn't that terrific?" P: "Yeah, but I've gotta eat something." "ON THE FARM" I was not, and did "I WANNA BE GOOD 'N' BAD!" More wine, more favorites, more fun, and the evening flew by, as, indeed, the years have. Now, many people will be treated to an evening of these gems as I once was. The feeling of that evening never leaves me, and neither does my love for the gem most precious to me.

Happy 70, Steve!

Peter E. Jones

Dear Stephen,

Congratulations on this celebration of your brilliant contribution to the American musical Theatre. We are so proud that our song "Home" was included in your list. We are prouder still that you are our friend.

With many, many bravos for you and your work and much love,

John Kander and Fred Ebb

A writer I knew greeted people with names of theatre greats. Instead of "Hello" he'd say, "Luigi Pirandello!" "See you later" was, say "Oscar Wilde . . .," or, if he were in a rush, "O'Neill!" Going in to see *Company* I waved over at him and he called back, "Euripides!" During intermission we ran into one another in the lobby and both of us shouted, "Steve Sondheim!"

Hockney said Picasso was his main man because Pablo gave him the permission and courage to go all the way. Sondheim did it for lyricists, composers and playwrights. What a dandy thing to discover our number from the original *Kelly* among his list of "Songs He Wishes He'd Written." (Such a generous notion.) If Moose Charlap were around we'd have taken an ad.

Eddie Lawrence

Stephen Sondheim's unique talent, extraordinary craftsmanship, and enormous "ears" have changed musical theater forever and set the standard for everyone who follows.

Happy Birthday!

Michael Leonard

Dear Steve,

We couldn't be more delighted to have one of our songs on your wish list, since there is no song of yours we wouldn't want on ours. Your mentorship when we were fledglings, your encouragement, the inspiration of your work throughout our entire career—for all this we are profoundly grateful. You have always shown us what was possible and what to reach for.

Happy, happy birthday! Don't ever stop singing.

With Love,

> Richard Maltby, Jr. and David Shire

Fond I'm
Of Sondheim
He's my muse-ical God!
For where would the world be
Without *Sweeney Todd?*
Where would it be
Without *Gypsy* or *Forum?*
For those two alone
I'll forever adore'm!
And with *Story, Night Music*
And *Follies* and *Passion,*
It's a sure bet
S. Sondheim
Won't pass out of fashion!
Yes, where would the world be
Without Sundays with George?
Or the fact that Steve's written music
On which we happily gorge?
He's let us keep
Company
With his ingenious styles
Which accounts for the reason
Most days, "I'm All Smiles"!
Now with just a word
Or two more
I'll finally end this epistle:
Happy Birthday,

Steve Sondheim

Please keep on making us
Whistle

> Herbert E. Martin

When I saw *Anyone Can Whistle* during its pre-Broadway tryout period, I seemed to hear History whispering in my ear, "I'm getting ready to send in a new era of the American Musical Theater." When I saw *Company*, I whispered back, "Don't bother, it's here." By the time I saw *Sunday in the Park with George* and *Into the Woods*, the whispers had turned to shouts of joy.

Thank you, dear Stephen, for a never-ending stream of new beginnings. Your grateful fan,

Hugh Martin

As for a comment on Stephen, I can only say that since "Anyone Can Whistle" I have been an unswervable fan of his work, musically as well as lyrically, and in the unlikely event that someone should ask me for a list of fifty-five songs I wish I had written, I could easily fill the list with songs of Stephen's, with no effort at all. As a composer, the pleasure for me has been in not only discovering his words and his music, but also in learning from them.

William Roy

I've known Stephen Sondheim for longer than either of us would like to admit.

He said to me a long time ago, that "writing music was, for him, relatively easy, but lyrics he sweated and sweated over."

That remark still gets me crazy.

Happy Birthday Stephen.

Love,

Charles Strouse

Steve's misfortune is to be an Apollonian artist set down in a Dionysian era; despite this he has established himself as our theater's preeminent musical dramatist, and it has been my privilege to have served him as orchestrator these many years.

In my more wistful moments I've considered a few items that I wish that he *had* written:

1. *Phantom of the Opera* (what happens when the writers take over the theater)
2. *Sunset Boulevard* (what happens when the actors take over the theater)
3. *La Cage Aux Folles* (as Rossini remarked regarding a good melody written by an otherwise unworthy composer: "Troppo buone per questo coglione!"—Too good for that bastard!)
4. *Les Miserables* (just for the money)

Steve's graciousness towards me is of long standing—to him I owe a career, my sanity and an appreciation of his ability to observe with a knowing chuckle, the human condition. Thanks for all that, Steve, and for always treating me as an Old Friend.

Jonathan Tunick

Things I wish *I'd* written: "Ode to Joy," "Lovely" (*Funny Thing*), "Lullaby" (Brahms), "The Ladies Who Lunch" (*Company*), "I'm Still Here" (*Follies*), "In the Still of the Night" (Porter), "In the Still of the Night" (Doo Wop), "Send in the Clowns," "Aba Daba Honeymoon," "Back in Business" (*Dick Tracy*), *A Little Night Music* (Mozart), *A Little Night Music* (Sondheim), "Smile" (Chaplin), "Children Will Listen" (*Into the Woods*), *Winterreise* (All), *Sweeney Todd* (All), "A Little Priest" (*this one gets a special mention*), "Please, no grass . . . the theater is a temple, not a class!" (*The Frogs*, Yale Pool), "Someone to Watch Over Me" (Gershwin), "Not While I'm Around," *Sunday in the Park* (All), etc. etc.

Living national treasure. Member of the Pantheon. Thanks for saving the last quarter of the century . . .

Maury Yeston

Part III

SONGLISTING, DISCOGRAPHY AND PUBLISHING INFORMATION

Explanatory Notes

I have tried to make the following songlisting as useful, informative, and easy to use as possible, but some further clarification is necessary. First, "songlisting" is slightly misleading, as all of Sondheim's known musical works, published and unpublished, whatever their genre, are listed here in alphabetical order, ignoring initial articles "The," "A," and "An." Works with commonly used alternate titles, such as "Buddy's Blues" and "The God-Why-Don't-You-Love-Me Blues," are cross-referenced. Particularly in his later scores, such as *Into the Woods* and *Passion*, published scores reflect titles such as "Opening (Part IV)," whereas recordings refer to these sections with titles like "Jack, Jack, Jack." I have attempted to cross-reference as many of these as seemed useful, or at least include the score information parenthetically with the more commonly known title. "See also" references refer to a related song, often a later or earlier version of the same song, or to indicate songs that are usually linked, such as "Love Will See Us Through" and "You're Gonna Love Tomorrow."

Each song title is followed by its source—be it a stage musical, film, or television show. "From" is self-explanatory. "Cut from" generally means that the song was not used in the final version of the show, but in some cases, the song may never have been rehearsed. However, the difference between "cut" and "unused" seems either too subtle, or too difficult to track down, to be worthy of the distinction. Songs that were written for revivals of shows, or, as in the case of *Saturday Night*, decades after the majority of the score was written, are described as being "written for the [year given] production of [show title]." "For" generally means that the show was unproduced or the song was unfinished.

Most show titles are clear and unambiguous, but one unproduced show that Sondheim worked on as lyricist to Leonard Bernstein has been variously known as *A Pray by Blecht*, *The Exception and the Rule*, and *The Race to Urga*; the last is the title I have decided to use here. The show *Gold!*, on which he is currently working, was previously known as *Wise Guys*, and it has been rumored that its title may change yet again.

After a show's title is a year in parentheses. For produced shows, this is the year that the show opened; for unproduced works this is the year or years in which the show was predominantly written. Unproduced shows are described as "unproduced" after the date. Any composer and lyricist collaborators are noted after the date information. Other notes or points of interest are placed in square brackets.

For songs that have been published, that information is conveyed in the next line. At the end of this section are the definitions of the codes that indicate the title of the published vocal scores, vocal selections, and songbooks referenced. Not all of these are in print, but between libraries and various auction catalogs, used bookstores, and music websites, all should be available to the determined collector. The codes for the published songs are usually followed by information on the vocal range. If no range is given, it is either described as a "company number," meaning for multiple voices, or "instrumental." The ranges are given using the standard designation of middle C as "c^1," the C an octave above as "c^2," and an octave above that as "c^3"; the C below middle C is "c," and the C below that is "C." Most songs are written in the treble clef, even if they are specifically for men and sung an octave lower than written. The primary exception is in *Sweeney Todd* in which Sweeney and the Judge are written in the bass clef in the piano-vocal score, and are so designated here. The range information is given here for two primary purposes: to inform singers if they have the range for a given song, and, in the cases where a song has been published in various keys, to determine which publication best suits the singer's tessitura. For instance, there are versions of "Being Alive" listed here in which the lowest note is either F, G, B, or D. When ranges are given for duets, or trios, the information is given in the order that the voices are heard in the work, separated by slashes. Not included here are Sondheim songs published in general collections of songs, most individual sheet music, and instrumental or choral arrangements.

Next appears the discographical information. This includes only published, commercially available recordings—not personal tapes or pirated recordings, which abound. It also includes only vocal recordings of songs with lyrics by Sondheim but music by another composer—wherever it is possible to distinguish them (with the exception of a listing at the end of the major instrumental albums of *West Side Story, Gypsy,* and *Do I Hear A Waltz).*

The listings under each title are divided into two sections. First are the show recordings (in the broadest sense) in chronological order—as closely as can be determined. For these, the album title is followed by the performer's name, followed by the recording information. Second are the recordings by singers, singing groups, and instrumentalists, listed alphabetically by lead performer or group name. This list includes the performer's name, followed by the album title, followed by the recording information. For recordings that contain three or more songs by Sondheim, a code is given (in SMALLCAPS) to direct the reader to the recording information found in the section at the end of this guide (beginning on page 340). In essence, those pages contain the heart of what would be the most significant collection of Sondheim recordings. For recordings which contain only one or two Sondheim songs, all the available information for the recording is listed under the individual songs. There are a few show recordings that are out of chronological order, as I discovered their existence after codes had already been used throughout the songlisting. There are also a few cases where a recording includes less than three Sondheim songs, but it was included in the second portion of the discography in order to display, for instance, all known *Candide* recordings together. I hope these examples are clear and will cause no confusion.

There are currently four albums that comprise collections of previously recorded Sondheim songs: *A Collector's Sondheim, The Stephen Sondheim Songbook, The Sondheim Collection,* and *The MUSICality of Sondheim* (see page 386). Cuts included in these are indicated in the body of this discography with the superscript numbers [1,2,3] or [4] appearing after the title of the source recording. Not included in this discography are previously issued recordings that are included in non-Sondheim collections, usually with titles like "Broadway's Greatest Hits."

Credit must be given to the appendix to Stephen Banfield's book, *Sondheim's Broadway Musicals,* which proved to be an invaluable starting point for much of the title and show information. There were dozens of sources for the discographical information and I am grateful to all who contributed citations and missing pieces of information. Any compilation of this type is inevitably incomplete and dated by the time it is printed, but it is hoped that the benefits will outweigh the imperfections. My fervent wish is that Sondheim will write many more shows and all of his works will continue to be published and recorded. Annotate this listing as you see fit, and for those obsessive-compulsive types, I shall try to correct it and keep it updated for future editions.

CODES FOR PUBLISHED MUSIC:

ACWPVS	*Anyone Can Whistle* piano-vocal score, Hal Leonard 312012
ACWVS	*Anyone Can Whistle* vocal selections, Hal Leonard 312010
APVS	*Assassins* piano-vocal score, Warner Bros. VF1765
ASI	*All Sondheim vol. I*, Warner Bros. VAL2023
ASII	*All Sondheim vol. II*, Warner Bros. VAL2024A
ASIII	*All Sondheim vol. III*, Warner Bros. VAL2025A
ASIV	*All Sondheim vol. IV*, Warner Bros. 0283B
ATGVS	*All That Glitters* vocal selections, Broadcast Music Inc., 1949
AVS	*Assassins* vocal selections—revised, Warner Bros. VF1928
BOB	*Bernstein On Broadway*, Amberson/G. Schirmer
BSBA	Barbra Streisand *The Broadway Album*, Hal Leonard HL00358239
BSBB	Barbra Streisand *Back to Broadway*, Cherry Lane Music/Hal Leonard 02502132
BSC	Barbra Streisand *The Concert*, Cherry Lane Music/Hal Leonard 02502164
CaPVS	*Candide* piano-vocal score, Macmillan/Schirmer Books; current edition, Boosey & Hawkes M051966103
CaVS	*Candide* vocal selections, Amberson Enterprises/G. Schirmer; current edition, Boosey & Hawkes M051922338
CPVS	*Company* piano-vocal score, Hal Leonard HL00362136
CVS	*Company* vocal selections, Valando Music, 1970
CVS2	*Company* vocal selections, 25th Anniversary Edition, Hal Leonard HL00359494
DIHPVS	*Do I Hear a Waltz?* piano-vocal score, Hal Leonard 312116
DIHVS	*Do I Hear a Waltz?* vocal selections, Hal Leonard 312115
DTVS	*Dick Tracy* vocal selections, Hal Leonard HL00490516
FLVS	*Follies* London vocal selections, Carlin Music Group/IMP 89042/Hal Leonard HL00359869
FPVS	*Follies* piano-vocal score, Hal Leonard 362215
FTPVS	*A Funny Thing . . . Forum* piano-vocal score, Hal Leonard 312152
FTVS	*A Funny Thing . . . Forum* vocal selections, Hal Leonard 312151
FVS	*Follies* vocal selections, Charles Hansen
GPVS	*Gypsy* piano-vocal score, Hal Leonard 312188
GVS	*Gypsy* vocal selections, Hal Leonard 312187
HTSS	*Hansen Treasury of Stephen Sondheim Songs*, Charles Hansen Music & Books, Inc.
ITWPVS	*Into the Woods* piano-vocal score, Warner Bros. VF1544

ITWVS	*Into the Woods* vocal selections, Warner Bros. VF1445
LNMPVS	*A Little Night Music* piano-vocal score, Warner Bros. VAL2014A
LNMVS	*A Little Night Music* vocal selections, Warner Bros. VAL2013A
MWRPVS	*Merrily We Roll Along* piano-vocal score, Revelation Music & Rilting Music/Tommy Valando
MWRVS	*Merrily We Roll Along* vocal selections, Warner Bros. VAL2015A
POPVS	*Pacific Overtures* piano-vocal score, Warner Bros. VAL2017
PPVS	*Passion* piano-vocal score, Warner Bros. PF9608
PRSM	*Phinney's Rainbow* sheet music, Broadcast Music Inc., 1948
PVS	*Passion* vocal selections, Warner Bros. VF2164
SCCH	*Sondheim A Celebration at Carnegie Hall,* Warner Bros. VAL2022A
SNVS	*Saturday Night* vocal selections, Hal Leonard HL00313107
SPGPVS	*Sunday in the Park with George* piano-vocal score, Warner Bros. VAL2019A
SPGVS	*Sunday in the Park with George* vocal selections, Warner Bros. VAL2018A
SSFTS	*stephen sondheim film and television songs* Warner Bros. 0098B
SSS	*The Stephen Sondheim Songbook,* Chappell & Company/Elm Tree Books, London, 1979
STPVS	*Sweeney Todd* piano-vocal score (revised), Warner Bros. VAL2021B
STVS	*Sweeney Todd* vocal selections, Warner Bros. VAL2020A
WSSFS	*West Side Story* full score, Boosey & Hawkes MO51211760
WSSPVS	*West Side Story* piano-vocal score, Boosey & Hawkes MO51970209
WSSVS	*West Side Story* vocal selections, Boosey & Hawkes MO51933457

Songlisting, Discography, and Publishing Information

SONGLISTING

"A-1 March" from *Anyone Can Whistle* (1964), [also known as "Hooray for Hapgood"]
ACWPVS d^1-$g\#^2$
Anyone Can Whistle Original Cast (Ensemble) [part of "A Parade in Town"], see ANYONE1
Anyone Can Whistle Live at Carnegie Hall (Ensemble), see ANYONE2

"Act I Prologue" from *Pacific Overtures* (1976)
POPVS d-$b\flat^1$

"Act Two Opening" added to *Merrily We Roll Along* (1989) [includes "He's Only a Boy" and a modified version of "Good Thing Going"]
Merrily We Roll Along Revival Cast (Michelle Pawk), see MERRILY2
Merrily We Roll Along London Cast (Louise Gold), see MERRILY3

"Ad" from *Mary Poppins* (1950, unproduced)

"Addison's Trip Around the World" written for *Gold!* (forthcoming)

"The Advantages of Floating in the Middle of the Sea" from *Pacific Overtures* (1976)
POPVS company number
Pacific Overtures Original Cast (Mako, Company), see PACIFICOVER1

Pacific Overtures English National Opera (Richard Angas, Company), see PACIFICOVER2

Sondheim (Book-of-the-Month) (instrumental), see SOND1

A Gala Concert for Hal Prince (The Munich Radio Orchestra), see GALA1

East West Players/*East West Overtures* (Mako, Tim Dang & Ensemble), see EASTWEST1

New York City Opera Orchestra/*Broadway's Best* (instrumental) ["*Pacific Overtures* Suite, First Movement"], see NEWYORKCITYOP1

"Advice" from *Climb High* (1950–52, unproduced)

"After All" from *By George* (1946)

"Afternoon in Benicia" for *The Legendary Mizners* (unproduced)

"Agony" from *Into the Woods* (1987)

ITWPVS duet b-e^2/c♯^{1}-e^2, reprise b-e♯^{2}/c♯^{1}-e^2, ITWVS duet d^1-f^2 [both]

Into the Woods Original Cast (Robert Westenberg, Chuck Wagner), see INTOTHE1

Into the Woods London Cast (Clive Carter, Mark Tinkler), see INTOTHE2

Symphonic Sondheim (Instrumental) [part of the "Into the Woods Suite"], see SYMPHONICSON1

No One is Alone . . . (Greg Hart & Kynan Johns), see NONONEIS1

Into the Woods Revival Cast (Greg Edelman, Christopher Sieber), see INTOTHE3

East West Players/*East West Overtures* (Scott Watanabe, Andrew Djang), see EASTWEST1

"Ah, But Underneath . . ." from London revival of *Follies* (1987)

ASIII f-b♭^{1}, FLVS f-e♭^{2}

Follies London Cast (Diana Rigg), see FOLLIES03

Putting It Together (Julie Andrews) [incomplete], see PUTTINGIT1

Follies, The Complete Recording (Dee Hoty, Gentlemen of the Ensemble), see FOLLIES05

Moving On (Company), see MOVINGON [with "Pretty Women"]

Kreutz, Michael/*Since You Stayed Here*, Blue Moon Music [n.n.], 2001

Laine, Cleo/*Cleo Sings Sondheim*, see LAINEC2

"Ah, Miss" from *Sweeney Todd* (1979)

STPVS c^1-f^2

Sweeney Todd Original Cast (Victor Garber, Sarah Rice, Merle Louise), see SWEENEYT1

Sweeney Todd Barcelona Cast (Pep Molina, Ma. Josep Peris, Teresa Vallicrosa), see SWEENEYT3

Sweeney Todd Live at the NYP (Davis Gaines, Heidi Grant Murphy, Audra McDonald), see SWEENEYT4

"Ah, Paree!/Ah, Paris!" from *Follies* (1971)
FLVS, FVS, HTSS g♯-c², FPVS c♯¹-g² [for "montage" ending low note of a]
Follies Original Cast (Fifi D'Orsay), see FOLLIES01
*Side by Side by Sondheim*¹ (Millicent Martin), see SIDEBYS1
Side by Side... Australian Cast (Jill Perryman), see SIDEBYS2
Follies in Concert (Liliane Montevecchi), see FOLLIES02
Follies London Cast (Maria Charles), see FOLLIES03
Follies, The Complete Recording (Liliane Montececchi), see FOLLIES05
Singers Unlimited/*A Little Light Music* (Beryl Korman), see SINGERSUN1
[with "Parisaian Pierrot" & "The Last Time I Saw Paris"]

"Airport at Biarritz" from *Stavisky* (1974)
Stavisky (instrumental), see STAVISKY1

"Alarms," see "Four Black Dragons"

"All for You" from *Saturday Night* (1954)
SNVS d¹-g²
Unsung Sondheim (Davis Gaines), see UNSUNGS1
Saturday Night Bridewell Cast (Anna Francolini), see SATURDAYN1
Saturday Night Original New York Cast (Lauren Ward), see SATURDAYN2

"All I Need Is the Girl/Boy" from *Gypsy* (1959), music by Jule Styne
GPVS e¹-g², GVS c♯¹-e²
Gypsy Original Cast (Paul Wallace), see GYPSY01
Gypsy Film (Paul Wallace), see GYPSY02
Gypsy London Cast (Andrew Norman), see GYPSY03
Gypsy Revival Cast (Robert Lambert), see GYPSY04
Gypsy TV Cast (Jeffrey Broadhurst), see GYPSY05
Celebrating Gypsy . . . (Tim Flavin), see CELEBRATGYP
Kay Medford in "Gypsy" (Richard Fox), see GYPSY09
Baker, Darrin/*What's a Nice Girl Like You . . .*, Car-Jam Records/2die4 99012, 1999 [in medley with "Hundreds of Girls"]
Broadway Theatre Chorus/*Fiddler on the Roof; Gypsy*, see BROADWAYTHEAT1
Burnett, Carol/*Carol Burnett Sings*, Decca (S)7-4437, 1967 [reissued on CD as *Let Me Entertain You*, Decca 012 159 402-2, 2000]
Chakiris, George/*George Chakiris*, Capitol (S)ST-1750, 1962
Damone, Vic/*Don't Let Me Go*, United Talent/Buddah (S) UTS-4501, 1960-69

Damone, Vic/. . . *Live in Concert*, Classic World #12A, 2000 [?]

Feinstein, Michael/*Michael Feinstein Sings the Jule Styne Songbook*, see FEINSTEIN1

Harnar, Jeff/*Jeff Harnar Sings the 1959 Broadway Songbook*, see HARNARJ1

Malmberg, Sue/*Musical Theatre Classics: Tenor*, H. Leonard Pub. Corp HL00660152, 1990 [cassette]

Manilow, Barry/*Showstoppers*, Arista 18687-2, 1991

Marcovicci, Andrea/*Andrea Marcovicci Sings Movies*, DRG 91405, 1991 [in medley]

McKechnie, Donna/*Inside the Music*, see mckechnied1 [in medley]

Myles, Meg/*Meg Myles at the Living Room*, Mercury MG-20686, (S)SR-60686, 1963

Ross, Annie/*Gypsy*, see ROSSANNIE

Roy Budd Trio/*Everything's Coming Up Roses: The Musical . . . Sondheim*, see ROYBUDD1

Sinatra, Frank/*Francis A. Sinatra & Edward K. Ellington*, Reprise 10242-2, 1967

Sinatra, Frank/*The Reprise Collection*, Reprise 9 26340-2, 1990

Singing Hoosiers/*Twentieth Anniversary Concert 1970*, Century Records 38142, 1970

Styne, Jule/*My Name is Jule*, see STYNEJ1

Tormé, Mel/*Tormé Swings Shubert Alley*, Verve (S)6-2132, 1960, Verve 821 581-2 YH [MGM 1960, reissued by PolyGram 1984]

Tormé, Mel/*'Round Midnight: A Retrospective*, Stash Records ST-CD-4, 1988

"All Things Bright and Beautiful" cut from *Follies* (1971), [see also "Prologue"]

ASII duet e^1-$f\!\!\#^2$/e^1-g^2, FPVS instrumental as "Prologue"

Marry Me a Little[1] (Craig Lucas, Suzanne Henry), see MARRYME1

A Little Sondheim Music (Los Angeles Vocal Arts Ensemble), see LITTLES1

Follies, The Complete Recording (Laurence Guittard, Donna McKechnie), see FOLLIES05

Dow, Judith/*Regards to Broadway*, see DOWJ1

Mayes, Sally/*Boys and Girls Like You and Me* (with Brent Barrett), see MAYESS1 [with "Your Eyes are Blue"]

New York City Gay Men's Chorus/*New York, New York, A Broadway Extravaganza*, see NEWYORKCITYGAY1

"All's Fair" from *By George* (1946)

"Alma Mater" from *Phinney's Rainbow* (1948)

"Alms . . . Alms . . ." from *Sweeney Todd* (1979) [included in "No Place Like London"]
STPVS a-d$\sharp^2$
Sweeney Todd Original Cast (Merle Louise), see SWEENEYT1
Sweeney Todd Barcelona Cast (Teresa Vallicrosa), see SWEENEYT3
Sweeney Todd Live at the NYP (Audra McDonald), see SWEENEYT4

"Alumnum's Song" from *Phinney's Rainbow* (1948)

"America" from *West Side Story* (1957), music by Leonard Bernstein
BOB, WSSPVS duet + company, WSSVS c^1-e^2
West Side Story Original Cast (Chita Rivera, Marilyn Cooper, Reri Grist, Shark Girls), see WESTSIDE01
West Side Story film (Bety Wand, George Chakiris, The Sharks, Their Girls), see WESTSIDE02
West Side Story Studio Cast (Louise Edeiken, Tatiana Troyanos, Chorus), see WESTSIDE03
Sondheim: A Musical Tribute (Chita Rivera, Pamela Myers), see SONDAMUST1
Jerome Robbins Broadway (Charlotte d'Ambrosia, Debbie Shapiro, Barbara Yeager, Nancy Hess, Elaine Wright, Renée Stork), see JEROMER1
West Side Story Studio Cast London (La Vern Williams, Mary Carewe, Jenny O'Grady, Lee Gibson), see WESTSIDE04
West Side Story Studio Cast Leicester Haymarket (Caroline O'Connore, Julie Paton, Girls), see WESTSIDE05
West Side Story Studio Cast Leicester Haymarket (Caroline O'Connore, Nick Ferranti, Sharks), see WESTSIDE05 [Alternate Motion Picture Version]
West Side Story, The Songs of (Natalie Cole, Pati Labelle, Sheila E.), see WESTSIDE06
West Side Story, Dave Grusin presents (background vocalists), see WESTSIDE07
West Side Story London Studio Cast (Mary Preston, Venita Ernandes, Lorraine Hart, Lorraine Smith), see WESTSIDE09
Blackwell, Harolyn/*A Simple Song: Blackwell Sings Bernstein*, see BLACKWELL1 [duet with Vanessa Williams]
Darin, Bobby/*West Side Story*, see DARIN1
Davis Jr., Sammy/*Sammy Davis Jr. at the Cocoanut Grove*, see DAVISS [part of *West Side Story* medley]
Kaufmann, Anna Maria/*Spotlight—Musical Moments*, Polydor [n.n.], 1999[?]
Lopez, Trini/*Trini at PJ's*, Reprise (S)6093, 1968
Lyman, Arthur/*Many Moods of Arthur Lyman*, Hi-Fi (S)SL-1007, 45rpm 5057, 1962

Martin, Denny/*Taste of Honey*, Libery LRP-3237, (S)LST-7237, 1962
O'Connor, Caroline/*What I Did for Love*, JAY Records CDJAY 1314, 1998
Stephens, Dave/*Broadway Originals*, Cameo (S)CS-4006, 1962

"Another Hundred People" from *Company* (1970)
ASI, CPVS, CVS [2 versions], CVS2, HTSS, SSS c^1-eb^2
Company Original Cast (Pamela Myers), see COMPANY01
Sondheim: A Musical Tribute (Pamela Myers), see SONDAMUST1
Side by Side by Sondheim (Julia McKenzie), see SIDEBYS1
Side by Side . . . Australian Cast (Geraldene Morrow), see SIDEBYS2
A Stephen Sondheim Evening (Judy Kaye), see STEPHENSE1
A Broadway Extravaganza (instrumental), see BROADWAYEX [in medley]
Stephen Sondheim's Company . . . in Jazz (The Trotter Trio), see COMPANY03
Company Revival Cast (La Chanze), see COMPANY05
Second City Divas (Kathy Santen), M.A.M. Records [n.n.], 1996
Company London Revival Cast (Anna Francolini), see COMPANY04
Sondheim Tonight (The West End Chorus), see SONDTON1 [with "Being Alive" & "Sunday in the Park with George"]
The Stephen Sondheim Album (Alice Ripley), see STEPHENSA1
Moving On (Company), see MOVINGON
Company Brazilian Cast (Sabrina Korgut), see COMPANY06
Beechman, Laurie/*Time Between the Time*, DRG 5230, 1993
Boston Pops Orchestra/*Songs of the '60s* (instrumental), see BOSTON1
Cook, Barbara/*Barbara Cook sings Mostly Sondheim* (sung by Malcolm Gets), see COOKB1 [with "So Many People"]
Dartmouth Aires/*Colors*, Dynamic Recording XPL-1026 [n.d.], [Men's Chorus]
Di Novi, Gene/*Softly*, Di 123 Pedimega, 1977 [solo piano]
East West Players/*East West Overtures* (Deborah Nishimura), see EASTWEST1
Gillies, Jodie/*Jodie Gillies*, TVD 93371 (Festival Records), [n.d.]
Heller, Marc/*Take Me to the World: Songs by Stephen Sondheim*, see HELLERM1
Lemper, Ute/*City of Strangers*, see LEMPER1
Michuda, Marie/*It's a Grand Night for Singing*, Southport S-SSD 0074, 1999
New York City Gay Men's Chorus/*Love Lives On*, see NEWYORKCITYGAY2
Roy Budd Trio/*Everything's Coming Up Roses: The Musical . . . Sondheim*, see ROYBUDD1
Swingle Singers/*1812*, Swing CD4, 1989 [reissued on Virgin Classics CDC 5 45134 2, 1995]
Turner, Geraldine/*Old Friends*, see TURNERG1
Wilk, Oystein/*Too Many Mornings*, see WILKO1

"Another National Anthem" from *Assassins* (1991)
 APVS company number
 Assassins Original Cast (Company), see ASSASSINS1
 No One Is Alone . . . (Company), see NONONEIS1

"Another World" from *The Lady or the Tiger* (1954, unproduced), music by
 Mary Rodgers

"Any Moment" from *Into the Woods* (1987)
 ITWPVS duet b♭-e♭²/c¹-d²
 Into the Woods Original Cast (Robert Westenberg, Joanna Gleason), see
 INTOTHE1
 Into the Woods London Cast (Clive Carter, Imelda Staunton), see INTOTHE2
 No One Is Alone . . . (Kynan Johns), see NONONEIS1
 Into the Woods Revival Cast (Greg Edelman, Kerry O'Malley), see INTOTHE3
 Peters, Bernadette/*Sondheim, Etc.*, see PETERSB1 [with "Hello Little Girl"]

"Anyone Can Whistle" from *Anyone Can Whistle* (1964)
 ACWPVS g-c², reprise g-d♭², ACWVS, ASI, HTSS, SCCH, SSS b♭-e♭²
 Anyone Can Whistle² Original Cast (Lee Remick), see ANYONE1
 Sondheim: A Musical Tribute (Stephen Sondheim), see SONDAMUST1
 Side by Side by Sondheim (David Kernan), see SIDEBYS1
 Side by Side . . . Australian Cast (Bartholomew John), see SIDEBYS2
 Songs of Sondheim Irish Cast (Tony Kenny), see SONGSOFSOND1
 Sondheim, Book-of-the-Month Records (Betsy Joslyn), see SOND1
 A Broadway Extravaganza (instrumental), see BROADWAYEX [in medley]
 Sondheim: A Celebration at Carnegie Hall (Billy Stritch), see SONDACELATC1
 Color and Light: Jazz Sketches . . . (Nancy Wilson), see COLOR1
 Anyone Can Whistle Live at Carnegie Hall (Bernadette Peters), see ANYONE2
 A Little Light Music (Beryl Korman and/or Julia Meadows), see LITTLEL1
 The Stephen Sondheim Album (Jane Krakowski), see STEPHENSA1
 Stephen Sondheim Songs (instrumental accompaniment), see STEPHENSS1
 Ballingham, Pamela/*Magical Melodies*, Earth Mother Productions
 EMPD06B, 1991
 Barrowman, John/*Reflections from Broadway⁴*, see BARROWMAN1
 Bennett, Richard Rodney/*A Different Side of Sondheim*, see BENNETTR1
 Breach, Joyce and William Roy/*Love Is the Thing*, Audiophile ACD–314,
 2001
 Buckley, Betty/*heart to heart*, KO Productions 0001-2, 2000
 Campbell, James, Gene Di Novi, Dave Young/*Manhattan Echoes*, Mar-
 quis Records 267, 2000
 Campbell, Mike/*My Romance*, Audiophile 287, 1997
 Clary, Robert/*Louis Lebeau Remembers . . . Stephen Sondheim . . .*, see CLARYR1

Cook, Barbara/*Barbara Cook Sings Mostly Sondheim*, see COOKB1

Desmond, Trudy/*Tailor Made*, The Jazz Alliance TJA-10015, 1992

Ellis, Anita with Ellis Larkins/*A Legend Sings*, Orion ORS 79358, 1979

Ellis, Anita/*Look to the Rainbow*, Audiophile ACD-310, 2000

Gaines, Davis/*Against the Tide*, LAP Records 76628 2, 1996

Hateley, Linzi/*True Colours*, Dress Circle [n.n.], 2001 [with "The Girl I Meant to Be"]

Heller, Marc/*Take Me to the World: Songs by Stephen Sondheim*, see HELLERM1

Intimate Broadway/*With One Look*, Intersound 8309, 1996

Jackie & Roy/*A Stephen Sondheim Collection*, see JACKIE&1

Laine, Cleo/*Cleo Sings Sondheim*, see LAINEC2

Laine, Cleo & James Galway/*Sometimes When We Touch*, RCA ARL1-3628, 1980

Markey, Enda/*Another Place and Time*, see MARKEY1

Mendelssohn Choir/*Mendelssohn Sings Sondheim*, see MENDELSSOHN1 [with "See What it Gets You"]

Patinkin, Mandy/*Mandy Patinkin*, see PATINKIN1

Prowse, Juliet/*What Are You Afraid Of?*, Columbia 454-43016, 1965

Roy Budd Trio/*Everything's Coming Up Roses: The Musical . . . Sondheim*, see ROYBUDD1

Saxe, Emily/*Whistling-Broadway to Berk'ley Square*, Orchard 3285, 1999

Singers Unlimited/*A Little Light Music* (Julia Meadows), see SINGERSUN1

Straight Out/*Long Black Flat White*, [n.l.], 2000 [Australian]

Tormé, Mel & George Shearing/*A Vintage Year*, Concord Jazz CJ-341, 1988 [solo piano By George Shearing]

Turner, Geraldine/*Old Friends*, see TURNERG1

Warlow, Anthony/*Midnight Dreaming*, Polydor 523612-2, 1994

Wilk, Oystein/*Too Many Mornings*, see WILKO1

Wopat, Tom/*The Still of the Night*, Angel CDC 7243 5 23623 2 5, 2000

York, Joe/*My Favorite Year*, see YORKJ1

"Arlette and Stavisky" from *Stavisky* (1974)
   Stavisky (instrumental), see STAVISKY1

"Arlette by Day" from *Stavisky* (1974)
   Stavisky (instrumental), see STAVISKY1

"Arlette by Night" from *Stavisky* (1974)
   Stavisky (instrumental), see STAVISKY1

"Art Isn't Easy," see "Putting It Together"

"Atom Bomb Baby (Mambo)" cut from *West Side Story* (1957), music by Leonard Bernstein

"Auto da fé (What a Day)" from 1974 revival of *Candide*, music by Leonard Bernstein, lyrics also by John LaTouche and Richard Wilbur
CaPVS company number
Candide Revival Cast (Company), see CANDIDE01
Candide New Broadway Cast (Company), see CANDIDE05
Candide Royal National Theatre (Company), see CANDIDE06

"Auto Show" from *Stavisky* (1974) [based on "Beautiful Girls (Bring On the Girls)" cut from *Follies*]
Stavisky[1] (instrumental), see STAVISKY1

"Ave alumnum" from *Phinney's Rainbow* (1948)

"Baby June and Her Newsboys" from *Gypsy* (1959), music by Jule Styne
GPVS e^1-e^2, GVS e^1-e^2 [as intro to "Let Me Entertain You"]
Gypsy Revival Cast (no credits), see GYPSY04
Gypsy TV Cast (Lacey Chabert, Elisabeth Moss, Joey Cee, Blake Armstrong, Teo Weiner), see GYPSY05
The Broadway Kids/*The Broadway Kids Sing Broadway*, Lightyear 54174-2, 1994

"Back in Business" from *Dick Tracy* (1990)
SCCH, SSFTS g-e^2
Sondheim: A Celebration at Carnegie Hall (Liza Minnelli, Billy Stritch, Ensemble), see SONDACELATC1
Putting It Together (Company), see PUTTINGIT1
Sondheim—A Celebration (Julia McKenzie, Millicent Martin, David Kernan), see SONDACEL1
Sondheim at the Movies (Alet Oury with others), see SONDATTHEM1
Kitt, Eartha/*Back in Business*, DRG 91431, 1994

"Back to the Palace" cut from *Into the Woods* (1987)

"Balcony Scene" cut from *West Side Story* (1957), music by Leonard Bernstein [an early version of "Tonight"]

"The Ballad of Booth" from *Assassins* (1991)
APVS, AVS, SCCH duet c$\sharp^1$-a$\sharp^2$/f$\sharp$-f$\sharp^2$
Assassins Original Cast (Patrick Cassidy, Victor Garber, Marcus Olson), see ASSASSINS1
Sondheim: A Celebration at Carnegie Hall (Patrick Cassidy, Victor Garber), see SONDACELATC1
No One Is Alone . . . (Michael Denholm & Kynan Johns), see NONONEIS1 [with "The Ballad of *Sweeney Todd*"]

Sondheim: A Celebration (Patrick Cassidy, Scott Waara), see SONDACEL2
Mendelssohn Choir/*Mendelssohn Sings Sondheim* (Robert Shoup), see
MENDELSSOHN1

"The Ballad of Czolgosz" from *Assassins* (1991)
  APVS, AVS d^1-g^2 + company
  Assassins Original Cast (Patrick Cassidy, Company), see ASSASSINS1

"The Ballad of Guiteau" from *Assassins* (1991)
  AVS duet a-$g^{\flat 2}$/c^1-g^2
  Assassins Original Cast (Jonathan Hadary, Patrick Cassidy), see ASSASSINS1

"The Ballad of Sweeney Todd" from *Sweeney Todd* (1979)
  ASI, SCCH, STVS solo version f-c^2, STPVS company number
  Sweeney Todd Original Cast (Len Cariou, Company), see SWEENEYT1
  A Little Sondheim Music (Los Angeles Vocal Arts Ensemble), see LITTLES1
  Symphonic Sondheim (instrumental) [part of the "*Sweeney Todd* Suite,"
    see SYMPHONICSON1
  Sondheim: A Celebration at Carnegie Hall (instrumental), see SONDACE-
    LATC1
  Stephen Sondheim's Sweeney Todd . . . In Jazz (The Trotter Trio), see
    SWEENEYT2
  No One Is Alone . . . (Company), see NONONEIS1 [with "The Ballad of
    Booth"]
  Sweeney Todd Barcelona Cast (Constantino Romero, Company), see
    SWEENEYT3
  A Gala Concert for Hal Prince (Len Cariou, Company), see GALA1
  Sondheim: A Celebration (James Matthew Campbell, Leo Daignault,
    Larry Raben, George Miserlis), see SONDACEL2
  Sondheim Tonight (Len Cariou, The Soloists), see SONDTON1
  Sweeney Todd Live at the NYP (George Hearn, Company), see SWEENEYT4
  DeLaria, Lea/*Play It Cool*, see DELARIA1
  East West Players/*East West Overtures* (Robert Almodovar & Ensemble),
    see EASTWEST1
  Gay Men's Chorus of Los Angeles/*Simply Sondheim*, see GAYMENSCLA1
    [in medley]
  His Master's Fish[1], featuring Gordon Grody, RCA "Red Seals Disco" 12"
    single PD-11687 (S) [n.d.], [later included in *A Collector's Sondheim*]

"Bang!" cut from *A Little Night Music* (1973)
  ASIII duet a$\sharp$-f^2/b$\sharp$-f^2
  Marry Me a Little[1] (Craig Lucas, Suzanne Henry), see MARRYME1
  Putting It Together (Michael Rupert, Rachel York), see PUTTINGIT1

"The Barber and His Wife" from *Sweeney Todd* (1979)
STPVS A-d[1]
Sweeney Todd Original Cast (Len Cariou), see SWEENEYT1
Sweeney Todd Barcelona Cast (Constantino Romero), see SWEENEYT3

"Barcelona" from *Company* (1970)
CPVS, CVS2, HTSS, SCCH, SSS duet b♭-f^2/c^1-f^2
Company Original Cast[2] (Dean Jones, Susan Browning), see COMPANY01
Side By Side By Sondheim (Julia McKenzie, David Kernan), see SIDEBYS1
Side By Side . . . Australian Cast (Geraldene Morrow, Bartholomew John), see SIDEBYS2
Songs of Sondheim Irish Cast (Tony Kenny, Loreto O'Connor), see SONGS-OFSOND1
Symphonic Sondheim (Instrumental), see SYMPHONICSON1
Sondheim: A Celebration at Carnegie Hall (Instrumental), see SONDACELATC1
Stephen Sondheim's Company . . . In Jazz (The Trotter Trio), see COMPANY03
Company London Revival Cast (Adrian Lester, Hannah Jones), see COMPANY04
Company Revival Cast (Boyd Gaines, Jane Krakowski), see COMPANY05
Sondheim: A Celebration (Patrick Cassidy, Joely Fisher), see SONDACEL2
Sondheim Tonight (Julia McKenzie, David Kernan), see SONDTON1
Company Brazilian Cast (Claudio Botelho, Patricia Levy), see COMPANY06
Company German Cast (Felix Powroslo, Anina Doinet), see COMPANY07
Bennett, Richard Rodney/*A Different Side of Sondheim*, see BENNETTR1
East West Players/*East West Overtures* (Alvin Ing, Jennifer Paz), see EASTWEST1
Jackie & Roy/*A Stephen Sondheim Collection*, see JACKIE&1

"Bargaining" from *Do I Hear a Waltz?* (1965), music by Richard Rodgers
DIHPVS b♭-e♭^{3}
Do I Hear a Waltz? Original Cast (Sergio Franchi, Elizabeth Allen), see DOIHEAR1

"Beautiful" from *Sunday in the Park with George* (1984)
ASIII, SPGPVS, SPGVS duet f♯-b^1/c♯^{1}-f♯^{2}
Sunday in the Park . . . Original Cast (Barbara Bryne, Mandy Patinkin), see SUNDAYIN1
No One Is Alone . . . (Michelle Burgan & Craig Weatherill), see NONONEIS1

"Beautiful Girls" from *Follies* (1971)
ASIV, FLVS, FVS, HTSS c^1-e^2 [g^2 opt. in ASIV], FPVS solo + company e^1-a^2/d^1-f♯^{2}
Follies Original Cast (Michael Bartlett and Company), see FOLLIES01

Sondheim: A Musical Tribute (Ron Holgate), see SONDAMUST1

Side by Side by Sondheim[1] (David Kernan), see SIDEBYS1

Side by Side . . . Australian Cast (Bartholomew John), see SIDEBYS2

Follies in Concert (Arthur Rubin and Company), see FOLLIES02

Follies London Cast (Paul Bentley and Company), see FOLLIES03

A Gala Concert for Hal Prince (Robert DuSold, Company), see GALA1

Follies, The Complete Recording (Vahan Khanzadian & Company), see FOLLIES05

Sondheim Tonight (Michael Ball, Company), see SONDTON1

Clary, Robert/*Louis Lebeau Remembers . . . Stephen Sondheim. . . .*, see CLARYR1

McMahon, Ed, Capitol 45rpm 3213, [n.d.]

Roy Budd Trio/*Everything's Coming Up Roses: The Musical . . . Sondheim*, see ROYBUDD1

Wilson, Julie/*Julie Wilson at Brothers & Sisters* Vol. Two, see WILSONJ1 [with "[The Story of] Lucy and Jessie," "Losing My Mind" & "Could I Leave You"]

Wilson, Julie/*Julie Wilson Sings the Stephen Sondheim Songbook*, see WILSONJ2

"Beautiful Girls (Bring On the Girls)" cut from *Follies* (1971) [music used as "Auto Show" in *Stavisky*]

Follies, The Complete Recording (Vahan Khanzadian, Peter Davenport), see FOLLIES05

"[Beggar Woman's] Lullaby" from *Sweeney Todd* (1979) [lyric added after original production]

Sweeney Todd Live at the NYP (Audra McDonald), see SWEENEYT4 [included in the "City on Fire" segment]

"Being Alive" from *Company* (1970)

ASI, CVS, HTSS, g^1-a^2, BSBA b-d♭^{2} [f-e♭^{2} optional], CPVS f^1-g♯^{2}, CVS, SCCH, SSS d^1-e^2

Company Original Cast[2] (Dean Jones and Company), see COMPANY01 [the Larry Kert recording, overdubbed for the original London cast, is included on the 1998 reissue]

Sondheim: A Musical Tribute (Larry Kert), see SONDAMUST1

Side by Side by Sondheim (David Kernan, Millicent Martin, Julia McKenzie), see SIDEBYS1

A Stephen Sondheim Evening[1] (Judy Kaye), see STEPHENSE1

Everyone's a Love Song, see EVERYONE1

Songs of Stephen Sondheim/You Sing the Hits, see SONGSOFSTEP1

Putting It Together (Company), see PUTTINGIT1

Sondheim: A Celebration at Carnegie Hall (Patti Lupone), see SONDACELATC1

Being Alive!—The Art of German Musical Stars (Paul Kribbe), Sound of Music Records SOMCD 001, [n.d.], [with "No More"]

Stephen Sondheim's Company . . . in Jazz (The Trotter Trio), see COMPANY03

Company London Revival Cast (Adrian Lester), see COMPANY04

Company Revival Cast (Boyd Gaines), see COMPANY05

Sondheim—A Celebration (Julia McKenzie, Millicent Martin, David Kernan), see SONDACEL1

Hey, Mr. Producer! (Bernadette Peters), see HEYMRP

Celebrating Sondheim (Claire Moore), see CELEBRATSON

Showstoppers from Broadway[4] (Stephen Bogardus), JAY Records, CDJAY 1266, 199[?]

Sondheim Tonight (The Soloists, The West End Chorus), see SONDTON1 [with "Another Hundred People" and "Sunday in the Park with George"]

Company Brazilian Cast (Claudio Botelho), see COMPANY06

Company German Cast (Felix Powroslo), see COMPANY07

Stephen Sondheim Songs (instrumental accompaniment), see STEPHENSS1

Barrowman, John/*Reflections from Broadway*, see BARROWMAN1

Beavis, Rinchard/*In the Spotlight*, Silverword [n.n.], 2001

Beechman, Laurie/*No One Is Alone*, see BEECHMAN1

Billings, Alexandra/*Being Alive*, Southport S-SSD 0080, [n.d.]

Bogart, Matt/*Simple Song*, JAY Records CDJAY 1363, 2002

Boston Pops Orchestra/*Songs of the '60s* (instrumental), see BOSTON1

Budd, Julie/*If You Could See Me Now*, After 9 [n.n.], 2000

Burton, Paul/*Songs on a Steinway*, Imperial Digital Limited IDID1, 1996

Byrne, Debra/*New Ways to Dream*, see BYRNED1

Cerna, Jo-Jo de la/*Trust the Wind*, Dress Circle JJDLC9901, 1999 [with "No More"]

Combo fiasco/*here*, italic entertainment [n.n, n.d.], [with "Not a Day Goes By" & "Not While I'm Around"]

Connelli, Judi/*Judi Connelli Live in London*, see CONNELLI2 [with "In Buddy's Eyes"]

De Ferranti, Margie/*Margie De Ferranti*, see DEFERRANT1 [with "It Only Takes a Moment"]

Dore, Michael/*Simply*, [?], 2002 [with "Not a Day Goes By" & "Take Me to the World"]

Dow, Judith/*Regards to Broadway*, see DOWJ1

Ford, Anne Kerry/*Something Wonderful*, see FORDA1

Heller, Marc/*Take Me to the World: Songs by Stephen Sondheim*, see HELLERM1

Hickland, Catherine/ *. . . Sincerely, Broadway*, After Nine [n.n.], 1997

Jahana, Raishel/*Sondheim Songs*, see JAHANA1

Joseph, Alexander/*Being Alive!*, [n.l., n.n.], 1999[?]

Keegan, Ted/*Ted Keegan Sings*, LML TKS001CD, 2001

Kostelanetz, Andre/*Everything Is Beautiful*, Columbia [n.n.], 1970 [instrumental]

Laine, Cleo/*Cleo Laine Return to Carnegie*, see LAINEC1

Lemper, Ute/*City of Strangers*, see LEMPER1

Lupone, Patti/*Patti Lupone Live!*, RCA Victor 09026-61797-2, 1993

McDermott, Sean/*My Broadway*, see MCDERMOTTS1

Mendelssohn Choir/*Mendelssohn Sings Sondheim*, see MENDELSSOHN1

Mitchell, Keith/*Keith Mitchell Sings Broadway*, Spark SPA-03, 1972

O'May, John/*Unusual Way*, MEM-004, 2000

Ost, Martha/*Something New, Something Blue*, Kendroit Productions [n.n.], 1979

Patinkin, Mandy/*Dress Casual*, see PATINKIN2

Peters, Bernadette/*Sondheim, Etc.*, see PETERSB1

Prince, Peter/*Being Alive*, RP Media [n.n.], 2001

Ruffelle, Frances/*Frances Ruffelle*, Dress Circle DRESSCD05, [n.d.]

Smith, Martin/*A Handful of Keys*, MSCD001, [n.d.]

Streisand, Barbra/*The Broadway Album*, see STREISAND

Streisand, Barbra/*Timeless*, see STREISAND3 [with "Something Wonderful"]

Turner, Geraldine/*Old Friends*, see TURNERG1

Warlow, Anthony/*On the Boards*, Polydor 513 402 2, 1992, [also included in Warlow's *The Best of Act One*, Polydor 533152-2, 1996]

Whiting, Margaret/*The Lady's in Love with You*, Audiophile ACD 207, 1985, 1989

Williams, Gary/*Recipe for Love*, [n.l., n.n., n.d.]

"Benicia" written for *Gold!* (forthcoming)

"Birthday Prayer" (1962) [piano piece written for Bernstein, contains cryptic message]

"Bitterness" from *By George* (1946)

"The Blob" from *Merrily We Roll Along* (1981)
    MWRPVS company number
    Merrily We Roll Along Revival Cast (Michelle Pawk, Company), see MERRILY2
    Merrily We Roll Along London Cast (Louise Gold, Company), see MERRILY3

"Bluebird Incidental 1 and 2," see "I'm Like the Bluebird"

"Bobby and Jackie and Jack" from *Merrily We Roll Along* (1981)
    MWRPVS quartet
    Merrily We Roll Along Original Cast (Lonny Price, Sally Klein, Jim Walton, David Loud), see MERRILY1

Merrily We Roll Along Revival Cast (Adam Heller, Anne Bobby, Malcolm Gets, Danny Burstein), see MERRILY2
Merrily We Roll Along London Cast (Evan Pappas, Michael Cantwell, Jacqueline Dankworth), see MERRILY3

"Bobby-Baby" from *Company* (1970), [also referred to as "Overture" & wed throughout score]
CPVS company number
Company Original Cast (Company), see COMPANY01
Company London Revival Cast (Company), see COMPANY04
Company Revival Cast (Company), see COMPANY05
Company Brazilian Cast (Company), see COMPANY06
Company German Cast (Ensemble), see COMPANY07

"Bolero d'Amour" from *Follies* (1971) [theme by Sondheim and a dance development by John Berkman]
FPVS instrumental
Follies, The Complete Recording (Orchestra), see FOLLIES05

"Boom Crunch!" cut from *Into the Woods* (1987)

"The Bordelaise" from *All That Glitters* (1949)

"A Bowler Hat" from *Pacific Overtures* (1976)
POPVS g-e♭²
Pacific Overtures Original Cast (Isao Sato), see PACIFICOVER1
Pacific Overtures English National Opera (Malcolm Rivers), see PACIFIC-OVER2

"The Boy from . . ." from *The Mad Show* (1966), music by Dorothy Rodgers
HTSS a-c²
The Mad Show² (Linda Lavin), Columbia Records OL-6530, OS-2930, 1966
Side by Side by Sondheim (Julia McKenzie), see SIDEBYS1
Side by Side . . . Australian Cast (Jill Perryman), see SIDEBYS2
Songs of Sondheim Irish Cast (Gemma Craven), see SONGSOFSOND1
hey, love (Faith Prince), see HEYLOVE1
Barnett, Peter & Julia Early/*In So Many Words*, see BARNETTEARLY1
McKenzie, Julia/*The Musicals Album*, see MCKENZIEJ1
Prior, Marina/*Somewhere*, see PRIORM1

"A Boy Like That" from *West Side Story* (1957), music by Leonard Bernstein
WSSPVS duet f-d♭²/d♭¹-b♭² [leads into "I Have a Love"]
West Side Story Original Cast (Carol Lawrence, Chita Rivera), see WESTSIDE01

West Side Story film (Betty Wand), see WESTSIDE02
West Side Story Studio Cast (Tatiana Troyanos, Kiri Te Kanawa), see WESTSIDE03
Side by Side by Sondheim (Millicent Martin, Julia McKenzie), see SIDEBYS1
West Side Story Studio Cast London (Barbara Bonney, La Vern Williams), see WESTSIDE04
West Side Story Studio Cast Leicester Haymarket (Caroline O'Connore, Tinuke Olafimihan), see WESTSIDE05
West Side Story, The Songs of (Selena), see WESTSIDE06
West Side Story London Studio Cast (Mary Preston, Jill Martin), see WESTSIDE09
The 3 Divas (Judi Connelli, Suzanne Johnston, Jennifer McGregor), [n.l., n.n.], 2000
Blackwell, Harolyn/*A Simple Song: Blackwell Sings Bernstein* (duet with Vanessa Williams), see BLACKWELL1
Callaway, Ann Hampton & Liz/*Sibling Revelry*, see CALLAWAYA&1 [in medley]
Garrett, Lesley/*Travelling Light* (duet with Denyce Graves), EMI/Angel Classics 5T20Z, 2002 [with "I Have a Love"]
Prior, Marina/*Somewhere*, see PRIORM1 [in medley]
Singers Unlimited/*A Little Light Music* (Beryl Korman, Julia Meadows), see SINGERSUN1
Vroman, Lisa/*Broadway Classics*, Offplanet 59057 02602, 1999 [with "I Have a Love"]

"Bright Star" from *Climb High* (1950–52, unproduced)

"Bring Me My Bride" from *A Funny Thing Happened on the Way to the Forum* (1962)
FTPVS b-f♯^{2} + company
A Funny Thing . . . Original Cast (Ronald Holgate, Zero Mostel, Company), see FUNNY01
A Funny Thing . . . London Cast (Leon Greene, Frankie Howerd, Company), see FUNNY02
A Funny Thing . . . Film (Leon Greene, Company), see FUNNY03 [listed as "My Bride"]
A Funny Thing . . . Revival Cast (Cris Groenendaal, Nathan Lane, Company), see FUNNY05

"Bring On the Girls," see "Beautiful Girls"

"Broadway" from *Gypsy* (1959), music by Jule Styne [recordings under "Dainty June and Her Farm Boys"]
GPVS company a♮-g^1, solo e♯^{1}-d^2

"Broadway Baby" from *Follies* (1971)
ASI, HTSS, SSS c^1-e♭^{2}, FLVS, FVS, SCCH c^1-e^2, FPVS g-b^1 [with medley ending]
Follies Original Cast (Ethel Shutta), see FOLLIES01
Sondheim: A Musical Tribute (Ethel Shutta), see SONDAMUST1
Side by Side by Sondheim[1] (Julia McKenzie), see SIDEBYS1
Side by Side . . . Australian Cast (Geraldene Morrow), see SIDEBYS2
Songs of Sondheim Irish Cast (Gemma Craven), see SONGSOFSOND1
Follies in Concert (Elaine Stritch), see FOLLIES02
Follies London Cast (Margaret Courtenay), see FOLLIES03
Sondheim: A Celebration at Carnegie Hall (Daisy Eagan), see SONDACELATC1
A Gala Concert for Hal Prince (Debbie Shapiro Gravitte), see GALA1
Follies/Themes from the Legendary Musical (The Trotter Trio), see FOLLIES04
Hey, Mr. Producer! (Maria Friedman, Julia McKenzie, Bernadette Peters & The Broadway Babies), see HEYMRP
Follies, The Complete Recording (Kaye Ballard), see FOLLIES05
Showstoppers from Broadway[4] (Carolee Carmello), JAY Records [n.n.], CDJAY 1266, 199[?]
Sondheim Tonight (Michael Ball), see SONDTON1
The Stephen Sondheim Album (Lea Delaria), see STEPHENSA1
Moving On (Company), see MOVINGON
Stephen Sondheim Songs (instrumental accompaniment), see STEPHENSS1
Blaine, Vivian/*For You*, see BLAINEV1
Campbell, David/*Yesterday Is Now*, Philips 522714-2, 1996
Criswell, Kim/*Back to Before*, JAY Records, CDJAY 1317, 1999
Florida Symphonic Pops/*The Phantom of the Opera*, see FLORIDA1 [instrumental]
Friedman, Maria/*Maria Friedman*, Carlton Sounds 30360 00012, 1995
Jahana, Raishel/*Sondheim Songs*, see JAHANA1
Laine, Cleo/*Cleo Laine Return to Carnegie*, see LAINEC1
Loudon, Dorothy/*Broadway Baby*, DRG CDSL 5203, 1986
Markey, Enda/*Another Place and Time*, see MARKEY1
Peters, Bernadette/*Bernadette*, MCA MCAD-10612, 1992 [LP 1980-81]
Peters, Bernadette/*Sondheim, Etc.*, see PETERSB1
Rochester Pops Orchestra/*Opening Night*, see ROCHESTERP1 [instrumental]
Singers Unlimited/*A Little Light Music* (Beryl Korman), see SINGERSUN1
Stritch, Elaine/*Elaine Stritch at Liberty*, see STRITCHE1

"Brotherly Love" written for *Gold!* (forthcoming)

"Buddy's Blues" from *Follies* (1971), [also known as "The God-Why-Don't-You-Love-Me Blues"]
FLVS, FVS, HTSS, SSS solo version c^1-e♭^{2}, FPVS trio version d^1-f^2/d^1-a^2 [both women's voices later range]

Follies Original Cast (Gene Nelson), see FOLLIES01

Sondheim: A Musical Tribute (Larry Blyden, Donna McKechnie, Chita Rivera), see SONDAMUST1

Side by Side by Sondheim[1] (David Kernan, Millicent Martin, Julia McKenzie), see SIDEBYS1

Side by Side . . . Australian Cast (Bartholomew John), see SIDEBYS2

Sondheim, Book-of-the-Month Records (Bob Gunton, Betsy Joslyn, Debbie Shapiro), see SOND1

Follies in Concert (Mandy Patinkin), see FOLLIES02

Follies London Cast (David Healey), see FOLLIES03

Sondheim—A Celebration (Julia McKenzie, Millicent Martin, David Kernan), see SONDACEL1

Follies/Themes From the Legendary Musical (The Trotter Trio), see FOLLIES04

Celebrating Sondheim (Tudor Davies, Claire Moore, Rosemary Ashe), see CELEBRATSON

Follies, The Complete Recording (Tony Roberts, Pamela Jordan, Danette Holden), see FOLLIES05

Brussell, Barbara/*patterns*, see BRUSSELL1

Jackie & Roy/*A Stephen Sondheim Collection*, see JACKIE&1

McMahon, Ed, Capitol 45rpm 3213, [n.d.]

Roy Budd Trio/*Everything's Coming Up Roses: The Musical . . . Sondheim*, see ROYBUDD1

Turner, Geraldine/*Old Friends*, see TURNERG1

"By the Sea" from *Sweeney Todd* (1979)

ASI, STVS a-e^2, STPVS duet g♯-e^2/G♯-b

Sweeney Todd Original Cast (Angela Lansbury, Len Cariou), see SWEENEYT1

A Little Sondheim Music (Janet Smith, Michael Gallup), see LITTLES1

Stephen Sondheim's Sweeney Todd . . . in Jazz[3] (The Trotter Trio), see SWEENEYT2

Sweeney Todd Barcelona Cast (Vicky Pena, Constantino Romero), see SWEENEYT3

Sondheim—A Celebration (Millicent Martin), see SONDACEL1

Sweeney Todd Live at the NYP (Patti Lupone, George Hearn), see SWEENEYT4

"The Cadys" from *All That Glitters* (1949)

"Can That Boy Foxtrot!" cut from *Follies* (1971)

HTSS b♭-e♭^{2}

Side by Side by Sondheim (Millicent Martin, Julia McKenzie), see SIDEBYS1

Side by Side . . . Australian Cast (Jill Perryman, Geraldene Morrow), see SIDEBYS2

Marry Me a Little[1] (Craig Lucas, Suzanne Henry), see MARRYME1

The Birdcage (Nathan Lane), see BIRDCAGE
A Little Light Music (Beryl Korman and/or Julia Meadows), see LITTLEL1
Sondheim: A Celebration (Carole Cook), see SONDACEL2
Follies, The Complete Recording (Ann Miller), see FOLLIES05
Alexander, Roberta/*With You*, see ALEXR1
Ameling, Elly/*Sentimental Me*, Phillips 412 433-1, 1984
Fuller, Mark/*Songs About Adam*, see FULLERM1
Singers Unlimited/*A Little Light Music* (Julia Meadows), see SINGERSUN1
Turner, Geraldine/ . . . *Sings the Stephen Sondheim Songbook, Vol. 2*, see
    TURNERG2
Wilson, Julie/*Julie Wilson Sings the Stephen Sondheim Songbook*, see
    WILSONJ2

"C'est moi," see "Operetta"

"Charley Prince Birthday" (unfinished)

"[The] Chase" cut from *A Funny Thing Happened on the Way to the Forum*
    (1962)
A Funny Thing . . . Film (instrumental), see FUNNY03

"Chéri" cut from *Follies* (1971)

"Children and Art" from *Sunday in the Park with George* (1984)
    SPGPVS g♭-d♭^{2}, SPGVS g-d^2
    Sunday in the Park . . .[1] Original Cast (Bernadette Peters, Mandy
        Patinkin), see SUNDAYIN1
    Color and Light: Jazz Sketches . . . (Holly Cole), see COLOR1
    Buckley, Betty/*Children Will Listen*, see BUCKLEYB1
    Michaels, Marilyn/*A Mother's Voice*, MEW MEW10002, 1998

"Children Will Listen (Finale, Part III)" from *Into the Woods* (1987)
    BSBB g-d♯^{2} [extended], ITWPVS company number, SCCH g-f^2 [ex-
        tended; also in sheet music Warner Bros. VS6207]
    Into the Woods[1] Original Cast (Bernadette Peters, Company), see IN-
        TOTHE1
    Into the Woods London Cast (Julia McKenzie, Company), see INTOTHE2
    Symphonic Sondheim (instrumental) [part of the "Into the Woods Suite"],
        see SYMPHONICSON1
    Sondheim: A Celebration at Carnegie Hall (Betty Buckley), see SONDACELATC1
    No One Is Alone . . . (Michelle Burgan), see NONONEIS1
    Sondheim: A Celebration (Loretta Devine), see SONDACEL2 [with "Not
        While I'm Around"]

Out on Broadway (Tracy Collins & Company), see OUTONB1 [with "You Are the Light"]
The Stephen Sondheim Album (Ruthie Henshall), see STEPHENSA1
Stephen Sondheim Songs (instrumental accompaniment), see STEPHENSS1
Into the Woods Revival Cast (Vanessa Williams, Company), see INTOTHE3
Anthony, Julie/*Lush*, MHM [n.n.], 2001 [Australian]
Buckley, Betty/*Children Will Listen*, see BUCKLEYB1
Byrne, Debra/*New Ways to Dream* (with Hugh Jackman), see BYRNED1
Cinncinnati Pops Orchestra, Erich Kunzel &/*On Broadway*, Telarc CD-80498, 1999
Clark, Petula, see CLARKP1
Combo Fiasco/*Live at the Adelaide Cabaret Festival*, 2002 [with "One Tin Soldier"]
Guest, Rob/*Unmasked*, Thom 488648-2 (Sony/Australia), 1998 [piano solo]
Jahana, Raishel/*Sondheim Songs* (instrumental), see JAHANA1 [with "Everybody Says Don't"]
Mathis, Johnny/*Mathis on Broadway*, Columbia CK 63892, 2000 [with "Our Children"; duet with Betty Buckley"]
McKinley, Bill/*Everything Possible*, Everything Possible EPCD922-0, 1992
Patinkin, Mandy/*Oscar and Steve*, see PATINKIN4 [in medley]
Streisand, Barbra/*Back to Broadway*, see STREISAND2 [additional music and lyrics by Sondheim]

"Chris and David I (Stars Give Light)" cut from *Climb High* (1950–52, unproduced)

"Chris and David II (No Star of Night)" cut from *Climb High* (1950–52, unproduced)

"Christmas Carol" from *I Know My Love* (1951)

"Christmas Island at Christmas Time" written with Mary Rodgers (1957)
Anderson, D.C./*All Is Calm, All Is Bright*, LML CD-136, 2001

"Chromolume #7" from *Sunday in the Park with George* (1984)
SPGPVS (instrumental)
Sunday in the Park . . . Original Cast (instrumental), see SUNDAYIN1

"Chrysanthemum Tea" from *Pacific Overtures* (1976)
POPVS d^1-f^2 + company
Pacific Overtures Original Cast (Alvin Ing, Mako, Mark Hsu Syers, Timm Fujii, Gedde Watanabe, Patrick Kinser-Lau, Conrad Yama, Jae Woo Lee, Ernest Harada, Freda Foh Shen), see PACIFICOVER1

Pacific Overtures English National Opera (Edward Byles, Simon Masterton-Smith, Ian Comboy, Harry Nicoll, Gordon Christie, John Cashmore, Terry Jenkins, Richard Angas), see PACIFICOVER2

Yoshida, Fusaka/*Koto Recital Classical and Modern Works*, Major TJV FY1/2 (S), [n.d.], [instrumental for Koto, played by Yoshida—Shamisen in original cast]

"Cinderella at the Grave" from *Into the Woods* (1987)
ITWPVS duet c^1-e^2/f^1-f^2
Into the Woods Original Cast (Kim Crosby, Merle Louise), see INTOTHE1
Into the Woods London Cast (Jacqueline Dankworth, Eunice Gayson), see INTOTHE2
Into the Woods Revival Cast (John McMartin, Laura Benanti, Pamela Myers), see INTOTHE3

"City On Fire" from *Sweeney Todd* (1979)
STPVS company number
Sweeney Todd Original Cast (Merle Louise, Company), see SWEENEYT1
Sweeney Todd Barcelona Cast (Teresa Vallicrosa, Company), see SWEENEYT3
Sweeney Todd Live at the NYP (Audra McDonald, Company), see SWEENEYT4

"Civilization" cut from *Pacific Overtures* (1976)

"Class" from *Saturday Night* (1954)
SNVS [primary voice] b-e^2
Saturday Night Bridewell Cast (Sam Newman, Company), see SATURDAYN1
Saturday Night Original New York Cast (David Campbell, Company), see SATURDAYN2

"Climb High" from *Climb High* (1950, unproduced)

"Cocktail Party" cut from *Climb High* (1950, unproduced)

"Color and Light" from *Sunday in the Park with George* (1984)
SPGPVS duet b♭-g^2/b-e^2 [-c^2 optional]
Sunday in the Park . . . Original Cast (Mandy Patinkin, Bernadette Peters), see SUNDAYIN1
Color and Light: Jazz Sketches . . . (Herbie Hancock, piano), see COLOR1
No One Is Alone . . . (Craig Weatherill), see NONONEIS1 [with "Sunday in the Park with George"]
Starobin, David/*New Music with Guitar, Volume 3* (Patrick Mason), see STAROBIND1

"Come Over Here" music by Jule Styne (1960)

"Come Play Wiz Me" from *Anyone Can Whistle* (1964)
ACWPVS duet a-d^2/a-e^2, ACWVS solo version b-e^2
Anyone Can Whistle Original Cast (Lee Remick, Harry Guardino), see
ANYONE1
Anyone Can Whistle Live at Carnegie Hall (Bernadette Peters, Scott
Bakula), see ANYONE2

"Comedy Tonight" from *A Funny Thing Happened On the Way to the Forum*
(1962)
ASI, FTVS, HTSS, SCCH, SSS solo version a-e♭^{2} [-g^2 optional], FTPVS
company number
A Funny Thing . . .[1] Original Cast (Zero Mostel, Company), see FUNNY01
A Funny Thing . . . London Cast (Frankie Howerd, Company), see FUNNY02
A Funny Thing . . . Film (Zero Mostel, Company), see FUNNY03
Side by Side by Sondheim (Millicent Martin, Julia McKenzie, David Ker-
nan), see SIDEBYS1 [with "Love Is in the Air"]
Side by Side . . . Australian Cast (Jill Perryman, Bartholomew John, Ger-
aldene Morrow), see SIDEBYS2 [with "Love Is in the Air"]
Songs of Sondheim Irish Cast (Company), see SONGSOFSOND1 [with "Love
Is in the Air"]
Sondheim, Book-of-the-Month Records (Bob Gunton, Company), see
SOND1
Jerome Robbins Broadway (Jason Alexander, Scott Wise, Joey McKneely,
Michael Kubala, Company), see JEROMER1
Symphonic Sondheim (Instrumental), see SYMPHONICSON1
Sondheim: A Celebration at Carnegie Hall (instrumental), see SONDACELATC1
A Gala Concert for Hal Prince (Company), see GALA1
Stephen Sondheim's A Funny Thing . . . Forum . . . In Jazz (The Trotter Trio),
see FUNNY04
A Funny Thing . . . Revival Cast (Nathan Lane, Company), see FUNNY05
Sondheim—A Celebration (Julia McKenzie, Millicent Martin, David Ker-
nan), see SONDACEL1 [incomplete]
Celebrating Sondheim (Ensemble), see CELEBRATSON
More West End the Concert, see MOREWEST
Sondheim Tonight (The Soloists), see SONDTON1
Amor al Reves es Roma [A Funny Thing . . .] Mexican Cast, see FUNNY06
Stephen Sondheim Songs (instrumental accompaniment), see STEPHENSS1
Live at the Commander Boardwalk Cabaret, [n.l.] NR11810, [n.d.]
Boston Pops/*Music of the Night*/*Pops on Broadway*, see BOSTON2 [in-
strumental]
Ferrante & Teicher/*A Man and a Woman: The Other Motion Picture
Themes*, United Artists UAL 3572, 1967 [two pianos]

Florida Symphonic Pops/*The Phantom of the Opera*, see FLORIDA1 [instrumental]
Heller, Marc/*Take Me to the World: Songs by Stephen Sondheim*, see HELLERM1
Holloway, Stanley/`Ello Stanley*, MGM E 4284, 1965
Jackie & Roy/*A Stephen Sondheim Collection*, see JACKIE&1
Mendelssohn Choir/*Mendelssohn Sings Sondheim*, see MENDELSSOHN1
Moore, Wayne & Brenda Silas Moore/*What's a Brayne & Wenda?*, Ducy Lee Recordings DLR900103, [n.d.]
Nagano, Jerry/*Meet Jerry Nagano*, Jerri-Co Productions [n.n.], 1978 [Organ]
Pot Pourri/*Something Familiar, Something Peculiar*, Move MCD086, 2000
Rochester Pops Orchestra/*Opening Night*, see ROCHESTERP1 [instrumental]
Tony Hatch Singers/*The Stereo Sound of Stage and Screen*, Marble Arch (s) MST-21, [n.d.]
Will Bronson Singers/*Best of Broadway*, Solid State SS 17011, (S) SS 18011, 1967

"Company" from *Company* (1970)
CPVS, CVS [2 versions], CVS2 company number, HTSS g-d^2 [f♯ optional]
Company Original Cast (Dean Jones, Company), see COMPANY01
Side by Side by Sondheim (Millicent Martin, Julia McKenzie, David Kernan), see SIDEBYS1
Side by Side . . . Australian Cast (Jill Perryman, Bartholomew John, Geraldene Morrow), see SIDEBYS2
Sondheim: A Celebration at Carnegie Hall (The Tonics), see SONDACELATC1
Stephen Sondheim's Company . . . *in Jazz* (The Trotter Trio), see COMPANY03
Company London Revival Cast (Adrian Lester, Company), see COMPANY04
Company Revival Cast (Boyd Gaines, Company), see COMPANY05
More West End the Concert (Kim Criswell, Graham Bicley, Simon Bowman), see MOREWEST
Sondheim Tonight (The Soloists), see SONDTON1
Company Brazilian Cast (Claudio Botelho, Company), see COMPANY06
Company German Cast (Ensemble), see COMPANY07
Boston Pops Orchestra/*Songs of the '60s* (instrumental), see BOSTON1
Laine, Cleo/*Cleo Laine Return to Carnegie*, see LAINEC1
Nero, Peter, Columbia 45rpm 4-45167, 1970
Winterhalter, Hugo/*Applause*, Musicor (S)3190, 1970

"The Contest" from *Sweeney Todd* (1979) ["Part II" is optional in score]
STPVS b-c^3 [part II is a duet with the 2nd voice c-a^2, or alternate c^3]
Sweeney Todd Original Cast (Joaaquín Romaguera), see SWEENEYT1
Stephen Sondheim's Sweeney Todd . . . *in Jazz* (The Trotter Trio), see SWEENEYT2
Sweeney Todd Barcelona Cast (Esteve Ferrer, Muntsa Rius), see SWEENEYT3
Sweeney Todd Live at the NYP (Stanford Olsen), see SWEENEYT4

"Cool" from *West Side Story* (1957), music by Leonard Bernstein
BOB, WSSVS c^1-eb^2, WSSPVS solo + company & dance c^1-eb^2
West Side Story Original Cast (Mickey Calin, The Jets), see WESTSIDE01
West Side Story film (Tucker Smith, The Jets), see WESTSIDE02
West Side Story Studio Cast (Kurt Ollman, The Jets), see WESTSIDE03
Bernstein on Broadway (Peter Hofmann), see BERNSTEINON1
Jerome Robbins Broadway (Scott Wise, The Jets), see JEROMER1
West Side Story Studio Cast London (Christopher Howard, Boys), see WESTSIDE04
West Side Story Studio Cast Leicester Haymarket (Nicholas Warnford, Jets), see WESTSIDE05
West Side Story, The Songs of (Patti Austin, Mervyn Warren, Bruce Hornsby), see WESTSIDE06
West Side Story London Studio Cast (Franklyn Fox), see WESTSIDE09
Carroll, David/*Showstopers from the Fabulous 50's*, Mercury MG-20411, (S)SR-60060, 1960
Davis Jr., Sammy/*Sammy Davis Jr. at the Cocoanut Grove*, see DAVISS [part of *West Side Story* medley]
DeLaria, Lea/*Play It Cool*, see DELARIA1
Fasano, Barbara/*The Girls of Summer*, Human Child Records hcr400, 1998
Kalin Twins, Decca 45rpm ED-2641, 1960
Kalin Twins/*Top Teen Hits*, Decca (S)ED7-2661, 1960
Martin, Denny/*Another Taste of Honey*, Liberty LRP-3277, (S)LST-7277, 1964
Nelson, Oliver/*Full Nelson*, Verve (S)V6-8508, 1964

"Cora's [The Cookie] Chase (Ballet)" from *Anyone Can Whistle* (1964)
ACWPVS a-e + quartet & soprano b^1-d^3
Anyone Can Whistle Original Cast (Angela Lansbury, Don Doherty, Gabriel Dell, Lee Remick, Ensemble), see ANYONE1
A Little Sondheim Music (Los Angeles Vocal Arts Ensemble), see LITTLES1 [listed as "Waltz I"]
Anyone Can Whistle Live at Carnegie Hall (Madeline Kahn, Walter Bobbie, Chip Zien, Ken Page, Harolyn Blackwell, Ensemble), see ANYONE2

"Could I Leave You?" from *Follies* (1971)
ASI, FLVS, FVS, HTSS, SSS b#-e^2, FPVS f#-bb^1
Follies Original Cast (Alexis Smith), FOLLIES01
Sondheim: A Musical Tribute (Alexis Smith), see SONDAMUST1
Side by Side by Sondheim[1] (David Kernan), see SIDEBYS1
Side by Side . . . Australian Cast (Bartholomew John), see SIDEBYS2
Songs of Sondheim Irish Cast (Gay Bryne), see SONGSOFSOND1
Follies in Concert (Lee Remick), see FOLLIES02

Follies London Cast (Dianna Rigg), see FOLLIES03
Putting It Together (Julie Andrews), see PUTTINGIT1
Songs of Stephen Sondheim / You Sing the Hits, see SONGSOFSTEP1
Sondheim—A Celebration (Julia McKenzie) see SONDACEL1
Follies / Themes from the Legendary Musical (The Trotter Trio), see FOLLIES04
Follies, The Complete Recording (Dee Hoty), see FOLLIES05
Company German Cast (Andreas Ziemons), see COMPANY07
Stephen Sondheim Songs (instrumental accompaniment), see STEPHENSS1
Connelli, Judy / *Back to Before—A Life in Song*, ABC 461 883-2, 2001
Gay Men's Chorus of Los Angeles / *Simply Sondheim*, see GAYMENSCLA1
Harvey, Jane / *The Other Side of Sondheim*, see HARVEYJ1
Kitt, Eartha / *Eartha Kitt Live in London*, Ariola 353825, 1990
Lear, Evelyn / *Evelyn Lear Sings Sondheim and Bernstein*, see LEARE1
Malmberg, Myrra / *What Can You Lose?*, see MALMBERG1
Turner, Geraldine / *Old Friends*, see TURNERG1
Wilson, Julie / *Julie Wilson at Brothers & Sisters* Vol. Two, see WILSONJ1
   [with "Beautiful Girls," "[The Story of] Lucy and Jessie," and "Losing
   My Mind"]
Wilson, Julie / *Julie Wilson Sings the Stephen Sondheim Songbook*, see
   WILSONJ2

"Country House" from the 1987 London revival of *Follies*
   ASIII, FLVS duet a♭-e² / a♭-f²
   Follies London Cast (Dianna Rigg, Daniel Massey), see FOLLIES03
   Putting It Together (Julie Andrews), see PUTTINGIT1

"Cow Song" from *Gypsy* (1959), music by Jule Styne [recordings under
   "Dainty June and Her Farm Boys"]
   GPVS company c¹-f²

"Crazy Piano" for *Reds* (1981) [unused]

"Crickets (Not Quite Night-IV)" cut from *A Little Night Music* (1973)

"Crime Doesn't Pay" cut from *The Lady or the Tiger?* (1954, unproduced)

"Cross Questions" cut from *Anyone Can Whistle* (1964)

"Cuckoo" cut from *Do I Hear a Waltz?* (1965), music by Richard Rodgers

"Dainty June and Her Farmboys" from *Gypsy*, music by Jule Styne
   GPVS company a¹-a²
   Gypsy Original Cast (Company), see GYPSY01
   Gypsy London Cast (Company), see GYPSY03

Gypsy Revival Cast (Company), see GYPSY04

Gypsy TV Cast (Jennifer Beck, Jeffrey Broadhurst, Peter Lockyer, Michael Moore, Patrick Boyd, Terry Lindholm, Gregg Russell, Cynthia Gibb), see GYPSY05

"Damon and Pythias" for *Gold!* (forthcoming)

"The Dance at the Gym" from *West Side Story* (1957), music by Leonard Bernstein, [no lyric]
WSSPVS instrumental

"Darling (Kissing Song)" cut from *Merrily We Roll Along* (1981)

"Darling!" cut from *Merrily We Roll Along* (1981)

"Dawn" for *Singing Out Loud* (1992–93, unproduced)
ASIV a♯–f♯² [for multiple voices]
Sondheim at the Movies (Jolie Jenkins, Bryan Batt, Sanny Burstein, James Hindman), see SONDATTHEM1

"The Day Off" from *Sunday in the Park with George* (1984)
SPGPVS company number, but "Part I"—the Spot & Fifi sequence—ranges a♯–g²
Sunday in the Park . . . Original Cast (Mandy Patinkin, Barbara Byrne, Judith Moore, Nancy Opel, Brent Spiner, Melanie Vaughn, Mary D'arcy, Robert Westenberg, William Parry), see SUNDAYIN1

"Delighted, I'm Sure" completed for the 1999 Pegasus Players production of *Saturday Night*
SNVS company number
Saturday Night Original New York Cast (Andrea Burns, Rachel Ulanet, Clarke Thorell, Chrisopher Fitzgerald, Michael Benjamin Washington, Kirk McDonald, Greg Zola, Joey Sorge), see SATURDAYN2

"Delta Iota Mu" cut from *Climb High* (1950-52, unproduced)

[*Dick Tracy*]
Jenson Publications/*New Music for Concert Band: Vol. 27*, Jenson Publications, HLP-74, 1990 [Dick Tracy soundtrack highlights]

"The Dim Dinner" from *Phinney's Rainbow* (1948)

"Dinner Table Scene," see "Night Waltz II"
A Little Night Music Royal National Theatre (Company), see LITTLEN05

"Distant Past" from *Stavisky* (1974)
  Stavisky (instrumental), see STAVISKY1

"Do I Hear a Waltz?" for *Do You Hear a Waltz?* (1963, unproduced TV show)
  ASIV ab-db^2

"Do I Hear a Waltz?" from *Do I Hear a Waltz?* (1965), music by Richard
  Rodgers
  DIHPVS a-db^2, DIHVS, SSS b-d^2
  Do I Hear a Waltz? Original Cast (Elizabeth Allen, Ensemble), see
    DOIHEAR1
  Sondheim: A Musical Tribute (Dorothy Collins), see SONDAMUST1
  Do I Hear a Waltz? Pasadena Playhouse Production (Alyson Reed), see
    DOIHEAR2
  Stephen Sondheim Songs (instrumental accompaniment), see STEPHENSS1
  Andrews, Julie/*The Music of Richard Rodgers*, Philips 442 603-2, 1994 [in
    medley]
  Barr, John/*A Small Affair*, Dress Circle MBJB 1, [n.d]
  Bennett, Tony/*If I Ruled the World: Songs for the Jet Set*, Columbia CL
    2343, 1965
  Christy, June/*Something Broadway Something Latin*, Capitol ST 2410, 1965?
  Christy, June/*Through the Years*, Hindsight HCD260, 1995
  Connelli, Judi & Suzanne Johnston/*Perfect Strangers*, see CONNELLI3 [in
    Rodgers medley]
  Davis Jr., Sammy/*Sammy's Back on Broadway*, Reprise 6169, 1965
  De Lorenzo, Brian/*Found Treasures*, see DELORENZO1 [in "A Waltz Medley"]
  Dow, Judith/*Regards to Broadway*, see DOWJ1
  Gorme, Eydie/*After You've Gone*, Columbia 45rpm 4-43225, 1965
  Gorme, Eydie/*The Golden Encore: Hit Tunes That Sold Over a Million*, Co-
    lumbia Special Products, CSP-248, 196[?]
  Herman, Jerry/*Hello, Jerry*, United Artists UAL 3432, (S)6432, 1965
  Jolly, Pete/*Too Much, Baby*, Columbia CL-2397, (S)CS-9197, 1967
  Lee, Peggy/*Disc Jockey Sampler: November 1968*, Capitol Records SRRO/
    4651, 1968
  Lee, Peggy/*Peggy Lee in Concert*, The Entertainers CD 346, 1996
  Mendelssohn Choir/*Mendelssohn Sings Sondheim*, see MENDELSSOHN1
  Roy Budd Trio/*Everything's Coming Up Roses: The Musical . . . Sondheim*,
    see ROYBUDD1
  Stafford, Jo/*Do I Hear a Waltz?*, Dot DLP 3673, (S)25673, 1967
  Stevens, Kaye/*Feelin' Good*, Capitol 45rpm 5393, 1965
  Sullivan, KT/*Sings the Sweetest Sounds of Richard Rodgers*, DRG 91462,
    2000 [with "When You're Dancing a Waltz"]
  Woodfield, Ann/*Shades of Reflection*, Guild Music Ltd/Zah Zah ZZCD
    9805, 1998 [with "Lover"]

"Doctor" from *The Jet-Propelled Couch* (1958, unproduced)

"Dogma Nu" from *Phinney's Rainbow* (1948)

"Don't Ballet," see "Everybody Says Don't"

"Don't Give It a Thought" cut from *The Race to Urga* (1968, unproduced), music by Leonard Bernstein

"Don't Laugh" from *Hot Spot* (1963), music by Dorothy Rodgers, lyrics with Martin Charnin
Newman, Phyllis/*The Mad Woman of Central Park*, DRG CDSL 5212, 1990

"Don't Look at Me" from *Follies* (1971)
FPVS duet a-b^1/c$^{\#1}$-c$^{\#2}$
Follies Original Cast (Dorothy Collins, John McMartin), see FOLLIES01
Follies in Concert (Barbara Cook, George Hearn), see FOLLIES02
Follies London Cast (Julia McKenzie, Daniel Massey), see FOLLIES03
Follies, The Complete Recording (Donna McKechnie, Laurence Guittard), see FOLLIES05

"Dowagers" cut from *Gold!* (forthcoming)

"Dream Ballet" from *Phinney's Rainbow* (1948)

"Drink to Zee Moon" from *All That Glitters* (1949)

"Dueling Pianos" from *Hey, Mr Producer! (The Musical World of Cameron Mackintosh)* , 1997 [contrived from "Send in the Clowns" and Andrew Lloyd Webber's "Music of the Night" with new lyrics by Sondheim]
Hey, Mr. Producer! (Stephen *Sondheim* & Andrew Lloyd Webber), see HEYMRP

"Easy Life" from *Stavisky* (1974)
Stavisky (instrumental), see STAVISKY1

"[The] Echo Song (Questions)" cut from *A Funny Thing Happened on the Way to the Forum* (1962)
A Stephen Sondheim Evening (Liz Callaway, Steven Jacob), see STEPHENSE1

"The Emperor of Japan" cut from *Pacific Overtures* (1976), [see also "Civilization"]

"The Emperor's New Clothes" cut from *Do I Hear a Waltz?* (1965), music by Richard Rodgers

"Epiphany" from *Sweeney Todd* (1979)
STPVS B♭-f¹ [2nd voice for 2 m. d♯¹-c♯²]
*Sweeney Todd*¹ Original Cast (Len Cariou), see SWEENEYT1
Sweeney Todd Barcelona Cast (Constantino Romero), see SWEENEYT3
Sweeney Todd Live at the NYP (George Hearn, Patti LuPone), see SWEENEYT4
Lee, Christopher/*Christopher Lee Sings Devils, Rogues & Other Villains*, Wolfslair [n.n.], 1996

"Erna" from *Stavisky* (1974)
Stavisky (instrumental), see STAVISKY1

"Erna Remembered" from *Stavisky* (1974)
Stavisky (instrumental), see STAVISKY1

"Eulogies" from *Sunday in the Park with George* (1984)
SPGPVS instrumental

"Ever After (Finale, Part IV)" from *Into the Woods* (1987)
ITWPVS company number
Into the Woods Original Cast (Tom Aldredge, Company) see INTOTHE1
Into the Woods London Cast (Nicholas Parsons, Company), see INTOTHE2
Into the Woods Revival Cast (John McMartin, Company), see INTOTHE3

"Every Day a Little Death" from *A Little Night Music* (1973)
ASI, LNMVS, SSS duet a-c² [both], LNMPVS g♯-b¹ [both]
*A Little Night Music*² Original Cast (Patricia Elliott, Victoria Mallory), see LITTLEN01
A Little Night Music London Cast (Maria Aitken, Veronica Page), see LITTLEN02
A Little Night Music Film (Diana Rigg), see LITTLEN03
A Little Night Music Studio Cast (Susan Hampshire, Janis Kelly), see LITTLEN04
Putting It Together (Julie Andrews, Rachel York), see PUTTINGIT1
Color and Light: Jazz Sketches . . . (Grover Washington Jr., tenor sax), see COLOR1
A Little Night Music Royal National Theatre (Patricia Hodge, Joanna Riding), see LITTLEN05
A Little Night Music Barcelona Cast (Mireia Ros, Alicia Ferer), see LITTLEN06 [and reprise by the Quintet]
Buckley, Betty/*An Evening at Carnegie Hall* (with Carol Maillard), see BUCKLEYB3
Byrne, Debbie/*Caught in the Act*, Mushroom Records [Australia] RMD53342/TVD93342, 1991
Callaway, Ann Hampton & Liz/*Sibling Revelry*, see CALLAWAYA&L [in medley]

Day, Courtenay/*Courtenay Day Live at Don't Tell Mama*, see DAYC1 [with "Pretty Women"]

Ferreri, Michael/*Sweet Dreams*, see FERRERI1 [with "I Don't Want to Know"]

McLaren, Morag/*I Never Do Anything Twice*, see MCLAREN1

Randwyck, Issy van/*It's Oh So Issy*, Dress Circle IVR-CD-1, 1996 [with "My Husband the Pig"]

Skinner, Emily & Alice Ripley/*Duets*[3], Varese Sarabande VSD-5958, 1998

Trotter, Terry/*Stephen Sondheim's A Little Night Music*, see TROTTERT1 [piano solo]

"Everybody Loves Leona" cut from *Do I Hear A Waltz?* (1965), music by Richard Rodgers
Do I Hear a Waltz? Pasadena Playhouse Production (Alyson Reed), see DOIHEAR2

"Everybody Loves Louis" from *Sunday in the Park with George* (1984) SPGPVS a-c#[2]
Sunday in the Park . . . Original Cast (Bernadette Peters), see SUNDAYIN1
Sondheim: A Celebration (Sally Mayes), see SONDACEL2
Celebrating Sondheim (Mary Carewe), see CELEBRATSON
Malmberg, Myrra/*What Can You Lose?*, see MALMBERG1

"Everybody Ought to Have a Maid" from *A Funny Thing Happened on the Way to the Forum* (1962)
FTPVS quartet c#[1]-e[2] [all voices], FTVS, SSS solo version b-d[2]
A Funny Thing . . . Original Cast (David Burns, Zero Mostel, Jack Gilford, John Carradine), see FUNNY01
A Funny Thing . . . London Cast ('Monsewer' Eddie Gray, Frankie Howerd, Kenneth Connor, Jon Pertwee), see FUNNY02
A Jolly Theatrical Season (Robert Morse, Charles Nelson Reilly), Capitol (S) ST 1862, 1963
A Funny Thing . . . Film (Michael Horderm, Zero Mostel, Jack Gilford, Phil Silvers), see FUNNY03
Side by Side . . . Australian Cast (John Laws, Bartholomew John, Geraldene Morrow, Jill Perryman), see SIDEBYS2
Putting It Together (Stephen Collins, Christopher Durang, Michael Rupert), see PUTTINGIT1
A Funny Thing . . . Revival Cast (Lewis J. Stadlen, Nathan Lane, Mark Linn-Baker, Ernie Sabella), see FUNNY05
Stephen Sondheim's A Funny Thing . . . Forum . . . In Jazz (The Trotter Trio), see FUNNY04
Sondheim: A Celebration (Michael Jeter), see SONDACEL2
Stephen Sondheim Songs (instrumental accompaniment), see STEPHENSS1
Lorin & the Robins, Capitol 45rpm 4775, 1964

"Everybody Says Don't" from *Anyone Can Whistle* (1964)
ACWPVS, ACWVS, ASIII, HTSS, SSS g-e², BSBB f-d², BSC [special lyrics; in medley with "I'm Still Here" and "Don't Rain On My Parade"]
Anyone Can Whistle Original Cast (Harry Guardino), see ANYONE1
Side by Side by Sondheim (Millicent Martin, David Kernan, Julia McKenzie), see SIDEBYS1
Side by Side . . . Australian Cast (Geraldene Morrow, Jill Perryman, Bartholomew John), see SIDEBYS2
Sondheim, Book-of-the-Month Records (Timothy Nolan), see SOND1
Anyone Can Whistle Live at Carnegie Hall (Scott Bakula), see ANYONE2
The Stephen Sondheim Album (Liz Callaway), see STEPHENSA1
Moving On (Company), see MOVINGON [with "Move On," "I Know Things Now," and "Take Me to the World"]
Stephen Sondheim Songs (instrumental accompaniment), see STEPHENSS1
Barr, John/*A Small Affair*, Dress Circle MBJB 1, [n.d.]
Beechman, Laurie/*Listen to My Heart*, DRG 5216, 1990
Bogart, Matt/*Simple Song*, JAY Records CDJAY 1363, 2002
Brussell, Barbara/*patterns*, see BRUSSELL1
Connelli, Judi & Suzanne Johnston/*Perfect Strangers*, see CONNELLI3 [with "Our Time"]
Cook, Barbara/*Barbara Cook Sings Mostly Sondheim*, see COOKB1
Harvey, Jane/*The Other Side of Sondheim*, see HARVEYJ1
Heller, Marc/*Take Me to the World: Songs by Stephen Sondheim*, see HELLERM1
Hubbard, Bruce/*For You, For Me*, EMI/Angel CDC 7 49928 2, 1990
J's/*Jamie*, Columbia 45rpm 4-43017, 1964
Jackie & Roy/*A Stephen Sondheim Collection*, see JACKIE&1
Jahana, Raishel/*Sondheim Songs*, see JAHANA1 [with "Children Will Listen"]
Laine, Cleo/*Cleo Sings Sondheim*, see LAINEC2
McKechnie, Donna/*Inside the Music*, see MCKECHNIED1
Patinkin, Mandy/*Kidults*, Nonesuch 79534-2, 2001 [with "The King's New Clothes"]
Starr, Lynn/*Lynn Starr Live! "It's Only Love,"* [n.l., n.n., n.d.]
Streisand, Barbra/*Back to Broadway*, see STREISAND2
Streisand, Barbra/*The Concert*, Columbia C2K 66109, 1994
Ventura, Carol/*Carol!*, Prestige PRST 7358, 1964[?]
Victor, Larry/*Our Time Will Soon Go By*, Original Cast Records OC 9330, 1993

"Everybody's Got the Right (Finale)" from *Assassins* (1991), [also included in the "Opening"]
APVS, AVS company number
Assassins Original Cast (Victor Garber, Terence Mann, Debra Monk, Jonathan Hadary, Eddie Korbich, Lee Wilkof, Greg Germann, Annie Golden, Jace Alexander), see ASSASSINS1

No One Is Alone . . . (Company), see NONONEIS1

Sondheim: A Celebration (John Allen, Paul Carr, Bridget Hoffman, David Holladay, Jean Kauffman, Kevin Loreque, Alan Safier, Sean Smith, Steve Wilde), see SONDACEL2

"Everything's Coming Up Roses" from *Gypsy* (1959), music by Jule Styne [revised version of "I'm Betwixt And Between" cut from *High Button Shoes*]

GPVS b♭-c#^{2}, GVS c^1-d^2

Gypsy Original Cast (Ethel Merman), see GYPSY01

Herb Geller and his all-stars play selections from *Gypsy* (Barbara Lang), see GELLERH

Gypsy Film (Rosalind Russell or Lisa Kirk?), see GYPSY02

Broadway's Big Hits (David Carroll), Mercury SR 60811/(M) MG 20811, 1963

Gypsy London Cast (Angela Lansbury), see GYPSY03

Gypsy Revival Cast (Tyne Daly), see GYPSY04

Gypsy TV Cast (Bette Midler), see GYPSY05

Celebrating Gypsy . . . (Libby Moore), see CELEBRATGYP

Gypsy German Cast (Angelika Milster), see GYPSY07

Selections From "Gypsy" and "Flower Drum Song" (Florence Henderson), see GYPSY08

Kay Medford in "Gypsy" (Kay Medford), see GYPSY09

Basile, Jo/*Hit Broadway Musicals*, Audio Fidelity AF-1972, (S)SD-5972, 1962

Bassey, Shirley/*Bassey Belts the Best*, United Artists UAL-3419, (S)UAS-6419, 1965

Blaine, Vivian/*For You*, see BLAINEV1

Bryan, Joy/*Make the Man Love Me*, Contemporary M-3604, (S)S-7604, 1962

Burnett, Carol/*Burnett Sings*, Decca (S)DL7-4437, 1965 [reissued on CD as *Let Me Entertain You*, Decca 012 159 402-2, 2000]

Carroll, Diahann/*Diahann Carroll at the Persian Room*, United Artists UAL-3080, (S)UAS-6080, 1961

Carroll, Diahann/*Stands Up and Sings*, United Artists UAL-3331, (S)UAS-6331, 1965

Clooney, Rosemary/*Clap Hands, Here Comes Rosie*, Victor (S)LSP-2212, 1961

Davies, Lew/*Cheerful Earful*, Command (S)RS-861, 1965

Ellis, Ray/*Our Man on Broadway*, RCA Victor LPM-2615, 1960

Feinstein, Michael/*Michael Feinstein Sings the Jule Styne Songbook*, see FEINSTEIN1

Gene Lowell Singers/*Voices in Song: American Musical Theater*, Time S/2003, 1960

Harvey, Jane/*The Other Side of Sondheim*, see HARVEYJ1 [part of "Rose's Medley"]

Henshall, Ruthie/*The Ruthie Henshall Album*, Tring002, 1996

Hi-Lo's, The/*Broadway Playbill*, see HILOS

Harnar, Jeff/*Jeff Harnar Sings the 1959 Broadway Songbook*, see HARNARJ1

Holmes, Leroy/*Golden Hits of Broadway*, United Artists UAL-3234, (S)UAS-6234, 1962

John Cacavas Singers/*The Broadway Songbook*, Gallery (S) LPG-3200, MIO International MUS 5007, 1965

King Family/ . . . *Live! In the Round* (Marilyn King), Warner Bros. (S)1660, 1960

Kuhn, Judy/*Just in Time—Judy Kuhn Sings Jule Styne*, Varese Sarabande VSD-5472, 1995

Lawrence, Steve/*Lawrence Goes Latin*, United Artists UAL-3114, (S)UAS-6114, 1962

Lee, Donna/ . . . *At the School of Arts Café*, Larrikin LRF 394, [n.d.]

Lewis, Jerry, Decca 45rpm 9-3115, 1961

Lewis, Monica/ . . . *Swings Jule Styne*, DRG 802, 1991

Mathis, Johnny/*Ballads & Rhythms of Broadway*, Columbia C2L-17, (S)CS2-803, 1961

McKenzie, Rita/*Ethel Merman's Broadway*, see MCKENZIER1

Merman, Ethel/*This Is Broadway's Best*, Columbia B2W, (S)B2WS-1, 1961;

Merman, Ethel/*The Lindsay Record*, Columbia CSP 261, [n.d.], [*Sondheim* wrote special lyrics for this recording supporting John Lindsay's candidacy for Mayor of New York]

Merman, Ethel/*Merman in Vegas*, Reprise R9-6062, 1962

Merman, Ethel/*Merman Sings Merman*, London Records XPS-901, 1972

Merman, Ethel/*A Gala Tribute to Joshua Logan*, [n.l., n.n, n.d.]

Merman, Ethel/*The Disco Album*, A&M Records SP-4775, 1979

Merman, Ethel/*Mermania!*, see MERMANE1 [2 versions, 1 in medley]

Miller, Roger/*King of the Road (The Best of . . .)*, Laser Light 15 478, 1992

Modernaires/*Like Swing*, Mercury MG-20546, (S)SR-60220, 1961

Parker, Frank/*Golden Favorites of Broadway*, Liberty LRP-3252, (S)LST-7252, 1962

Pastor, Tony/*Shakin' Up Vegas*, Capitol (S)ST-1415, 1961

Roberts, Geo/*Bottoms Up*, Columbia CL-1520, (S)CS-8320, 1961

Ross, Annie/*Gypsy*, see ROSSANNIE

Roy Budd Trio/*Everything's Coming Up Roses: The Musical . . . Sondheim*, see ROYBUDD1

Rydell, Bobby/*Bobby Rydell Salutes the Great Ones*, Cameo (S)1010, 1961

Sands, Tommy/*Sands at the Sands*, Capitol (S)ST-1364, 1961

Squires, Dorothy, HMV 45-POP 1097, [n.d.]

Steele,Tommy/*Everything's Coming Up Broadway*, Liberty LRP-3426, (S)LST-7426, 1965
Stevens, Kay/*Ruckus at the Riviera*, Columbia CL-1716, (S)CS-8516, 1962
Styne, Jule/*My Name is Jule*, see STYNEJ1
Williams, Andy/*Music from Shubert Alley*, Sinclair, SS-2250, 1959

"Everything's Perfect" cut from *Merrily We Roll Along* (1981)

"Evoe for the Dead" from The Frogs (1974), [also known as *Paean*]
   The Frogs/Evening Primrose Studio Recording (Chorus), see FROGS1

"Exhibit 'A'" from *Saturday Night* (1954)
   SNVS b♭-e♭²
   Saturday Night Bridewell Cast (James Miillard), see SATURDAYN1
   Saturday Night Original New York Cast (Christopher Fitzgerald), see SATURDAYN2

"*Exodus*: (The Sound of Poets)" from *The Frogs* (1974)
   The Frogs/Evening Primrose Studio Recording (Chorus), see FROGS1

"Faculty Song" from *Phinney's Rainbow* (1948)

"Fair Brooklyn" part of "That Kind of a Neighborhood" from *Saturday Night* (1954)
   A Stephen Sondheim Evening (Company), see STEPHENSE1

"Fair Lady" (incomplete) cut from *The Lady or the Tiger* (1954, unproduced)

"Fanfare (for 3 Trumpets)" (1976)

"Fanfare and Arena Sequence" cut from *The Lady or the Tiger* (1954, unproduced) [incomplete]

"Fanfare" from *The Frogs* (1974)
   The Frogs/Evening Primrose Studio Recording (Orchestra), see FROGS1

"Farewell" added to the 1972 revival of *A Funny Thing Happened on the Way to the Forum*

"Farewell Letter (Scene Thirteen)" from *Passion* (1995)
   PPVS duet a-d♯²/a♯-f²
   Passion Original Cast (Marrin Mazzie, Jere Shea), see PASSION1
   Passion London Concert (Helen Hobson, Michael Ball), see PASSION3

"Farm Sequence" from *Gypsy* (1959), music by Jule Styne, [see also "Broadway," "Cow Song," "Dainty June and Her Farmboys"; same music as "Gone Are the Days" cut from *High Button Shoes*]
Brinberg, Steven/*Simply Barbra*, JAY Records, CDJAY 1329, 1999

"Fear No More" added to the 1975 Cleveland revival of *The Frogs*, setting of a lyric by William Shakespeare
ASII a♭-b♭^{2}
A Stephen Sondheim Evening[1] (George Hearn), see STEPHENSE1 [not on cd, available on *A Collector's Sondheim*]
Sondheim (Book-of-the Month) (Timothy Nolen), see SOND1
Shakespeare on Broadway (Ron Raines), Varese Sarabande VSD-5622, 1996
The Frogs/Evening Primrose Studio Recording (Davis Gaines), see FROGS1

"Final Scene" from *Sweeney Todd* (1979)
STPVS duet G-g♭^{1}/b♭-d♭^{2}
Sweeney Todd Original Cast (Len Cariou) see SWEENEYT1
Stephen Sondheim's Sweeney Todd . . . In Jazz (The Trotter Trio), see SWEENEYT2 [listed as "Finale"]
Sweeney Todd Barcelona Cast (Constantino Romero), see SWEENEYT3
Sweeney Todd Live at the NYP (Patti LuPone, George Hearn, Neil Patrick Harris), see SWEENEYT4

"Finale" from *By George* (1946)

"Finale" from *Phinney's Rainbow* (1948)

"Finale" from *Into the Woods* (1987) [see also "Into the Woods" & "Ever After"]
ITWPVS company number

"Finale" from *Passion* (1995)
PPVS company number
Passion Original Cast (William Parry, Cris Groendaal, Francis Ruivivar, Marrin Mazzie, Matthew Porretta, Marcus Olson, Gregg Edelman, Company, Jere Shea, Donna Murphy), see PASSION1
Passion London Concert (Helen Hobson, Michael Ball, Helen Hobson, Company), see PASSION3

"Finale-Chaos" from *Follies* (1971)
FPVS primarily instrumental
Follies Original Cast (Company), FOLLIES01

Follies in Concert (Company), see FOLLIES02
Follies, The Complete Recording (Company), see FOLLIES05

"Finaletto" from *Phiney's Rainbow* (1948)

"Finishing the Hat" from *Sunday in the Park with George* (1984)
ASII, SPGPVS, SPGVS b♭-a♭²
Sunday in the Park . . . Original Cast (Mandy Patinkin), see SUNDAYIN1
Sondheim (Book-of-the Month) (Cris Groenendaal), see SOND¹
Symphonic Sondheim (instrumental), see SYMPHONICSON1
No One Is Alone . . . (Craig Weatherill), see NONONEIS1
Buckley, Betty/*The London Concert*, see BUCKLEYB2
Friedman, Maria/*Maria Friedman*, Carlton Sounds 30360 00012, 1995
Marcovicci/Andrea/*Live from London*, Cabaret Records 5023-2, 1997
Marien, Robert/*Broadway-Montreal*, 1997 [sung in French]
Starobin, David/*New Music with Guitar, Volume 3* (Patrick Mason), see
   STAROBIND1
Wilk, Oystein/*Too Many Mornings*, see WILKO1
Wilson, Lambert/*Musicals*, see WILSONL1

"First Letter" from *Passion* (1995)
PPVS duet b♭-c²/b♭-g¹
Passion Original Cast (Marrin Mazzie, Jere Shea), see PASSION1
Passion London Concert (Helen Hobson, Michael Ball), see PASSION3

"First Midnight" from *Into the Woods* (1987)
ITWPVS company number, mostly spoken
Into the Woods Original Cast (Company), see INTOTHE1
Into the Woods London Cast (Company), see INTOTHE2
Symphonic Sondheim (Instrumental) [part of the "Into the Woods Suite"],
   see SYMPHONICSON1
Into the Woods Revival Cast (Company), see INTOTHE3

"Flag Song" cut from *Assassins* (1991)

"Flashback" from *Passion* (1995)
PPVS company number
Passion Original Cast (Gregg Edelman, Donna Murphy, Linda Bal-
   gord, John Leslie Wolfe, Matthew Porretta, Juliet Lambert), see
   PASSION1
Passion London Concert (Paul Bentley, Maria Friedman, Monica
   Ernesti, Nigel Williams, Simon Green, Freya Copeland), see PASSION3

"Fly Birds (Opening, Part IIA)" from *Into the Woods* (1987), [see "Opening"
   for recordings] ITWPVS trio g-d²/c¹-g¹/c¹-a¹

"Fogg's Asylum/Fogg's Passacaglia" from *Sweeney Todd* (1979)
Sweeney Todd Original Cast (Company), see SWEENEYT1
Sweeney Todd Barcelona Cast (Company), see SWEENEYT3
Sweeney Todd Live at the NYP (Company), see SWEENEYT4

"Forty Days" from *Passion* (1995)
PPVS b♭-e^2
Passion Original Cast (Marrin Mazzie), see PASSION1
Passion London Concert (Helen Hobson), see PASSION3

"Four Black Dragons" from *Pacific Overtures* (1976)
POPVS trio + chorus c♯^{1}-g♭^{2}/b♭-e^2/d♭^{1}-e^2
Pacific Overtures Original Cast (Jea Woo Lee, Mark Hsu Syers, Mako, Company), see PACIFICOVER1
Pacific Overtures English National Opera (Terry Jenkins, John Cashmore, Company), see PACIFICOVER2
Scott, Phil/*Serious Cabaret*, Middle Eight Music [n.n.], 2002

"Fourth Letter" from *Passion* (1995)
PPVS f-d♭^{2}
Passion Original Cast (Marrin Mazzie, Jere Shea), see PASSION1
Stephen Sondheim's Passion . . . in Jazz (The Trotter Trio), see PASSION2
Passion London Concert (Helen Hobson, Michael Ball), see PASSION3

"Franklin Shepard, Inc." from *Merrily We Roll Along* (1981)
MWRPVS d♭^{1}-a♭^{2}
Merrily We Roll Along Original Cast (Lonny Price), see MERRILY1
Merrily We Roll Along Revival Cast (Adam Heller), see MERRILY2
Merrily We Roll Along London Cast (Evan Pappas), see MERRILY3
Sondheim: A Celebration (Kirby Tepper), see SONDACEL2
Celebrating Sondheim (Claire Moore, Glyn Kerslake), see CELEBRATSON

"Free" from *A Funny Thing Happened on the Way to the Forum*, (1962) [a new lyric was written for the film, but was not used]
FTPVS duet b-f^2/g^1-f^2 [a^2 optional]
A Funny Thing . . . Original Cast (Zero Mostel, Brian Davies), see FUNNY01
A Funny Thing . . . London Cast (Frankie Howerd, John Rye), see FUNNY02
A Funny Thing . . . Revival Cast (Nathan Lane, Jim Stanek), see FUNNY05
Stephen Sondheim's A Funny Thing . . . Forum . . . In Jazz (The Trotter Trio) see FUNNY04

"Free" (first version) cut from *A Funny Thing Happened on the Way to the Forum* (1962)

"French Waltz" cut from *A Little Night Music* (1973)

"The Frogs," see *"Parados"* from *The Frogs* (1974)

"Fumblington Girls' Song" from *Phinney's Rainbow* (1948)

"Funeral Sequence" from *A Funny Thing Happened on the Way to the Forum* (1962)
FTPVS company number
A Funny Thing . . . Original Cast (Zero Mostel, Ronald Holgate, Company), see FUNNY01
A Funny Thing . . . London Cast (Frankie Howerd, Leon Greene, Company), see FUNNY02
A Funny Thing . . . Film (Leon Greene, Company), see FUNNY03 [listed as "The Dirge"]
A Funny Thing . . . Revival Cast (Cris Groenendaal, Nathan Lane, Company), see FUNNY05

"The Future" from *Stavisky* (1974)
Stavisky (instrumental), see STAVISKY1

"The Gaggle of Geese (Hornpipe)" cut from *A Funny Thing Happened on the Way to the Forum* (1962)

"The Game" written for *Gold!* (forthcoming)

"Garden Sequence" from *Passion* (1995)
PPVS b♭-d^2
Passion Original Cast (Jere Shea, Marrin Mazzie, Donna Murphy), see PASSION1
Passion London Concert (Michael Ball, Helen Hobson, Maria Friedman), see PASSION3

"Gavotte" see "Life Is Happiness Indeed" from *Candide* (1974)

"Gee, Officer Krupke" from *West Side Story* (1957), music by Leonard Bernstein
WSSPVS company number
West Side Story Original Cast[2] (Eddie Roll, Grover Dale, The Jets), see WESTSIDE01
West Side Story film (Russ Tamblyn, The Jets), see WESTSIDE02
West Side Story Studio Cast (David Livingston, Quartet, Todd Lester, Marty Nelson, Peter Thom, Stephen Bogardus), see WESTSIDE03
West Side Story Studio Cast London (Derrek Chessor, Boys), see WESTSIDE04
West Side Story Studio Cast Leicester Haymarket (Kieran Daniels, Jets), see WESTSIDE05

West Side Story Studio Cast Leicester Haymarket (Nicholas Warnford, Jets), see WESTSIDE05 [Motion Picture Version]

West Side Story, The Songs of (Salt-N-Peppa, Def Jam, Lisa "Left Eye" Lopes of TLC, TheJerky Boys, Paul Rodriguez), see WESTSIDE06

West Side Story London Studio Cast (Leo Karibian, Norman Fuber, Vince Logan), see WESTSIDE09

Canadian Brass/*The Canadian Brass Plays Bernstein*, RCAVictor 09026/68633-4, 1997

Clary, Robert/*Robert Clary Sings at the Jazz Bakery in Los Angeles*, Original Cast OC-9799, 1997

Davis Jr., Sammy/*Sammy Davis Jr. at the Cocoanut Grove*, see DAVISS [part of *West Side Story* medley]

Drake, Alfred & Peters, Roberta/*Alfred Drake & Roberta Peters Sing the Popular Music of Leonard Bernstein* (The Ray Charles Singers), see DRAKEA

"George School Frowns" from *By George* (1946)

"George's Moon" from *The World of Jules Feiffer* (1962)

"Get Out" written for *Gold!* (forthcoming)

"Getting Married Today" from *Company* (1970)
CPVS trio e^1-a♭^{2}/b-g♭^{2}/a-d♭^{2} [+ chorus], CVS2 f^1-a^2/c^1-g^2/a♭-c^2 [+ chorus], HTSS g^1-g^2/d^1-f^2/b♭-c^2, SCCH f♯^{1}-a♭^{2}/b-g♭^{2}/a-d♭^{2} [+ chorus]
Company Original Cast (Beth Howland, Steve Elmore, Teri Ralston, Company), see COMPANY01
Sondheim: A Musical Tribute (Beth Howland, Teri Ralston, Steve Elmore), see SONDAMUST1
Side by Side by Sondheim (Millicent Martin, Julia McKenzie, David Kernan), see SIDEBYS1
Side by Side . . . Australian Cast (Jill Perryman, Bartholomew John, Geraldene Morrow), see SIDEBYS2
Sondheim: A Celebration at Carnegie Hall (Jeanne Lehman, Mark Jacoby, Madeline Kahn), see SONDACELATC1
Putting It Together (Julie Andrews, Company), see PUTTINGIT1
Company London Revival Cast (Michael Simkins, Sophie Thompson), see COMPANY04
Company Revival Cast (Veanne Cox, Patricia Ben Peterson, Danny Burstein), see COMPANY05
Sondheim: A Celebration (Nancy Dussault), see SONDACEL2
The Stephen Sondheim Album (Eydie Alyson, Juliana A. Hansen, Tami Tappan), see STEPHENSA1 [*Note*: This is a "hidden track" at the end of the CD]

Company Brazilian Cast (Claudia Netto, Raul Serrador, Cidalia Castro), see COMPANY06
Company German Cast (Alexandra Seefisch, Alen Hodzovic, Carolin Soyka), see COMPANY07

"Giants in the Sky" from *Into the Woods* (1987)
ASIV, ITWPVS c1-f_2
Into the Woods Original Cast (Ben Wright), see INTOTHE1
Into the Woods London Cast (Richard Dempsey), see INTOTHE2
The Stephen Sondheim Album (Brian D'Arcy James), see STEPHENSA1
Into the Woods Revival Cast (Adam Wylie), see INTOTHE3
Cook, Barbara/*Barbara Cook sings Mostly Sondheim* (sung by Malcolm Gets), see COOKB1 [with "Into the Woods"]
De Lorenzo, Brian/*Found Treasures*, see DELORENZ1
East West Players/*East West Overtures* (Robert Lee), see EASTWEST1
Patinkin, Mandy/*Dress Casual*, see PATINKIN2
Sandford, Luke/*Shimmer*, see SANDFORD1 [piano solo]

"The Girls of Summer" from *The Girls of Summer* (1956)
ASIII b-e^2
Marry Me a Little (Suzanne Henry), see MARRYME1
Fasano, Barbara/*The Girls of Summer*, Human Child Records hcr400, 1998
Hobson, Helen/*Hobson's Choice*, Upbeat Recordings/Showbiz/U.K. UR124, 1996-97
O'Donnell, Kerryn/*What More Do I Need?*, [n.l., n.n.], 2001, [Australian]
Upshaw, Dawn/*I Wish It So*, see UPSHAWD1
Woodfield, Ann/*Shades of Reflection*, Guild Music Ltd./Zah Zah ZZCD 9805, 1998

"Glad t' See Ya" from *By George* (1946)

"The Glamorous Life" from *A Little Night Music* (1973)
LNMPVS company number
A Little Night Music Original Cast (Judy Kahan, Glynis Johns, Hermione Gingold, Teri Ralston, Beth Fowler, Barbara Lang, Benjamin Rayson, Gene Varrone), see LITTLEN01
A Little Night Music[1] London Cast (Christine McKenna, Jean Simmons, Hermione Gingold, John J. Moore, Chris Melville, Liz Robertson, David Bexon, Jacquey Chappell), see LITTLEN02
A Little Night Music Studio Cast (Megan Kelly, Sian Phillips, Elisabeth Welch, Dinah Harris, Hilary Western, Susan Flannery, Michael Bulman, Martin Nelson), see LITTLEN04
The Great Waltz (Hollywood Bowl Orchestra), see HOLLYWOODB1 [part of "The Night Waltzes"]

A Little Night Music Royal National Theatre (Claire Cox, Judi Dench, Sian Phillips, Ernestina Quarco, Stephen Hanley, Tim Goodwin, Morag McLaren, Di Botcher), see LITTLEN05 [includes "The Letter Song" version from the film]

A Little Night Music Barcelona Cast (Miranda Gas, Vicky Pena, Montserrat Carulla, Xavier Fernandez, Muntsa Rius, Ana Feu, Alberto Demestres, Teresa de la Torre), see LITTLEN06

Trotter, Terry/*Stephen Sondheim's A Little Night Music*, see TROTTERT1 [piano solo]

"The Glamorous Life (The Letter Song)" from the film of *A Little Night Music* (1978)

ASII, SSFTS c^1-e^2

A Little Night Music[1] Film (Chloe Franks, sung by Elaine Tomkinson), see LITTLEN03 [also included on the 1998 reissue of the original cast recording, see LITTLEN01]

Sondheim (Book-of-the Month) (Betsy Joslyn), see SOND1

A Little Night Music Royal National Theatre (Company), see LITTLEN05 [see entry above]

Sondheim at the Movies (Cassidy Ladden), see SONDATTHEM1

Malmberg, Myrra/*What Can You Lose?*, see MALMBERG1

Trotter, Terry/*Stephen Sondheim's A Little Night Music*, see TROTTERT1 [piano solo]

"God, That's Good!" from *Sweeney Todd* (1979)

STPVS company number

Sweeney Todd Original Cast (Ken Jennings, Angela Lansbury, Len Cariou, Company), see SWEENEYT1

Sweeney Todd Barcelona Cast (Muntsa Rius, Vicky Pena, Constantino Romero, Company), see SWEENEYT3

Sweeney Todd Live at the NYP (Neil Patrick Harris, Patti LuPone, George Hearn, Company), see SWEENEYT4

"The God-Why-Don't-You-Love-Me Blues," see "Buddy's Blues"

"Gold" written for *Gold!* (forthcoming)

"The Good Life" written for *Gold!* (forthcoming)

"Good Thing Going" from *Merrily We Roll Along* (1981)

ASII, MWRPVS, MWRVS, SCCH c^1-f^2

Merrily We Roll Along Original Cast (Lonny Price, Jim Walton), see MERRILY1

Sondheim (Book-of-the Month) (Timothy Nolen), see SOND1
Sondheim: A Celebration at Carnegie Hall (The Tonics), see SONDACELATC1
Merrily We Roll Along Revival Cast (Adam Heller, Malcolm Gets), see
    MERRILY2
Merrily We Roll Along London Cast (Evan Pappas, Michael Cantwell),
    see MERRILY3
No One Is Alone . . . (Michelle Burgan), see NONONEIS1 [with "Not a Day
    Goes By"]
Sondheim: A Celebration ('Nita Whitaker), see SONDACEL2
Sondheim Tonight (David Kernan), see SONDTON1 [with "Not a Day Goes
    By"]
Alexander, Roberta/*With You*, see ALEXR1
Andrew, Leo/*A World of Possibilities*, [n.l.] LAVW 1, 2001 [with "Not a
    Day Goes By"]
Barrowman, John/*Reflections from Broadway*, see BARROWMAN1
East West Players/*East West Overtures* (Zar Acayan), see EASTWEST1
Gay Men's Chorus of Los Angeles/*Simply Sondheim*, see GAYMENSCLA1
Harvey, Jane/*The Other Side of Sondheim*, see HARVEYJ1
Heller, Marc/*Take Me to the World: Songs by Stephen Sondheim*, see HELLERM1
LaMott, Nancy/*My Foolish Heart*, Midder Music, MM CD003, 1993
Markey, Enda/*Another Place and Time*, see MARKEY1 [with "Not a Day
    Goes By"]
McDermott, Sean/*My Broadway*, see MCDERMOTTS1
McGillin, Howard/*Where Time Stands Still*, [n.l.], HFM 5497, 2002 [with
    "Not While I'm Around"]
Nease, Byron/*When I Fall in Love*, Audible (Audiophile) Difference AD
    CD002, 1992 [with "Think of Me"]
Noll, Christiane/*A Broadway Love Story*, Varese Sarabande VSD-5956,
    1988
Patinkin, Mandy/*Experiment*, see PATINKIN3
Roy, William/*When I Sing Alone*, Audiophile (D)AP-213, 1986; ACD-213,
    1996
Sullivan, KT/*Crazy World*, DRG 91413, 1993
Turner, Geraldine/*When We Met*, Desiree [n.n.], 1999
Sinatra, Frank/*She Shot Me Down*, Reprise Records FS 2305, 1981
Wilk, Oystein/*Too Many Mornings*, see WILKO1
Wilson, Julie/*Julie Wilson Sings the Stephen Sondheim Songbook*, see WILSONJ2

"Goodbye Arlette" from *Stavisky* (1974)
    Stavisky (instrumental), see STAVISKY1

"Goodbye for Now" from *Reds* (1981) [vocal version of the "Theme from
    Reds"]
    ASIII, SSFTS f-e^2

Reds Soundtrack, see REDS1
Sondheim (Book-of-the Month) (Mary D'Arcy), see SOND1
Unsung Sondheim[3] (Liz Callaway), see UNSUNGS1
Sondheim at the Movies (Orchestra), see SONDATTHEM1
Moving On (Company), see MOVINGON [with "I Wish I Could Forget You"]
Academy Film Orchestra, The/*Great Movie Themes*, The Special Music
   Co. Inc., SCD 4501, 1986 [instrumental]
Breach, Joyce & William Roy/*Love Is the Thing*, Audiophile, ACD–314,
   2001
Como, Perry/*So It Goes*, RCA Victor AFL1-4272, 1983
Ford, Anne Kerry/*Something Wonderful*, see FORDA1 [with "Edelweiss"]
Gay Men's Chorus of Los Angeles/*Simply Sondheim*, see GAYMENSCLA1
Jiear, Alison/*Simply Alison Jiear*, Dress Circle DAD 007/1, 1995
Marcovici, Andrea/*What Is Love?*, DRG 91401, 1990
Rampal, Jean-Piere/*Music My Love*, CBS Masterworks MK 45548, 1989
   [flute with Claude Bolling at the piano]
Turner, Geraldine/*Old Friends*, see TURNERG1

"Gossip Sequence" from *Sunday in the Park with George* (1984)
SPGPVS company number
Sunday in the Park . . . Original Cast (Melanie Vaughn, Mary D'Arcy, Bar-
   bara Bryne, Judith Moore, William Parry), see SUNDAYIN1
No One Is Alone . . . (Sybil Williams, Kerry Sampson) see NONONEIS1

"[Gotta] Keep `Em Humming" cut from *Sunday in the Park with George* (1984)

"Gracious Living Fantasy" added to 2000 production of *Saturday Night*
Saturday Night Original New York Cast (instrumental based on "Class"
   with dialogue), see SATURDAYN2

"Green Finch and Linnet Bird" from *Sweeney Todd* (1979)
ASI, SCCH, STVS a♭-e♭[2], STPVS c[1]-g[2]
Sweeney Todd Original Cast (Sarah Rice), see SWEENEYT1
A Little Sondheim Music (Delcina Stevenson), see LITTLES1
Sondheim: A Celebration at Carnegie Hall (Harolyn Blackwell), see
   SONDACELATC1
Stephen Sondheim's Sweeney Todd . . . *In Jazz* (The Trotter Trio), see
   SWEENEYT2
Sweeney Todd Barcelona Cast (Ma. Josep Peris), see SWEENEYT3
Sondheim Tonight (Julia Migenes), see SONDTON1
Sweeney Todd Live at the NYP (Heidi Grant Murphy), see SWEENEYT4
Collins, Judy/*Running for My Life*, Elektra 6E-253, 1980
East West Players/*East West Overtures* (Linda Igarashi), see EASTWEST1
Emerson, Karen Smith/*Songs of the Nightingale*, Centaur 2232, 1995

Gay Men's Chorus of Los Angeles/*Simply Sondheim*, see GAYMENSCLA1 [in medley]
Heller, Marc/*Take Me to the World: Songs by Stephen Sondheim*, see HELLERM1
Lear, Evelyn/*Evelyn Lear Sings Sondheim and Bernstein*, see LEARE1
Prior, Marina/*Somewhere*, see PRIORM1

"Greens, Greens (Opening, Part III)" from *Into the Woods* (1987), [see "Opening" for recordings]
ITWPVS rap number, approximate pitches

"Growing Up" added to 1985 production of *Merrily We Roll Along*
ASIV b-d^2
Merrily We Roll Along Revival Cast (Malcolm Gets, Michele Pawk), see MERRILY2
Merrily We Roll Along London Cast (Michael Cantwell, Louise Gold), see MERRILY3

"Gun Song" from *Assassins* (1991)
APVS quartet
Assassins Original Cast (Terence Mann, Victor Garber, Jonathan Hadary, Debra Monk), see ASSASSINS1
Putting It Together (Christopher Durang, Julie Andrews, Stephen Collins, Michael Rupert, Rachel York), see PUTTINGIT1
No One Is Alone . . . (Greg Hart), see NONONEIS1 [with "My Friends"]
Mars, Susannah/*Take Me to the World*, see MARSS1 [with "Regretting What I Said"]

"Gwendolen and Yolanda" from *Phinney's Rainbow* (1948)

[*Gypsy* Medley] from *Gypsy* (1959), music by Jule Styne
Stevlekar, Steven/*Jule Styne Remembered*, Starlight Records SLR29626, 1996 [individual numbers not listed]

"Gypsy Strip Routine" from *Gypsy* (1959), music by Jule Styne [see also "Let Me Entertain You"]
GPVS f♯-c^2
Gypsy Original Cast (Sandra Church), see GYPSY01
Gypsy Film (Natalie Wood), see GYPSY02
Gypsy London Cast (Zan Charise), see GYPSY03
Gypsy Revival Cast (Crista Moore), see GYPSY04
Gypsy TV Cast (Cynthia Gibb), see GYPSY05
Gypsy German Cast (Susanne Eisenkolb), see GYPSY07

"Hal Prince 50th Birthday" (1978)

"Hal Prince 65th Birthday" (1993)

"Happily Ever After" cut from *Company* (1970)
ASIII c^1-f^2
Sondheim: A Musical Tribute (Larry Kert), see SONDAMUST1 [incomplete]
Marry Me a Little[1] (Craig Lucas), see MARRYME1

"Happiness" from *Passion* (1995)
ASIV solo version c^1-$g\flat^2$, PPVS duet a-e^2/a-$d\sharp^2$, PVS duet c^1-$g\flat^2$/b-f^2
Passion Original Cast (Marrin Mazzie, Jere Shea), see PASSION1
Stephen Sondheim's Passion . . . In Jazz (The Trotter Trio), see PASSION2
Passion London Concert (Helen Hobson, Michael Ball), see PASSION3
Cook, Barbara/*Barbara Cook Sings Mostly Sondheim*, see COOKB1
Peters, Bernadette/*Sondheim, Etc.*, see PETERSB1

"Happy Ending" cut from *A Funny Thing Happened on the Way to the Forum* (1962)

"Have I Got a Girl for You" from *Company* (1970)
CPVS, CVS2 quintet
Company Original Cast (Charles Braswell, John Cunningham, Steve Elmore, George Coe, Charles Kimbrough, Company), see COMPANY01
Putting It Together (Michael Rupert, Stephen Collins), see PUTTINGIT1
Company London Revival Cast (Paul Bentley, Gareth Snook, Men), see COMPANY04
Company Revival Cast (Timothy Landfield, Jonathan Dokuchitz, Men), see COMPANY05
Company Brazilian Cast (Paulo Mello, Rica Barros, Raul Serrador, Mauro Gorini, Daniel Boaventura), see COMPANY06
Company German Cast (Ensemble), see COMPANY07
A'Hearn, Patrick/*Patterns of the Heart*, Patrick A'Hearn/DAN Productions Inc. PAI503, 1997

"Have to Give Her Someone" cut from *Into the Woods* (1987)

"Have You Been Waiting Long?" from *Climb High* (1950, unproduced)

"Hello, Doughboy" unused from *Follies* (1971) [incomplete, lyrics only]

"Hello, Little Girl" from *Into the Woods* (1987)
ITWPVS duet $b\flat$-$g\flat^2$/f^1-d^2
Into the Woods Original Cast (Robert Westenberg, Danielle Ferland), see INTOTHE1
Into the Woods London Cast (Clive Carter, Tessa Burbridge), see INTOTHE2
Putting It Together (Stephen Collins, Rachel York), see PUTTINGIT1
No One Is Alone . . . (Kynan Johns) see NONONEIS1

Into the Woods Revival Cast (Greg Edelman, Christopher Sieber, Molly Ephraim), see INTOTHE3
Peters, Bernadette/*Sondheim, Etc.*, see PETERSB1 [with "Any Moment"]
Warlow, Anthony/*On the Boards*, Polydor 513 402 2, 1992

"Here We Are Again" from *Do I Hear a Waltz?* (1965), music by Richard Rodgers
DIHPVS company number [lead vocal $g\sharp$-b^1], DIHVS c^1-$e\flat^2$
Do I Hear a Waltz? Original Cast (Carol Bruce, Madeleine Sherwood, Jack Manning, Elizabeth Allen, Julienne Marie, Stuart Damon), see DOIHEAR1
Do I Hear a Waltz? Pasadena Playhouse Production (Alyson Reed), see DOIHEAR2

"A Hero Is Coming" cut from *Anyone Can Whistle* (1964)

"Hideout at Chamonix" from *Stavisky* (1974)
Stavisky (instrumental), see STAVISKY1

"High Life" cut from *The Last Resorts* (1956, unproduced)

"High Tor" from *High Tor* (1949, unproduced)

"The Hills of Tomorrow" from *Merrily We Roll Along* (1981)
ASIII, MWRVS solo version $c1$-$g\flat^2$, MWRPVS company number
Merrily We Roll Along Original Cast (Company), see MERRILY1
A Little Sondheim Music (Ensemble), see LITTLES1
Heller, Marc/*Take Me to the World: Songs by Stephen Sondheim*, see HELLERM1
Jobson, Mark deVille/*My House*, see JOBSON1

"Hold Me" unused from *Company* (1970) [incomplete]

"Hollywood and Vine" from *Twigs* (1971), written with George Furth

"Home Is the Place" music by Jule Styne (1960)
Bennett, Tony/*Yesterday I Heard the Rain*, Columbia LE-10056, 1968
Feinstein, Michael/*Michael Feinstein Sings the Jule Styne Songbook*, see FEINSTEIN1

"Honey" cut from *Merrily We Roll Along* (1981)
ASIII, MWRVS $c\sharp^1$-f^2
Sondheim (Book-of-the Month) (instrumental), see SOND1
Lost in Boston III (Liz Callaway, Jason Graae), Varese Sarabande VSD-5563, 1995
The MUSICality of Sondheim[4] (Jacqueline Dankworth, Maria Friedman, Michael Cantwell), JAY Records CDJAZ 9006, 2002

"Hooray for Hapgood," see "A-1 March"

"The House of Marcus Lycus" from *A Funny Thing Happened on the Way to the Forum* (1962)
FTPVS d^1-d^2 [b♭-optional], mostly instrumental
A Funny Thing . . . Revival Cast (Ernie Sabella, Girls), see FUNNY05

"The House of Marcus Lycus" (version 1) cut from *A Funny Thing Happened on the Way to the Forum* (1962)
A Stephen Sondheim Evening[1] (George Hearn, Bob Gunton, Women), see STEPHENSE1

"How Do I Know?" from *Phinney's Rainbow* (1948)

"How I Saved Roosevelt" from *Assassins* (1991) [music based on John Philip Sousa "March" from *El Capitan*]
APVS company number
Assassins Original Cast (Company, Eddie Korbich), see ASSASSINS1

"*Hymnos*: Evoe! (Hymn to Dionysos)" from *Frogs* (1974)
The Frogs/Evening Primrose Studio Recording (Nathan Lane, Brian Stokes Mitchell & Chorus), see FROGS1

"I Believe in You" see "They Ask Me Why I Believe in You"

"I Do Like You" cut from *A Funny Thing Happened on the Way to the Forum* (1962)
ASII duet b-f♯^{2}/b-d^2
Sondheim (Book-of-the Month) (Bob Gunton, Timothy Nolen), see SOND1
Moving On (Company), see MOVINGON [with "Old Friends" and "Side by Side"]
Bennett, Richard Rodney/*A Different Side of Sondheim*, see BENNETTR1
Herman, Woody/*My Kind of Broadway*, Columbia CL-2357, (S)CS-9157, 1965 [instrumental]
Jackie & Roy/*A Stephen Sondheim Collection*, see JACKIE&1
Wilson, Julie/*Julie Wilson Sings the Stephen Sondheim Songbook*, see WILSONJ2 [duet with William Roy]

"I Don't Want to Fall in Love with You" from *Climb High* (1950–52, unproduced)

"I Feel Pretty" from *West Side Story* (1957), music by Leonard Bernstein
BOB, WSSPVS solo + trio c^1-a^2 + trio, WSSVS solo version c^1-g^2

West Side Story Original Cast (Carol Lawrence, Marilyn Cooper, Carmen Guiterrez, Elizabeth Taylor), see WESTSIDE01

West Side Story film (Marni Nixon, Yvonne Othon, Suzie Kaye, Joanne Miya), see WESTSIDE02

West Side Story Studio Cast (Kiri Te Kanawa, Girls), see WESTSIDE03

Bernstein on Broadway (Debbie Sasson), see BERNSTEINON1

West Side Story Studio Cast London (Barbara Bonney, Girls), see WESTSIDE04

West Side Story Studio Cast Leicester Haymarket (Tinuke Olafimihan, Elinor Stephenson, Julie Paton, Nicole Carty), see WESTSIDE05

West Side Story, The Songs of (Little Richard), see WESTSIDE06

West Side Story London Production (Marlys Watters), see WESTSIDE08

West Side Story London Studio Cast (Jill Martin, Venita Ernandes, Lorraine Hart, Lorraine Smith), see WESTSIDE09

Ambrose, Amanda/*Amanda*, Dunwich (S)668, 1967

Andrews, Julie/*Broadway's Fair Julie*, Columbia CL-1712, (S)CS-8512, 1962

Burroughs, Marilyn/*I Feel Pretty*, Philips PHS 600-137, 1964

Lester, Ketty/*Where Is Love?*, Victor (S)LSP-3326, 1965

Nicholson, Carla & Michael/*Just Duet*, see NICHOLSONC1 [with "Somewhere," & "Tonight"]

Peters, Roberta/*Alfred Drake & Roberta Peters Sing the Popular Music of Leonard Bernstein*, see DRAKEA

Ross, Annie/*Annie Ross Sings a Song with Mulligan*, World Pacific Records WP-1253, (S)ST-1020, 1959

Smith, Ethel/*Lady Fingers*, Decca 8744, 1962

Sommers, Joanie/*For Those Who Think Young*, Warner Bros. (S)WS-1436, 1962

Stafford, Wanda/*In Love for the Very First Time*, Roulette (S)SR-25140, 1962

Te Kanawa, Kiri/*Kiri Te Kanawa Sings*, Westminster (S)8232, 1973

Te Kanawa, Kiri/*The Young Kiri*, [n.l., n.n., n.d.]

Upshaw, Dawn/*I Wish It So*, see UPSHAWD1

Vaughn, Sarah/*Sassy Swings the Tivoli*, Mercury MG-20831, (S)SR-60831, 1964, CD: EMARCY 832 788-2, 1987

Vroman, Lisa/*Broadway Classics*, Offplanet 59057 02602, 1999

"I Guess This Is Goodbye" from *Into the Woods* (1987)
ITWPVS d$\sharp^1$-d$\sharp^2$

Into the Woods Original Cast (Ben Wright), see INTOTHE1

Into the Woods London Cast (Richard Dempsey), see INTOTHE2

Into the Woods Revival Cast (Adam Wylie), see INTOTHE3

"I Have a Love" from *West Side Story* (1957), music by Leonard Bernstein

BSBB duet [with "One Hand, One Heart"], WSSPVS duet b$\flat$-g^2/b-a^1 [preceeded by "A Boy Like That"]

West Side Story Original Cast (Carol Lawrence, Chita Rivera), see WESTSIDE01
West Side Story film (Marni Nixon, Betty Wand), see WESTSIDE02
West Side Story Studio Cast (Kiri Te Kanawa, Tatiana Troyanos), see WESTSIDE03
West Side Story Studio Cast London (Barbara Bonney, La Vern Williams), see WESTSIDE04
West Side Story Studio Cast Leicester Haymarket (Tinuke Olafimihan, Caroline O'Connor), see WESTSIDE05
West Side Story, The Songs of (Trisha Yearwood), see WESTSIDE06
West Side Story London Studio Cast (Jill Martin), see WESTSIDE09
Stage2/the human heart (Francis Cruz, Charlie Owens), DINK Records DIDX 045940, 1997 [with "I Wish I Could Forget You"]
Blackwell, Harolyn/*A Simple Song: Blackwell Sings Bernstein* (duet with Vanessa Williams), see BLACKWELL1
Garrett, Lesley/*Travelling Light* (duet with Denyce Graves), EMI/Angel Classics 5T20Z, 2002 [with "I Have a Love"]
Prior, Marina/*Somewhere*, see PRIORM1 [in medley]
Streisand, Barbra/*Back to Broadway* (duet with Johnny Mathis), see STREISAND2
Vroman, Lisa/*Broadway Classics*, Offplanet 59057 02602, 1999 [with "A Boy Like That"]

"I Have the Funniest Feeling" (unfinished)

"I Know" see "Who Knows?"

"I Know Things Now" from *Into the Woods* (1987)
ITWPVS c^1-$e♭^2$
Into the Woods Original Cast (Daniele Ferland), see INTOTHE1
Into the Woods London Cast (Tessa Burbridge), see INTOTHE2
No One Is Alone . . . (Leonie Harris), see NONONEIS1
Moving On (Company), see MOVINGON [with "Move On," "Everybody Says Don't," "Take Me to the World"]
Into the Woods Revival Cast (Molly Ephriam), see INTOTHE3

"I Love You, Etcetera" from *All That Glitters* (1949)
ATGVS g-d^2

"I Must Be Dreaming" from *All That Glitters* (1949)
ATGVS c^1-f^2
The Stephen Sondheim Album (Emily Skinner), see STEPHENSA1 [available on "Special Edition" CD only]

"I Need Love" from *All That Glitters* (1949)
ATGVS b♭-f^2

"I Never Do Anything Twice (Madam's Song)" from *The Seven Percent Solution* (1976)
ASI, SCCH, SSFTS b-e♭²
*Side by Side by Sondheim*¹ (Millicent Martin), see SIDEBYS1
Side by Side . . . Australian Cast (Jill Perryman), see SIDEBYS2
Songs of Sondheim Irish Cast (Gemma Craven), see SONGSOFSOND1
Sondheim: A Celebration at Carnegie Hall (BETTY), see SONDACELATC1
Sherlock Holmes Classic Themes From 221B Baker Street (Judy Kaye). Varese Sarabande VSD-5692, 1996
Sondheim Tonight (Millicent Martin), see SONDTON1
Clark, Petula/*here for you*, see CLARKP1
Harpsichord Pieces, Hungaroton/White Label 31729, 1999
Kennedy, Barbara/*You'd Be Surprised!*, Globe GLO 6045, 1998
LuPone, Patti/*matters of the heart*, Varese Sarabande VSD-6058, 1999 [with "When the World Was Young"]
McLaren, Morag/*I Never Do Anything Twice*, see MCLAREN1
McNight, Sharon/*Songs to Offend Almost Everyone*, [n.l., n.n.], 2002
Montevecchi, Liliane/*On the Boulevard*, JAY Records CDJAY 1286, 1998
Shannon, Hugh/*Saloon Singer*, Audiophile AP 171/172, 1982
Turner, Geraldine/ . . . *Sings the Stephen Sondheim Songbook, Vol. 2*, see TURNERG2
Wilson, Julie/*Julie Wilson Sings the Stephen Sondheim Songbook*, see WILSONJ2

"I Opened a Book" from *Phinney's Rainbow* (1948)

"I Read (Fosca's Entrance)" from Passion (1995)
PPVS f-d² , PVS b♭-g²
Passion Original Cast (Donna Murpy), see PASSION1
Passion London Concert (Maria Friedman), see PASSION3

"I Remember" from *Evening Primrose* (1966)
ASI, HTSS, SSFTS c¹-d²
Sondheim: A Musical Tribute (Victoria Mallory), see SONDAMUST1
*Side by Side by Sondheim*¹ (David Kernan), see SIDEBYS1
Side by Side . . . Australian Cast (Bartholomew John), see SIDEBYS2
*Sondheim at the Movies*³ (Liz Calaway), see SONDATTHEM1
Celebrating Sondheim (Claire Moore), see CELEBRATSON
*Sondheim Tonight*⁴ (Julia Migenes), see SONDTON1
The Frogs/Evening Primrose Studio Recording (Theresa McCarthy), see FROGS1
Alexander, Roberta/*With You*, see ALEXR1
Bennett, Richard Rodney/*A Different Side of Sondheim*, see BENNETTR1

Brandes, Jeanie/*Love in the World I Remember*, JBD6130, 1995
Brightman, Sarah/*Songs That Got Away*, R.U. 8391162, 1989; reissued on Decca 422 839 116-2
Buckley, Betty/*Children Will Listen*, see BUCKLEYB1
Clary, Robert/*Louis Lebeau Remembers . . . Stephen Sondheim . . .*, see CLARYR1
Collins, Judy/*Hard Times for Lovers*, Elektra 6E-171, 1979
Ford, Anne Kerry/*In the Nest of the Moon*, Illyria Records 001, 1996 [with "Try to Remember"]
Gay Men's Chorus of Los Angeles/*Simply Sondheim*, see GAYMENSCLA1
Jackie & Roy/*A Stephen Sondheim Collection*, see JACKIE&1
Jackson, Lynne & Mike Palter/*Rememberings*, Redlyn Ltd. JP-1A, 1983
Laine, Cleo/*Cleo Sings Sondheim*, see LAINEC2
Lear, Evelyn/*Evelyn Lear Sings Sondheim and Bernstein*, see LEARE1
LeMel, Gary/*Lost in Your Arms*, Atlantic 83443-2, 2001
Little, Brad/*Unmasked*, (Angels Unlimited) [n.n.], 1999
Major, Malvina/*I Remember*, Kiwi Pacific CD SLC-221, [n.d.]
Malmberg, Myrra/*What Can You Lose?*, see MALMBERG1
McCarthy, Michael/*Broadway*, Haili Limited MCPS HLB CD1, 1994
McDonough, Megan/*My One and Only Love*, Shanachie 5027, 1996
McGovern, Maureen/*Another Woman in Love*, CBS MK 42314, 1987
Mendelssohn Choir/*Mendelssohn Sings Sondheim*, see MENDELSSOHN1
Murphy, Mark/*Song for the Geese*, RCA [n.n.], 1997
Patinkin, Mandy/*Dress Casual* (sung by Bernadette Peters), see PATINKIN2
Reeves, Dianne/*I Remember*, Blue Note CDP 7 90264 2, 1991
Streisand, Barbra/*Christmas Memories*, Columbia CK 85920, 2001 [new verse added by Sondheim]
Sullivan, Christine/*Live at Miettas*, Larrikin CD LRJ 297, 1993
Turner, Geraldine/*Old Friends*, see TURNERG1
Wilk, Oystein/*Too Many Mornings*, see WILKO1
Wilson, Nancy/*Love Nancy*, Columbia CK 57425, 1994

"I Remember That" from *Saturday Night* (1954)
ASIV, SNVS duet b-e^2 [both]
Saturday Night Bridewell Cast (Mark Haddigan, Tracie Bennett), see SATURDAYN1
Saturday Night Original New York Cast (Clarke Thorell, Andrea Burns), see SATURDAYN2

"I Wish (Opening, Part I; Once Upon a Time)" from *Into the Woods* (1987)
[see "Opening" for recordings]
ITWPVS company number

"I Wish" for unproduced film version of *Into the Woods* (1996)

"I Wish I Could Forget You" from *Passion* (1995)
  PPVS f-c^2 , PVS a-e^2
  Passion Original Cast (Donna Murpy, Jere Shea), see PASSION1
  Stephen Sondheim's Passion . . . in Jazz (The Trotter Trio), see PASSION2
  Stage2/the human heart (Francis Cruz, Charlie Owens), DINK Records
    DIDX 045940, 1997 [with "I Have a Love"]
  Passion London Concert (Maria Friedman, Michael Ball), see PASSION3
  Moving On (Company), see MOVINGON [with "Goodbye for Now"]
  Patinkin, Mandy/*Oscar and Steve*, see PATINKIN4
  Turner, Geraldine/*Old Friends*, see TURNERG1 [added to 1997 reissue]

"I Wouldn't Change a Thing" cut from *Happily Ever After* (1959, unproduced)

"If," see "It Would Have Been Wonderful"

"If I Had Three Wishes for Christmas" cut from Gypsy (1959), music by
  Jule Styne
  Groenendaal, Cris/*A Christmas Wish*, [n.l.] 45990/2, [n.d.]
  Anderson, D.C./*All Is Calm, All Is Bright*, LML CD-136, 2001

"If Momma Was Married" from *Gypsy* (1959), music by Jule Styne
  GPVS duet g-b^1/g-c#^{2}, HTSS, SSS duet g-c^2 [both]
  Gypsy Original Cast (Sandra Church, Lane Bradbury), see GYPSY01
  Sondheim: A Musical Tribute (Alice Playten, Virginia Sandifur), see
    SONDAMUST1
  Gypsy London Cast (Zan Charise, Debbie Bowen), see GYPSY03
  Side by Side by Sondheim (Millicent Martin, Julia McKenzie), see SIDEBYS1
  Side by Side . . . Australian Cast (Jill Perryman, Geraldene Morrow), see
    SIDEBYS2
  Gypsy Revival Cast (Crista Moore, Tracy Venner), see GYPSY04
  Gypsy TV Cast (Cynthia Gibb, Jennifer Beck), see GYPSY05
  Gypsy German Cast (Ruth Rauer, Susanne Eisenkalb), see GYPSY07
  Kay Medford in "Gypsy" (Lorraine Smith, Sonya Petrie), see GYPSY09
  Live at the Commander Boardwalk Cabaret, NR11810, [n.d.]
  Callaway, Ann Hampton & Liz/*Sibling Revelry*, see CALLAWAYA&L [in
    medley]
  Skinner, Emily & Alice Ripley/*Duets*, Varese Sarabande VSD-5958, 1998

"If There's Anything I Can't Stand" from *By George* (1946)

"If You Can Find Me I'm Here" from *Evening Primrose* (1966)
  ASIV, SSFTS a-f#^{2}
  Sondheim at the Movies (Gary Beach), see SONDATTHEM1

The Frogs/Evening Primrose Studio Recording (Neil Patrick Harris), see FROGS1
Patinkin, Mandy/*Dress Casual*, see PATINKIN2

"I'll Meet You at the 'Donut'" from *By George* (1946)

"I'm a Fast Worker" from *By George* (1946)

"I'm Above All That" from *The Lady or the Tiger* (1954, unproduced), music by Mary Rodgers

"I'm Calm" from *A Funny Thing Happened on the Way to the Forum* (1962)
FTPVS d^1-f$\sharp^2$
A Funny Thing . . . Original Cast (Jack Gilford), see FUNNY01
A Funny Thing . . . London Cast (Kenneth Connor), see FUNNY02
Putting It Together (Michael Rupert, Julie Andrews), see PUTTINGIT1
A Funny Thing . . . Revival Cast (Mark Linn-Baker), see FUNNY05
Stephen Sondheim's A Funny Thing . . . Forum . . . In Jazz (The Trotter Trio), see FUNNY04
Clary, Robert/*Louis Lebeau Remembers . . . Stephen Sondheim . . .*, see CLARYR1
Laine, Cleo/*Cleo Sings Sondheim*, see LAINEC2

"I'm in Love with a Boy" from *Climb High* (1950–52, unproduced)

"I'm Like the Bluebird" from *Anyone Can Whistle* (1964)
ACWPVS b-c$\sharp^2$
Anyone Can Whistle Live at Carnegie Hall ("The Cookies"), see ANYONE2 [included in "Miracle Introduction"]

"I'm Still Here" from *Follies* (1971)
ASI, FLVS, FVS, HTSS, SSS g-d^2, BSC [special lyrics; in medley with "Everybody Says Don't" & "Don't Rain on My Parade"], FPVS e♭-b^1 [c^2 optional], an individual sheet was published of the version written for the film *Postcards From the Edge*, Hal Leonard HL00355893 g-d^2
Follies Original Cast (Yvonne DeCarlo), FOLLIES01
Sondheim: A Musical Tribute (Nancy Walker), see SONDAMUST1
Side by Side by Sondheim[1] (Millicent Martin), see SIDEBYS1
Side by Side . . . Australian Cast (Jill Perryman), see SIDEBYS2
Songs of *Sondheim* Irish Cast (Gemma Craven), see SONGSOFSOND1
Songs of Stephen Sondheim/You Sing the Hits, see SONGSOFSTEP1
Follies in Concert (Carol Burnett), see FOLLIES02
Follies London Cast (Dolores Gray), see FOLLIES03

Follies/Themes from the Legendary Musical (The Trotter Trio), see FOLLIES04
Follies, The Complete Recording (Ann Miller), see FOLLIES05
The Stephen Sondheim Album (Dorothy Loudon), see STEPHENSA1
Stephen Sondheim Songs (instrumental accompaniment), see STEPHENSS1
Guevera, Nacha/*Aqui Estoy*, [n.l., n.n.], ca. 1980 [in Spanish]
Harvey, Jane/*The Other Side of Sondheim*, see HARVEYJ1
Kitt, Eartha/*I'm Still Here*, [n.l., n.n., n.d.]
Kitt, Eartha/*Eartha Kitt Live in London*, Ariola 353825, 1990
Laine, Cleo/*Cleo Sings Sondheim*, see LAINEC2
Lucas, Lee/*The Big Strapping Fag Show*, Ducy Lee Recordings 900105,
1997 [special lyrics by Lee Lucas]
Streisand, Barbra/*The Concert*, Columbia C2K 66109, 1994 [lyrics rewritten by *Sondheim*]
Stritch, Elaine/*Elaine Stritch at Liberty*, see STRITCHE1
Turner, Geraldine/ . . . *Sings the Stephen Sondheim Songbook, Vol. 2*, see
TURNERG2
Wilson, Julie/*Julie Wilson Sings the Stephen Sondheim Songbook*, see WILSONJ2

"Impossible" from *A Funny Thing Happened on the Way to the Forum* (1962)
FTPVS duet b♭-g♭² [both], FTVS, SSS duet a-f² [both]
A Funny Thing . . . Original Cast (David Burns, Brian Davies), see FUNNY01
A Funny Thing . . . London Cast ("Monsewer" Eddie Gray, John Rye),
see FUNNY02
Putting It Together (Julie Andrews, Stephen Collins), see PUTTINGIT1
A Funny Thing . . . Revival Cast (Lewis J. Stadlen, Jim Stanek), see
FUNNY05
Stephen Sondheim's A Funny Thing . . . Forum . . . In Jazz (The Trotter Trio)
see FUNNY04

"In a Year from Now" from *Climb High* (1950–52, unproduced)

"In Buddy's Eyes" from *Follies* (1971)
FLVS, FVS b♭-e♭², FPVS f♯-d²
Follies Original Cast (Dorothy Collins), FOLLIES01
Follies in Concert (Barbara Cook), see FOLLIES02
Sondheim (Book-of-the-Month) (Betsy Joslyn), see SOND1
Follies London Cast (Julia McKenzie), see FOLLIES03
Sondheim—A Celebration (Julia McKenzie), see SONDACEL1
Follies/Themes from the Legendary Musical (The Trotter Trio), see FOLLIES04
Celebrating Sondheim (Rosemary Ashe), see CELEBRATSON
Follies, The Complete Recording (Donna McKechnie), see FOLLIES05
Moving On (Company), see MOVINGON

Connelli, Judi/*Judi Connelli Live in London*, see CONNELLI2 [with "Being Alive"]

Cook, Barbara/*All I Ask of You*, DRG 91456, 1999

Harrow, Nancy/*Two's Company*, Emarcy PHCE 5029, [n.d.]

Harvey, Jane/*The Other Side of Sondheim*, see HARVEYJ1

McKechnie, Donna/*Inside the Music*, see MCKECHNIED1

"In Praise of Women" from *A Little Night Music* (1973)
LNMPVS c^1-f^2

A Little Night Music Original Cast (Laurence Guittard), see LITTLEN01

A Little Night Music[1] London Cast (David Kernan), see LITTLEN02

A Little Sondheim Music (Michael Gallup), see LITTLES1

A Little Night Music Studio Cast (Jason Howard), see LITTLEN04

Putting It Together (Michael Rupert, Christopher Durang, Stephen Collins), see PUTTINGIT1

A Little Night Music Royal National Theatre (Lambert Wilson), see LITTLEN05 [with "My Husband the Pig"]

A Little Night Music Barcelona Cast (Jordi Boixaderas), see LITTLEN06

Hubbard, Bruce/*For You, For Me*, EMI/Angel CDC 7 49928 2, 1990

"In Someone's Eyes" cut from *Follies* (1971) [almost identical to "In Buddy's Eyes" with the addition of a duet counter-melody]

"In the Movies" from *Saturday Night* (1954)
SNVS company number

Unsung Sondheim (Marilyn Cooper), see UNSUNGS1

Saturday Night Bridewell Cast (Tracie Bennett, Ashleigh Sendin, Jeremy David, Simon Greiff, Maurice Yeoman, Mark Haddigan), see SATURDAYN1

Saturday Night Original New York Cast (Michael Benjamin Washington, Kirk McDonald, Greg Zola, Joey Sorge, Clarke Thorell, Andrea Burns, Rachel Ulanet), see SATURDAYN2

"In the Tradition (Greek)" cut from *Climb High* (1950–52, unproduced)

"In There" for *The Race to Urga* (1968, unproduced), music by Leonard Bernstein

"Incidental Music" from *Invitation to a March* (1960)
Unsung Sondheim (instrumental), see UNSUNGS1

"Incidental Music" from *The Enclave* (1973)
Unsung Sondheim (instrumental), see UNSUNGS1

"Interesting Questions" cut from *Into the Woods* (1987)

"Interrogations," see "Simple"

"Into the Woods (Act I Opening, Parts II and VIII; Act I Finale, Part IV; Act II Opening, Part IX; Act II Finale, Part IV)" from *Into the Woods* (1987) (Act I Opening, Part II) ITWPVS, ITWVS b♭-e♭^{2}, all other versions, included in ITWPVS, are company numbers
    Into the Woods Original Cast (Tom Aldredge, Company), see INTOTHE1
    Into the Woods London Cast (Nicholas Parsons, Company), see INTOTHE2
    Symphonic Sondheim (instrumental) [part of the "Into the Woods Suite"], see SYMPHONICSON1
    Into the Woods Revival Cast (John McMartin, Company), see INTOTHE3
    Cook, Barbara/*Barbara Cook Sings Mostly Sondheim* (sung by Malcolm Gets), see COOKB1 [with "Giants in the Sky"]
    East West Players/*East West Overtures* (Amy Hill), see EASTWEST1 ["Opening Part III"—Witch's sequence only]

"Into the Woods" for unproduced film version of *Into the Woods* (1996)

"Invocation" cut from *A Funny Thing Happened on the Way to the Forum* (1962)
    A Stephen Sondheim Evening[1] (Bob Gunton, Company), see STEPHENSE1

"Invocation and Instructions to the Audience" from *Frogs* (1974), [also known as *Prologos*]
    ASII b♭-a♭^{2} [includes portions for additional voices]
    Putting It Together (Christopher Durang), see PUTTINGIT1 [new lyrics by Sondheim]
    Sondheim: A Celebration (Jane Carr, Roger Rees), see SONDACEL2
    The Frogs/Evening Primrose Studio Recording (Nathan Lane, Brian Stokes Mitchell and Chorus), see FROGS1

"Invocation to the Muses" from *Frogs* (1974)
    The Frogs/Evening Primrose Studio Recording (Nathan Lane & Chorus), see FROGS1

"Is This What You Call Love? (Scene 9)" from *Passion* (1995)
    PPVS g-f^2
    Passion Original Cast (Jere Shea), see PASSION1
    Passion London Concert (Michael Ball), see PASSION3

"Isn't It?" from *Saturday Night* (1954)
    ASII, SNVS a-e^2
    A Stephen Sondheim Evening (Victoria Mallory), see STEPHENSE1

Saturday Night Bridewell Cast (Anna Francolini), see SATURDAYN1
Saturday Night Original New York Cast (Lauren Ward), see SATURDAYN2
Malmberg, Myrra/*What Can You Lose?*, see MALMBERG1

"It Must Be Spring" cut from *By George* (1946)

"It Takes All Kinds" cut from *The Birdcage* (1996)
   Sondheim at the Movies (Bryan Batt, Danny Burstein, Robert Randle, Jim Ryan, Kevin Parisceau, Alec Timerman), see SONDATTHEM1

"It Takes Two" from *Into the Woods* (1987)
   ITWPVS, ITWVS duet a-f$\sharp^2$/a$\flat$-d$\sharp^2$
   Into the Woods Original Cast (Joanna Gleason, Chip Zien), see INTOTHE1
   Into the Woods London Cast (Imelda Staunton, Ian Bartholomew), see INTOTHE2
   Sondheim—A Celebration (Julia McKenzie, David Kernan), see SONDACEL1
   Into the Woods Revival Cast (Stephen DeRosa, Kerry O'Malley), see INTOTHE3
   Wright, Bill/*"It Takes Two,"* see WRIGHTB1 [with "(I've Got) Beginner's Luck" & "Lucky Day"]
   Wright, Bill/*"It Takes Two,"* see WRIGHTB1 [with "Taking a Chance on Love"]

"It Wasn't Meant to Happen" cut from *Follies* (1971)
   Marry Me a Little[1] (Craig Lucas, Suzanne Henry), see MARRYME1
   The Stephen Sondheim Album (Michele Pawk), see STEPHENSA1
   Harvey, Jane/*The Other Side of Sondheim*, see HARVEYJ1

"It Would Have Been Wonderful" from *A Little Night Music* (1973)
   LNMPVS duet c^1-e^2 [both]
   A Little Night Music Original Cast (Len Cariou, Laurence Guittard), see LITTLEN01
   A Little Night Music London Cast (Joss Ackland, David Kernan), see LITTLEN02
   A Little Night Music Film (Len Cariou, Laurence Guittard), see LITTLEN03
   A Little Night Music Studio Cast (Eric Flynn, Jason Howard), see LITTLEN04
   A Little Night Music Royal National Theatre (Laurence Guittard, Lambert Wilson), see LITTLEN05
   A Little Night Music Barcelona Cast (Constantino Romero, Jordi Boixaderas), see LITTLEN06

"It's a Grand Country" from *All That Glitters* (1949)

"It's a Hit!" from *Merrily We Roll Along* (1981)
   MWRPVS quartet
   Merrily We Roll Along[1] Original Cast (Jason Alexander, Jim Walton, Ann Morrison, Lonny Price), see MERRILY1

Sondheim (Book-of-the-Month) (Cris Groenendaal, Steven Jacob, Betsy Joslyn, Timothy Nolen), see SOND1

Merrily We Roll Along Revival Cast (Paul Harman, Malcolm Gets, Adam Heller, Amy Ryder, Anne Bobby), see MERRILY2

Merrily We Roll Along London Cast (Michael Cantwell, Evan Pappas, Maria Friedman, Gareth Snook, Jacqueline Dankworth, Theatergoers), see MERRILY3

"It's Hot Up Here" from *Sunday in the Park with George* (1984) SPGVS company number

Sunday in the Park . . . Original Cast (Company), see SUNDAYIN1

"It's in Your Hands Now" written for *Gold!* (forthcoming)

"It's Only a Play," see "Parabasis"

"It's That Kind of a Neighbourhood," see "That Kind of a Neighborhood"

"I've Got You to Lean On" from *Anyone Can Whistle* (1964) ACWPVS solo + trio a-g♭^{2} + trio, ACWVS solo version b-e^2

Anyone Can Whistle Original Cast (Angela Lansbury, Gabriel Dell, Arnold Soboloff, James Frawley, The Boys), see ANYONE1

Anyone Can Whistle Live at Carnegie Hall (Walter Bobbie, Ken Page, Madeline Kahn, Chip Zien), see ANYONE2, includes introduction

Cano, Eddie/*Broadway Right Now*, Reprise (S)RS-6124, 1965

Day, Courtenay/*Courtenay Day Live at Don't Tell Mama*, see DAYC1 [with "The Little Things You Do Together"]

Ver Planck, Marlene/*A Warmer Place*, Audiophile AP-169, 1982

"Jack, Jack, Jack[, Head in a Sack] (Opening, Part IV)" from *Into the Woods* (1987) [also listed under "Opening"] ITWPVS b♭-g♭^{2}

Into the Woods Original Cast (Barbara Bryne), see INTOTHE1

Into the Woods London Cast (Patsy Rowlands), see INTOTHE2

"Jerry Beaty Birthday" (1955) [Mary Rodgers' first husband]

"Jet Song" from *West Side Story* (1957), music by Leonard Bernstein WSSPVS company number

West Side Story Original Cast (Company), see WESTSIDE01

West Side Story film (Russ Tamblyn, The Jets), see WESTSIDE02

West Side Story Studio Cast (Kurt Ollmann, Peter Thom, Stephen Bogardus, David Livingston, Chorus), see WESTSIDE03

West Side Story Studio Cast London (Christopher Howard, Boys), see WESTSIDE04

West Side Story Studio Cast Leicester Haymarket (Nicholas Warnford, Jets), see WESTSIDE05
West Side Story, The Songs of (Brian Setzer), see WESTSIDE06
West Side Story London Studio Cast (Franklyn Fox, Norman Furber, Vince Logan, Leo Karibian), see WESTSIDE09
Davis Jr., Sammy/*Sammy Davis Jr. at the Cocoanut Grove*, see DAVISS [part of *West Side Story* medley]

"Jitterbug" from *By George* (1946)

"Johanna (Act 1) (Anthony)" from *Sweeney Todd* (1979)
ASI, STPVS, STVS c^1-e^2
Sweeney Todd Original Cast (Victor Garber), see SWEENEYT1
Sondheim (Book-of-the-Month) (Chamber Ensemble), see SOND1
A Stephen Sondheim Evening (Cris Groendaal), see STEPHENSE1
Symphonic Sondheim (instrumental) [part of the "*Sweeney Todd* Suite,"], see SYMPHONICSON1
Sondheim: A Celebration at Carnegie Hall (Jerry Hadley), see SONDACELATC1
Stephen Sondheim's Sweeney Todd . . . In Jazz (The Trotter Trio), see SWEENEYT2
Sweeney Todd Barcelona Cast (Pep Molina), see SWEENEYT3
Celebrating Sondheim (Glyn Kerslake), see CELEBRATSON
Sweeney Todd Live at the NYP (Davis Gaines), see SWEENEYT4
Moving On (Company), see MOVINGON [with "Someone Is Waiting," "Multitudes of Amys," "No, Mary Ann"]
Cant, Donald/*Donald Cant*, see CANTD1 [in medley]
Connelli, Judi & Suzanne Johnston/*Perfect Strangers*, see CONNELLI3 [with "Pretty Women"]
Conrads, Norbert/*I'll Be There (Musical Ballads)*, Fresh Arts/GEM LC3834, [n.d.]
Gay Men's Chorus of Los Angeles/*Simply Sondheim*, see GAYMENSCLA1 [in medley]
Heller, Marc/*Take Me to the World: Songs by Stephen Sondheim*, see HELLERM1
Jackie & Roy/*A Stephen Sondheim Collection*, see JACKIE&1
McVey, J. Mark/*Broadway and Beyond*, [n.l., n.n.] 1998
Mendelssohn Choir/*Mendelssohn Sings Sondheim*, see MENDELSSOHN1
Orchestra Manhattan (Byron Olson)/*Digital Broadway* (1986), see OR-CHESTRAMAN1 [instrumental]
Peters, Bernadette/*Sondheim, Etc.*, see PETERSB1
Ramey, Sam/*Sam Ramey on Broadway/So in Love*, Teldec 4509-90865-2, 1993
Silberschlag, Jeffrey/*The American Trumpet*, Delos Record 3187, 1998
Warlow, Anthony/*Centre Stage*, Polydor [n.n., n.d.]
Wilk, Oystein/*Too Many Mornings*, see WILKO1 [in medley]
Wilson, Lambert/*Musicals*, see WILSONL1

"Johanna (Act 2)" from *Sweeney Todd* (1979)
STPVS quartet A♭-d♭^{1}/a♭-e^2/c^1-f^2 [optional g♭^{2}]/a♭^{1}-e♭^{2}
Sweeney Todd Original Cast (Victor Garber, Len Cariou, Merle Louise, Sarah Rice), see SWEENEYT1
Sweeney Todd Barcelona Cast (Pep Molina, Constantino Romero, Teresa Vallicrosa), see SWEENEYT3
Sweeney Todd Live at the NYP (Davis Gaines, George Hearn, Audra McDonald, Heidi Grant Murphy), see SWEENEYT4

"Johanna (Judge Turpin)" from *Sweeney Todd* (1979) [not included in all productions]
STPVS B♭-f^1
Sweeney Todd Original Cast (Edmund Lyndeck), see SWEENEYT1
Stephen Sondheim's Sweeney Todd . . . In Jazz (The Trotter Trio), see SWEENEYT2 [included as part of "Finale"]
Sweeney Todd Barcelona Cast (Xavier Ribera), see SWEENEYT3
Sweeney Todd Live at the NYP (Paul Plishka), see SWEENEYT4

"The Judge's Return" from *Sweeney Todd* (1979) [based on "Pretty Women"]
STPVS duet C♯-e^1/G-d^1 [end section 1st voice goes down to G♯]
Sweeney Todd Live at the NYP (George Hearn, Paul Plishka), see SWEENEYT4

"Jules and Freida," see "No Life"

"Just Another Love Story" from *Passion* (1995)
PPVS duet a-d♯^{2}/a♯-f^2
Passion London Concert (Michael Ball), see PASSION3

"Just Like Last Night," cut from *Into the Woods* (1987)

"Kids Ain't," see "Like Everybody Else"

"King and Queen Duet" for *The Lady or the Tiger?* (1954, unproduced), written with Mary Rodgers [incomplete?]

"Kiss Me" from *Sweeney Todd* (1979)
(Part I) STPVS duet c♯^{1}-g♯^{2}/b-f♯^{2}, (Part II) STPVS quartet d♯^{1}-c^3/c♯^{1}-f♯^{2}/c♯^{1}-a^2/b-f♯^{1}
Sweeney Todd Original Cast (Sarah Rice, Victor Garber), see SWEENEYT1
Stephen Sondheim's Sweeney Todd . . . In Jazz (The Trotter Trio), see SWEENEYT2
Sweeney Todd Barcelona Cast (Ma. Josep Peris, Pep Molina), see SWEENEYT3
Sweeney Todd Live at the NYP (John Aler, Davis Gaines, Heidi Grant Murphy, Paul Plishka), see SWEENEYT4

"Kissing Song," see "Darling"

"Ladies in Their Sensitivities" from *Sweeney Todd* (1979)
STPVS e^1-a^2
Sweeney Todd Original Cast (Jack Eric Williams, Edmund Lyndeck), see SWEENEYT1
Sweeney Todd Barcelona Cast (Xavier Ribera, Pedro Pomares), see SWEENEYT3
Sweeney Todd Live at the NYP (John Aler, Paul Plishka), see SWEENEYT4

"The Ladies Who Lunch" from *Company* (1970)
ASI, CVS a-e$\flat^2$, BSBA g-d^2 [with "Pretty Women"], CPVS, CVS2 e-b$\flat^1$
Company^2 Original Cast (Elaine Stritch), see COMPANY01
Stephen Sondheim's Company . . . In Jazz (The Trotter Trio), see COMPANY03
Company London Revival Cast (Sheila Gish), see COMPANY04
Company Revival Cast (Debra Monk), see COMPANY05
Sondheim—A Celebration (David Kernan), see SONDACEL1
Sondheim Tonight (Dame Edna Everage, a.k.a. Barry Humphries), see SONDTON1
Company Brazilian Cast (Totia Meireles), see COMPANY06
Company German Cast (Nicole Johannhanwahr), see COMPANY07
Stephen Sondheim Songs (instrumental accompaniment), see STEPHENSS1
Blaine, Vivian/*For You*, see BLAINEV1
Boston Pops Orchestra/*Songs of the '60s* (instrumental), see BOSTON1
Byron, Don/*A Fine Line: Arias and Lieder* (clarinet with Cassandra Wilson vocal), Blue Note Records 7243 5 26801 2 2V, 2000
Harvey, Jane/*The Other Side of Sondheim*, see HARVEYJ1
Laine, Cleo/*Cleo Sings Sondheim*, see LAINEC2
Lemper, Ute/*City of Strangers*, see LEMPER1
Mendelssohn Choir/*Mendelssohn Sings Sondheim*, see MENDELSSOHN1
Streisand, Barbra/*The Broadway Album*, see STREISAND1 [lyric changes by Sondheim]
Stritch, Elaine/*Elaine Stritch at Liberty*, see STRITCHE1
Wilson, Julie/*Julie Wilson at Brothers & Sisters* Vol. Two, see WILSONJ1
Wilson, Julie/*Julie Wilson Sings the Stephen Sondheim Songbook*, see WILSONJ2

"The Lame, the Halt, and the Blind" cut from *Anyone Can Whistle* (1964)

"Last Midnight" from *Into the Woods* (1987)
ITWPVS f-d$\flat^2$
Into the Woods Original Cast (Bernadette Peters), see INTOTHE1
Into the Woods London Cast (Julia McKenzie), see INTOTHE2
Into the Woods Revival Cast (Vanessa Williams), see INTOTHE3

"Last Week, Americans" from *Do I Hear a Waltz?* (1965), music by Richard
  Rodgers
  DIHPVS a-a[1]
  Do I Hear a Waltz? Pasadena Playhouse Production (Carol Lawrence),
  see DOIHEAR2

"Later" from *A Little Night Music* (1973)
  LNMPVS b♯-b[2]
  A Little Night Music Original Cast (Mark Lambert), see LITTLEN01
  A Little Night Music London Cast (Terry Mitchell), see LITTLEN02
  A Little Night Music Film (Christopher Guard), see LITTLEN03
  A Little Night Music Studio Cast (Bonaventura Bottone), see LITTLEN04
  A Little Night Music Royal National Theatre (Brendan O'Hea), see LIT-
  TLEN05
  A Little Night Music Barcelona Cast (Angel Llacer), see LITTLEN06
  Heller, Marc/*Take Me to the World: Songs by Stephen Sondheim*, see
  HELLERM1
  Trotter, Terry/*Stephen Sondheim's A Little Night Music*, see TROTTERT1 [pi-
  ano solo]

"The Lay of a Gay Young Man" from *Climb High* (1950–52, unproduced)

"LE5-5539" (approx. 1960) [birthday song for Mary Rodgers]

"Lenny" music by Kurt Weill [new lyrics to the song "Jenny" from *Lady in
  the Dark*; for Leonard Bernstein 70th birthday concert at Tanglewood]

"Lesson #8" from *Sunday in the Park with George* (1984)
  SPGPVS g♯-f[2]
  Sunday in the Park . . . Original Cast (Mandy Patinkin), see SUNDAYIN1
  Starobin, David/*New Music with Guitar, Volume 3* (Patrick Mason), see
  STAROBIND1

"Let It Happen," see "Take the Moment"

"Let Me Entertain You" from *Gypsy* (1959), music by Jule Styne, [see also
  "May We Entertain You" and "Gypsy Strip Routine"]
  GPVS duet f[1]-e♯[2], solo b♯-e[2], GVS a♯-d[2] [e[2] with intro], SSS a♯-e[2]
  Celebrating Gypsy . . . (Claire Moore, Tim Flavin, Libby Morris), see
  CELEBRATGYP
  Kay Medford in "Gypsy" (Sonya Petrie, Kay Medford), see GYPSY09
  Ann-Margret/*Bachelor's Paradise*, Victor (S)LSP-2659, 1964 (reissued in
  Ann-Margret/Let Me Entertain You, RCA 66882-2, 1996)

Anthony, Ray, Capitol 45rpm 4876, 1962

Bailey, Pearl/*Come on Let's Play with Pearlie Mae*, Roulette (S)SR-25181, 1964

Burnett, Carol/*Carol Burnett Sings*, Decca (S)DL7-4437, 1964 [reissued on CD as *Let Me Entertain You*, Decca 012 159 402-2, 2000]

Church, Sandra/*Let Me Entertain You*, Columbia CL-1461, (S)CS-8253, 1961

Crewe, Bob/*Kicks with Bob Crewe*, Warwick T-52027, (S)ST-2027, 1961

Fisher, Eddie/*Tonight with Eddie Fisher*, Ramrod (S)ST-6002, 1962

Gibson, Deborah/*Long Island Sounds*, Two Young Kids TYK003, [n.d.]

Harnar, Jeff/*Jeff Harnar Sings the 1959 Broadway Songbook*, see HARNARJ1

Mendelssohn Choir/*Mendelssohn Sings Sondheim*, see MENDELSSOHN1

Muller, Werner/*Werner Muller on Broadway*, London (S)SP-44047, 1964

Pringle, Anne & Mark Burnell/*Little Things We Do Together*, Spectrum SR003, [n.d.]

Ross, Annie/*Gypsy*, see ROSSANNIE

Styne, Jule/*My Name Is Jule*, see STYNEJ1

"Let's Go to the Movies" cut from *Gypsy* (1959), music by Jule Styne

"Let's Not Fall in Love" from *All That Glitters* (1949)
ATGVS b♭-d♯²

"Let's Run Away" cut from *Follies* (1971), [see also "Vincent and Vanessa"]

"The Letter" from *Sweeney Todd* (1979)
STPVS quintet
Sweeney Todd Original Cast (Len Cariou, Carole Doscher, Skip Harris, Betsy Joslyn, Craig Lucas, Robert Ousley), see SWEENEYT1
Sweeney Todd Barcelona Cast (Company), see SWEENEYT3
Sweeney Todd Live at the NYP (George Hearn, Tania Batson, Jacqueline Pierce, James Bassi, Lewis White, Frank Barr), see SWEENEYT4

"(The) Letter Song," see "The Glamorous Life" from the film of *A Little Night Music*

"Liasons" from *A Little Night Music* (1973)
ASIII, LNMVS, SSS a-c♯², LNMPVS d-f♯¹
A Little Night Music² Original Cast (Hermione Gingold), see LITTLEN01
A Little Night Music¹ London Cast (Hermione Gingold), see LITTLEN02
Sondheim (Book-of-the-Month) (Chamber Ensemble), see SOND1
A Little Night Music⁴ Studio Cast (Elisabeth Welch), see LITTLEN04
A Little Night Music Royal National Theatre (Sian Phillips), see LITTLEN05

Sondheim—A Celebration (Millicent Martin), see SONDACEL1
A Little Night Music Barcelona Cast (Montserrat Carulla), see LITTLEN06
Laine, Cleo/*Cleo Sings Sondheim*, see LAINEC2

"Life Is Happiness Indeed" for 1974 revival of *Candide*, music by Leonard
   Bernstein
   CaPVS, CaVS company number
   Candide Revival (Mark Baker, Maureen Brennan, Sam Freed, Deborah
      St. Darr), see CANDIDE01
   Candide New York City Opera (David Eisler, John Lankston, Erie Mills,
      Scott Reeve, Maris Clement), see CANDIDE02
   Candide Leonard Bernstein Conducting (Jerry Hadley, Kurt Ollmann,
      June Anderson, Della Jones), see CANDIDE04
   Candide New Broadway Cast (Jim Dale, Jason Danieley, Harolyn Black-
      well, Brent Barrett, Stacey Logan, Ensemble), see CANDIDE05, (see also
      "Old Lady's False Entrance")
   Candide Royal National Theatre (Daniel Evans, Alex Kelly, Simon Day,
      Elizabeth Renhan), see CANDIDE05, [includes "Life Is Happiness Un-
      ending," which may include Sondheim lyrics]

"Like Everybody Else" cut from *West Side Story* (1957), music by Leonard
   Bernstein
   Lost in Boston (Judy Malloy, Richard Roland, Sal Viviano), Varese Sara-
      bande VSD- 5475, 1994

"Like It Was" from *Merrily We Roll Along* (1981)
   ASIII, MWRVS d^1-f^2, MWRPVS a-c^2 [intro. of "Old Friends" f-a^1]
   Merrily We Roll Along Original Cast (Ann Morrison, Lonny Price), see
      MERRILY1
   Sondheim (Book-of-the-Month) (Steven Jacob, Debbie Shapiro), see SOND1
   Putting It Together (Julie Andrews), see PUTTINGIT1
   Merrily We Roll Along Revival Cast (Amy Ryder, Adam Heller), see
      MERRILY2
   Merrily We Roll Along London Cast (Maria Friedman, Evan Pappas), see
      MERRILY3
   Malmberg, Myrra/*What Can You Lose?*, see MALMBERG1
   Turner, Geraldine/*Old Friends*, see TURNERG1 [in medley]
   Upshaw, Dawn/*I Wish It So*, see UPSHAWD1

"Lion Dance" from *Pacific Overtures* (1976) [based on American Admiral's
   section of "Please Hello"]
   POPVS instrumental
   Pacific Overtures[4] English National Opera (instrumental), see PACIFICOVER2

"List a While, Lady" from *High Tor* (1949, unproduced)

"Little Dream" from the film *The Birdcage* (1996)
SSFTS c-e♭²
The Birdcage (Nathan Lane), see BIRDCAGE
Sondheim at the Movies (Susan Egan), see SONDATTHEM1
Music from The Birdcage, HSE Records, HTCD 33/34-2, 1996

"Little Lamb" from *Gypsy* (1959), music by Jule Styne
GPVS d♭¹-e♭², GVS c¹-d²
Gypsy Original Cast (Sandra Church), see GYPSY01
Gypsy Original Cast (Ethel Merman), see GYPSY01, [included on 1999 reissue; with "Mr. Goldstone"]
Gypsy London Cast (Zan Charisse), see GYPSY03
Gypsy Revival Cast (Crista Moore), see GYPSY04
Gypsy TV Cast (Cynthia Gibb), see GYPSY05
Bluebells & Hugo Montenegro/*All About Kids*, 20th Fox, (S)SFX-3034, 1961
Hi-Lo's, The/*Broadway Playbill*, see HILOS
Limeliters/*Sing Out*, Victor (S)LSP-2445, 1961
Merman, Ethel/*Forgotten Broadway vol. II*, [n.l.], T102, [n.d.]
Merman, Ethel/*Mermania!*, see MERMANE1 [with "Mr. Goldstone"]
Murphy, Rose/*Jazz, Joy & Happiness*, United Artists UAJ-14025, (S)UAJS-15025, 1963

"A Little Priest" from *Sweeney Todd* (1979)
STPVS duet g-c♯²/G-g♭¹
*Sweeney Todd*¹ Original Cast (Angela Lansbury, Len Cariou), see SWEENEYT1
Sondheim (Book-of-the-Month) (Joyce Castle, Timothy Nolen), see SOND1
Putting It Together (Company), see PUTTINGIT1 [lyric changes by Sondheim]
Stephen Sondheim's Sweeney Todd . . . In Jazz (The Trotter Trio), see SWEENEYT2
Sweeney Todd Barcelona Cast (Vicky Pena, Constantino Romero), see SWEENEYT3
Sweeney Todd Live at the NYP (Patti LuPone, George Hearn), see SWEENEYT4

"(The) Little Things (You Do Together)" from *Company* (1970)
ASI, CVS, HTSS, SSS solo version a-d², CPVS, CVS2 company number
Company Original Cast² (Elaine Stritch, Barbara Barrie, Charles Kimbrough, Company), see COMPANY01
Sondheim: A Musical Tribute (Mary McCarty), see SONDAMUST1
Side by Side by Sondheim (Julia McKenzie, David Kernan), see SIDEBYS1
Side by Side . . . Australian Cast (Bartholomew John, Geraldene Morrow), see SIDEBYS2

Songs of Sondheim Irish Cast (Tony Kenny, Loreto O'Connor), see SONGS-OFSOND1

Sondheim (Book-of-the-Month) (Joyce Castle, Timothy Nolen), see SOND1

Company London Revival Cast (Sheila Gish, Company), see COMPANY04

Company Revival Cast (Debra Monk, Company), see COMPANY05

Company Brazilian Cast (Totia Meireles, Company), see COMPANY06

Day, Courtenay/*Courtenay Day Live at Don't Tell Mama*, see DAYC1 [with "I've Got You to Lean On"]

Gay Men's Chorus of Los Angeles/*Simply Sondheim*, see GAYMENSCLA1

Horne, Marilyn/*The Men in My Life*, RCA Victor CD 9026-62647-2, 1994 (duet with Spiro Malas)

Jackie & Roy/*A Stephen Sondheim Collection*, see JACKIE&1

Laine, Cleo/*Cleo Sings Sondheim*, see LAINEC2

Pringle, Anne & Mark Burnell/*Little Things We Do Together*, Spectrum SR003, [n.d.]

Mendelssohn Choir/*Mendelssohn Sings Sondheim*, see MENDELSSOHN1

Turner, Geraldine/ . . . *Sings the Stephen Sondheim Songbook, Vol. 2*, see TURNERG2

Wright, Bill/*"It Takes Two,"* see WRIGHTB1

"Little White House" *and* "Who Could Be Blue?" cut from *Follies* (1971) [music used for "Salon at the Claridge #2" in *Stavisky*]
ASII duet $d\flat^{41}$-$g\flat^{2}$/$b\flat$-$g\flat5^{2}$

Marry Me a Little[1] (Suzanne Henry), see MARRYME1

Follies, The Complete Recording (Laurence Guittard, Dee Hoty), see FOLLIES05

"Live Alone and Like It" from *Dick Tracy* (1990)
SCCH, SSFTS b-$e\flat^{2}$

Sondheim: A Celebration at Carnegie Hall (James Naughton), see SOND-ACELATC1

Putting It Together (Michael Rupert), see PUTTINGIT1

Barnett, Peter & Julia Early/*In So Many Words*, see BARNETTEARLY1

Gillan, James/*James Gillan*, [n.l., n.n.], 2001

Minnelli, Liza/*Liza Live from Radio City Music Hall*, Columbia CD 7464-53169-2, 1992

Torme, Mel/*Mel Torme at the Movies*, Rhino R275481, 1999

Wright, Bill/*"It Takes Two,"* see WRIGHTB1 [with "Anyplace I Hang My Hat Is Home"]

"Live, Laugh, Love" from *Follies* (1971)
FPVS c-f^{2} [+ chorus]

Follies Original Cast (John McMartin, Chorus), see FOLLIES01

Follies in Concert (George Hearn, Chorus), see FOLLIES02

No One Is Alone . . . (Michael Denholm), see NONONEIS1
Follies/Themes from the Legendary Musical (The Trotter Trio), see FOLLIES04
Follies, The Complete Recording (Laurence Guittard, Company), see FOLLIES05
Clary, Robert/*Louis Lebeau Remembers* . . . *Stephen Sondheim* . . . , see CLARYR1

"Looks" for *Singing Out Loud* (1992–93, unproduced)

"Losing My Mind" from *Follies* (1971)
ASI, FLVS, FVS, HTSS, SCCH c^1-$e\flat^2$, FPVS f-b1
Follies Original Cast (Dorothy Collins), see FOLLIES01
Sondheim: A Musical Tribute (Dorothy Collins), see SONDAMUST1
Side by Side by Sondheim[1] (Julia McKenzie), see SIDEBYS1
Side by Side . . . Australian Cast (Geraldene Morrow), see SIDEBYS2
Sondheim (Book-of-the-Month) (Debbie Shapiro), see SOND1
Follies in Concert (Barbara Cook), see FOLLIES02
Follies London Cast (Julia McKenzie), see FOLLIES03
Songs of Stephen Sondheim/You Sing the Hits, see SONGSOFSTEP1
Symphonic Sondheim (instrumental), see SYMPHONICSON1
Sondheim: A Celebration at Carnegie Hall (Dorothy Loudon), see SONDACELATC1
The Magic of the Musicals (Marti Webb, Mark Rattray), see MAGICOF1
Color and Light: Jazz Sketches . . . (Holly Cole), see COLOR1
A Gala Concert for Hal Prince (Kelli James Chase), see GALA1
Sondheim: A Celebration (Tim Curry), see SONDACEL2
No. 1 Australian Musicals Album (Judy Connelli), Polydor 539 736-2, 1998
Follies/Themes from the Legendary Musical (The Trotter Trio), see FOLLIES04
Hey, Mr. Producer! (Michael Ball), see HEYMRP
Follies, The Complete Recording (Donna McKechnie), see FOLLIES05
Sondheim Tonight (Maria Friedman), see SONDTON1
The Stephen Sondheim Album (Dame Edna, Barry Humphries), see STEPHENSA1
Stephen Sondheim Songs (instrumental accompaniment), see STEPHENSS1
Ball, Michael/*The Musicals*, see BALLM1
Bassey, Shirley/*I Capricorn*, United Artists Records UAS-5565, 1972
Burgess, Sally/*Sally Burgess Sings Jazz*, [n.l., n.n., n.d.]
Burton, Paul/*Songs on a Steinway*, Imperial Digital Limited IDID1, 1996
Cant, Donald/*Donald Cant*, see CANTD1
Clark, Petula/*here for you*, see CLARKP1
Clary, Robert/*Robert Clary Sings at the Jazz Bakery in Los Angeles*, Original Cast Records 9799, 1997 [with "Not While I'm Around," and "You Could Drive a Person Crazy"]
Cole, Holly/*It Happened One Night*, Caravan CDP 7243 8 5269 05, 1996
Connelli, Judy/*On My Way to You*, see CONNELLI1

Cook, Barbara/*Live from London*, DRG 91430, 1994

Cook, Barbara/*Barbara Cook Sings Mostly Sondheim*, see COOKB1 [with "Not a Day Goes By"]

Corry, Peter/*Peter Corry in Concert*, Pet Cor CD 001, 2001 [with "Send in the Clowns"; recorded in 1993]

DeLaria, Lea/*Play It Cool*, see DELARIA1

Edwards, Stan/*Play Me Hearts and Flowers*, OC 41117-46502, 1997

Fuller, Mark/*Songs About Adam*, see FULLERM1 [with "Not a Day Goes By" & "Isn't This Better?"]

Fulton, Eileen/*I Think About You*, Original Cast 04399, 2000 [with "Dinner for One Please James" and "I Don't Care Much"]

Hamilton, Lindsay/*It's Me!*, Dress Circle CD HAM 1, 1999 [with "So in Love"]

Harpsichord Pieces, Hungaroton/White Label 31729, 1999

Harvey, Jane/*The Other Side of Sondheim*, see HARVEYJ1

Jo, Sumi/*Only Love*, Erato 8573-80241-2, 2000

Heller, Marc/*Take Me to the World: Songs by Stephen Sondheim*, see HELLERM1

Keller, Gretta/*Gretta Keller in Concert*, Stanyan SR10041, 1975

Kendall, Trent/*So Much to Say*, Dress Circle/Trent, 1995

Kennedy, Barbara/*You'd Be Surprised!*, Globe GLO 6045, 1998

Kostelanetz, Andre/*For All We Know*, Columbia C 30672, 1971

Laine, Cleo/*Cleo Sings Sondheim*, see LAINEC2

La Rue, Danny/*I Am What I Am*, Elite PMPCD 1201, 1995

Lear, Evelyn/*Evelyn Lear Sings Sondheim and Bernstein*, see LEARE1

Lee, Peggy/*Where Did They Go?*, Capitol ST-810, 1971

Lipton, Celia/*As Time Goes By*, Independent Record Group, CML 1393/vol. II, 1988

Lemper, Ute/*City of Strangers*, see LEMPER1

Marjorie-Jean/*Losing My Mind*, Carmel Records MJ10001, 1988, 1989

Markey, Enda/*Another Place and Time*, see MARKEY1

Martino, Al/*Summer of '42*, Capitol ST-793, 1971

McBryde, Deian/*Love . . . & Other Distractions*, EvAnMedia evan-35700CD, 2000

McDonough, Megan/*My One and Only Love*, Shanachie 5027, 1996

McKenzie, Julia/*The Musicals Album*, see MCKENZIEJ1

Mendelssohn Choir/*Mendelssohn Sings Sondheim* (Barbara Cohen), see MENDELSSOHN1

Minnelli, Liza/*Results*, Epic EK45098, 1989

Murray, Todd/*When I Sing Low*, Zate Entertainment ZE91002, 2002

Orchestra Manhattan (Byron Olson)/ *Digital Broadway* (1986), see ORCHESTRAMAN1 [instrumental]

Paige, Elaine/*A Musical Touch of Elaine Paige*, Dominion Records DN 6221, 1984

Paige, Elaine/*Stages*, Atlantic 81776-1, 1987

Prior, Marina/*Leading Lady*, Columbia 469214-2, [n.d.]
Saxe, Emily/*Broadway & All That Jazz*, see SAXEE1
Sheldon, Jack with Ross Tompkins/*On My Own*, Concord Jazz, CCD-4529, 1992 [trumpet]
Short, Bobby/*Live at the Cafe Carlyle*, see SHORTB1
Singers Unlimited/*A Little Light Music* (Julia Meadows), see SINGERSUN1
Southern, Sheila/*Sheila Southern with Love*, [n.l., n.n., n.d.]
Thomas, Richard/*I Need to Know*, [n.l., n.n.], 2002
Tompkins, Sheldon/*On My Own*, Concord Jazz 04529, 1992
Tormé, Mel/*Night at the Concord Pavilion*, Concord Jazz CCD-4433, 1990
Turner, Geraldine/*Old Friends*, see TURNERG1
Warlow, Anthony/*Midnight Dreaming*, Polydor 523612-2, 1994
Webb, Marti/*Performance*, Telstar/First Night Records TCD2391, 1989
Welch, Elisabeth/*This Thing Called Love*, RCA 60366-2-RC, 1989
Wilk, Oystein/*Too Many Mornings*, see WILKO1
Wilson, Julie/*Julie Wilson at Brothers & Sisters* Vol. Two, see WILSONJ1 [with Beautiful Girls," "[The Story of] Lucy and Jessie" and "Could I Leave You"]
Wilson, Julie/*Julie Wilson Sings the Stephen Sondheim Songbook*, see WILSONJ2

"Love, I Hear" from *A Funny Thing Happened on the Way to the Forum* (1962)
FTPVS b-d^2, FTVS, SSS, SCCH b-f$\sharp$^{2} [g^2 optional]
A Funny Thing . . . Original Cast (Brian Davies), see FUNNY01
A Funny Thing . . . London Cast (John Rye), see FUNNY02
Sondheim: A Celebration at Carnegie Hall (Michael Jeter), see SONDACELATC1
A Funny Thing . . . Revival Cast (Jim Stanek), see FUNNY05
Stephen Sondheim's A Funny Thing . . . Forum . . . In Jazz (The Trotter Trio), see FUNNY04
Amor al Reves es Roma [*A Funny Thing* . . .] Mexican Cast, see FUNNY06
Clary, Robert/*Louis Lebeau Remembers . . . Stephen Sondheim. . . .*, see CLARYR1
Heller, Marc/*Take Me to the World: Songs by Stephen Sondheim*, see HELLERM1
Land, Peter & Robert Meadmore/*That's What Friends Are For*, First Night CD52, [n.d.]
Turner, Geraldine/*Old Friends*, see TURNERG1 [with "What Can You Lose"; added to 1997 reissue]
Wilson, Julie/*Julie Wilson Sings the Stephen Sondheim Songbook*, see WILSONJ2

"Love Is Going Around," see "Love Is in the Air"

"Love Is in the Air" cut from *A Funny Thing Happened on the Way to the Forum* (1962)
FTPVS instrumental, HTSS c^1-e$\flat$^{2}
Sondheim: A Musical Tribute (Larry Blyden, Susan Browning), see SONDAMUST1

Side by Side by Sondheim[1] (Millicent Martin, Julia McKenzie, David Kernan), see SIDEBYS1 [with "Comedy Tonight"]
Side by Side . . . Australian Cast (Jill Perryman, Bartholomew John, Geraldene Morrow), see SIDEBYS2 [with "Comedy Tonight"]
Songs of Sondheim Irish Cast (Company), see SONGSOFSOND1 [with "Comedy Tonight"]
The Birdcage (Christine Baranski, Robin Williams), see BIRDCAGE
Live at the Commander Boardwalk Cabaret, [n.l.] NR11810, [n.d.]
Jackie & Roy/*A Stephen Sondheim Collection*, see JACKIE&1
Paich, Marty with Carol and Cathy, Groove 58-0002 (N2PW-0388) 45rpm, 1961[?]

"Love Like Ours (Scene 3, Part II)" from *Passion* (1995)
PPVS, PVS duet b-e^2/a-e^2
Stephen Sondheim's Passion . . . *In Jazz* (The Trotter Trio), see PASSION2

"Love Story (Your Eyes Are Blue)" cut from *A Funny Thing Happened on the Way to the Forum* (1962), [see also "Your Eyes Are Blue"]

"Love Takes Time" for film version of *A Little Night Music* (1978) [new lyrics for "Night Waltz"]
A Little Night Music Film (Company), see LITTLEN03
Putting It Together (Company), see PUTTINGIT1

"Love Will See Us Through" from *Follies* (1971), [see also "You're Gonna Love Tomorrow"]
Follies Original Cast (Harvey Evans, Marti Rolph), see FOLLIES01
Follies[1] in Concert (Jim Walton, Liz Callaway), see FOLLIES02
Follies London Cast (Evan Pappas, Deborah Poplett), see FOLLIES03
Follies, The Complete Recording (Billy Hartung, Danette Holden), see FOLLIES05

"Loveland" from *Follies* (1971)
FPVS c-b^2
Follies in Concert (Company), see FOLLIES02
Sondheim: A Celebration at Carnegie Hall (Ensemble), see SONDACELATC1
Follies/Themes from the Legendary Musical (The Trotter Trio), see FOLLIES04
Follies, The Complete Recording (Company), see FOLLIES05

"Loveland" from the 1987 London production of *Follies*
ASIII, FLVS, SCCH [misidentified as 1971 version] b♭-g^2
Follies London Cast (Paul Bentley, Company), see FOLLIES03

"Lovely" from *A Funny Thing Happened on the Way to the Forum* (1962)
FTPVS duet $c\sharp^1$-f^2/d^1f^2, FTVS, SSS solo version c^1-$e\flat^2$
A Funny Thing . . . Original Cast (Brian Davies, Preshy Marker), see
 FUNNY01
A Funny Thing . . . London Cast (John Rye, Isla Blair), see FUNNY02
A Funny Thing . . . Film (Annette Andre, Michael Crawford), see FUNNY03
Putting It Together (Rachel York), see PUTTINGIT1
Stephen Sondheim's A Funny Thing . . . *Forum* . . . *In Jazz* (The Trotter Trio)
 see FUNNY04
A Funny Thing . . . Revival Cast (Jessica Boevers, Jim Stanek), see FUNNY05
Amor al Reves es Roma [*A Funny Thing* . . .] Mexican Cast, see FUNNY06
The MUSICality of Sondheim[4] (Emily Loesser, Don Stephenson), JAY
 Records CDJAZ 9006, 2002
Allen, Steve/*Steve Allen Sings*, Dot DLP-35530, (S)DLP-25530, 1964
Jazz at the Movies Band/*Sax on Broadway*, Discovery 77068, 1997
Johnson, J.J./*J.J. Johnson's Broadway*, Verve V6-8530, 1964 [trombone]
MacCrae, Gordon/*Warmer Than a Whisper*, Capitol 45rpm 4773, 1962
McKechnie, Donna/*Inside the Music*, see MCKECHNIED1 [with "Will He
 Like Me" & "A Secretary Is Not a Toy"]
The Platters/*I Love You 1,000 Times*, Musicor 2091, (S)3091, 1969
Puma, Joe with Hod O'Brien & Red Mitchell/*Shining Hour*, Reservoir
 102, 1987 [trio]

"Lovely" (Reprise) from *A Funny Thing Happened on the Way to the Forum*
 (1962)
FTPVS duet d^1-f^2/e^1-g^2
A Funny Thing . . . Original Cast (Zero Mostel, Jack Gilford), see FUNNY01
A Funny Thing . . . London Cast (Frankie Howerd, Kenneth Connor), see
 FUNNY02
A Funny Thing . . . Film (Zero Mostel, Jack Gilford), see FUNNY03
A Funny Thing . . . Revival Cast (Nathan Lane, Mark Linn-Baker), see
 FUNNY05

"Lovely Ladies" cut from *The Lady or the Tiger?* (1954, unproduced)

"Love's a Bond" from *Saturday Night* (1954)
SNVS b-e^2
Unsung Sondheim (Walter Willison), see UNSUNGS1
Saturday Night Bridewell Cast (Gavin Lee), see SATURDAYN1
Saturday Night Original New York Cast (Donald Corren), see SATUR-
 DAYN2
Saturday Night Original New York Cast (Natascia A. Diaz), see SATUR-
 DAYN2 ["Blues" version]

"Loving You" from *Passion* (1995)

PPVS f♯-c², PVS b♭-e♭²; [an extended version combining aspects of "Loving You" and the "Finale" was published as an individual sheet as Warner Bros. PV9587]

Passion Original Cast (Donna Murphy), see PASSION1

Stephen Sondheim's Passion . . . In Jazz (The Trotter Trio), see PASSION2

Color and Light: Jazz Sketches . . . (Nancy Wilson and Peabo Bryson), see COLOR1

Stage1/how I love you (William Reilly, Ralph Pena, Michael Fawcett, Richard True, Francis Cruz), DINK Records DIDX 037070, 1996 [with "If I Loved You"]

Sondheim: A Celebration (Ellen Harvey), see SONDACEL2

Passion London Concert (Maria Friedman), see PASSION3

Sondheim Tonight (Michael Ball), see SONDTON1

Moving On (Company), see MOVINGON [with "Not a Day Goes By," "So Many People"]

Stephen Sondheim Songs (instrumental accompaniment), see STEPHENSS1

Ball, Michael/*The Musicals*, see BALLM1

Ball, Michael/*Secrets of Love*, Spectrum 544 100-2, 2000

Cole, Holly/*Romantically Helpless*, EMI B00004U8U7, 2000

Cook, Barbara/*Barbara Cook Sings Mostly Sondheim*, see COOKB1

Gay Men's Chorus of Los Angeles/*Simply Sondheim*, see GAYMENSCLA1

Heller, Marc/*Take Me to the World: Songs by Stephen Sondheim*, see HELLERM1

Mars, Susannah/*Take Me to the World*, see MARSS1 [with "Not a Day Goes By"]

Mathis, Johnny/*Mathis on Broadway*, Columbia CK 63892, 2000

McDermott, Sean/*My Broadway*⁴, see MCDERMOTTS1

Michuda, Marie/*It's a Grand Night for Singing*, Southport S-SSD 0074, 1999

Nicastro, Michelle/*On My Own*³, Varese Sarabande VSD-5810, 1997

Patinkin, Mandy/*Oscar and Steve*, see PATINKIN 4

Strassen, Michael/*Loving You* (with Vicki Emery), Dress Circle 32796 00122, 1997 [with "No One Has Ever Loved Me"]

Turner, Geraldine/ *. . . Sings the Stephen Sondheim Songbook, Vol. 2*, see TURNERG2

Vannatter, Dane/*Double Standards*, Avitus Productions [n.n.], 2001

"Lucy and Jessie," see "The Story of Lucy and Jessie"

"Lullaby" from *Phinney's Rainbow* (1948)

"Lunch" for *Singing Out Loud* (1992–93, unproduced)

"Madam's Song," see "I Never Do Anything Twice"

"Make the Most of Your Music" from the 1987 London production of *Follies*
    ASIII, FLVS b-g^2 [includes a small amount of choral accompaniment]
    Follies London Cast (Daniel Massey, Company), see FOLLIES03
    The Stephen Sondheim Album (Brent Barrett), see STEPHENSA1
    McLaren, Morag/*I Never Do Anything Twice*, see MCLAREN1

"March to the Treaty House" from *Pacific Overtures* (1976) [from American
    Admiral's section of "Please Hello"]
    POPVS instrumental
    Sondheim (Book-of-the-Month) (instrumental), see SOND1
    A Gala Concert for Hal Prince (The Munich Radio Orchestra), see GALA1
    Sondheim Tonight (Orchestra), see SONDTON1
    New York City Opera Orchestra/*Broadway's Best* (instrumental) ["Pa-
    cific Overtures Suite, Third Movement"], see NEWYORKCITYOP1

"Maria" from *West Side Story* (1957), music by Leonard Bernstein
    BOB, SSS, WSSVS a♭-g^2, WSSPVS b-b♭^{2} [a^2 alternate]
    West Side Story Original Cast (Larry Kert), see WESTSIDE01
    West Side Story film (Jim Bryant), see WESTSIDE02
    Broadway's Big Hits (Herman Clabanoff), Mercury SR 60811/(M) MG
    20811, 1963
    West Side Story Studio Cast (José Carreras), see WESTSIDE03
    Met Stars on Broadway (Eileen Farrell), MET/RCA MET-204, 1980; MET
    204CD, 1989
    Bernstein on Broadway (Peter Hofmann), see BERNSTEINON1
    West Side Story Studio Cast London (Michael Ball), see WESTSIDE04
    West Side Story Studio Cast Leicester Haymarket (Paul Manuel), see
    WESTSIDE05
    West Side Story London Production (Marlys Waters), see WESTSIDE07
    West Side Story London Production (Don McKay), see WESTSIDE08
    West Side Story London Studio Cast (David Holliday), see WESTSIDE09
    Alban, Manny/*West Side Story*, Decca (S)DL7-4517, 1965
    Baker, Don/*The Sound of Music & West Side Story*, KAPP KL-1411, (S)KS-
    3411, 1965
    Basile, Jo/*Movie Theme Hits*, Audio Fidelity AF-1979, (S)SD-5979, 1965
    Bibb, Leon/*Leon Bibb Sings*, Columbia CL-1762, (S)CS-8562, 1963
    Bonnemere/*Bound of Memory*, Roost (S)2241, 1960
    Cashmore, John/*Musical Cocktail*, GEMA LC8248, [n.d.]
    Chakiris, George/*George Chakiris*, Capitol (S)ST-1750, 1963
    Chakiris, George, Capitol 45rpm 4844, 1963
    Clebanoff, O., Mercury 45rpm 71905, 1961

Clebanoff, O./*King of Kings*, Mercury MG-20640, (S)SR-60640, 1961

Como, Perry/*By Request*, Victor (S)LSP-2567, 1963

Cousens, Peter/*Corner of the Sky*, First Night OCRCD 6043, 1994

Crawford, Michael/*Songs from the Stage and Screen*, see CRAWFORDM1

Damone, Vic/*On the Street Where You Live*, see DAMONE1

Davis Jr., Sammy/*Sammy Davis Jr. at the Cocoanut Grove*, see DAVISS [part of *West Side Story* medley]

Drake, Alfred/*Alfred Drake & Roberta Peters Sing the Popular Music of Leonard Bernstein*, see DRAKEA

Eddy, Nelson/*Of Girls I Sing*, Everest 9006, (S)8006, 1965

Farnon, Robert/*Portrait of Johnny Mathis*, Phillips PHM-200167, (S)PHS-600167, 1965

Fisher, [David] Du Du/*Over the Rainbow*, Helicon Records HL 8064, 1989 [in Hebrew]

Fisher, David "Dudu" and London Symphony Orchestra/Showstoppers, Pickwick Music PY, PK-4141, 1993

Fisher, Eddie/ . . . *At the Wintergarden*, Ramrod Records RR1-2, Taragon TARCD-1054, 1962, 69 [with "Something's Coming" and "Tonight"]

Fortunes, Press (S)83002, 1969

Four Tops/*Four Tops on Broadway*, Motown (S)657, 1969

Franchi, Sergio/*Women in My Life*, Victor (S)LSC-2696, 1965

Garland, Judy/*Judy Duets* (with Vic Damone), see GARLAND [in *West Side Story* medley]

Goulet, Robert/*Sincerely Yours*, Columbia CL-1931, (S)CS-8731

Guest, Rob/*Standing Ovation*, EMI Music (Australian Group) 7986212, 1991 [in medley]

Harmonicats/*Love Theme from "El Cid,"* Columbia CL-1753, (S)CS-8553, 1962

Heywood, Eddie/*Eddie Heywood's Golden Encores*, Liberty LPP-3250, (S)LST-7250, 1963

Holmes Singers, Leroy/*Golden Hits of Broadway*, United Artists UAL-3234, 1963

Hooper, Jeff/*As Long As I'm Singing*, Silverword CDSMG0004, 2001 [with "An Affair to Remember"]

Jay and the Americans/*Sunday and Me*, United Artists (S)6474, 1969

Jay and the Americans/*Jay and the Americans Greatest Hits*, United Artists (S)6555, 1969

Keating, John/*Temptation*, London (S)PS-44019, 1963

Kert, Larry/*Larry Kert Sings Leonard Bernstein*, SEECO CE-467, (S)CES-4670, 1963

King, Wayne/*Music from Broadway and Hollywood*, Decca (S)DL7-4517, 1963

La Staya, Pepe/*MacDougal St.*, Everest 45rpm 19423, 1961

Leyton, Jeff/*Music of the Night*, Linn AKD098, 1998
Mathis, Johnny, Columbia 45rpm 4-41684, 1960
Mathis, Johnny/*Faithfully*, Columbia EPB-14221, CL-1422, (S)CS-8219, 1960
Mathis, Johnny, Columbia 45rpm 4-33042, 1965
Mathis, Johnny/*The Greatest Years*, Columbia C2L-34, (S)C²S-834, 1965
McDermott, Sean/*My Broadway*, see MCDERMOTTS1
Mighty Sparrow/*Mighty Sparrow Sings for Lovers*, Victor LPB-3015, 1965
Peerce, Jan, United Artists 45rpm 574, 1963
Peerce, Jan/*Music to Remember from "Lawrence of Arabia,"* United Artists UAL-3278, (S)UAS-6278, 1963
Peerce, Jan/*Jan on Broadway*, United Artists UAL-3248, (S)UAS-6248, 1963
Peterson, Jimmy/*Inside of Me*, Chess 45rpm 1886, 1965
Pitney, Gene/*Looking Through the Eyes of Love*, Musicpr 2069, (S)3069, 1966
Proby, P.J., Liberty 45rpm 55850, 1966
Quisano, Joe/*Ah, Camminare*, Columbia 3-42493, 1963
Roberts, Malcolm, Victor 45rpm 47-9245, 1968
Roberts, Malcolm/*The Talk of the Town*, Right RIGHT018, 2002
Rydell, Bobby/*Era Reborn*, Cameo (S)SC-4017, 1963
Salems, Epic 45rpm S-9480, 1961
Sinatra, Frank/*Frank Sinatra Conducts Music from Pictures and Plays*, Reprise (S)R9- 6045
Thomas, Richard/*The Impossible Dream*, [n.l., n.n.], 1999[?] [Australian]
Touzet, Rene/*Rene Touzet Goes to the Movies*, Crescendo (S)GNPS-81, 1963
Vale, Jerry/*Great Moments on Broadway*, Columbia CL2489, (C)CS-9289, 1966
Vardi, Emmanuel O./*More Sounds of Hollywood*, Kapp KL-1289, (S)3266, 1963
Wade, Adam/*Very Good Year for Girls*, Epic LN-24056, (S)BN-26056, 1963
Wess, Richard/*Mack the Knife*, United Artists UAL-3203, (S)UAS-6202, 1963
Whitfield, David/*I Believe*, London 45rpm 9506, 1962-63
Whitfield, David/*Million Stars*, London LL-3332, 1966
Wilkinson, Colm/*Stage Heroes*, BMG/RCAVictor 74321-25856-2, 1997
Williams, Andy/*Moon River*, Columbia CL-1809, (S)CS08609, 1963
Williams, Roger/*Eventide*, Kapp 45rpm 437, 1961
Williams, Roger/*Maria*, Kapp KL-1266, (S)KS-3266, 1963
Wilson, Lambert/*Musicals*, see WILSONL1
Zentner, Si/*Desafinado*, Liberty LRP-3273, (S)LST-7273, [n.d.]

"Marriage Proposal," see "Goodbye for Now"

"Marry Me a Little" cut from *Company* (1970) [reinstated in later productions]
ASII, CVS2 g♯-f♯²
Marry Me a Little[1] (Suzanne Henry), see MARRYME1
Side by Side . . . Australian Cast (Bartholomew John), see SIDEBYS2
Putting It Together (Michael Rupert), see PUTTINGIT1
Company London Revival Cast (Adrian Lester), see COMPANY04
Company Revival Cast (Boyd Gaines), see COMPANY05
Company Brazilian Cast (Claudio Botelho), see COMPANY06
Barnett, Peter & Julia Early/*In So Many Words*, see BARNETTEARLY1
Brussell, Barbara/*patterns*, see BRUSSELL1
Buckley, Betty/*The London Concert*, see BUCKLEYB2
Callaway, Liz/*The Story Goes On: On and Off Broadway*, Varese Sarabande VSD-5585, 1995
Clary, Robert/*Louis Lebeau Remembers . . . Stephen Sondheim . . .*, see CLARYR1
Ferreri, Michael/*Sweet Dreams*, see FERRERI1
Malmberg, Myrra/*What Can You Lose?*, see MALMBERG1
Noll, Christiane/*A Broadway Love Story*[3], Varese Sarabande VSD-5956, 1988

"May We Entertain You?" from *Gypsy* (1959), music by Jule Styne, [see also "Let Me Entertain You"]
Gypsy TV Cast (Lacey Chabert, Elisabeth Moss), see GYPSY05

"Maybe They're Magic" from *Into the Woods* (1987)
ITWPVS g♯-e²
Into the Woods Original Cast (Joanna Gleason), see INTOTHE1
Into the Woods London Cast (Imelda Staunton), see INTOTHE2
Into the Woods Revival Cast (Stephen DeRosa, Kerry O'Malley), see INTOTHE3

"Maybe They're Magic" (first version) cut from *Into the Woods* (1987)

"Me and My Town" from *Anyone Can Whistle* (1964)
ACWPVS a-e♭² + trio
Anyone Can Whistle Original Cast (Angela Lansbury, Sterling Clark, Harvey Evans, Larry Roquemore, Tucker Smith), see ANYONE1
Sondheim: A Musical Tribute (Angela Lansbury, Harvey Evans, Tony Stevens), see SONDAMUST1
Sondheim (Book-of-the-Month) (Debbie Shapiro), see SOND1
Anyone Can Whistle Live at Carnegie Hall (Madeline Kahn, Sterling Clark, Harvey Evans, Evan Pappas, Eric Riley, Tony Stevens), see ANYONE2
Celebrating Sondheim (Rosemary Ashe, Tudor Davies, Glyn Kerslake), see CELEBRATSON
Moving On (Company), see MOVINGON

"Men" from *By George* (1946)

"Merrily We Roll Along" from *Merrily We Roll Along* (1981)
ASIII, MWRVS c^1-a^2 [includes section with background vocal], MWR-
PVS company number
Merrily We Roll Along Original Cast (Company), see MERRILY1
Putting It Together (Christopher Durang), see PUTTINGIT1
Merrily We Roll Along Revival Cast (Company), see MERRILY2
Merrily We Roll Along London Cast (Company), see MERRILY3
Gay Men's Chorus of Los Angeles/*Simply Sondheim*, see GAYMENSCLA1
Jackie & Roy/*A Stephen Sondheim Collection*, see JACKIE&1

"Miles Gloriosus" cut from *A Funny Thing Happened on the Way to the Forum* (1962)

"The Miller's Son" from *A Little Night Music* (1973)
ASI, LNMVS, SSS g-c^2, LNMPVS $f\sharp$-b^1
A Little Night Music Original Cast (D. Jamin-Bartlett), see LITTLEN01
A Little Night Music^1 London Cast (Diane Langton), see LITTLEN02
A Little Night Music Studio Cast (Maria Freedman), see LITTLEN04
A Stephen Sondheim Evening (Liz Callaway), see STEPHENSE1
Putting It Together (Rachel York), see PUTTINGIT1
A Little Night Music Royal National Theatre (Issy Van Randwyck), see
LITTLEN05
Sondheim: A Celebration (Tia Riebling), see SONDACEL2
Moving On (Company), see MOVINGON
A Little Night Music Barcelona Cast (Nuria Canals), see LITTLEN06
Company German Cast (Alexandra Seefisch), see COMPANY07
Ford, Anne Kerry/*Something Wonderful*, see FORDA1
Kostelanetz, Andre/*Andre Kostelanetz Plays Great Hits of Today*, Colum-
bia KC 32415, 1973 [later released on "Quadrophonic Pop Concert"
Columbia CQ 32856, 1974]
Laine, Cleo/*Cleo Laine Return to Carnegie*, see LAINEC1
Laine, Cleo/*Cleo Sings Sondheim*, see LAINEC2
Morris, Joan/*Lime Jello: An American Cabaret*, RCA AML1-5830, 1986
Ruffelle, Frances/*Frances Ruffelle*, Dress Circle DRESSCD05, [n.d.]
Skinner, Emily/*Unsuspecting Hearts*, Varese Sarabande 302 066 074 2, 1999
Turner, Geraldine/*Old Friends*, see TURNERG1

"Miracle Song" from *Anyone Can Whistle* (1964)
ACWPVS $f\sharp g^2$ + company
Anyone Can Whistle Original Cast (Arnold Soboloff, Ensemble, Angela
Lansbury, Peg Murray), see ANYONE1
Anyone Can Whistle Live at Carnegie Hall (Madeline Kahn, Maureen
Moore, Chip Zien, Ensemble), see ANYONE2

"Miss Andrew" for *Mary Poppins* (1950, unproduced) [incomplete]

"Mr. A" (lyrics only?) (1959) [for Ginger Rogers' nightclub act]

"Mr. Goldstone" from *Gypsy* (1959), music by Jule Styne
  GPVS f-b♭[1] [+ company at end]
  Gypsy Original Cast (Ethel Merman, Company), see GYPSY01
  Gypsy Original Cast (Ethel Merman), see GYPSY01 [included on 1999
    reissue; with "Little Lamb"]
  Gypsy Film (Rosalind Russell, Company), see GYPSY02
  Gypsy London Cast (Angela Lansbury, Company), see GYPSY03
  Gypsy Revival Cast (Tyne Daly, Company), see GYPSY04
  Gypsy TV Cast (Bette Midler, Peter Riegert, Jennifer Beck, Jeffrey Broad-
    hurst, Peter Lockyer, Michael Moore, Patrick Boyd), see GYPSY05
  Kay Medford in "Gypsy" (Kay Medford), see GYPSY09
  Four Lads/*Dixieland Doin's*, Kapp KL-1254, (S)KS-3255, 1962
  Hi-Lo's, The/*Broadway Playbill*, see HILOS
  Merman, Ethel/*Mermania!*, see MERMANE1 [2 versions, 1 with "Little Lamb"]

"Mix!" cut from *West Side Story* (1957), music by Leonard Bernstein [mu-
  sic later used in *Chichester Psalms*]

"A Moment with You" from *Saturday Night* (1954)
  SNVS duet c♯[1]-f[2]/c♯[1]-d♭[2]
  Marry Me a Little (Suzanne Henry, Craig Lucas), see MARRYME1
  Saturday Night Bridewell Cast (Gavin Lee, Anna Francolini, Sam New-
    man), see SATURDAYN1
  Saturday Night Original New York Cast (Donald Corren, David Camp-
    bell, Lauren Ward), see SATURDAYN2
  The Stephen Sondheim Album (Theresa Finamore and Andrew Lippa), see
    STEPHENSA1

"Moments in the Woods" from *Into the Woods* (1987)
  ITWPVS g-d[2]
  Into the Woods Original Cast (Joanna Gleason), see INTOTHE1
  Into the Woods London Cast (Imelda Staunton), see INTOTHE2
  No One Is Alone . . . (Kerry Sampson), see NONONEIS1
  Into the Woods Revival Cast (Kerry O'Malley), see INTOTHE3
  Turner, Geraldine/ *. . . Sings the Stephen Sondheim Songbook, Vol. 2*, see
    TURNERG2 [with "No More"]

"Momma's Talkin' Soft" cut from *Gypsy* (1959), music by Jule Styne
  Gypsy Original Cast (Laura Leslie), see GYPSY01 [included on 1999 reissue]
  Herb Geller and his all-stars play selections from *Gypsy* (Barbara Lang),
    see GELLERH

The Unknown Theater Songs of Jule Styne/ (singer unknown), Blue Pear Records BP 1011, [n.d.]

Lost in Boston III[3] (Lindsay Ridgeway and Sarah Chapman), Varese Sarabande VSD- 5563, 1995

Clark, Petula/*Uptown with Petula Clark,* Imperial 9281, 9079, (S)12027, 1962

Clark, Petula/*This Is Petula Clark!,* Sunset Records/Liberty, SUM-1101, [n.d.]

"Montage," see "Rain on the Roof," "Ah, Paris!" and "Broadway Baby"

"Montalvo at Biarritz" from *Stavisky* (1974)
Stavisky (instrumental), see STAVISKY1

"Montana Chem" completed for the 1999 Pegasus Players production of *Saturday Night*
SNVS company number
Saturday Night Original New York Cast (Michael Benjamin Washington, Kirk McDonald, Greg Zola, Joey Sorge, Clarke Thorell, Andrea Burns), see SATURDAYN2

"Moon in My Window" from *Do I Hear a Waltz?* (1965), music by Richard Rodgers
DIHPVS trio $g\sharp$-d^2/g-a^1/$g\sharp$-b^1, DIHVS c^1-$e\flat^2$
Do I Hear a Waltz? Original Cast[2] (Julienne Marie, Carol Bruce, Elizabeth Allen), see DOIHEAR1
Do I Hear a Waltz? Pasadena Playhouse Production (Annie Wersching, Carol Lawrence, Alyson Reed), see DOIHEAR2
Intimate Broadway/*My Favorite Things,* Intersound 8311, 1996

"More" from *Dick Tracy* (1990)
DTVS f-b^1 + chorus, SSFTS $b\flat$-e^2 + chorus
Sondheim at the Movies[3] (Jennifer Simard), see SONDATTHEM1
Sondheim: A Celebration (The Tonics), see SONDACEL2
Sondheim Tonight (Maria Friedman, The Soloists), see SONDTON1
Madonna/*I'm Breathless,* see MADONNA1

"Mother's Day I" cut from *Gypsy* (1959), music by Jule Styne

"Move On" from *Sunday in the Park with George* (1984)
ASIV, SPGVS solo version $g\sharp$-g^2, BSBB $f\sharp$-$e\flat$ [with new lyrics and incorporating "We Do Not Belong Together"], SPGPVS duet $d\sharp^1$-g^2/$g\sharp$-$c\sharp^2$
Sunday in the Park . . .[1] Original Cast (Mandy Patinkin, Bernadette Peters), see SUNDAYIN1

Sondheim: A Celebration (Dale Kristien), see SONDACEL2

Celebrating Sondheim (Claire Moore, Stephen Hill), see CELEBRATSON

Moving On (Company), see MOVINGON [with "I Know Things Now," "Everybody Says Don't," and "Take Me to the World"]

Company German Cast (Karsten Oliver Wollm), see COMPANY07

Brussell, Barbara/*patterns*, see BRUSSELL1

Buckley, Betty/*With One Look*, Sterling S1007-2, 1994

Connelli, Judy/*On My Way to You*, see CONNELLI1, [includes "We Do Not Belong Together"]

Connelli, Judi/*Judi Connelli Live in London*, see CONNELLI2 [with "Married," "You Better Sit Down Kids," and "Stay with Me" ("Move On" includes "We Do Not Belong Together")]

Cook, Barbara/*Barbara Cook Sings Mostly Sondheim* (duet with Malcolm Gets), see COOKB1

Ferreri, Michael/*Sweet Dreams*, see FERRERI1

Harris, Sam/*Different Stages*, ZHQ Recordz ZHQ3001, 1994 [in medley]

Jahana, Raishel/*Sondheim Songs*, see JAHANA1

Jobson, Mark deVille/*My House*, see JOBSON1

Osborne, George/*Now Available in Stores*, Original Cast OC166, 2000

Peters, Bernadette/*Sondheim, Etc.*, see PETERSB1

Prior, Marina/*Somewhere*, see PRIORM1

Streisand, Barbra/*Back to Broadway*, see STREISAND2 [with lyric changes by Sondheim]

Vannatter, Dane/*Double Standards*, Avitus Productions [n.n.], 2001

"Multitudes of Amy's" cut from *Company* (1970)

ASIV b♭-f²

Symphonic Sondheim (instrumental), see SYMPHONICSON1

Unsung Sondheim (Michael Rupert), see UNSUNGS1

Sondheim: A Celebration (Jamie Anderson), see SONDACEL2

Moving On (Company), see MOVINGON [with "Someone Is Waiting," "No, Mary Ann," and "Johanna"]

Barr, John/*In Whatever Time We Have*, see BARRJ1

McDermott, Sean/[TBD], JAY Records, 2002

Patinkin, Mandy/*Experiment*, see PATINKIN3

"My Friends" from *Sweeney Todd* (1979)

STPVS duet B♭-e¹/b-e♭²

Sweeney Todd Original Cast (Len Cariou, Angela Lansbury), see SWEENEYT1

No One Is Alone . . . (Kynan Johns), see NONONEIS1, [with "Gun Song"]

Sweeney Todd Barcelona Cast (Constantino Romero, Vicky Pena), see SWEENEYT3

Sweeney Todd Live at the NYP (George Hearn, Patti LuPone), see SWEENEYT4

East West Players/*East West Overtures* (Orville Mendoza, Freda Foh Shen), see EASTWEST1

Gay Men's Chorus of Los Angeles/*Simply Sondheim*, see GAYMENSCLA1 [in medley]

"My Greatest Day" cut from *West Side Story* (1957), music by Leonard Bernstein [related to "Jet Song"]

"My Husband the Pig" cut from *A Little Night Music* (1973) [related to "Every Day a Little Death"]
Putting It Together (Julie Andrews), see PUTTINGIT1
A Little Night Music Royal National Theatre (Patricia Hodge), see LITTLEN05 [with "In Praise of Women"]
Randwyck, Issy van/*It's Oh So Issy*, Dress Circle IVR-CD-1, 1996 [with "Every Day a Little Death"]

"My Last K.O.B." from *By George* (1946)

"My Two Young Men" written for *Gold!* (forthcoming)

"The Natives Are Restless" cut from *Anyone Can Whistle* (1964)

"The New York Follies" from *Climb High* (1950–52, unproduced)

"Next" from *Pacific Overtures* (1976)
POPVS company number
Pacific Overtures Original Cast (Mako, Company), see PACIFICOVER1
Pacific Overtures English National Opera (Richard Angas, Company), see PACIFICOVER2
Sondheim (Book-of-the-Month) (instrumental), see SOND1
A Gala Concert for Hal Prince (The Munich Radio Orchestra), see GALA1
Sondheim Tonight (Orchestra), see SONDTON1
East West Players/*East West Overtures* (Tim Dang and Ensemble), see EASTWEST1

"Next to You" written for *Gold!* (forthcoming)

"Nice She Ain't" cut from *Gypsy* (1959), music by Jule Styne
Gypsy Original Cast (Bernie Knee), see GYPSY01, [included on 1999 reissue]
Feinstein, Michael/*Michael Feinstein Sings the Jule Styne Songbook*, see FEINSTEIN1
Mayes, Sally/*Boys and Girls Like You and Me* (with Boyd Gaines), see MAYESS1 [with "You're Awful"]

"Nice Town, But—" from *Climb High* (1950–52, unproduced)

"The Night Is the Best Time of the Day" from Ginger Rogers' nightclub act (1959)

"Night Waltz (I)(The Sun Won't Set)" from *A Little Night Music* (1973)
LNMPVS quintet & instrumental versions, LNMVS instrumental
A Little Night Music Original Cast (Barbara Lang, Beth Fowler, Teri Ralston, Benjamin Rayson, Gene Varrone), see LITTLEN01
*A Little Night Music*1 London Cast (John J. Moore, Chris Melville, Liz Robertson, David Bexon, Jacquey Chappell), see LITTLEN02
A Little Sondheim Music (Janet Smith, Darlene Romano, Paul Johnson, Rickie Weiner-Gole, Michael Gallup), see LITTLES1
A Little Night Music Film (instrumental), see LITTLEN03, (see also "Love Takes Time")
A Little Night Music Studio Cast (Dinah Harris, Hilary Western, Susan Flannery, Michael Bulman, Martin Nelson), see LITTLEN04
The Great Waltz (Hollywood Bowl Orchestra), see HOLLYWOODB1 [part of "The Night Waltzes"]
A Gala Concert for Hal Prince (The Munich Radio Orchestra), see GALA1
A Little Night Music Royal National Theatre (Di Botcher, Morag McLaren, Ernestina Quarcoo, Stephen Handley, Tim Goodwin), see LITTLEN05
Carousel Waltz and Other Waltzes from the Musical Theater, JAY Records CDJAY 1310, 1999
Sondheim Tonight (The Soloists), see SONDTON1
A Little Night Music Barcelona Cast (Xavier Fernandez, Teresa de la Torre, Muntsa Rius, Anna Feu, Alberto Demestres), see LITTLEN06
Bennett, Richard Rodney/*A Different Side of Sondheim*, see BENNETTR1 [piano solo]
Boston Pops Orchestra/*That's Entertainment*, Philips 416 499-2, 1981 [with "Send in the Clowns"; also, uses "Love Takes Time" version of "Night Waltz"]
Boston Pops Orchestra/*That's Entertainment*/*Pops on Broadway*, Philips 7144 124, 6302 124, 198?
Dow, Judith/*Regards to Broadway*, see DOWJ1
New York City Opera Orchestra/*Broadway's Best* (instrumental), see NEWYORKCITYOP1
Sandford, Luke/*Shimmer*, see SANDFORD1 [piano solo]
Trotter, Terry/*Stephen Sondheim's A Little Night Music*, see TROTTERT1 [piano solo]

"Night Waltz—II (The Sun Sits Low) (Liebeslieders)" from *A Little Night Music* (1973)
LNMPVS quintet

A Little Night Music[1] Original Cast (Teri Ralston, Gene Varone, Benjamin Rayson, Beth Fowler, Barbara Lang), see LITTLEN01 [included on the 1998 reissue only]
A Little Sondheim Music (Janet Smith, Darlene Romano, Paul Johnson, Rickie Weiner-Gole, Michael Gallup), see LITTLES1
A Little Night Music Studio Cast (Dinah Harris, Hilary Western, Susan Flannery, Michael Bulman, Martin Nelson), see LITTLEN04
A Little Night Music Royal National Theatre (Ernestina Quarcoo, Tim Goodwin, Stephen Hanley, Morag McLaren, Di Botcher), see LITTLEN05
A Little Night Music Barcelona Cast (Xavier Fernandez, Teresa de la Torre, Muntsa Rius, Anna Feu, Alberto Demestres), see LITTLEN06
Trotter, Terry / *Stephen Sondheim's A Little Night Music*, see TROTTERT1 [piano solo]

"Night Waltz III," see "Perpetual Anticipation"

"Night Waltz IV," see "Crickets"

"No Fussing" from *By George* (1946)

"No Life" from *Sunday in the Park with George* (1984)
SPGPVS duet g-d^2 [both]
Sunday in the Park . . . Original Cast (Charles Kimbrough, Dana Ivey), see SUNDAYIN1

"No, Mary Ann" cut from *The Thing of It Is* (1969, unproduced)
ASIV g-b^1
Unsung Sondheim (Jason Graae), see UNSUNGS1
Moving On (Company), see MOVINGON [with "Someone Is Waiting," "Multitudes of Amys," and "Johanna"]

"No More" from *Into the Woods* (1987)
ITWPVS duet a♭-e^2/g-e♭^{2}, ITWVS duet b♭^{1}-f^2/a-f^2
Into the Woods Original Cast (Chip Zien, Tom Aldredge), see INTOTHE1
Into the Woods London Cast (Ian Bartholomew, John Rogan), see INTOTHE2
Being Alive!—The Art of German Musical Stars (Paul Kribbe), Sound of Music Records SOMCD 001, [n.d.], [with "Being Alive"]
Sondheim: A Celebration (Wally Kurth), see SONDACEL2
Into the Woods Revival Cast (Stephen DeRosa, John McMartin), see INTOTHE3
Cerna, Jo-Jo de la / *Trust the Wind*, Dress Circle JJDLC9901, 1999 [with "Being Alive"]
Jahana, Raishel / *Sondheim Songs*, see JAHANA1
Patinkin, Mandy / *Mandy Patinkin*, see PATINKIN1
Richard, Lisa / *Born to Entertain*, LML Records, 200[?]

Smith, Martin/*A Handful of Keys*, MSCD001, [n.d.]
Turner, Geraldine/ . . . *Sings the Stephen Sondheim Songbook, Vol. 2*, see
TURNERG2 [with "Moments in the Woods"]

"No One Has Ever Loved Me (Scene 14)" from *Passion* (1995)
PPVS b-d², PVS b♭-f²
Passion Original Cast (Jere Shea, Donna Murphy), see PASSION1
Stephen Sondheim's Passion . . . in Jazz (The Trotter Trio), see PASSION2
Passion London Concert (Michael Ball, Maria Friedman), see PASSION3
Barnett, Eileen/*Live at the Cinegrill*, LML SDM-CD002, 1999 [with "Hold
     Out for the Real Thing"]
De Lorenzo, Brian/*Found Treasures*, see DELORENZ1
Strassen, Michael/*Loving You*, Dress Circle 32796 00122, 1997 [with
     "Loving You"]

"No One Is Alone" from *Into the Woods* (1987)
ITWPVS company number, ITWVS b♭-f² [d♭² optional]
Into the Woods Original Cast (Kim Crosby, Danielle Ferland, Chip Zien,
     Ben Wright), see INTOTHE1
Into the Woods London Cast (Jacqueline Dankworth, Tessa Burbridge,
     Ian Bartholomew, Richard Dempsey), see INTOTHE2
No One Is Alone . . . (Michael Denholm, Michelle Burgan) see NONONEIS1
Into the Woods Revival Cast (Laura Benanti, Molly Ephriam, Stephen
     DeRosa, Adam Wylie), see INTOTHE3
Ballingham, Pamela/*Magical Melodies*, Earth Mother Productions
     EMPD06B, 1991
Bays, Terri/*Spark of Creation*, [Great Britain n.n.], 1999[?]
Beechman, Laurie/*No One Is Alone³*, see BEECHMAN1
Boston Pops/*Music of the Night*/*Pops on Broadway*, see BOSTON2 (in-
     strumental)
Buckley, Betty/*Children Will Listen*, see BUCKLEYB1
Byrne, Debra/*New Ways to Dream*, see BYRNED1
Cant, Donald/*Donald Cant*, see CANTD1
De Ferranti, Margie/*Margie De Ferranti*, see DEFERRANT1 [with "Some-
     times a Day Goes By," "Just a Housewife"]
Draxl, Tim/*Ordinary Miracles*, Columbia [n.n.], 1999
Gay Men's Chorus of Los Angeles/*Diversity*, GMCLA, 1991
Gay Men's Chorus of Los Angeles/*Simply Sondheim*, see GAYMENSCLA1
Guest, Rob/*Standing Ovation*, EMI Music (Australian Group) 7986212,
     1991
Harris, Sam/*Standard Time*/*Different Stages*, ZHQ Recordz ZHQ3001, 1994
Jahana, Raishel/*Sondheim Songs*, see JAHANA1
Jobson, Mark deVille/*My House*, see JOBSON1 [with "Not a Day Goes By"]

Johnson, Maree/*Maree Johnson*, [n.l., n.n.], 1999[?]

Laine, Cleo/*Cleo Sings Sondheim*, see LAINEC2

Laine, Cleo/*The Very Best of Cleo Laine* (with Jacqui Dankworth), RCA-Victor 43215, 1997

Malmberg, Myrra/*What Can You Lose?*, see MALMBERG1

Mendelssohn Choir/*Mendelssohn Sings Sondheim*, see MENDELSSOHN1

New York City Gay Men's Chorus/*Love Lives On*, see NEWYORKCITYGAY2

O'May, John/*Unusual Way*, MEM-004, 2000

Patinkin, Mandy/*Mandy Patinkin*, see PATINKIN1

Peters, Bernadette/*I'll Be Your Baby Tonight*, Angel 54699, 1996

Peters, Bernadette/*Sondheim, Etc.*, see PETERSB1

Sterling, Clark/*Inspirational Broadway*, Sterling, 1994 [with "You'll Never Walk Alone"]

Wilk, Oystein/*Too Many Mornings*, see WILKO1

York, Joe/*My Favorite Year*, see YORKJ1

"No Place Like London" from *Sweeney Todd* (1979)

STPVS trio c^1f^2/$A\flat$-f^1/a-$d\sharp^2$

Sweeney Todd Original Cast (Victor Garber, Len Cariou, Merle Louise), see SWEENEYT1

Sweeney Todd Barcelona Cast (Pep Molina, Constantino Romero, Teresa Vallicrosa), see SWEENEYT3

Sweeney Todd Live at the NYP (Davis Gaines, George Hearn, Audra McDonald), see SWEENEYT4

"No Problem" for *Muscle* (1992, unproduced), [see also "Opening"]

"No Sad Songs for Me" from *Where To From Here* (1950, unproduced)

"No Star of Night," see "Chris and David II"

"No Understand" from *Do I Hear a Waltz?* (1965), music by Richard Rodgers

DIHPVS trio $a\sharp$-e^2/$c\sharp^1$-d^2/$c\sharp^1$-d^2

Do I Hear a Waltz? Original Cast (Stuart Damon, Fleury D'Antonakis, Carol Bruce), see DOIHEAR1

Do I Hear a Waltz? Pasadena Playhouse Production (Benjamin Sprunger, Carol Lawrence, Tina Gasbarra), see DOIHEAR2

"Nobody Reads Books" from *The Jet-Propelled Couch* (1958, unproduced)

"Not a Day Goes By" from *Merrily We Roll Along* (1981)

ASII, MWRVS, MWRPVS, SCCH d^1-$f\sharp^2$

Merrily We Roll Along Original Cast (Jim Walton), see MERRILY1

Fuller, Mark/*Songs About Adam*, see FULLERM1 [with "Losing My Mind" and "Isn't This Better?"]

Hampson, Thomas/*Leading Man (The Best of Broadway)*, Angel 55249, 1996

Harvey, Jane/*The Other Side of Sondheim*, see HARVEYJ1

Jackie & Roy/*A Stephen Sondheim Collection*, see JACKIE&1

Jahana, Raishel/*Sondheim Songs*, see JAHANA1

Jobson, Mark deVille/*My House*, see JOBSON1 [with "No One Is Alone"]

Jorback, Peter/*Personaliza val*, [n.l., n.n.], 2000 [in Swedish]

Laine, Cleo/*Cleo Sings Sondheim*, see LAINEC2

LaMott, Nancy/*My Foolish Heart*, Midder Music, MM CD003, 1993

LuPone, Patti/*matters of the heart*, Varese Sarabande VSD-6058, 1999

Markey, Enda/*Another Place and Time*, see MARKEY1 [with "Good Thing Going"]

Mars, Susannah/*Take Me to the World*, see MARSS1 [with "Loving You"]

Mendelssohn Choir/*Mendelssohn Sings Sondheim*, see MENDELSSOHN1

New York City Gay Men's Chorus/*Love Lives On*, see NEWYORKCITYGAY2

Patinkin, Mandy/*Oscar and Steve*, see PATINKIN4

Peters, Bernadette/*Sondheim, Etc.*, see PETERSB1

Simon, Carly/*Torch*, Warner Bros. Records BSK 3592, 1981

Streisand, Barbra/*The Concert*, Columbia C2K 66109, 1994

Turner, Geraldine/ . . . *Sings the Stephen Sondheim Songbook, Vol. 2*, see TURNERG2

Wilk, Oystein/*Too Many Mornings*, see WILKO1

Wilson, Julie/*Julie Wilson Sings the Stephen Sondheim Songbook*, see WILSONJ2

"Not a Day Goes By (Part II)" Reprise from *Merrily We Roll Along* (1981) MWRPVS duet

Merrily We Roll Along Original Cast (Jim Walton, Ann Morrison), see MERRILY1

Merrily We Roll Along Revival Cast (Anne Bobby, Malcolm Gets, Amy Ryder), see MERRILY2

Merrily We Roll Along London Cast (Michael Cantwell, Jacqueline Dankworth, Maria Friedman), see MERRILY3

"Not for Children" from *Climb High* (1950–52, unproduced)

"Not Quite Night," see "Crickets"

"Not While I'm Around" from *Sweeney Todd* (1979)
ASI, BSC, STVS b♭-f², BSBA a-e♭², STPVS duet e♭¹-a²/g-f¹

Sweeney Todd Original Cast (Ken Jennings, Angela Lansbury), see SWEENEYT1

Sondheim (Book-of-the-Month) (Steven Jacob), see SOND1

A Little Sondheim Music (Paul Johnson, Janet Smith), see LITTLES1

The Magic of the Musicals (Marti Webb, Mark Rattray), see MAGICOF1

Stephen Sondheim's Sweeney Todd . . . In Jazz (The Trotter Trio with vocal by Lorraine Feather), see SWEENEYT2

Sweeney Todd Barcelona Cast (Montsa Rius, Vicky Pena), see SWEENEYT3

A Gala Concert for Hal Prince (Dave Willetts), see GALA1

Sondheim—A Celebration (David Kernan), see SONDACEL1

Sondheim: A Celebration (Loretta Devine), see SONDACEL2 [with "Children Will Listen"}

Celebrating Sondheim (Michael Ball), see CELEBRATSON

Sondheim Tonight (Clive Rowe), see SONDTON1

Sweeney Todd Live at the NYP (Neil Patrick Harris, Patti LuPone), see SWEENEYT4

Stephen Sondheim Songs (instrumental accompaniment), see STEPHENSS1

Atwood, Eden/*Cat On a Hot Tin Roof,* Concord Jazz CCD-4599, 1994

Ball, Michael/*Centre Stage,* Hip-O 440 016 071-2, 2001

Barr, John/*In Whatever Time We Have,* see BARRJ1 [with "One Hand, One Heart"]

Barrowman, John/*Reflections from Broadway,* see BARROWMAN1 [hidden track, duet with his mother]

Besette, Mimi/*Lullabies of Broadway,* Music for Little People [n.n.], 1990, 91, 93

Buckley, Betty/*Children Will Listen,* see BUCKLEYB1

Cant, Donald/*Donald Cant,* see CANTD1 [in medley]

Clary, Robert/*Robert Clary Sings at the Jazz Bakery in Los Angeles,* Original Cast Records 9799, 1997 [with "Losing My Mind," and "You Could Drive a Person Crazy"]

Combo fiasco/*here,* italic entertainment [n.n, n.d.], [with "Not a Day Goes By" & "Being Alive"]

Cook, Barbara/*Barbara Cook Sings Mostly Sondheim* (duet with Malcolm Gets), see COOKB1

Elling, Kurt/*Flirting with Twilight,* Blue Note 31113 38, 2001

Feinstein, Michael/*Live at the Algonquin,* Parnassus Records PRO101, 1986; cd Elektra Nonesuch 9607432

Gay Men's Chorus of Los Angeles/*Simply Sondheim,* see GAYMENSCLA1 [in medley]

Groenendaal, Cris/*Always—Music for Our Children,* SunDial Records SDcd 85152, 1994

Guest, Rob/*Standing Ovation,* EMI Music (Australian Group) 7986212, 1991

Harvey, Jane/*The Other Side of Sondheim,* see HARVEYJ1

Heller, Marc/*Take Me to the World: Songs by Stephen Sondheim,* see HELLERM1

Kirchschlager, Angelika/*when night falls,* Sony Classical SK 64498, 1999

Laine, Cleo/*Cleo Sings Sondheim,* see LAINEC2

McGillin, Howard/*Where Time Stands Still*, HFM 5497, 2002 [with "Good Thing Going"]
Mendelssohn Choir/*Mendelssohn Sings Sondheim*, see MENDELSSOHN1
New York City Gay Men's Chorus/*New York, New York, A Broadway Extravaganza*, see NEWYORKCITYGAY1
Nesbitt, Bobby/*Big Time*, Mile Marker Music MMM2 44807, 2001
Osmond, Donny/*This Is the Moment* (duet with Vanessa Williams), Decca Broadway 44001 30522, 2001
Paris, Jackie/*Nobody Else But Me*, Audiophile APCD-245, 1988
Patinkin, Mandy/*Kidults*, Nonesuch 79534-2, 2001
Prince, Peter/*Being Alive*, RP Media [n.n.], 2001
Prior, Marina/*Somewhere*, see PRIORM1
Silberschlag, Jeffrey/*The American Trumpet*, Delos Record 3187, 1998
Streisand, Barbra/*The Broadway Album*, see STREISAND1
Taylor, Becky/*A Dream Come True*, [n.l., n.n.], 2001
Turner, Geraldine/*Old Friends*, see TURNERG1
Turtle Creek Chorale/*From the Heart*, Turtle Creek Chorale 113023-D5-0169-1, 1990
Wilk, Oystein/*Too Many Mornings*, see WILKO1 [in medley]
Wilson, Julie/*Julie Wilson Sings the Stephen Sondheim Songbook*, see WILSONJ2 (duet with William Roy)
York, Joe/*My Favorite Year*, see YORKJ1

"Now" from *A Little Night Music* (1973)
LNMPVS b♭-e^2
A Little Night Music Original Cast (Len Cariou), see LITTLEN01
A Little Night Music London Cast (Joss Ackland), see LITTLEN02
A Little Night Music Film (Len Cariou), see LITTLEN03
A Little Night Music Studio Cast (Eric Flynn), see LITTLEN04
Putting It Together (Christopher Durang), see PUTTINGIT1 (lyric changes by Sondheim)
A Little Night Music Royal National Theatre (Laurence Guittard), see LITTLEN05
A Little Night Music Barcelona Cast (Constantino Romero), see LITTLEN06
Trotter, Terry/*Stephen Sondheim's A Little Night Music*, see TROTTERT1 [piano solo]

"Now" (first version) cut from *A Little Night Music* (1973)

"Now You Know" from *Merrily We Roll Along* (1981)
MWRPVS g♭-e^2 + company
Merrily We Roll Along Original Cast (Ann Morrison, Company), see MERRILY1
Merrily We Roll Along Revival Cast (Amy Ryder, Company), see MERRILY2

Merrily We Roll Along London Cast (Matthew White, Maria Friedman, Alan Mosley, Michael Cantwell, Company), see MERRILY3
Buckley, Betty/*An Evening at Carnegie Hall*, see BUCKLEYB3
Rubano, Craig/*Finishing the Act* (duet with Marsh Hanson), see RUBANOC1

"Nowhere to Go" cut from *Sunday in the Park with George* (1984) [related to "We Do Not Belong Together"]

"Numbers" cut from *A Little Night Music* (1973)

"Old Friends" from *Merrily We Roll Along* (1981)
ASII, MWRVS, SCCH b♭-f^2 [solo with trio ending], MWRPVS trio
Merrily We Roll Along Original Cast (Ann Morrison, Jim Walton, Lonny Price), see MERRILY1
Sondheim (Book-of-the-Month) (Steven Jacob, Debbie Shapiro), see SOND1
A Stephen Sondheim Evening[1] (Stephen Sondheim, Angela Lansbury, Company), see STEPHENSE1
Sondheim: A Celebration at Carnegie Hall (Liza Minnelli), see SONDACELATC1
Merrily We Roll Along Revival Cast[3] (Amy Ryder, Malcolm Gets, Adam Heller), see MERRILY2
Merrily We Roll Along London Cast (Michael Cantwell, Evan Pappas, Maria Friedman), see MERRILY3
A Little Light Music (Beryl Korman and/or Julia Meadows) see LITTLEL1
Sondheim—A Celebration (Julia McKenzie, Millicent Martin, David Kernan), see SONDACEL1
Celebrating Sondheim (Ensemble), see CELEBRATSON
Moving On (Company), see MOVINGON [with "I Do Like You," and "Side by Side by Side"]
Buckley, Betty/*The London Concert*, see BUCKLEYB2
Buckley, Betty/*Stars and Moon*, see BUCKLEYB4
Carroll, Diahann/*The Time of My Life*, Sterling S1015-2, 1997
Clary, Robert/*Louis Lebeau Remembers . . . Stephen Sondheim . . .*, see CLARYR1
Clooney, Rosemary/*Demi-Centennial!*, Concord Jazz CCD-4633, 1995
Feinstein, Michael/*Live at the Algonquin*, Parnassus Records PRO101, 1986; cd Elektra Nonesuch 9607432
Gay Men's Chorus of Los Angeles/*Simply Sondheim*, see GAYMENSCLA1
Harvey, Jane/*The Other Side of Sondheim*, see HARVEYJ1
Horne, Lena/*We'll Be Together Again*, Blue Note CDP 7243 8 28974 2 2, 1994
Horne, Lena/*An Evening with Lena Horne*, Blue Note CDP7243 8 32877 2, 1995
Lewis, Monica/*Why Did I Choose You?*, Equinox EQCD 7003, 199?
Manilow, Barry/*Showstoppers*, Arista 18687-2, 1991
Mendelssohn Choir/*Mendelssohn Sings Sondheim*, see MENDELSSOHN1
Minnelli, Liza/*Liza Minnelli at Carnegie Hall*, Telarc CD-85502, 1987

Minnelli, Liza/*Liza Live from Radio City Music Hall*, Columbia CD 7464-53169-2, 1992

Postillo, Tom/*What Matters Most*, ELBA CACD 4002-2, 1993

Saxe, Emily/*Broadway & All That Jazz*, see SAXEE1

Singers Unlimited/*A Little Light Music* (Beryl Korman, Julia Meadows), see SINGERSUN1

Turner, Geraldine/*Old Friends*, see TURNERG1 [in medley]

Wright, Bill/*It Takes Two*, see WRIGHTB1

"Old House" from *Stavisky* (1974)
Stavisky (instrumental), see STAVISKY1

"Old Lady's False Entrance/Old Lady's Second False Entrance" from 1997 revival of *Candide*, music by Leonard Bernstein [same music as "Life Is Happiness Indeed"]
Candide New Broadway Cast (Andrea Martin with Jim Dale), see CANDIDE05

"On My Left" written for *Gold!* (forthcoming)

"On the River" cut from *The Last Resorts* (1956, unproduced), [see also "High Life"]

"On the Steps of the Palace" from *Into the Woods* (1987)
ITWPVS a-e^2
Into the Woods Original Cast (Kim Crosby), see INTOTHE1
Into the Woods London Cast (Jacqueline Dankworth), see INTOTHE2
No One Is Alone . . . (Sybil Williams), see NONONEIS1
Cinderella/Songs from the Classic Fairy Tale (Pamela Winslow), Varese Sarabande VSD-5875, 1998
Into the Woods Revival Cast (Laura Benanti, Molly Ephraim, Adam Wylie), see INTOTHE3

"Once I Had a Friend" cut from *The Lady or the Tiger* (1954, unproduced), music and lyrics with Mary Rodgers
hey, love (Jason Workman), see HEYLOVE1

"Once in Your Life" cut from *West Side Story* (1957), music by Leonard Bernstein [related to "I Have a Love"]

"Once Upon a Time," see "Your Eyes Are Blue"

"One" cut from *West Side Story* (1957), music and lyric by Leonard Bernstein [an early version of what became "One Hand, One Heart"]
Stafford, Jo/*Jo Stafford: The Portrait Edition*, Sony Music Distribution A3K 57836, 1994 [previously unreleased, recorded in 1957]

"One Hand, One Heart" from *West Side Story* (1957), music by Leonard Bernstein

 BOB, WSSPVS duet $e\flat^1$-$g\flat^2$/$g\flat^1$-$a\flat^2$, BSBB duet [with "I Have a Love"], WSSVS solo version $e\flat^1$-$e\flat^2$

 West Side Story Original Cast (Larry Kert, Carol Lawrence), see WESTSIDE01

 West Side Story film (Jim Bryant, Marni Nixon), see WESTSIDE02

 West Side Story Studio Cast (José Carreras, Kiri Te Kanawa), see WESTSIDE03

 Bernstein on Broadway (Peter Hofmann, Debbie Sasson), see BERNSTEINON1

 West Side Story Studio Cast London (Michael Ball, Barbara Bonney), see WESTSIDE04

 West Side Story Studio Cast Leicester Haymarket (Paul Manuel, Tinuke Olafimihan), see WESTSIDE05

 West Side Story, The Songs of (Tevin Campbell), see WESTSIDE06

 West Side Story London Production (Don McKay, Marlys Watters), see WESTSIDE08

 West Side Story London Studio Cast (David Holliday, Jill Martin), see WESTSIDE09

 Leonard Bernstein's New York (Dawn Upshaw, Richard Muenz), see LEONARDB1

 Ames, Ed/*My Kind of Songs*, Victor (S)LSP3390, 1965

 Barr, John/*In Whatever Time We Have*, see BARRJ1 [with "Not While I'm Around"]

 Beechman, Laurie/*No One Is Alone*, see BEECHMAN1 [in medley]

 Cook, Barbara/*It's Better with a Band*, MMG MCD 10010, 1986

 Damone, Vic/*You're Just Another Pretty Face*, Victor/Capitol 45rpm 4947, 1963;

 Escorts/*I Can't Be Free*, Coral 45rpm 62349, 1963

 Harnar, Jeff/*Jeff Harnar Sings the 1959 Broadway Songbook*, see HARNARJ1

 Lanning, Jerry/*Jerry Lanning Sings*, MGM (S)4500, 1970

 Migenes, Julia/*Live at the Olympia*, see MIGENES1

 Prior, Marina/*Somewhere*, see PRIORM1

 Streisand, Barbra/*Back to Broadway* (duet with Johnny Mathis), see STREISAND2

 Te Kanawa, Kiri/*The Young Kiri*, [n.l., n.n., n.d.]

 Warwick, Dionne/*On Stage and in the Movies*, Scepter (S)SRM 559, 1967

 Warwick, Dionne/*Dionne Warwick's Greatest*, Scepter (S)575, 1970 (45rpm 21044)

 Zamora, Marie/*Comedies Musicales* (with Michael Ball), [n.l., n.n.], 2000

"One More Kiss" from *Follies* (1971)

 ASI, FLVS, FVS solo version e^1-$a\flat^2$, FPVS duet d^1-$g\flat^2$/$e\flat^1$-a^2

 Follies Original Cast (Justine Johnston, Victoria Mallory), FOLLIES01

 Sondheim: A Musical Tribute (Justine Johnston, Victoria Mallory), see SONDAMUST1

Follies in Concert (Licia Albanes, Erie Mills), see FOLLIES02
Follies London Cast (Adele Leigh, Michelle Todd), see FOLLIES03
Color and Light: Jazz Sketches . . . (Jim Hall, guitar), see COLOR1
Follies, The Complete Recording (Carol Skarimbas, Ingrid Ladendorf), see FOLLIES05
Heller, Marc/*Take Me to the World: Songs by Stephen Sondheim*, see HELLERM1
Tune, Tommy/*Slow Dancin'*, RCAVictor/BMG 09026-68322-2, 1997

"The One on the Left" cut from *Sunday in the Park with George* (1984) [a portion of this song is included in the "Day Off" sequence]

"One Wonderful Day" from *Saturday Night* (1954)
SNVS company number
Saturday Night Bridewell Cast (Company), see SATURDAYN1
Saturday Night Original New York Cast (Andrea Burns, Clarke Thorell, Christopher Fitzgerald, Rachel Ulanet, Natascia A. Diaz, Michael Benjamin Washington, Kirk McDonald, Greg Zola, Joey Sorge), see SATURDAYN2
Saturday Night Original New York Cast (Company), see SATURDAYN2 ["Finale" version]

"Opening" for *The Lady or the Tiger?* (1954, unproduced) [incomplete]

"Opening" cut from *West Side Story* (1957), music by Leonard Bernstein, lyrics by Sondheim and Bernstein

"Opening" from *Into the Woods* (1987) [see "I Wish," "Into the Woods," "Fly, Birds," "Greens, Greens," "Jack, Jack, Jack," "You Wish to Have the Curse Reversed?" "Ladies, Our Carriage Waits," and "The Spell Is on My House" for recording and music information]

"Opening" from *Assassins* (1991), [see "Everybody's Got the Right" for recording information]
APVS company number

"Opening" for *Muscle* (1992, unproduced), [see also "No Problem" and "Poses"]

"Opening" for *Gold!* (forthcoming), [see also "On My Left"]

"Opening Doors" from *Merrily We Roll Along* (1981)
MWRPVS company number
Merrily We Roll Along Original Cast (Jim Walton, Lonny Price, Ann Morrison, Jason Alexander, Marianna Allen, Sally Klein), see MERRILY1

Merrily We Roll Along Revival Cast (Malcolm Gets, Adam Heller, Amy
  Ryder, Paul Harman, Cass Morgan, Anne Bobby), see MERRILY2
Merrily We Roll Along London Cast (Evan Pappas, Michael Cantwell,
  Maria Friedman, Gareth Snook, Jacqueline Dankworth), see MERRILY3
Moving On (Company), see MOVINGON [with "Our Time"]

"Opening Number" from *Phinney's Rainbow* (1948)

"Operetta (C'est moi)" from *Stavisky* (1974) [based on "The World's Full
  of Boys/Girls" cut from *Follies*]
Stavisky (singer unidentified), see STAVISKY1

"Our Little World" added to the 1991 London production of *Into the Woods*
Into the Woods London Cast (Julia McKenzie, Mary Lincoln), see INTOTHE2
Into the Woods Revival Cast (Vanessa Williams, Melissa Dye), see INTOTHE3

"Our Time" from *Merrily We Roll Along* (1981)
MWRPVS company number, MWRVS, SCCH duet version d♭¹-g♭²/b♭-e♭²
*Merrily We Roll Along*¹ Original Cast (Jim Walton, Lonny Price, Ann
  Morrison, Company), see MERRILY1
Sondheim: A Celebration at Carnegie Hall (Boys Choir of Harlem), see SOND-
  ACELATC1
Merrily We Roll Along Revival Cast (Malcolm Gets, Adam Heller, Amy
  Ryder, Company), see MERRILY2
Merrily We Roll Along London Cast (Michael Cantwell, Evan Pappas,
  Maria Friedman, Company), see MERRILY3
Sondheim A Celebration (The Company), see SONDACEL2 [with "Side by
  Side" and "Sunday"]
Celebrating Sondheim (Ensemble), see CELEBRATSON
Out on Broadway (Tracy Collins, Quenten Schumacher, Company), see
  OUTONB1 [with "Do You Hear the People Sing?"]
Moving On (Company), see MOVINGON [with "Opening Doors" and 2nd
  medley with "With So Little to Be Sure of"]
Callaway, Ann Hampton & Liz/*Sibling Revelry*, see CALLAWAYA&1
Callaway, Liz/*The Story Goes On: On and Off Broadway* (with Ann
  Hampton Callaway), Varese Sarabande VSD-5585, 1995
Connelli, Judi & Suzanne Johnston/*Perfect Strangers*, see CONNELLI3
  [with "Everybody Says Don't"]
East West Players/*East West Overtures* (Kym Hoy, Randy Guiaya, En-
  semble) see EASTWEST1
Gay Men's Chorus of Los Angeles/*Diversity*, GMCLA [n.n.], 1991
Gay Men's Chorus of Los Angeles/*Simply Sondheim*, see GAYMENSCLA1
Mendelssohn Choir/*Mendelssohn Sings Sondheim*, see MENDELSSOHN1

New York City Gay Men's Chorus/*New York, New York, A Broadway Extravaganza*, see NEWYORKCITYGAY1
O'Brien, Joanne and Lee Lessack/*An Enchanted Evening: The Music of Broadway*, LML Music, LML CD-104, 1998
Pot Pourri/*Rhythm of Life*, Move MCD058, 1999[?]
Sterling, Clark/*Inspirational Broadway*, Sterling, 1994

"Overture" from 2000 production of *Saturday Night*
Saturday Night Original New York Cast (Orchestra), see SATURDAYN2

"Overture" from *A Funny Thing Happened on the Way to the Forum* (1962)
FTPVS instrumental
A Funny Thing . . . Original Cast (Orchestra), see FUNNY01
A Funny Thing . . . London Cast (Orchestra), see FUNNY02
A Funny Thing . . . Revival Cast (Orchestra), see FUNNY05

"Overture" (first version) cut from *A Funny Thing Happened on the Way to the Forum* (1962)

"Overture" from *Anyone Can Whistle* (1964), [see "Prelude Act I"]

"Overture" from *Company* (1970), [see also "Bobby-Baby"]

"Overture" from *Follies* (1971) [based on "All Things Bright and Beautiful" cut from *Follies*]
FPVS instrumental
Follies Original Cast (Orchestra), see FOLLIES01
Follies in Concert (Orchestra), see FOLLIES02
Follies/Themes from the Legendary Musical[3] (The Trotter Trio), see FOLLIES04 [listed as "Opening"]
Follies, The Complete Recording (Orchestra), see FOLLIES05

"Overture" from the London production of *Follies* (1987)

"Overture" from *A Little Night Music* (1973)
LNMPVS vocal quintet
A Little Night Music Original Cast (Barbara Lang, Beth Fowler, Teri Ralston, Benjamin Ralston, Gene Varrone), see LITTLEN01
A Little Night Music London Cast (John J. Moore, Chris Melville, Liz Robertson, David Bexon, Jacquey Chappell), see LITTLEN02
A Little Night Music Film (Company), see LITTLEN03
A Little Sondheim Music (Michael Gallup, Darlene Romano, Delcina Stevenson, Jeffrey Araluce, Rickie Weiner-Gole), see LITTLES1

A Little Night Music Studio Cast (Dinah Harris, Hilary Western, Susan Flannery, Michael Bulman, Martin Nelson), see LITTLEN04
A Little Night Music Royal National Theatre (Morag McLaren, Di Botcher, Ernestina Quarcoo, Stephen Hanley, Tim Goodwin), see LITTLEN05
A Little Night Music Barcelona Cast (Xavier Fernandez, Teresa de la Torre, Muntsa Rius, Anna Feu, Alberto Demestres), see LITTLEN06

"Overture" from *Merrily We Roll Along* (1981)
MWRPVS instrumental
Merrily We Roll Along Original Cast (Orchestra), see MERRILY1
Merrily We Roll Along Revival Cast (Orchestra), see MERRILY2
Merrily We Roll Along London Cast (Orchestra), see MERRILY3
Celebrating Sondheim (instrumental), see CELEBRATSON

"Paean: Evoe for the Dead," see "Evoe for the Dead"

"Parabasis: It's Only a Play" from *The Frogs* (1974)
The Frogs/Evening Primrose Studio Recording (Chorus), see FROGS1

"Paradise" for *Gold!* (forthcoming)

"Parados: The Frogs" from *The Frogs* (1974)
The Frogs/Evening Primrose Studio Recording (Nathan Lane, Brian Stokes Mitchell, Chorus), see FROGS1

"Parlor Songs" from *Sweeney Todd* (1979), [see "Sweet Polly Plunkett" and "The Tower of Bray" for music]
Sweeney Todd Original Cast (Jack Eric Williams, Angela Lansbury, Ken Jennings), see SWEENEYT1
Stephen Sondheim's Sweeney Todd . . . In Jazz (The Trotter Trio), see SWEENEYT2
Sweeney Todd Barcelona Cast (Pedro Pomares, Vicky Pena), see SWEENEYT3
Sweeney Todd Live at the NYP (John Aler, Patti LuPone, Neil Patrick Harris), see SWEENEYT4

"Party, Party" from *Climb High* (1950–52, unproduced)

"Pavement Pounding Sequence" from *Climb High* (1950–52, unproduced)

"The People Will Hear" from *All That Glitters* (1949)

"Perfectly Lovely Couple" from *Do I Hear a Waltz?* (1965), music by Richard Rodgers
DIHPVS company number, but all voices c^1-d^2
Do I Hear a Waltz? Original Cast (Stuart Damon, Madeleine Sherwood, Julienne Marie, Carol Bruce, Jack Manning, Elizabeth Allen, Sergio Franchi, Fleury D'Antonakis), see DOIHEAR1

Do I Hear a Waltz? Pasadena Playhouse Production (The Company), see DOIHEAR2

"Perhaps" cut during the New Haven tryout from *Do I Hear a Waltz?* (1965), music by Richard Rodgers

"Perpetual Anticipation" from *A Little Night Music* (1973)
LNMPVS trio b♭-g^2/b♭-f^2/b♭-f^2
A Little Night Music Original Cast (Teri Ralston, Beth Fowler, Barbara Lang), see LITTLEN01
A Little Night Music London Cast (Chris Melville, Liz Robertson, Jacquey Chappell), see LITTLEN02
A Little Night Music Studio Cast (Dinah Harris, Hilary Western, Susan Flannery), see LITTLEN04
Putting It Together (Rachel York), see PUTTINGIT1
A Little Night Music Royal National Theatre (Ernestina Quarcoo, Morag McLaren, Di Botcher), see LITTLEN05
A Little Night Music Barcelona Cast (Teresa de la Torre, Muntsa Rius, Anna Feu), see LITTLEN06

"Philadelphia!" cut from *Do I Hear a Waltz?* (1965), music by Richard Rodgers

"Phinney's Rainbow" from *Phinney's Rainbow* (1948)
PRSM d^1-f^2

"Piano Practice" from *A Little Night Music* (1973) [based on cut song "Two Fairy Tales"]
LNMPVS instrumental

"Piazza Promenade" cut from *Do I Hear a Waltz?* (1965), music by Richard Rodgers [related to "Bargaining"]

"Pirelli's Death" from *Sweeney Todd* (1979)
STPVS e♭^{1}-c^3
Sweeney Todd Barcelona Cast (Esteve Ferrer), see SWEENEYT3
Sweeney Todd Live at the NYP (Stanford Olsen), see SWEENEYT4

"Pirelli's Miracle Elixir" from *Sweeney Todd* (1979)
STPVS b-a^2 + company
Sweeney Todd Original Cast (Ken Jennings, Len Cariou, Angela Lansbury, Joaquín Romaguera, Company), see SWEENEYT1
Sweeney Todd Barcelona Cast (Muntsa Rius, Constantino Romero, Vicky Pena, Company), see SWEENEYT3
Sweeney Todd Live at the NYP (Neil Patrick Harris, Company), see SWEENEYT4

"The Plan" cut from *Into the Woods* (1987)

"Pleasant Little Kingdom" cut from *Follies* (1971) [conceived as lead into "Too Many Mornings"]
   ASIV duet a♯-e♭² [both]
   Sondheim: A Musical Tribute (Dorothy Collins, John McMartin), see SON-
     DAMUST1 [sung with "Too Many Mornings"]
   Follies, The Complete Recording (Laurence Guittard, Donna McKech-
     nie), see FOLLIES05
   Gay Men's Chorus of Los Angeles/*Simply Sondheim* (Joanna Gleason),
     see GAYMENSCLA1
   Patinkin, Mandy/*Oscar and Steve*, see PATINKIN4 (duet with Judy Blazer)
     [sung with "Too Many Mornings"]

"Please Hello" from *Pacific Overtures* (1976)
   POPVS company number
   Pacific Overtures[1] Original Cast (Alvin Ing, Yuki Shimoda, Ernest
     Harada, Mako, Patrick Kinser-Lau, Mark Hsu Syers, James Dybas),
     see PACIFICOVER1
   Pacific Overtures English National Opera (Alan Woodrow, John
     Kitchiner, Eric Roberts, Paul Strathearn, Ian Comboy, Harry Nicoll),
     see PACIFICOVER2

"Poems" from *Pacific Overtures* (1976)
   POPVS duet e♭¹-g²/d¹-f²
   Pacific Overtures Original Cast (Isao Sato, Sab Shimono), see PACIFICOVER1
   A Stephen Sondheim Evening (George Hearn, Bob Gunton), see STEPHENSE1
   Pacific Overtures English National Opera (Malcolm Rivers, Christopher
     Booth-Jones), see PACIFICOVER2
   Color and Light: Jazz Sketches . . . (Terrence Blanchard, trumpet), see COLOR1
   Patinkin, Mandy/*Oscar and Steve*, see PATINKIN4 (duet with Michael
     Yukon Grody)

"Poor Baby" from *Company* (1970)
   CPVS, CVS2 company number
   Company Original Cast (Barbara Barrie, Teri Ralston, Merle Louise,
     Beth Howland, Elaine Stritch, Charles Kimbrough, George Coe),
     see COMPANY01
   Company London Revival Cast (Rebecca Front, Clive Rowe, Liza Sadoy,
     Teddy Kempner, Clare Burt, Sophie Thompson, Sheila Gish), see
     COMPANY04
   Company Revival Cast (Kate Burton, Robert Westenberg, Diana Canova,
     John Hillner, Patricia Ben Peterson, Veanne Cox, Debra Monk), see
     COMPANY05

Company Brazilian Cast (Solange Badim, Daniel Boaventura, Reginah Restelieux, Mauro Gorini, Claudia Netto, Totia Meireles), see COMPANY06

Boston Pops Orchestra/*Songs of the '60s* (instrumental), see BOSTON1

"Poor Thing" from *Sweeney Todd* (1979)
STPVS f♯-b[1]
Sweeney Todd Original Cast (Angela Lansbury), see SWEENEYT1
Sweeney Todd Barcelona Cast (Vicky Pena), see SWEENEYT3
Sweeney Todd Live at the NYP (Patti LuPone), see SWEENEYT4

"Poses" for *Muscle* (1992, unproduced), [see also "Opening"]

"Potpourri" for *Gold!* (forthcoming)

"Pour le sport" from *The Last Resorts* (1956, unproduced)
Marry Me a Little[1] (Suzanne Henry, Craig Lucas), see MARRYME1

"Prayer" cut from *Pacific Overtures* (1976)

"Prayers" cut from *Pacific Overtures* (1976) [a portion was used in "Chrysanthemum Tea"]

"Prelude" from *Invitation to a March* (1960)

"Prelude" from *Sweeney Todd* (1979)
STPVS Instrumental
Sweeney Todd Original Cast (instrumental), see SWEENEYT1
Sweeney Todd Live at the NYP (instrumental), see SWEENEYT4

"Prelude Act I [Overture]" from *Anyone Can Whistle* (1964)
ACWPVS Instrumental
Anyone Can Whistle Original Cast (Orchestra), see ANYONE1

"Pretty Lady" from *Pacific Overtures* (1976)
ASI, POPVS, SCCH, SSS trio c^1-f^2/a-f^2/f-d^2
Pacific Overtures Original Cast (Patrick Kinser-Lau, Timm Fujii, Mark Hsu Syers), see PACIFICOVER1
Side by Side by Sondheim (Millicent Martin, Julia McKenzie, David Kernan), see SIDEBYS1
Side by Side . . . Australian Cast (Bartholomew John, Geraldene Morrow, Jill Perryman), see SIDEBYS2
Songs of Sondheim Irish Cast (Company), see SONGSOFSOND1
Sondheim (Book-of-the-Month) (instrumental), see SOND1

A Little Sondheim Music (Jeffrey Araluce, Dale Morich, Michael Gallup), see LITTLES1

Pacific Overtures English National Opera (Leon Berger, Edward Byles, Alan Woodrow), see PACIFICOVER2

Symphonic Sondheim (instrumental), see SYMPHONICSON1

Sondheim: A Celebration at Carnegie Hall (Mark Jacoby, Eugene Perry, Herbert Perry), see SONDACELATC1

East West Players/*East West Overtures* (Radmar Agana Jao, Daniel Kim, Paul Wong), see EASTWEST1

Mendelssohn Choir/*Mendelssohn Sings Sondheim* (Timothy Cornetti, John Niederberger, Robert Shoup), see MENDELSSOHN1

Nesbitt, Bobby/*Big Time*, Mile Marker Music MMM2 44807, 2001

O'May, John/*Unusual Way*, MEM-004, 2000

Patinkin, Mandy/*Mandy Patinkin*, see PATINKIN1

"Pretty Little Picture" from *A Funny Thing Happened on the Way to the Forum* (1962)

FTPVS trio b-f#^{2}/b-g#^{2}/b-f#^{2}, FTVS solo version b♭-f^2

A Funny Thing . . . Original Cast (Zero Mostel, Brian Davies, Preshy Marker), see FUNNY01

A Funny Thing . . . London Cast (Frankie Howerd, John Rye, Isla Blair), see FUNNY02

A Stephen Sondheim Evening[1] (Bob Gunton, Liz Callaway, Steven Jacob), see STEPHENSE1

A Funny Thing . . . Revival Cast (Nathan Lane, Jessica Boevers, Jim Stanek), see FUNNY05

Amor al Reves es Roma [A Funny Thing . . .] Mexican Cast, see FUNNY06

Scott, Phil/*Serious Cabaret*, [n.l., n.n.], 2002

Turner, Geraldine/ . . . *Sings the Stephen Sondheim Songbook, Vol. 2*, see TURNERG2

"Pretty Women" from *Sweeney Todd* (1979)

ASI, STVS solo version c^1-e^2, BSBA g-d^2 [with "The Ladies Who Lunch"], STPVS duet E-f^1/A-f^1 + whistling, reprise c#-e^1/G-d^1

Sweeney Todd[1] Original Cast (Edmund Lyndeck, Len Cariou), see SWEENEYT1

A Little Sondheim Music (Dale Morich, Michael Gallup), see LITTLES1

A Broadway Celebration, see BROADWAYCEL

Sondheim: A Celebration at Carnegie Hall (Eugene Perry, Herbert Perry), see SONDACELATC1

Putting It Together (Michael Rupert, Stephen Collins), see PUTTINGIT1

Color and Light: Jazz Sketches . . . (Peabo Bryson), see COLOR1

Stephen Sondheim's Sweeney Todd . . . *In Jazz* (The Trotter Trio), see SWEENEYT2

Sweeney Todd Barcelona Cast (Xavier Ribera, Constantino Romero), see SWEENEYT3

Leading Men Don't Dance, 1997

Sweeney Todd Live at the NYP (Paul Plishka, George Hearn, Davis Gaines), see SWEENEYT4

Moving On (Company), see MOVINGON [with "Ah, But Underneath"]

Barnes, Buddy/*The Magic Time,* Audiophile AP-139, 1980

Buckley, Betty/*Much More,* Sterling S1014-2, 1997

Clary, Robert/*Louis Lebeau Remembers . . . Stephen Sondheim . . .,* see CLARYR1

Collins, Judy/*Running for My Life,* Elektra 6E-253, 1980

Connelli, Judi & Suzanne Johnston/*Perfect Strangers,* see CONNELLI3 [with "Johanna"]

Day, Courtenay/*Courtenay Day Live at Don't Tell Mama,* see DAYC1 [with "Every Day a Little Death"]

Gay Men's Chorus of Los Angeles/*Simply Sondheim,* see GAYMENSCLA1 [in medley]

Harvey, Jane/*The Other Side of Sondheim,* see HARVEYJ1

Heller, Marc/*Take Me to the World: Songs by Stephen Sondheim,* see HELLERM1

The Marian McPartland Trio/*Live at Yoshi's Nitespot,* Concord Jazz CCD-4712, 1996

Orchestra Manhattan (Byron Olson)/*Digital Broadway* (1986), see ORCHESTRAMAN1 [instrumental]

Pizzarelli, Bucky & John/*Solos & Duets,* Jazz Classics JZCL-5007, 1997 (2 Guitars)

Ramey, Sam/*Sam Ramey on Broadway/So in Love,* Teldec 4509-90865-2, 1993

Ripley, Alice & Emily Skinner/*Unsuspecting Hearts,* Varese Sarabande 302 066 074 2, 1999

Ross, Steve/*Steve Ross Live at the Algonquin,* Stolen Moments SM 1939, 1986

Streisand, Barbra/*The Broadway Album,* see STREISAND1

Wilk, Oystein/*Too Many Mornings,* see WILKO1 [in medley]

Young, Thomas/*Clair De Lune & Sister Moon,* Ocean Records/Allegra, 1997

"Professors' Reports" from *Phinney's Rainbow* (1948)

Prologos, see "Invocation and Instructions to the Audience"

"Prologue" from *Follies,* see "Overture"

"Prologue" from *Into the Woods,* see "Into the Woods" and "So Happy"

"Prologue" (sung version) cut from *West Side Story,* see "Opening"

"Puccini" cut from *Do I Hear a Waltz?* (1965), music by Richard Rodgers

"Puppy Love" from *By George* (1946)

"Putting It Together" from *Sunday in the Park with George* (1984) [in addition to the changed lyrics cited below, Sondheim also wrote a set of lyrics that were performed by Bernadette Peters at the 66th Academy Awards Ceremony in 1994]
   ASIII Streisand version g-e^2, BSBA g-d^2, SPGPVS company number [George's range is c^1-g$\flat^2$]
   Sunday in the Park . . . Original Cast (Mandy Patinkin, Company), see SUNDAYIN1
   Putting It Together (Stephen Collins, Rachel York, Michael Rupert, Julie Andrews, Christopher Durang, Scott Frankel), see PUTTINGIT1 [lyric changes by *Sondheim*]
   Stephen Sondheim Songs (instrumental accompaniment), see STEPHENSS1
   Anthony, Julie/*Julie Anthony Live at the Tilbury,* Cue/Polygram ORO21, 1996
   Orchestra Manhattan (Byron Olson)/*Digital Broadway* (1986), see ORCHESTRAMAN1 [instrumental]
   Starobin, David/*New Music with Guitar, Volume 3* (Patrick Mason), see STAROBIND1
   Streisand, Barbra/*The Broadway Album,* see STREISAND1 [lyric changes by Sondheim]
   Streisand, Barbra/*Timeless,* see STREISAND3

"The Q-Ladies' Waltz" from *Phinney's Rainbow* (1948)

"Quintet," see "Tonight (Quintet)" from *West Side Story*

"Rag Me That Mendelssohn March" from *A Mighty Man Is He* (1955)

"Rain on the Roof" from *Follies* (1971)
   FPVS duet b$\flat$-d^2 [both]
   Follies in Concert (Betty Comden, Adolph Green), see FOLLIES02
   Follies London Cast (Pearl Carr, Teddy Johnson), see FOLLIES03
   Follies, The Complete Recording (Natalie Mosco, Donald Saddler), see FOLLIES05

"Rainbows" for unproduced film version of *Into the Woods (1996)*

"Ready for the Woods," see "Moments in the Woods"

"The Reason Why" from *By George* (1946)

"Recent Past" from *Stavisky* (1974)
Stavisky (instrumental), see STAVISKY1

"Reds" *Theme from the Motion Picture "Reds"* from *Reds* (1981), [see also "Goodbye for Now"]
Piano score, Columbia Pictures Publications 1482RMX
Reds Soundtrack, see REDS1

"Remember?" from *A Little Night Music* (1973)
ASI, LNMVS solo version $c^{\sharp1}$-g^2, LNMPVS vocal quintet
A Little Night Music Original Cast (Barbara Lang, Beth Fowler, Teri Ralston, Benjamin Ralston, Gene Varrone), see LITTLEN01
A Little Night Music London Cast (John J. Moore, Chris Melville, Liz Robertson, David Bexon, Jacquey Chappell), see LITTLEN02
A Little Night Music Studio Cast (Dinah Harris, Hilary Western, Susan Flannery, Michael Bulman, Martin Nelson), see LITTLEN04
Sondheim: A Celebration at Carnegie Hall (Ron Baker, Peter Blanchet, Carol Meyer, Bronwyn Thomas, Blythe Walker), see SONDACELATC1
Putting It Together (Stephen Collins, Julie Andrews), see PUTTINGIT1
The Great Waltz (Hollywood Bowl Orchestra), see HOLLYWOODB1 [part of "The Night Waltzes"]
A Little Night Music Royal National Theatre (Morag McLaren, Di Botcher, Ernestina Quarcoo, Stephen Hanley, Tim Goodwin), see LITTLEN05
A Little Night Music Barcelona Cast (Xavier Fernandez, Teresa de la Torre, Muntsa Rius, Anna Feu, Alberto Demestres), see LITTLEN06
Patinkin, Mandy/*Oscar and Steve*, see PATINKIN4 [in medley]
Trotter, Terry/*Stephen Sondheim's A Little Night Music*, see TROTTERT1 [piano solo]

"Rich and Happy" from *Merrily We Roll Along* (1981) [replaced by "That Frank" in subsequent productions]
MWRPVS c^1-g^2 + company
Merrily We Roll Along Original Cast (Jim Walton, Company), see MERRILY1
Putting It Together (Stephen Collins, Julie Andrews, Michael Rupert, Christopher Durang, Rachel York, see PUTTINGIT1 [lyric changes by Sondheim]

"The Right Girl" from *Follies* (1971)
FPVS c^1-f^2
Follies Original Cast (Gene Nelson), see FOLLIES01
Follies in Concert (Mandy Patinkin), see FOLLIES02

Follies London Cast (David Healy), see FOLLIES03
Follies, The Complete Recording (Tony Roberts), see FOLLIES05

"Riot at the Funeral" from the 1966 film of *A Funny Thing Happened on the Way to the Forum*
A Funny Thing . . . Film (instrumental), see FUNNY03

"The Road You Didn't Take" from *Follies* (1971)
FPVS a-e^2
Follies Original Cast (John McMartin), see FOLLIES01
Follies in Concert (George Hearn), see FOLLIES02
Follies, The Complete Recording (Laurence Guittard), see FOLLIES05
Patinkin, Mandy/*Experiment*, see PATINKIN3

"Rose's Turn" from *Gypsy* (1959), music by Jule Styne
GPVS g-c^2
Gypsy Original Cast (Ethel Merman), see GYPSY01
Gypsy Film (Rosalind Russell), see GYPSY02
Gypsy London Cast (Angela Lansbury), see GYPSY03
Stairway to the Stars (Dolores Gray), First Night CD6021, 1989
Gypsy Revival Cast (Tyne Daly), see GYPSY04
Gypsy TV Cast (Bette Midler), see GYPSY05
Celebrating Gypsy . . . (Libby Morris), see CELEBRATGYP
Kay Medford in "Gypsy" (Kay Medford), see GYPSY09
Buckley, Betty/*An Evening at Carnegie Hall*, see BUCKLEYB3
Buckley, Betty/*The London Concert*, see BUCKLEYB2
Connelli, Judy/*Back to Before—A Life in Song*, ABC 461 883-2, 2001
MacKenzie, Gisele/ . . . *In Person at the Empire Room of the Waldorf-Astoria*, Everest LPBR 5069, 1960 [in medley]
Merman, Ethel/*Mermania!*, see MERMANE1 [early version titled "Mama's Turn"]
Turner, Geraldine/ . . . *Sings the Stephen Sondheim Songbook, Vol. 2*, see TURNERG2

"Routine Blues" from *By George* (1946)

"The Rumble" from *West Side Story* (1957), no lyric, music by Leonard Bernstein

"Salon at the Claridge #1" from *Stavisky* (1974) [based on "Yes" for *The Jet-Propelled Couch*]
Stavisky (instrumental), see STAVISKY1
Bennett, Richard Rodney/*A Different Side of Sondheim*, see BENNETTR1

"Salon at the Claridge #2 " from *Stavisky* (1974) [based on "Who Could Be Blue?" cut from *Follies*]
Stavisky[1] (instrumental), see STAVISKY1
Sandford, Luke/*Shimmer*, see SANDFORD1 [piano solo]

"Sand" for *Singing Out Loud* (1992–93, unproduced)
ASIV c^1-f^2
Sondheim at the Movies (Christiane Noll), see SONDATTHEM1

"Saturday Night" from *Saturday Night* (1954)
ASIV, SNVS quartet a-f^2
Marry Me a Little (Craig Lucas, Suzanne Henry), see MARRYME1
A Stephen Sondheim Evening (Company), see STEPHENSE1
Unsung Sondheim (Stan Chandler, David Engel, Larry Raben, Guy Stroman), see UNSUNGS1
Saturday Night Bridewell Cast (Maurice Yeoman, James Millard, Simon Greiff, Jeremy David), see SATURDAYN1
Saturday Night Original New York Cast (Michael Benjamin Washington, Kirk McDonald, Greg Zola, Joey Sorge), see SATURDAYN2

Saturday Night (reprise) from *Saturday Night* (1954)
Saturday Night Bridewell Cast (Maurice Yeoman, Simon Greiff, Jeremy David, James Millard), see SATURDAYN1
Saturday Night Original New York Cast (Michael Benjamin Washington, Kirk McDonald, Greg Zola, Joey Sorge), see SATURDAYN2 [2 versions]

"Searching" from *Sweeney Todd* (1979)
STPVS company number
Sweeney Todd Original Cast (Angela Lansbury, Len Cariou), see SWEENEYT1
Sweeney Todd Barcelona Cast (Vicky Pena, Constantino Romero), see SWEENEYT3

"Seattle to Los Angeles," see "Some People"

"Second Letter" from *Passion* (1995)
PPVS duet a-a^1 [both]
Passion Original Cast (Marrin Mazsie, Jere Shea), see PASSION1
Passion London Concert (Helen Hobson, Michael Ball), see PASSION3

"Second Midnight" from *Into the Woods* (1987)
ITWPVS company number [spoken]

"Second Midnight" cut from *Into the Woods* (1987)

"Secret of Night" from *Stavisky* (1974)
    Stavisky (instrumental), see STAVISKY1

"See What It Gets You" from *Anyone Can Whistle* (1964)
    Anyone Can Whistle Original Cast (Lee Remick), see ANYONE1
    Anyone Can Whistle Live at Carnegie Hall (Bernadette Peters), see ANYONE2
    Mendelssohn Choir/*Mendelssohn Sings Sondheim*, see MENDELSSOHN1
    [with "Anyone Can Whistle"]

"Send in the Clowns" from *A Little Night Music* (1973)
    ASI, BSBA [additional lyrics], LNMVS, SCCH, SSS a♭-b♭¹, LNMPVS g♭-a♭¹
    A Little Night Music Original Cast² (Glynis Johns), see LITTLEN01
    A Trip to the Circus, Silver Touch Tunes for Children SS1000, 1978
    A Little Night Music London Cast (Jean Simmons), see LITTLEN02
    Side by Side by Sondheim (Millicent Martin), see SIDEBYS1
    Side by Side . . . Australian Cast (Jill Perryman), see SIDEBYS2
    Songs of Sondheim Irish Cast (Gemma Craven), see SONGSOFSOND1
    A Little Night Music Film (Elizabeth Taylor), see LITTLEN03
    Music Box Waltzes and Popular Tunes (performed on the Porter twin disc music box), Porter Music Box [n.n.], 1984
    Sondheim (Book-of-the-Month) (Joyce Castle), see SOND1
    A Little Sondheim Music (Rickie Weiner-Gole, Dale Morich), see LITTLES1
    A Little Night Music Studio Cast (Sian Phillips), see LITTLEN04
    *A Stephen Sondheim Evening*¹ (Angela Lansbury, *Sondheim* at the piano), see STEPHENSE1
    Songs of Stephen Sondheim/You Sing the Hits, see SONGSOFSTEP1
    Met Stars on Broadway (Renata Scotto), MET/RCA MET-204, 1980, MET 204CD, 1989
    Aspects of West Side Story, A Little Night Music . . . (Orchestra of the Americas), ProArte CDB 8303, 1992
    The Magic of the Musicals (Marti Webb & Mark Rattray), see MAGICOF1
    A Broadway Celebration, see BROADWAYCE1
    Everyone's a Love Song, see EVERYONE1
    Symphonic Sondheim (Instrumental), see SYMPHONICSON1
    Sondheim: A Celebration at Carnegie Hall (Glenn Close), see SONDACELATC1
    A Little Night Music Royal National Theatre (Judi Dench), see LITTLEN05
    A Little Light Music (Beryl Korman and/or Julia Meadows), see LITTLEL1
    Showcase: The Musicals (Mary Carewe), Carlton Sounds/U.K. 30367 00672, 1995
    *Sondheim: A Celebration*³ (Glynis Johns), see SONDACEL2
    Scarlet and Gold Concert Royal Festival Hall, The Massed Bands of the Household Division (Grenadier Guards), The Valentine Music Group BNA 5131, 1997
    Broadway Classics, Victorian Arts Centre's "Morning Melodies" Volume 4 [n.n., Australia], 1998

Hey, Mr. Producer! (Judi Dench), see HEYMRP

Hey, Mr. Producer! (Stephen Sondheim, Andrew Lloyd Webber), see "Dueling Pianos"

Celebrating the Musicals . . . (Anita Dobson), see CELEBRATTHEM

More West End The Concert (Deborah Myers), see MOREWEST

Sondheim Tonight (Cleo Laine, Maria Friedman, Clive Rowe), see SONDTON1

A Little Night Music Barcelona Cast (Vicky Pena), see LITTLEN06

Adams Quintet, George/*Paradise Space Shuttlee*, Muse Records [n.n.], 1979

Akers, Karen/*Presenting Karen Akers*, Blackwood 81-750091, 1981; Rizzoli 1001

Allen Trio, Bob/*Bob Allen Trio Live*, Tetrachord Records 103142, 1980

Anderson, Ernestine/*Hello Like Before*, Concord Jazz CJ-31, 1977, CD CCD-4031

Andreas, Jamey/*Touched to My Tenderness—Guitar Classics*, Rebirth Records 3750, 1998

Andrews, Vince/*Hey, Vince!*, Gerard Records GR 1022, 1984 [saxophone]

Anthony, Julie/*You and I*, Polygram [n.n.], 1995/U&I, 1996

Apollo Stompers/*Phantasies II*, Soul Note 121175-2, 1991 [piano, jazz ensemble]

Arbors, The/*The Arbors*, Arbors Music Prod. Corp AR-67701, 197[?]

Arpin, John/*Broadway Baroque*, Pro-Arte/Fanfare RCD 451, 1990 [piano]

Artie Butler's Hollywood Rainbow Pops/*Classic Broadway*, K-tel International [n.n.], 1995

Arundel Middle School Concert Band/*Variations*, Recorded Publications Z573901 - 2573902, 1981

Auldridge, Mike/*Slidin' Smoke*, Flying Fish 080, 1979

Baker, Chet/*Live at Ronnie Scotts* (vocal: Van Morrison), DRG 91440, 1987

Ball, Michael/*Centre Stage*, Hip-O 440 016 071-2, 2001

Band of the Royal Irish Regiment/*Symphonic Celebration.* Bandleader 5147, 1999

Barduhn Big Band, Dave/*Dave Barduhn Big Band*, Barduhn RL-5135, 1977

Bassey, Shirley/*Good, Bad But Beautiful*, United Artists Records UA-LA542-G 0698, 1975

Bassey, Shirley/*I Am What I Am*, Towerbell Records VG 651 600065, 1984

Berner, Kenny/*Beauty Secrets*, BMG/RCAVictor 74321-69904-2, 1999

Bilk, Acker/*20 Greatest Hits*, Pye Records MCAB 20, 1977

Bilk, Acker/*The Best of Acker Bilk*, GNP Crescendo Records GNPD 2116, 1989 [clarinet and strings]

Blair Woodwind Quintet, Blair School of Music BSM-420, 198[?]

Boston Pops Orchestra/*The Two Sides of Fiedler*, London SPC 21190, 1979

Boston Pops Orchestra/*That's Entertainment*/*Pops on Broadway*, Philips 7144 124, 6302 124, 198[?]

Boston Pops Orchestra/*The Two Sides of Fiedler*, Decca MOR 527, 1979

Boston Pops Orchestra/*That's Entertainment*, Philips 416 499-2, 1981 [with "Night Waltz"]

Boston Pops/*Music of the Night*/*Pops on Broadway*, see BOSTON2 [instrumental]

Breau, Lenny & Brad Terry/*The Living Room Tapes: Volume 2*, Musical Heritage Society MHS 512627L, 1990 [guitar, clarinet]

Brewer, Teresa/*Teresa Brewer's New Album*, Image Records IM-306, 1977

Brewer, Teresa/*Teresa Brewer*, Audiofidelity Enterprises GAS-738, 1983

Britto, Carol & Michael Moore/*Inner Voices*, Town Crier TC 512, 1985 [piano, bass]

Bronhill, June/*June Bronhill at the Sydney Opera House*, M7 MLF-118, 1976 [reissued by BroadMusic BRCD073, or 510739, 1996]

Buckley, Betty/*The London Concert*, see BUCKLEYB2

Buckley, Betty/*Stars and Moon*/Live at the Donmar, Concord CCD-4949-2, 2001

Cacia, Paul Jazz Orchestra/*Quantum Leap: Digital Neophonics*, Outstanding Records OUTS 056, 1986

Cacia, Paul/*Quantum Leap*, Happy Hour Music [n.n.], 1987

Caine, Marti/*Marti*, BBC 17310 70042, 1994

Callicrate, Tim/*Serenade from Tahoe*, T. Callicrate TC100, 1988 [piano]

Canadian Brass/*Brass on Broadway*, Philips 442-133-2, 1994

Candlelight and Wine, CSP P2 15030, 1979 [Hagood Hardy]

Carreras, Jose/*Amigos para Siempre: Friends for Life: Romantic Songs of the World*, Atlantic 82413-2, 1992

Carroll, Barbara/*Barbara Carroll*, Blue Note [n.n.], 1976 [piano & instruments]

Castle Singers/*Cruisin' Down the River*, Design Studios [n.n.], 1984

Caymmi, Dori/*If Eve . . .*, Qwest/Warner Bros. 9 45604-2, 1994 [guitar, with Toots Thielemans on harmonica]

Clark, Petula/*My Greatest*, Madacy SA-2-6401, 1990[?]

Clef Hangers/*Take II: Carolina Fight Songs*, Clef Hangers, 1990? [A cappella men's chorus]

Coates, John F./ *Rainbow Road*, Omnisound N-1024, 1979 [Jazz piano]

Collins, Judy/*Judith*, Direct Disc Labs, SD 1660, 1976

Collins, Judy/*Judith*, Elektra 6E-111, 7E-1032, 1975

Collins, Judy/*Classic Broadway*, Platinum 15095-3752-2, 1999

Collins, Judy/*So Early in the Spring: The First 15 Years*, WEA Music of Canada, Elektra CEKJ-6002, 1977

Como, Perry/*For the Good Times*, Telstar STAR 2235, 1983

Como, Perry/*Perry Como Live on Tour*, RCA Victor, AQL1-3826, 1981

Conniff Singers, Ray/*Send in the Clowns*, Columbia KC 34170, 1976

Cook, Barbara/*Barbara Cook Sings Mostly Sondheim*, see COOKB1

Corry, Peter/*Peter Corry in Concert*, Pet Cor CD 001, 2001 [with "Losing My Mind"; recorded in 1993]

Crosby, Bing/*That's What Life Is All About*, United Artists Records [n.n.], 1976

Crosby, Bing/*Bing Crosby Live at the London Palladium*, K-Tel NE 951, 1976

Cruz, Edgar/*Those Were the Days*, ECI Recordings ECICS03, 1992 [guitar]

Damone, Vic/*Vic Damone in San Francisco*, Rebecca R-1214, 1979

Domingo, Placido/*The Broadway I Love*, see DOMINGO1

Dearie, Blossom/*1975 Vol. II*, Daffodil Records BMD 102 A&B, 1975

Denver Symphony Orchestra/*Fiedler's Favorites*, Maxiplay Pops CDM 8012, 1989

Denver Symphony Pops/*A Touch of Fiedler*, Pro-Arte Digital CDD 452, 1989

Dow, Judith/*Regards to Broadway*, see DOWJ1

East Tennessee School Band and Orchestra Association/*1981 All East Tennessee Clinic*, [Silver] Crest Records ET-1981, 1981?

Eaton, John/*Horchow Presents John Eaton*, [Horchow,] 409427, 1984 [piano]

Eckels, Steven/*Solo Guitar*, Eckels 37829, 1980 [guitar]

Elmhurst College Jazz Band/*Just Friends*, Elmhurst College, Music Dept. EC-1981, 1981

Ensemble Clarinesque/*Fascinating Rhythm*, Signum SIG 76-00, 1996

Faith, Percy/Summer Place '76, Columbia KC 33915, 1975

Ferrante & Teicher/*Killing Me Softly*, United Artists 1973 [two pianos]

Ferrante & Teicher/*30th Anniversary on Stage*, Bainbridge BT-8003, 1983

Fest, Manfredo/*Manifestations*, Tabu Records, 1979 [jazz ensemble]

Fiedler, Arthur/*The Two Sides of Fiedler*, London SPC5-21190, 1979

Fisher, [David] Du Du/*Over the Rainbow*, Helicon Records HL 8064, 1989 [in Hebrew]

Fisher, David "Dudu" and London Symphony Orchestra/*Showstoppers*, Pickwick Music PY, PK-4141, 1993

Florida State University Marching Chiefs, The/*FSU Marching Chiefs*, [n.l., n.n.], 1986

Florida Symphonic Pops/*The Phantom of the Opera*, see FLORIDA1 [instrumental]

Forrester, Maureen/*From Kern to Sondheim: Great American Theater Songs*, Fanfare CDD 374, 1984

Forsyth, Dianne/*Lady of the Landing*, Sun-Scape Records, KGOM 16, 1982

Forty-Five Minutes of Broadway, B. Keck and P. Demaree [n.n.], 1986

Francis Moore Orchesta/*Memories: Vol. 1.*, Bridge 100.011-2, 1987

Fredonia Brass Band, Mark Educational Recordings, Inc. MCBS-20736, 1986

Galway Pops Orchestra, James/*The Wind Beneath My Wings*, RCA Victor 60862-2-RC, 1991 [flute with orchestra]

Gay Men's Chorus of Los Angeles/*Simply Sondheim*, see GAYMENSCLA1

George Street/*George Street Live*, George Street Production GGS3424, 1984? [vocal group]

Gillies, Jodie/*Jodie Gillies*, TVD 93371 (Festival Records), [n.d.]

Go for Baroque/*Andante*, [n.l., n.n.] 1993[?] [instrumental group]

Goodman/*Live at Carnegie Hall: 40th Anniversary Concert*, London 422 820 349-4R-2, 1978 [clarinet and band]

Goodman, Benny/*Seven Come Eleven*, Columbia FC 38265, 1982

Goodman, Benny/*Benny Goodman and Friends*, Decca Record Co. 820 179-2, 1984

Gorme, Eydie/*Since I Fell for You*, Applause Records APLP 1002, 1981

Gorme, Eydie/*Eydie Gorme Sings/Canta*, President Records, PRCD 238, 1985

Greene, Ted/*Solo Guitar*, PMP Records A-5010, 1977, 1979 [guitar]

Grenadier Guards/*On Stage* (Anthony Lamb), Bandleader [n.n.], 1996

Griffin, Harvi/*Phase Three*, [n.l.] 40093, 1985[?] [harp]

Gustavus Adolphus College Band/*The Gustavus Stage Band: The Adolphus Stage Band*, Mark [Custom Recordings], 1980

Hall, Lani/*Sweet Bird*, A & M Records SP-4617, 1976

Hall Lani/*Lani Hall*, A&M Records CD 2517, 1987

Hamaty, Renee & Mystic Moods/*Stormy Memories*, Bainbridge BCD 6284, 1990 [New-Age piano]

Hardy, Hagood/*Maybe Tomorrow*, Capitol ST-11552, 1976 [piano and vibraphone with orchestra]

Harmon, Sally/*Snap, Classical Pop!*, Soulo SP108, 1991 [piano]

Hartman, Johnny/*This One's for Tedi*, Audiophile (D)AP-181, ACD-181, 1985, 1988

Hatch, David Glen/*My Romantic Favorites*, Covenant CCID-2800578, 1991 [piano]

Heller, Marc/*Take Me to the World: Songs by Stephen Sondheim*, see HELLERM1

Henderson, Bill/*Live at the Times*, Trend/Discovery Records DSCD-779, 1987

Hickland, Catherine/ . . . *Sincerely, Broadway*, After Nine [n.n.], 1997

Hirt, Al/*Candlelite Music Proudly Presents the Living Legend of Al Hirt*, Candlelite Music CU-754, 1983 [trumpet]

Hirt, Al/*A Living Legend*, ERA Records NU 9174, 1984

Houston Pops Orchestra/*Live from Carnegie*, The Orchestra H.P.O. 1001, 1977?

Houston Pops Orchestra/*Top of the Pops*, Tioch Records TD 1010, 1983

Hubbard, Edwin/*Edwin Hubbard*, Prana PL 12372, 1982 [flute, jazz ensemble]

Indiana University Jazz Ensemble/*Guest Recital*, [n.l., n.n.], 1988 [trombone ensemble]

Indios Tabajaras/*Beautiful Sounds*, RCA AFL1-3990, BMG Music 2379-2-RL, 1981 [guitar]

Jackie & Roy/*A Stephen Sondheim Collection*, see JACKIE&1

Jazz at the Movies Band/*Sax on Broadway*, Discovery 77068, 1997

Jenson Publications/*Marching Band '87: Vol. 1*, Jenson Publications, JP-8800, 1987

Jenson Publications/*New Music for Concert Band: Vol. 27*, Jenson Publications, HLP-74, 1990

Jo, Sumi/*Only Love*, Erato 8573-80241-2, 2000

John Bauer Brass/*John Bauer Brass*, Proprius PRCD 9163, 1997 [brass quintet; Swedish]

Jones, Grace/*Portfolio*, Island ILPS 9470, 1976

Jones, Jack/*The Full Life*, RCA APK1-2067, 1977

Keel, Howard/*With Love: For Yesterday and Today*, Silver Eagle Records SE 1026, 1984

Kenton, Stan/*Kenton '76*, Creative World ST1076, 1976, GNP/Crescendo Records STD 1076, 1991 [big band]

Kenton, Stan/*Street of Dreams*, Creative World [n.n.], 1979

Kidd, Carol/*That's Me*, Linn Records AKD 044, 1995

King, Morgana/*Portraits*, Muse Records MC 5301, 1984

Knorr Orchestra, Johnny/*Let's Go Dancing*, New Image Records NR 10294, 1980 [big band]

Kostelanetz, Andre/*Andre Kostelanetz Plays Broadway's Greatest Hits: From Annie, I Love My Wife, Side by Side by Sondheim, The King and I*, Columbia PC 34864, 1977

L.A. Connection/*Big Hits: Vol. III*, Springboard International SPB-4094, SLX-02487, 1977

Laine, Cleo/*A Beautiful Thing*, RCA Victor CPL1-5059, 1974

Laine, Cleo/*Cleo Laine Live at Carnegie Hall*, RCA Victor AYL1-3751, AFL1-5015, 09026-60960-2, 1973, 1974, 1975

Laine, Cleo/*Cleo Sings Sondheim*, see LAINEC2

Laine, Cleo/*Themes*, Sierra Records FEDC 2000, 1978[?]

Laine, Frankie/*Now and Then*, CSP P 15166, 1980

Larsen, Lyn/*Give My Regards!*, ProArte CDD 339, 1987 [organ]

Leahey Trio, Harry/*Still Waters*, Omnisound N 1031, 1980 [jazz trio]

Lear, Evelyn/*Evelyn Lear Sings Sondheim and Bernstein*, see LEARE1

LeMel, Gary/*How Fast Forever Goes*, Headfirst 10142, 1991

Lettermen/*The Time Is Right*, Capitol SW-11470, 1975 [vocal group]

Liberace/*Liberace's 40th Anniversary Collection*, Silver Eagle Records CE6651, 1984–1985

Liberace/*Showstoppers*, AVI AVIC-6071 Avi, 1979 [piano]

Lindroth, Lloyd/*Love Drops*, [n.l.] C-LL-100, 198[?] [harp]

Line, Lorie/*Out of Line*, Time Line Productions [n.n.], 1989 [piano]

Living Strings/*After the Lovin'*, Pickwick ACL-7039, 1977

Living Strings/*Feelings*, RCA APL1-2383, 1977 [instrumental]

London Brass/*Clowning Around: London Brass Entertains*, Teldec 2292-46069-2, 1990 [brass ensemble]

London Philharmonic Orchestra/*Broadway Gold*, Audio Award AA-101, 1981

London Philharmonic Orchestra/*A Pops Concert with the London Philharmonic Orchestra, Hits from 16 Shows*, Stage & Screen Productions SSC-710, 1983

Love Singers, Geoff/*Very Special Love Songs*, Moss Music Group MMG B-703, 1977

Lyles, Al/*My Shining Hour*, Alcraft Records A00-1, 1980

MacNeil, Madeline/*Soon It's Going to Rain*, Kicking Mule Records KMC-244, 1985 [vocals, hammer dulcimer, acc.]

Mancini, Henry/*Romantic Piano & Orchestra*, Readers' Digest RDK 5953, 1989, 1981

Manilow, Barry/*The Complete Collection and Then Some*, Arista 07822-18714-2, 1992

Mantovani Orchestra/*14 Dream Melodies*, CDMA : Soundsational CDMA-4012, 1978[?]

Mantovani Orchestra/*The Greatest Gift Is Love*, London Records LEF 5913, 1975

Mantovani Orchestra/*Live at Royal Festival Hall: Vol. II*, Bellaphon, 288-07-013, 1985

Mantovani Orchestra/*The Magic of Mantovani*, LDMI EGBR 2517, 198?

Mantovani Orchestra/*The Magic of the Mantovani Orchestra: Live at Royal Festival Hall*, Bainbridge BT 8001, BCD8001, RCA 224536, 1981

Mantovani Orchestra/*Mantovani*, Delta Music Inc. 15134, 79008 1990

Mantovani Orchestra/*Mantovani and His Orchestra: Live*, InterTape 500.005, 1987

Mantovani Orchestra/*Mantovani Magic*, Telstar Records/RCA STAC 2237, 1983

Mantovani Orchestra/*Mantovani Orchestra: A Tribute*, Breakaway Records BWY 80 & 81, 1983

Mantovani Orchestra/*Mantovani Salutes America's Great Songwriters*, London C213621, 1977

Marie, Gayle/*Lost and Found*, Gayleo GM003, 1988

Martens Paul & Donna/*First Gatherings*, Fat Patches Music ST-LP 2291, 197[?]

Martin, Wanda Mae/*Jubilation*, WM Productions [n.n.], 1979 [music for floor exercise]

Martino, Pat & Gil Goldstein/*We'll Be Together Again*, Muse Records [n.n.], 1976 [jazz piano & quitar]

Mathis, Johnny/*I Only Have Eyes for You*, Columbia AL or PC 34117, 1976

Mathis, Johnny/*Johnny Mathis Looks at Love*, CBS BT 16640, 1982

McCroby, Ron/*Breezin' the Classics*, Intersound, Inc. PAD 258 Pro Arte Digital, 1985 [whistler with the Arion Consort]

McCutcheon, Jim/*Jim McCutcheon & Company: Solos and Ensembles with Classical Guitar*, Guitar & Song 1002, 1986

McGlohon, Loonis/*Loonis in London*, Audiophile AP-166, 1982

McKenzie, Julia/*The Musicals Album*, see MCKENZIEJ1

McPartland, Marian/*A Fine Romance*, Improv 7115, 1976 [piano with jazz ensemble]

McPartland, Marian/*Solo Concert at Haverford*, Halcyon HAL 111, 1974, CD 111, 1990? [piano]

McRae, Carmen/*Carmen McCrae*, Who's Who in Jazz WWLP 21020, 1981

McRae, Carmen/*Sarah, Dedicated to You*, Novus/BMG Music (RCA) 3110-2-N, 1990

McVay, Ray & His Orchestra/*Playing Music from the Hit Parade*, Theatreland DS008 Dansan Records, 1979

Mendelssohn Choir/*Mendelssohn Sings Sondheim* (Kathryn Gibson, Todd Kuczawa), see MENDELSSOHN1

Mercer, Mabel/*Echoes of My Life*, Audiophile AP-161 and AP-162, 1980

Merman, Ethel & Mary Martin/*Together on Broadway* [n.l., n.n., n.d.]

Mottola, Tony/*I Only Have Eyes for You*, Project 3 PR 5094Sd, 1975 [guitar with orchestra]

Murphy, Julie/*Sophisticated Lady*, Melrose Records [n.n.], 1996

Mustin, Dene/*Dene Mustin Sings Your Requests*, Audiophile AP-134, [n.d.]

Nalle, Billy/*Billy Live!*, Wichita Theatre Organ WTO 1460, 1984 [organ]

Nero, Peter/*Peter Goes Pop*, Applause Records APLP 1013, 1982, Allegiance Records AVCD-5040, 1987

Nero, Peter/*The Wiz*, Crystal Clear Records CCS-6001, 1977 [piano]

New England Conservatory/*The Enchanted Circle Presents Harvey G. Phillips, Tuba: December 11, 1984, 8:00 p.m.*, [n.l., n.n., n.d.]

Newsome, Tommy/*Live from Beautiful Downtown Burbank*, Direct-Disc Labs DD103, 1978 [big band]

New Virginians/*Act III*, Major Recording Co. MRLP 2224, 197[?] [vocal group]

Nicholson, Carla & Michael/*Just Duet*, see NICHOLSONC1

Noel, Dick/*A Time for Love*, Legend Records SGS-5002, 1985

O'Brien, Sarah/*Dans Mes Rêves Je Reviens/In My Dreams I Return*, Orchard 1856, 2000

O'Connor, Larry/*Life in the Suburbs*, [n.l.], 41321, 1983[?]

O'Day, Anita/*Angel Eyes*, Emily ER-13081, 1981

Ogden, Nigel/*This Is the Moment*, Bandleader 8002, 2000

O'Meara, Serena/*Collage*, O'Meara Enterprises [n.n.], 199[?] [harp]

Opus II/*Music for Oboe and Guitar*, Fine Arts Recordings [n.n.], 1985

Orchestra Manhattan (Byron Olson)/*Digital Broadway* (1986), see OR-CHESTRAMAN1 [instrumental]

Paducah Tilghman High School Concert/*Symphonic and Jazz Bands* (Jetton Jr. High School Band, Brazelton Jr. High School Band), Audio Creations AC00087A, 1979, 1980

Paige, Elaine/*A Musical Touch of Elaine Paige*, Dominion Records DN 6221, 1984

Paige, Elaine/*Stages*, Atlantic 7 81776-1, 1987

Pandolfi, Emile/*By Request*, MagicMusic MMC-901, 1990 [piano]

Parris, Rebecca/*Double Rainbow*, Weston-Blair Productions BEC-3, 1987

Patterson, Frank/*Frank Patterson's Broadway*, Rego Irish Records & Tape [n.n.], 1995

Peacock, Christopher/*Pianoforte, Opus 1: Popular Requests*, [n.l., n.n., n.d.]

Penn State Blue Band/*1976 Penn State University Marching Blue Band*, Mark MC-9128, 1976?

Pizzarelli, Bucky/*Bucky's Bunch*, Monmouth Evergreen Records MES/7082, 198? [jazz band]

Prior, Marina/*Somewhere*, see PRIORM1

Ralston, Bob/*Feelings*, Ranwood R-8158, 1976 [keyboard/organ]

Random Lake High School Band and Choir/*Spring Concert 1979*, [n.l., n.n., n.d.]

Rawls, Lou/*Lou Rawls Live*, CBS/Philadelphia International [n.n.], 1978

Reeves, Dianne/*The Calling: Celebrating Sarah Vaughan*, Blue Note 2435-27694-2, 2001

Rochester Pops Orchestra/*Opening Night*, see ROCHESTERP1 [instrumental]

Ross, Diana/*An Evening with Diana Ross*, Motown Record Co. 3746352682, 1992, M7-877R2, 1977

Roy Budd Trio/*Everything's Coming Up Roses: The Musical . . . Sondheim*, see ROYBUDD1

Royal Scot Dragoon Guards/*In the Finest Tradition*, Attic Records Limited BLC-178 Attic/Bandleader, 1988, BNA 5017 [bagpipe and band]

Rubin, Vanessa/*I'm Glad There Is You*, RCA/BMG 01241 63170-2, 1994

Salonisti/*Transatlantic*, London Records 425 210-2, 1989 [salon orchestra]

Saxe, Emily/*Broadway & All That Jazz*, see SAXEE1

Schneider, Helen/*Right as the Rain*, Tomato R2 72244, 1995

Scott, Lee/*Lee Scott Volume 1*, Blue Heron 101, 1980 [jazz piano]

Scott's Pipes & Strings of Scotland, Tommy: *Vol 2: 'Tis a Gift*, Scotdisc KITV 394, 1985, CDITV 394, 1987 [bagpipe]

Send in the Clowns, Golden West College [n.n.], 1983[?] [recorded accompaniments]

Send in the Clowns, 20th Century Fox Records, 1979 (Walter Jackson?)

Shaw Bell Choir, Dorothy/*Here a Christmas-There a Christmas*, January Sound Studios JSS-DSBC-83, 1983? [handbells]

Shearing, George/*My Ship*, Verve/Polygram/MPS 821664-2, 821 664-1(2), G-22369, 1975, 1987? [piano]

Short, Bobby/*Live at the Cafe Carlyle*, see SHORTB1

Sims, Zoot/*Nirvana*, Groove Merchant GM 533, 1974

Sims, Zoot/*Somebody Loves Me*, Denon DC-8514, 1987

Sims, Zoot/*Somebody Loves Me*, LRC Ltd. CDC-8514, 1989

Sims, Zoot & Bucky Pizzarelli/*Send in the Clowns*, M.C.R. Productions 2625082, 1990

Sims, Zoot and Buddy Rich/*Zoot Sims*, CBS Records BT 18079, 1979

Sinatra, Frank/*Ol' Blue Eyes Is Back*, Reprise 2155-2, 1973

Sinatra, Frank/*The Reprise Collection*, Reprise 9 26349-2, 1990

Sinatra, Frank/*Sinatra Reprise: The Very Good Years*, Reprise 9 26501-2, 1991

Sinatra, Frank/*The Voice*, Dominion DN 6212, 1983

Singing Hoosiers in Concert, 1981, Indiana University School of Music no. 671

Singing Hoosiers in Concert, 1982, Indiana University School of Music no. 683

Singing Hoosiers in Concert, 1983, Indiana University School of Music no. 766

Singing Hoosiers in Concert, 1986, Indiana University School of Music no. 504

Singers Unlimited/*A Little Light Music* (Beryl Korman), see SINGERSUN1

SoundStroke/*Laser Woodcuts*, Second Hearing GS 9008, 1986

Starlight Orchestra/*Love Songs from the Movies*, Object Enterprise OP0038, 1991

Steele, Joan/*'Round Midnight*, Audiophile AP-94, 1976

Strazzeri, Frank/*Relaxin'*, Sea Breeze SB-1007, [n.d.]

Streisand, Barbra/*The Broadway Album*, see STREISAND1 [lyric changes by Sondheim]

Streisand, Barbra/*One Voice*, CBS Inc. CK 40788, 1987 [lyric changes by Sondheim, musical change by Streisand]

Streisand, Barbra/*Timeless*, see STREISAND3

Strolling Strings/*Over the Rainbow*, United States Air Force Band [n.n.], 198[?]

Sullivan, Ira/*Peace*, Galaxy [n.n.], 1979 [jazz quintet]

Summer Squash/*Of the Garden Wall*, [n.n.], 8506X59-A, 8506X59-B, 1985

Swingle II/*Lovin' You: Vol. II: Words & Music*, CBS S 81546, 1976

Syme, David/*Play It Again, Syme*, David Syme Concerts [n.n.], 1990[?] [piano]

Theatre Orchestra & Chorus/*Best of Broadway [Vol. 1]*, Til Records [n.n.], 1977

Thelin, Eje with E.T. Project/*E.T. Project Live at Nefertiti*, Dragon DRLP 128, 1986 [trombone with inst.]

Thomas, Mark/*Sounds of Gold*, Golden Crest Records [n.n.], 1980 [flute with piano]

Thomas, Richard "Cookie/*The Pleasure of Your Company*, [n.l., n.n.], 1998

Torme, Mel/*The London Sessions*, Sandstone Music D233083-2, 1990

Torme, Mel/*Torme, A New Album*, Gryphon Records G-916, 1980

Treorchy Male Chorus/*Music from Wales*, Bandleader 12, 2000

Trotter, Terry/*Stephen Sondheim's A Little Night Music*, see TROTTERT1 [piano solo]

Turner, Geraldine/ . . . *Sings the Stephen Sondheim Songbook, Vol. 2*, see TURNERG2

Two for the Blues, Pablo 2310-905, 1984 [jazz combo]

Ulster County Band/*1981 Ulster County Band Festival*, Mark Custom Recording Services MC-20123, 1981

University of Colorado Golden Buffalo Marching Band, University of Colorado USR 9275, 1975

University of Utah A Capella Choir, 1979-80, Location Recording Service CAV 0-2, 1980

University of Utah Ute Marching Band, Meteor Sound [n.n.], 1979

Vaughan, Sarah/*Thanks for the Memory*, Instant CD INS 5048, 1985

Vaughan, Sarah/*The Divine One*, Audiofidelity CRCD 2038 Chiaroscuro, 1985

Vaughan, Sarah/*A Foggy Day*, Astan Music 20117, 1984

Vaughan, Sarah/*Sarah Vaughan in the City of Lights*, Justin Time JTR 8474/5-2, 1999

Vaughan, Sarah/*Sarah Vaughn's 20 Hits*, Phoenix 20 P20-628, 1983

Vaughan, Sarah/*Send in the Clowns*, Mainstream [n.n.], 1974

Vaughan, Sarah The Count Basie Orchestra/*Send in the Clowns*, Pablo Records 2312-130, 1981

Vegas East Big Band/*Piece of the Action*, Century Productions LP 520604, LP33008, 198[?]

Venuti, Joe and Dave McKenna/*Alone at the Palace*, Chiaroscuro, 1977

Vondrackova, Helen/*The Broadway Album*, Supraphon LC 0358, 1993

Warner, Evelyn/*Here I Am*, Wuppertaler Stadtwerke [n.n.], 1999[?]

Whitaker, Roger/*The Best of Roger Whittaker*, Reader's Digest RD6A 141, RDK 5355, 1983

Whitaker, Roger/*Evergreens*, RCA C 234263, 1979

Whitaker, Roger/*Imagine*, RCA Victor AFL1-3077, 1978

Whitaker, Roger/*On Broadway*, RCAVictor 9026-68305-2, 1995

Whitaker, Roger/*The Roger Whittaker Album*, K-TEL International NE 1105, 1981

Whitaker, Roger/*The World of Roger Whittaker*, Pair Records PDC2-1212, 1988

Whitaker, Roger/*You Are My Miracle*, RCA Special Products DPC1-0955, 1991

Whitmore, Stan/*Piano on Broadway*, GreenHill GHD5009, 1994 [solo piano]
Wilk, Oystein/*Too Many Mornings*, see WILKO1
Williams, Darren/*Encore!*, [n.l., n.n.], 1999[?]
Wilson, Julie/*Julie Wilson Sings the Stephen Sondheim Songbook*, see WILSONJ2
Woodward, Edward/*Feelings*, Pickwick Music PWKS 4102P, [n.d.]
Woodward, Edward/*Love Is the Key*, DJM records DJF 20495, 1977
Wright Big Band, The Steve/*Nice 'n' Easy*, Jensen Pub. 603-14018 Dark Orchid Records, 1983
Wright, Danny/*Black and White*, Nichols-Wright Records NIW 101, 1986 [piano]
Yandall, Mary & Rodger Fox, Circular 11A, 11. 011, 1987
Young, Thomas/*High Standards*, Ess.A.Y Records CD1025, 1992
Zamfir, Gheorghe/*Love Songs*, Mercury 314 510 213-2, 1991 [panpipes with orchestra]
Zemarel Dance Band, The Zim/*The Swazze Sound of Zim Zemarel Dance Band: Featuring "Copacabana" and Other Favorites*, Columbia C 35616, 1978

"Send in the Clowns (Reprise)" from *A Little Night Music* (1973)
LNMPVS duet a-b[1] [both]
A Little Night Music Original Cast (Glynis Johns, Len Cariou), see LITTLEN01
A Little Night Music London Cast (Jean Simmons, Joss Ackland), see LITTLEN02
A Little Night Music Film (Elizabeth Taylor, Len Cariou), see LITTLEN03
A Little Night Music Studio Cast (Sian Phillips, Eric Flynn), see LITTLEN04
A Little Night Music Royal National Theatre (Judi Dench, Laurence Guittard), see LITTLEN05
A Little Night Music Barcelona Cast (Vicky Pena, Constantino Romero), see LITTLEN06

"Senior Waltz" from *By George* (1946)

"She Needs Me" cut from *Ilya Darling* (1967), music by Manos Hadjidakis

"Sheep's Song" from 1974 production of *Candide*, music by Leonard Bernstein
CaPVS quartet a-b[1]/a-b[1]/a-e[2]/a-b[1]
Candide Revival (Becky McSpadden, Renee Semes, Jim Corti, Deborah St. Darr), see CANDIDE01
Candide New York City Opera (Ivy Austin, Rhoda Butler, Robert Brubaker, Maris Clement, Chorus), see CANDIDE02
Candide New Broadway Cast (Nanne Puritz, D'vorah Bailey, Seth Malkin, Stacey Logan, Ensemble with Jim Dale), see CANDIDE05

"Show Me" from *Hot Spot* (1963), music with Mary Rodgers, lyric with
Martin Charnin, [see also "Don't Laugh"]
hey, love (Faith Prince), see HEYLOVE1

"Side by Side by Side" from *Company* (1970) [show versions include
"What Would We Do Without You?"]
CPVS, CVS2 company number, CVS, HTSS solo version c^1-e^2
Company Original Cast (Dean Jones, Company), see COMPANY01
Sondheim: A Musical Tribute (Company), see SONDAMUST1
Side by Side by Sondheim (Millicent Martin, Julia McKenzie, David Ker-
nan, Ned Sherrin, and pianists), see SIDEBYS1
Side by Side . . . Australian Cast (Company), see SIDEBYS2
Songs of Sondheim Irish Cast (Company), see SONGSOFSOND1
Symphonic Sondheim (Instrumental), see SYMPHONICSON1
Stephen Sondheim's Company . . . In Jazz (The Trotter Trio), see COMPANY03
Company London Revival Cast (Adrian Lester, Company), see COM-
PANY04
Company Revival Cast (Boyd Gaines, Company), see COMPANY05
A Gala Concert for Hal Prince (Raier Wallraf, Company), see GALA1
Sondheim: A Celebration (Julia McKenzie, Millicent Martin, David Ker-
nan), see SONDACEL1
Sondheim—A Celebration (The Company), see SONDACEL2 [with "Our
Time" and "Sunday"]
Hey, Mr. Producer! (David Kernan, Millicent Martin, Julia McKenzie,
Ned Sherrin, Stephen Sondheim), see HEYMRP
Sondheim Tonight (Company), see SONDTON1 [listed as "Finale"; includes
Sondheim]
Moving On (Company), see MOVINGON [with "I Do Like You," "Old
Friends"]
Company Brazilian Cast (Claudio Botelho, Company), see COMPANY06
Company German Cast (Ensemble), see COMPANY07
Boston Pops Orchestra/*Songs of the '60s* (instrumental), see BOSTON1
Jackie & Roy/*A Stephen Sondheim Collection*, see JACKIE&1

"Silly People" cut from *A Little Night Music* (1973)
ASII c^1-f^2
Sondheim: A Musical Tribute (George Lee Andrews), see SONDAMUST1
Marry Me a Little[1] (Craig Lucas), see MARRYME1
Heller, Marc/*Take Me to the World: Songs by Stephen Sondheim*, see
HELLERM1
New York City Gay Men's Chorus/*New York, New York, A Broadway Ex-
travaganza*, see NEWYORKCITYGAY1
Wilson, Lambert/*Musicals*, see WILSONL1

"Simple" from *Anyone Can Whistle* (1964) [waltz section originally private
birthday song for Mary Rodgers]
ACWPVS company number
Anyone Can Whistle Original Cast (Angela Lansbury, Harry Guardino,
Gabriel Dell, Larry Roquemore, Janet Hayes, Harvey Evans, Lester
Wilson, James Frawley, Arnold Soboloff, Ensemble), see ANYONE1
Anyone Can Whistle Live at Carnegie Hall (Scott Bakula, Walter Bobbie,
Madeline Kahn, David Lowenstein, Donna Lee Marshall, Harvey
Evans, Francis Ruvivar, Chip Zien, Ensemble), see ANYONE2

"Singing Out Loud" for *Singing Out Loud* (1992-93, unproduced)

"Small World" from Gypsy (1959), music by Jule Styne
GPVS f♯-a♯^{1} [+ duet at very end], GVS b♭-e♭^{2}
Gypsy Original Cast (Ethel Merman, Jack Klugman), see GYPSY01
Herb Geller and his all-stars play selections from *Gypsy* (Barbara Lang),
see GELLERH
Gypsy Film (Rosalind Russell, Lisa Kirk, Karl Malden), see GYPSY02
Gypsy London Cast (Angela Lansbury, Barrie Ingham), see GYPSY03
Gypsy Revival Cast (Tyne Daly, Jonathan Hadary), see GYPSY04
Gypsy TV Cast (Bette Midler, Peter Riegert), see GYPSY05
Celebrating Gypsy . . . (Libby Morris), see CELEBRATGYP
Selections from "Gypsy" and "Flower Drum Song" (Florence Henderson),
see GYPSY08
Kay Medford in "Gypsy" (Kay Medford, Jimmy Blackburn), see GYPSY09
Bailey, Pearl/*Come on Let's Play with Pearlie Mae*, Roulette (S)SR-25181,
1964
Bryant, Anita/*Anita Bryant*, Carlton (S)118, 1960
Chacksfield, Frank/*Lawrence of Arabia*, London LL-3298, (S)PS-298, 1964
Crawford, Jesse/*Sound of Jesse Crawford*, Decca (S)DL7-4028, 1962
Damme, Art Van/*Everything's Coming Up Music*, Columbia CL-1382,
(S)CS-8177, 1960
Feinstein, Michael/*Michael Feinstein Sings the Jule Styne Songbook*, see
FEINSTEIN1
Fields, Gracie, Decca F 11561, [n.d.]
Fisher, Eddie/*Tonight with Eddie Fisher*, Ramrod (S)ST-6002, 1962
Four Aces/*Four Aces Sing*, Decca (S)ED7-2665, 1960
Four Aces/*Hits from Broadway*, Decca (S)DL7-8855, 1959
Gary, John/*David Merrick Presents Hits from His Broadway Hits*, Victor
LPM/(S)LSP- 2947, 1964
Gorme, Eydie/*Sound of Music*, Columbia CL-2300, (S)CS-9100, 1966
Hi-Lo's, The/*Broadway Playbill*, see HILOS
Horne, Lena/ *. . . At the Sands*, RCA Victor LPM 2364, 1961 [in medley]

Horne, Marilyn/*The Men in My Life*, RCA Victor CD 9026-62647-2, 1994 (duet with Spiro Malas)

King, Wayne/*Listening Time*, Decca (S)DL7-8972, 1960

Kral, Irene/*Where Is Love?*, Candid Choice CHCD71012, 1974/1996 [with "A Time for Love"]

Lawrence, Steve/*Lawrence Goes Latin*, United Artists UAL-3114, (S)UAS-6114, 1962

Lawrence, Steve/*Steve Lawrence Conquers Broadway*, United Artists UAL-3368, (S)UAS- 6368, 1966

MacKenzie, Gisele/. . . *In Person at the Empire Room of the Waldorf-Astoria*, Everest LPBR 5069, 1960 [in medley]

Martin, Tony/*Days of Wine and Roses*, Chrysallis (S)CLS-100, 1964

Mathis, Johnny, Columbia 45rpm 4-41410, 1959

Mathis, Johnny/*You Are Everything to Me*, Columbia 33rpm (S)7-30410, 1959

Mathis, Johnny/*More Johnny's Greatest Hits*, Columbia CL-1344, (S)CS-8150, 1959

Mathis, Johnny/*Golden Dozen (Best of Jule Styne)*, Columbia CL-1462, 1960

Mathis, Johnny, Columbia 45rpm 4-33056, 1964

Mathis, Johnny/*The Great Years*, Columbia C2L-34, (S)C2S-834, 1964

McKenzie, Rita/*Ethel Merman's Broadway*, see MCKENZIER1

Melis, Jose/*Jose Melis on Broadway*, Mercury MG-20610, (S)SR-60610, 1962

Merman, Ethel/*A Gala Tribute to Joshua Logan*, [n.l., n.n., n.d.]

Merman, Ethel/*Merman in Vegas*, Reprise R9-6062, 1962

Merman, Ethel/*Mermania!*, see MERMANE1 [2 versions, 1 in medley]

Mozian, Roger King/*Spectacular Is the Sound of It*, MGM (S)SE-3883, 1962

O'Connell, Helen/*Era Reborn*, Cameo (S)SC-1045, 1964

Pringle, Anne & Mark Burnell/*Little Things We Do Together*, Spectrum SR003, [n.d.]

Ross, Annie/*Gypsy*, see ROSSANNIE

Roy Budd Trio/*Everything's Coming Up Roses: The Musical . . . Sondheim*, see ROYBUDD1

Sherwood, Roberta/*Live Performance*, Decca (S)DL7-4100, 1962

Smith, Ethel/*Ethel Smith on Broadway*, Decca (S)DL7-8993, 1962

Smith, Ethel/*Sound of Music*, Decca 45rpm 9-25518, 1962

Styne, Jule/*My Name Is Jule*, see STYNEJ1

Suzuki, Pat/*Looking at You*, Victor (S)LSP-2186, 1960

We Five, A&M 45rpm 770, 1966

We Five/*You Were on My Mind*, A&M (S)4-111, 1966

"Smile, Girls" cut from *Gypsy* (1959), music by Jule Styne

"So Happy (Act II Opening, Part II)" from *Into the Woods* (1987)
ITWPVS company number
Into the Woods Original Cast (Tom Aldredge, Company), see INTOTHE1
Into the Woods London Cast (Nicholas Parsons, Company), see INTOTHE2
Into the Woods Revival Cast (John McMartin, Company), see INTOTHE3

"So Many People" from *Saturday Night* (1954)
ASII, SNVS solo version b♭-e♭²
Sondheim: A Musical Tribute (Susan Browning, Jack Cassidy), see SOND-AMUST1
*Marry Me a Little*¹ (Suzanne Henry, Craig Lucas), see MARRYME1
Stage1/how I love you (Richard True, Michael Fawcett), DINK Records DIDX 037070, 1996
Saturday Night Bridewell Cast (Anna Francolini, Sam Newman), see SATURDAYN1
Saturday Night Original New York Cast (Lauren Ward, David Campbell), see SATURDAYN2
The Stephen Sondheim Album (Tami Tappan), see STEPHENSA1
Moving On (Company), see MOVINGON [with "Loving You," and "Not a Day Goes By"]
Bennett, Richard Rodney/*A Different Side of Sondheim*, see BENNETTR1
Bergman, Anna/*Souvenir*, LML 2002
Cook, Barbara/*Barbara Cook Sings Mostly Sondheim* (sung by Malcolm Gets), see COOKB1 [with "Another Hundred People"]
Jackie & Roy/*A Stephen Sondheim Collection*, see JACKIE&1
Mackay, Meg/*So Many People*, On Stage Music BP1234, 1994
Malmberg, Myrra/*What Can You Lose?*, see MALMBERG1
McKinley, Bill/*Everything Possible*, Everything Possible EPCD922-0, 1992
Patinkin, Mandy/*Experiment*, see PATINKIN3
Turner, Geraldine/ . . . *Sings the Stephen Sondheim Songbook, Vol. 2*, see TURNERG2

"Social Dancing" added to the 1987 London production of *Follies*
Follies London Cast (Company), see FOLLIES03

"Soldiers and Girls" cut from *Sunday in the Park with George* (1984), [see also "The One on the Left"]

"Soldier's Gossip (Scenes 8, 10 & 11)" from *Passion* (1995)
PPVS company numbers
Passion Original Cast (Francis Ruivivar, George Dvorsky, Cris Groenendaal, Marcus Olson, William Parry), see PASSION1
Passion London Concert (Michael Cantwell, Simon Green, Michael Dove, Nigel Williams), see PASSION3

"Some People" from *Gypsy* (1959), music by Jule Styne
  GPVS g♯-c², GVS c♯¹-e♯², SSS b-d♯²
  Gypsy Original Cast² (Ethel Merman), see GYPSY01
  Gypsy Film (Rosalind Russell, Lisa Kirk), see GYPSY02
  Gypsy London Cast (Angela Lansbury), see GYPSY03
  Gypsy Revival Cast (Tyne Daly), see GYPSY04
  Gypsy TV Cast (Bette Midler), see GYPSY05
  A Broadway Celebration, see BROADWAYCEL
  Celebrating Gypsy . . . (Libby Morris), see CELEBRATGYP
  Gypsy German Cast (Angelika Milster), see GYPSY07
  Selections from "Gypsy" and "Flower Drum Song" (Florence Henderson),
    see GYPSY08
  Kay Medford in "Gypsy" (Kay Medford), see GYPSY09
  Andreas, Christine/*Here's to the Ladies*, PS Classics [n.n.], 2002
  Arthur, Bea/*Bea Arthur on Broadway . . . Just Between Friends*, DRG 12993,
    2002
  Bailey, Jim/*Voices*, DCC Compact Classics DZS-164, 1998
  Billings, Alexandra/*Being Alive*, Southport S-SSD 0080, [n.d.]
  Garland, Judy/*Judy Garland Live!*, Capitol CDP 7923432, 1989
  Garland, Judy/*Just for Openers*, Capitol (S)DW-2062, 1964, M-12034, [1988]
  Hines, Mimi/*Mimi Hines Is a Happening*, Decca (S)74834, 1967, reissued
    as *The Mimi Hines Albums*, Cabaret Records CD 5017-2, 1995
  Horne, Lena/*Lena at the Sands*, RCA Victor LPM/(S)LSP-2364, 1961 [in
    medley]
  Lamond, Toni/ . . . *At the School of Arts Café*, Larrikin LRF 369, [n.d.]
  Lewis, Monica/ . . . *Swings Jule Styne*, DRG 802, 1991
  McKenzie, Rita/*Ethel Merman's Broadway*, see MCKENZIER1
  Merman, Ethel/*The Disco Album*, A&M Records SP-4775, 1979
  Merman, Ethel/*Ethel Merman at Carnegie Hall*, [n.l., n.n., n.d.]
  Merman, Ethel/*Ethel's Ridin' High*, Decca/London PS 909, 1974
  Merman, Ethel/*Mermania!*, see MERMANE1
  Minnelli, Liza/*Aznavour/Minelli: Paris-Palais Des Congres Integrale Du
    Spectacle*, EMI 8324272, [n.d.]
  Minnelli, Liza/*Liza Live from Radio City Music Hall*, Columbia CD 7464-
    53169-2, 1992
  Minnelli, Liza/*Liza Minnelli at Carnegie Hall*, Telarc CD-85502, 1987
  Minnelli, Liza/*Liza Minnelli Live at Carnegie Hall*, CALTEL [n.n.], 1981
  Peters, Bernadette/*Sondheim, Etc.*, see PETERSB1
  Ross, Annie/*Gypsy*, see ROSSANNIE
  Styne, Jule/*My Name Is Jule*, see STYNEJ1
  Syms, Sylvia/*Torch Song*, Koch KOC-CD-7936, 1997 [previously avail-
    able only as a Columbia 45rpm single, 1959]
  Whitfield, Weslia/*Weslia Whitfield Live in San Francisco*, Landmark
    LCD-1531-2, 1991

"Someone in a Tree" from *Pacific Overtures* (1976)
POPVS company number
Pacific Overtures[1] Original Cast (James Dybas, Mako, Gedde Watanabe, Mark Hsu Syers), see PACIFICOVER1
Sondheim (Book-of-the-Month) (instrumental), see SOND1
A Stephen Sondheim Evening (Bob Gunton, George Hearn, Steven Jacob, Cris Groenendaal), see STEPHENSE1
Pacific Overtures English National Opera (Eric Roberts, Richard Angas, Harry Nicoll, Alan Woodrow), see PACIFICOVER2
Sondheim: A Celebration (Deborah Nishimura, Sab Shimono, Gedde Watanabe), see SONDACEL2

"Someone Is Waiting" from *Company* (1970)
CPVS $c^{\sharp 1}$-$f^{\sharp 2}$ [+ chorus], CVS, SCCH c^1-f^2, CVS2 b-e^2
Company Original Cast (Dean Jones and the Vocal Minority), see COMPANY01
Sondheim: A Celebration at Carnegie Hall (Richard Muenz), see SONDACELATC1
Stephen Sondheim's Company . . . In Jazz (The Trotter Trio), see COMPANY03
Company Revival Cast (Boyd Gaines), see COMPANY05
Company London Revival Cast (Adrian Lester), see COMPANY04
Moving On (Company), see MOVINGON [with "Multitudes of Amys," "No, Mary Ann," "Johanna"]
Company Brazilian Cast (Claudio Botelho), see COMPANY06
Boston Pops Orchestra/*Songs of the '60s* (instrumental), see BOSTON1
Patinkin, Mandy/*Experiment*, see PATINKIN3
Wilk, Oystein/*Too Many Mornings*, see WILKO1

"Someone Like You" from *Do I Hear a Waltz?* (1965), music by Richard Rodgers
DIHPVS e^1-f^2, DIHVS d^1-$e\flat^2$
Do I Hear a Waltz? Original Cast (Sergio Franchi), see DOIHEAR1
Do I Hear a Waltz? Pasadena Playhouse Production (Anthony Crivello, Alyson Reed), see DOIHEAR2
Franchi, Sergio/*Songs of Richard Rodgers*, Victor (S)LSP-3365, 1966

"Someone to Trust" written for *Gold!* (forthcoming)

"Someone Woke Up" from *Do I Hear a Waltz?* (1965), music by Richard Rodgers
DIHPVS $a\flat$-b^1
Do I Hear a Waltz? Original Cast (Elizabeth Allen, Ensemble), see DOIHEAR1
Do I Hear a Waltz? Pasadena Playhouse Production (Alyson Reed, Eddy Martin), see DOIHEAR2

"Something Just Broke" added to the 1992 London production of *Assassins* APVS company number [included in reprint, also published as separate number Warner Bros. VS6153]

"Something's Coming" from *West Side Story* (1957), music by Leonard Bernstein

BOB, BSBA, SS, WSSVS d^1-f^2, WSSPVS e^1-g^2

West Side Story Original Cast[2] (Larry Kert), see WESTSIDE01

West Side Story film (Jim Bryant), see WESTSIDE02

West Side Story Studio Cast (José Carreras), see WESTSIDE03

Bernstein on Broadway (Peter Hofmann), see BERNSTEINON1

West Side Story Studio Cast London (Michael Ball), see WESTSIDE04

West Side Story Studio Cast Leicester Haymarket (Paul Manuel), see WESTSIDE05

West Side Story, The Songs of (All 4 One), see WESTSIDE06

West Side Story London Studio Cast (David Holliday), see WESTSIDE09

Ball, Michael/*The Musicals*, see BALLM1

Black, Stanley/*Broadway Blockbusters*, London (S)SP-44088, 1967

Buckley, Betty/*An Evening at Carnegie Hall*, see BUCKLEYB3

Burton, Gary/*Something's Coming*, Victor (S)LSP-2880, 1965

Connelli, Judi/*Judi Connelli Live in London*, see CONNELLI2 [with "Where Is It Written" & "The Way He Makes Me Feel"]

Connor, Chris & Maynard Ferguson/*Two's Company*, Roulette (S)SR-52068, 1961; cd: CDP 7243 8 37201 2 5, 1996

Connor, Chris/*'S Wonderful*, Blue Moon BMCD 3074 (rec. 1963) 1998[?]

Cook, Barbara/*Barbara Cook Sings Mostly Sondheim* (sung by Malcolm Gets), see COOKB1 [with "Tonight"]

Cousens, Peter/*Corner of the Sky*, First Night OCRCD 6043, 1994

Damone, Vic/*On the Street Where You Live*, see DAMONE1

Davis Jr., Sammy/*The Great Sammy Davis Jr.*, Columbia PCT 11299, 198[?]

Davis Jr., Sammy/*Sammy Davis Jr. at the Cocoanut Grove*, see DAVISS [part of *West Side Story* medley]

Davis Jr., Sammy/*Sammy Davis Jr. Belts the Best of Broadway*, Reprise (S)R9-2010, 1961

Davis Jr., Sammy/*What Kind of Fool Am I?*, Reprise (S)R9-6051, 1963

Dee & Tee, Coral 45rpm 62057, 1967

Desmond, Trudy/*Make Me Rainbows*, Koch Jazz KOC 3-7803, 1995

Fisher, Eddie/ . . . *At the Wintergarden*, Ramrod Records RR1-2, Taragon TARCD-1054, 1962, 69 [with "Maria" and "Tonight"]

Ford, Anne Kerry/*Something Wonderful*, see FORDA1

Garland, Judy/*Judy Duets* (with Vic Damone), see GARLAND [in *West Side Story* medley]

Garland, Judy/*Judy Garland Live!*, Capitol CDP 7923432, 1989

Group, The/*The Group*, Victor (S)LSP-2663, 1963

Hi-Lo's, The/*The Hi-Lo's and All That Jazz*, Columbia CL-1259, (S)CS-8077, 1960

Johnson, J.J./ *Broadway Express*, Victor (S)LSP-3544, 1967

Kert, Larry/*Larry Kert Sings Leonard Bernstein*, Seeco CE-467, (S)CES-4670, 1964

King's Singers, The/*The King's Singers Believe in Music*, Columbia/EMI SCX 6637, 1981

Lawrence, Carol/*Tonight at 8:30*, see LAWRENCEC

Mason, Karen/*Not So Simply Broadway*, Second Hearing GS 9015, 1986

Masse, Laurel/*Again*, Disques Beaupre DB820C, 1990

Mathis, Johnny/*The Global Collection*, Columbia/Legacy 64894, 1997

Mathis, Johnny/*The Shadow of Your Smile*, Mercury 21073, (S)61073, 1966

McDermott, Sean/*My Broadway*, see MCDERMOTTS1

McVey, J. Mark/*Broadway and Beyond*, [n.l., n.n.], 1998

Metzger, Derek/*Me and My Songs*, BMG METCD001, 1996

Migenes, Julia/*Live at the Olympia*, see MIGENES1

Patinkin, Mandy/*Experiment*, see PATINKIN3

Richards, Ann/*Many Moods of Ann Richards*, Capitol (S)ST-1406, 1960

Ross, Edmundo/*Broadway Goes Latin*, London LL-3277, (S)PS-277

Sommers, Joanie/*Let's Talk About Love*, Warner Bros. (S)WS-1474, 1962

Steele, Tommy/*Everything's Coming Up Broadway*, Liberty LRP-3426, (S)LST-7426, 1965

Storm, Rebecca/*We Never Said Goodbye*, Shearer Music Ltd./U.K., [n.n.], 1997

Streisand, Barbra/*The Broadway Album*, see STREISAND1

Streisand, Barbra/*One Voice*, CBS Inc. CK 40788, 1987

Streisand, Barbra/*Timeless* (with Lauren Frost), see STREISAND3

Tanner, Tony/*Something's Coming!*, Audio Fidelity AFLP 2171, 1967

Valente, Caterina/*I Happen to Like New York*, London LL-3362, (S)PS-362, 1964

Warren, Fran/*Something's Coming*, Warwick (S)ST 2012, 1960

Williams, Darren/*Something's Coming*, [n.l., n.n., n.d.]

"Somewhere" from *West Side Story* (1957), music by Leonard Bernstein
BOB, WSSPVS b-f♯², BSBA, BSC, SSS, WSSVS b♭-f²

West Side Story Original Cast (Reri Grist, Ensemble), see WESTSIDE01

West Side Story film (Jim Bryant, Marni Nixon), see WESTSIDE02

West Side Story Studio Cast (Marilyn Horne), see WESTSIDE03

Bernstein On Broadway (Debbie Sasson), see BERNSTEINON1

Jerome Robbins Broadway (Dorothy Benham, Christophe Caballero, Ensemble), see JEROMER1

West Side Story Studio Cast London (?), see WESTSIDE04

West Side Story Studio Cast Leicester Haymarket (Sally Burgess), see WESTSIDE05

West Side Story Studio Cast Leicester Haymarket (Paul Manuel, Tinuke Olafimihan), see WESTSIDE05 [Motion Picture Version]

West Side Story, The Songs of (Aretha Franklin), see WESTSIDE06

West Side Story, The Songs of (Phil Collins), see WESTSIDE06

Leonard Bernstein's New York (Dawn Upshaw), see LEONARDB1

West Side Story, Dave Grusin presents (Jon Secada), see WESTSIDE07

Afterglow (Tom Waits), Sony 2BTU, 1998

The 3 Divas (Judi Connelli, Suzanne Johnston, Jennifer McGregor), CDP 2000/DIVA003- 1, 2000

Ames, Ed/*Opening Nights*, Victor (S)LSP-2781, 1964

Ames, Ed/*Time for Living, A Time for Hope*, Victor (S)LSP-4128, 1970

Aznavour, Charles/*Of Flesh and Soul*, Monument (S)18130, 1970

Barry, Len, Decca 45rpm 62336, 1966

Barry, Sis/*Too Smart (For My Own Good)*, Colpix 45rpm 796, 1963

Bassey, Shirley/*Shirley Bassey Belts the Blues*, United Artists UAL-3419, (S)UAS-6419, 1965

Bassey, Shirley in Person, United Artists UAL-3463, (S)UAS-6463, 1967

Blackwell, Harolyn/*A Simple Song: Blackwell Sings Bernstein*, see BLACK-WELL1

Brothers Four, Columbia 45rpm 4-43211, 1965

Brothers Four/*Honey Wind Blows*, Columbia CL-2305, (S)CS-9105, 1965

Cant, Donald/*Donald Cant*, see CANTD1

Carreras, Jose/*Amigos para Siempre: Friends for Life: Romantic Songs of the World*, Atlantic 82413-2, 1992

Church, Charlotte/*Enchantment*, Columbia CK 89710, 2001

Cook, Barbara/*All I Ask of You*, DRG 91456, 1999

Cramer, Floyd/*Here's What's Happening*, Victor (S)LSP-3746, 1967

Crawford, Michael/*Songs from the Stage & Screen*, see CRAWFORDM1

Curtis, King/*Instant Groove*, Atco (S)293, 1970

D'Rone, Frank/*Brand New Morning*, Cadet (S)806, 1970

Darin, Bobby/*Venice Blue*, Capitol ST2322, [n.d.]

Darin, Bobby/*West Side Story*, see DARIN1

Davidson, John/*My Best to You*, Columbia CL-2648, (S)CS-9448, 1967

Diddley, Bo/*Bo Diddley Is a Gunslinger*, Checker 2977, 1961

Domingo, Placido/*The Broadway I Love*, see DOMINGO1

Douglas, Mike/*It's Time for Mike Douglas*, Epic LN-24169, (S)BN-26169, 1965

Drake, Alfred/*Alfred Drake & Roberta Peters Sing the Popular Music of Leonard Bernstein*, see DRAKEA

Dudley, Dave/*George*, Mercury (S)61242, 1970

Escorts, Coral 45rpm 62336, 1963

Feinstein, Michael/*Michael Feinstein with the Israel Philharmonic Orchestra*, Concord Records B00005Q6LL, 2002

Four Seasons/*Four Seasons Entertain You*, Phillips PHM-200164, (S)PHS-600164

Garland, Judy/*Judy Duets* (with Vic Damone), see GARLAND [in *West Side Story* medley]

Gary, John/*Choice*, Victor LPM/(S)LSP-3501, 1966

Goulet, Robert/*Traveling On*, Columbia CL-2541, (S)CS-9341, 1967

Guest, Rob/*Standing Ovation*, EMI Music (Australian Group) 7986212, 1991 [in medley]

Hall, Vince/*Vince Hall at the Club*, Tower (S)DT-5064, 1967

Holmes, Jerry/*Jerry Holmes Dramatic New Voice*, Warner Bros. (S)WS-1593, 1965

Horne, Lena/*Lena in Hollywood*, United Artists (S)6470, 1966; cd: EMI Records E2-37394, 1996

Horne, Marilyn/*The Men in My Life*, RCA Victor CD 9026-62647-2, 1994

Intimate Broadway/*My Favorite Things*, Intersound 8311, 1996

Ivir, Jasna/*Musical Diva Delights*, Jancowski JST 298, 1995

Jones, Jack/*If You Ever Leave Me*, Victor (S)LSP-3969, 1968

Kert, Larry/*Larry Kert Sings Leonard Bernstein*, Seeco CE-467, (S)CES-4670, 1964

King Richard's Fluegel Knights/*Knights on Broadway*, MTA (S)5008, 1970

King Sisters/*New Sounds of the Fabulous King Sisters*, Warner Bros. (S)1647, 1967

Knight, Bob/*Memories*, Four Josie 45rpm 899, 1963

Laine, Cleo/*Themes*, Sierra Records FEDC 2000, 1978[?]

Lee, Brenda/*Coming on Strong*, Decca (S)4825, 1967

LeMel, Gary/*Moonlighting*, Atlantic 831782, 1999

Leyton, Jeff/*Music of the Night*, Linn AKD098, 1998

Lymon, Frankie/*Sweet & Lovely*, Columbia 45rpm 4-43094, 1964

Lytle, Johnny/*Sound of Velvet Soul*, Solid State (S)18026, 1968

MacRae, Gordon/*If She Walked into My Life*, Capitol (S)ST-2578, 1967

Mann Singers, Johnny/*Daydream*, Liberty 3447, (S)7447, 1966

Martino, Al/*This Is Love*, Capitol (S)ST-2592, 1967

Mathis, Johnny/*Tender Is the Night*, Mercury MG-20890, (S)SR-60890, 1964

McDonald, Audra/*How Glory Goes*, Nonesuch 79580-2, 2000

McKenzie, Julia/*The Musicals Album*, see MCKENZIEJ1

Mirettes/*In the Midnight Hour*, Revue (S)7205, 1970

Mitchell, Keith/*Keith Mitchell Sings Broadway*, Spark SPA-03, 1972

Mitchell, Rubin/*Remarkable Rubin*, Capitol (S)ST-2658, 1967

Monro, Matt/*From Russia with Love*, Liberty LRP-3356, (S)LST-7356, 1964

Montgomery, Wes/*Fusion*, Riverside (S)RS9-472, 1964

Nash, Johnny, Atlantic 45rpm 2344, 1968

Newell, Norman/*I Gave My Love a Flower*, O:Epic 24323, (S)26323, 1968

Newton, Wayne/*One More Time*, MGM (S)4549, 1970

Nicholson, Carla & Michael/*Just Duet*, see NICHOLSONC1 [with "I Feel Pretty" and "Tonight"]

Ofarim, Esther/*Is It Really Me?*, Phillips PHM-200185, (S)PHS-600185, 1966

Paul, Billy/*Feelin' Good at the Cadillac Club*, Gamble (S)5002, 1970

Peter & Gordon/*Woman*, Capitol (S)ST-2477, [n.d.]

Price, Ray/*Sweetheart of the Year*, Columbia (S)CS-9822, 1970

Prior, Marina/*Somewhere*, see PRIORM1

Proby, P.J., Liberty 45rpm 55757, 1965

Proby, P.J./*Somewhere*, Liberty LRP-3406, (S)LST-7406, 1966

Ralston, Bob/*Lawrence Welk Presents Bob Ralston*, Raynote (S)8031, 1970

Reed, Vivian/*Vivian Reed*, Epic (S)26412, 1970

Righteous Brothers/*Standards*, Verve (S)6-5051, 1968

Stewart, Billy/*Billy Stewart*, Chess (S)1513, 1967

Storm, Rebecca/*Broadway by Storm*, [n.l., n.n., n.d.]

Strassen, Michael/*Chasing the Clouds*, Dress Circle [n.n.], 1999

Streisand, Barbra/*The Broadway Album*, see STREISAND1

Streisand, Barbra/*The Concert*, Columbia C2K 66109, 1994

Streisand, Barbra/*Timeless* (with Lauren Frost), see STREISAND3 [with "I Believe"]

Stuarti, Enzo, Jubilee 78rpm/45rpm 5234, 1961

Supremes, The/*Motortown Revue in Paris*, Tamla (S)264, 1966

Supremes, The/*The Supremes Live at the Copa*, Motown (S)636, 1966

Temptations/*In a Mellow Mood*, Gordy (S)924, 1968

Traits, Scepter 45rpm 12169, 1967

Tres Bien Quartet/*Four of a Kind*, Decca (S)7-4958, 1968

Tucker, Richard/*What Now My Love?*, Columbia ML-6295, (S)MS-6895, 1967

Vale, Jerry, Columbia 45rpm 4-43895, 1967

Vale, Jerry/*More Jerry Vale's Greatest Hits*, Columbia CL-2659, (S)CS-9459, 1967

Valente, Caterina/*Valente and Violins*, London LL-3363, (S)PS-363, 1964

Van Horn, John/*Sky High*, Moonglow 45rpm 225, 1963

Vondrackova, Helen/*The Broadway Album*, Supraphon LC 0358, 1993

Warner, Evelyn/*Here I Am*, Wuppertaler Stadtwerke [n.n.], 1999[?]

Warwick, Dionne/*The Windows of the World*, Scepter (S)SPS 563, 1968

Warwick, Dionne, Scepter 45rpm 21033, 1970

Warwick, Dionne/*Greatest*, Scepter (S)575, 1970

We Five, AAM 45rpm 800, 1966

We Five/*Make Someone Happy*, AAM (S)4-138, 1978

Weston, Kim/*This Is America*, MGM (!)4561, 1970

Whitaker, Roger/*On Broadway*, RCAVictor 9026-68305-2, 1995

Wilkinson, Colm/*Stage Heroes*, BMG/RCAVictor 74321-25856-2, 1997

Williams, Andy/*The Shadow of Your Smile*, Columbia CL-2499, (S)CS-9279, 1966

Wilson, Nancy/*From Broadway with Love*, Capitol (S)CST-2433, 1966
Younger Brothers/*High School Girl*, Warner Bros. 45rpm 5386, 1963

"A Song for Humming" from *Climb High* (1950-52, unproduced)

"Soon" from *A Little Night Music* (1973)
    LNMPVS c^1-$g\#^2$
    A Little Night Music Original Cast (Victoria Mallory), see LITTLEN01
    A Little Night Music London Cast (Veronica Page), see LITTLEN02
    A Little Night Music Film (Lesley-Anne Down), see LITTLEN03
    A Little Night Music Studio Cast (Janis Kelly), see LITTLEN04
    The Great Waltz (Hollywood Bowl Orchestra), see HOLLYWOODB1 [part of
        "The Night Waltzes"]
    A Little Night Music Royal National Theatre (Joanna Riding), see LIT-
        TLEN05
    A Little Night Music Barcelona Cast (Constantino Romero, Angel Llacer,
        Alicia Ferrer), see LITTLEN06 [and reprise by Teresa de la Torre]
    Trotter, Terry/*Stephen Sondheim's A Little Night Music*, see TROTTERT1 [pi-
        ano solo]

"Sooner or Later" from *Dick Tracy* (1990)
    ASIV, SSFTS b♭-e♭², DTVS, SCCH f-b♭¹
    Sondheim: A Celebration at Carnegie Hall (Karen Ziémba), see SONDACEL-
        ATC1
    Putting It Together (Rachel York), see PUTTINGIT1
    Sondheim at the Movies[3] (Jane Krakowski), see SONDATTHEM1
    Sondheim: A Celebration (David Cassidy), see SONDACEL2
    Out On Broadway (Keith Thompson), see OUTONB1
    Stephen Sondheim Songs (instrumental accompaniment), see STEPHENSS1
    Akers, Karen/*Unchained Melody*, DRG 5214, 1991
    Egan, Susan/*So Far*[4], JAY Records CDJAY 1359, 2002
    Hateley, Linzi/*Sooner or Later*, LHL 4, 1994
    Ivir, Jasna/*Musical Diva Delights*, Jonkowski JST 298, 1995
    Madonna/*I'm Breathless*, see MADONNA1
    McBryde, Deian/*Love . . . & Other Distractions*, EvAnMedia evan-
        35700CD, 2000 [with "The Man That Got Away"]
    O'Day, Anita/*Rules of the Road*, Pablo CD 2310-950-2, 1993
    Peters, Bernadette/*Sondheim, Etc.*, see PETERSB1
    Prior, Marina/*Somewhere*, see PRIORM1
    Saxe, Emily/*Whistling—Broadway to Berk'ley Square*, Orchard 3285, 1999
    Ver Planck, Marlene/*Marlene Ver Planck Meets Saxomania*, Audiophile
        ACD-288, 1994
    Wheatley, Rebecca/*Sooner or Later*, SB Music SB2401, [n.d.]
    Wilk, Oystein/*Too Many Mornings*, see WILKO1

"Sorry-Grateful" from *Company* (1970)
ASI, CVS, SSS solo version a-d^2, CPVS trio version b-e^2 [all 3], CVS2 c-f^2 [all 3]
Company Original Cast (Charles Kimbrough, George Coe, Charles Braswell, Dean Jones), see COMPANY01
Sondheim (Book-of-the-Month) (Timothy Nolen), see SOND1
Putting It Together (Stephen Collins), see PUTTINGIT1
Stephen Sondheim's Company . . . In Jazz (The Trotter Trio), see COMPANY03
Company Revival Cast (Robert Westenberg, John Hillner, Timothy Landfield), see COMPANY05
Company London Revival Cast (Clive Rowe, Teddy Kempner, Paul Bentley), see COMPANY04
Sondheim: A Celebration (Bill Hutton), see SONDACEL2
The Stephen Sondheim Album (Guy Haines), see STEPHENSA1
Company Brazilian Cast (Daniel Boaventura, Mauro Gorini, Paulo Mello), see COMPANY06
Buckley, Betty/*Children Will Listen*, see BUCKLEYB1
Gines, Christopher/*The Way It Goes*, Miranda [n.n.], 2001
Patinkin, Mandy/*Dress Casual*, see PATINKIN2
Short, Bobby/*Live at the Cafe Carlyle*, see SHORTB1
Wright, Bill/*It Takes Two*, see WRIGHTB1

"The Sound of Poets," see *"Exodus"*

"The Spell Is on My House (Opening Part VII)" from *Into the Woods* (1987) [see "Into the Woods" for recording information]
ITWPVS trio e♭^{1}-d♭^{2}/d♭^{1}-e♭^{2}/e♭^{1}-g♭^{2}

"A Star Is Born" (1954)

"Stars Give Light," see "Chris and David I"

"Stavisky Suite" (parts One, Two, and Three)
Sondheim at the Movies (Orchestra), see SONDATTHEM1

"Stavisky Suite"
Sondheim Tonight (Orchestra), see SONDTON1

"Stay" from *Do I Hear a Waltz?* (1965), music by Richard Rodgers
DIHPVS e♭^{1}-b♭^{2}, DIHVS c^1-g^2 [e^2 optional]
Do I Hear a Waltz? Original Cast (Sergio Franchi), see DOIHEAR1
Do I Hear a Waltz? Pasadena Playhouse Production (Alyson Reed, Anthony Crivello), see DOIHEAR2

Kirby Stone Four, Columbia 45rpm 4-43250, 1966
Sloane, Carol, Columbia 45rpm 4-43307, 1966
Sullivan, KT/*Sings the Sweetest Sounds of Richard Rodgers*, DRG 91462, 2000 [with "Can't You Do a Friend a Favor?" and "Look No Further"]

"Stay with Me" from *Into the Woods* (1987)
ITWPVS b♭-d♭², ITWVS d¹-f²
Into the Woods Original Cast (Bernadette Peters), see INTOTHE1
Into the Woods London Cast (Julia McKenzie), see INTOTHE2
No. 1 Australian Musicals Album (Judy Connelli), Polydor 539 736-2, 1998
Buckley, Betty/*Children Will Listen*, see BUCKLEYB1
Connelli, Judi/*Judi Connelli Live in London*, see CONNELLI2 [with "Married," "You Better Sit Down Kids," and "Move On," (which includes "We Do Not Belong Together")]
Connelli, Judy/*On My Way to You*, see CONNELLI1
Kirchschlager, Angelika/*when night falls*, Sony Classical SK 64498, 1999
O'Connor, Caroline/*What I Did for Love*⁴, JAY Records CDJAY 1314, 1998

"Still Got My Heart" from *Phinney's Rainbow* (1948)
PRSM c¹-e♭²

"The Story of Lucy and Jessie" from *Follies* (1971)
ASIV, FPVS g-b♭¹
Follies Original Cast (Alexis Smith), FOLLIES01
Follies in Concert (Lee Remick), see FOLLIES02
Follies, The Complete Recording (Dee Hoty, Ensemble), see FOLLIES05
Wilson, Julie/*Julie Wilson at Brothers & Sisters* Vol. Two, see WILSONJ1 [with "Beautiful Girls," "Losing My Mind," and "Could I Leave You?"]
Wilson, Julie/*Julie Wilson Sings the Stephen Sondheim Songbook*, see WILSONJ2

"Strength Through Sex" from *Phinney's Rainbow* (1948)

"Study Hall Dirge" from *By George* (1946)

"Suicide Sequence" from *All That Glitters* (1949)

"Suite at the Claridge" from *Stavisky* (1974)
Stavisky (instrumental), see STAVISKY1

"The Sun Is Blue" from *Mary Poppins* (1950, unproduced)

"The Sun Sits Low," see "Night Waltz II"

"The Sun Won't Set," see "Night Waltz I"

"Sunday" from *Sunday in the Park with George* (1984)
ASII, SCC2, SPGVS solo version $c\sharp^1$-a^2, SPGPVS company number [2 versions]
Sunday in the Park . . . Original Cast (Company), see SUNDAYIN1
Sondheim: A Celebration at Carnegie Hall (Bernadette Peters, Broadway Chorus), see SONDACELATC1
No One Is Alone . . . (Company), see NONONEIS1
Sondheim: A Celebration (The Company), see SONDACEL2 [with "Our Time and "Side by Side"]
Gay Men's Chorus of Los Angeles/*Simply Sondheim*, see GAYMENSCLA1
Heller, Marc/*Take Me to the World: Songs by Stephen Sondheim*, see HELLERM1
Rubano, Craig/*Finishing the Act*, see RUBANOC1
Singing Hoosiers, The/*The Singing Hoosiers in Concert, 1986*, Indiana University School of Music no. 504

"Sunday in the Park with George" from *Sunday in the Park with George* (1984)
SPGPVS e-d^2
Sunday in the Park . . . Original Cast (Bernadette Peters, Mandy Patinkin), see SUNDAYIN1
No One Is Alone . . . (Peta Belinda Ashton), see NONONEIS1 [with "Color & Light"]
Celebrating Sondheim (Mary Carewe, Stephen Hill), see CELEBRATSON
Sondheim Tonight (The Soloists, The West End Chorus), see SONDTON1 [with "Being Alive" and "Another Hundred People"]

"Sunrise Letter" from *Passion* (1995)
PPVS duet $a\flat$-e^2/$b\flat$-g^2
Passion Original Cast (Marrin Mazzie, Jere Shea), see PASSION1
Passion London Concert (Helen Hobson, Michael Ball), see PASSION3

"Sweet Polly Plunkett" from *Sweeney Todd* (1979), [see "Parlor Songs" for other recordings]
STPVS d^1-g^2
Putting It Together (Julie Andrews), see PUTTINGIT1

"Take Me to the World" from *Evening Primrose* (1966)
ASII, SSFTS solo version $b\flat$-$e\flat^2$
Sondheim: A Musical Tribute (Marti Rolph), see SONDAMUST1
Sondheim (Book-of-the-Month) (Mary D'Arcy), see SOND1
Sondheim at the Movies (Liz Callaway, Gary Beach), see SONDATTHEM1

Moving On (Company), see MOVINGON [with "Move On," "I Know Things Now," "Everybody Says Don't"]

The Frogs/Evening Primrose Studio Recording (Theresa McCarthy, Neil Patrick Harris), see FROGS1

Anthony, Julie/*Lush*, MHM [n.n.], 2001 [Australian]

Barnett, Peter & Julia Early/*In So Many Words*, see BARNETTEARLY1

Bennett, Richard Rodney/*A Different Side of Sondheim*, see BENNETTR1

Day, Courtenay/*State of Bliss*, LML Records [n.n.], 2002

Dore, Michael/*Simply*, [n.l., n.n.], 2002 [with "Being Alive" and "Not a Day Goes By"]

Heller, Marc/*Take Me to the World: Songs by Stephen Sondheim*, see HELLERM1

Jobson, Mark deVille/*My House*, see JOBSON1

Malmberg, Myrra/*What Can You Lose?*, see MALMBERG1

Mars, Susannah/*Take Me to the World*, see MARSS1

Nease, Byron/*When I Fall in Love*, Audible Difference AD CD002, 1992 [with "You and I"]

New York City Gay Men's Chorus/*New York, New York, A Broadway Extravaganza*, see NEWYORKCITYGAY1

Nova, Christian/*Walking Happy*, Original Cast Records OC9750, 1997 [with "Moon River"]

Patinkin, Mandy/*Dress Casual* (Bernadette Peters, Mandy Patinkin), see PATINKIN2

Roy Budd Trio/*Everything's Coming Up Roses: The Musical . . . Sondheim*, see ROYBUDD1

Turner, Geraldine/ *. . . Sings the Stephen Sondheim Songbook, Vol. 2*, see TURNERG2

Upshaw, Dawn/*I Wish It So*, see UPSHAWD1

"Take the Acorn" (incomplete) for *A Funny Thing Happened on the Way to the Forum* (1962)

"Take the Moment" from *Do I Hear a Waltz?* (1965), music by Richard Rodgers DIHPVS d^1-a♭^{2}, DIHVS c^1-e♭^{2}

Do I Hear a Waltz? Original Cast (Sergio Franchi), see DOIHEAR1

Leading Men Don't Dance, 1997

Do I Hear a Waltz? Pasadena Playhouse Production (Alyson Reed), see DOIHEAR2

Bennett, Tony/*If I Ruled the World—Tony Bennett Songs for the Jet Set*, Columbia CL- 2343, (S)CS-9143, 1965, CBS/Sony CD 25DP-5320, 199[?]

Davis Jr., Sammy/*Sammy's Back on Broadway*, Reprise (S) R-6169, 1968

Horne, Lena/*Feelin' Good*, United Artists (S)6433, 1968

Rubano, Craig/*Finishing the Act*, see RUBANOC1 [with "Before the Parade Passes By"]

"Tamate's Dance," see "There Is No Other Way"

"Tea" from *Mary Poppins* (1950, unproduced)

"Ten Years Old" cut from *The Fabulous Fifties* (1960), written with Burt Shevelove

"Thank You for Coming" cut from *Merrily We Roll Along* (1981)

"Thank You So Much" from *Do I Hear a Waltz?* (1965), music by Richard Rodgers
DIHPVS duet b♭-d^2/d^1-d^2, DIHVS, SSS duet c^1-c^2 [both]
Do I Hear a Waltz? Original Cast (Elizabeth Allen, Sergio Franchi), see DOIHEAR1
Do I Hear a Waltz? Pasadena Playhouse Production (Alyson Reed, Anthony Crivello), see DOIHEAR2

"That Dirty Old Man" from *A Funny Thing Happened on the Way to the Forum* (1962)
FTPVS b-f♯^{2}
A Funny Thing . . . Original Cast (Ruth Kobart), see FUNNY01
A Funny Thing . . . London Cast (Linda Gray), see FUNNY02
Stephen Sondheim's A Funny Thing . . . Forum . . . In Jazz (The Trotter Trio), see FUNNY04
A Funny Thing . . . Revival Cast (Mary Testa), see FUNNY05

"That Frank" added to 1985 revival of *Merrily We Roll Along* [replaces "Rich and Happy"]
Merrily We Roll Along Revival Cast (Malcolm Gets, Company), see MERRILY2
Merrily We Roll Along London Cast (Michael Cantwell, Company), see MERRILY3

"That Good Old American Dollar" from *All That Glitters* (1949)

"That Kind of a Neighborhood" from *Saturday Night* (1954), [includes "Fair Brooklyn"]
SNVS company number
Saturday Night Bridewell Cast (Maurice Yeoman, Simon Greiff, Jeremy David, Ashleigh Sendin, Tracie Bennett, Mark Haddigan, James Millard), see SATURDAYN1
Saturday Night Original New York Cast (Michael Benjamin Washington, Kirk McDonald, Greg Zola, Joey Sorge), see SATURDAYN2

"That Old Piano Roll" cut from *Follies* (1971) [included as instrumental in 1st section of the "Overture," and used in "Social Dancing" for the London revival]
ASIV c^1-e^2, FPVS instrumental [in "Overture"]
Unsung Sondheim[3] (Harry Groener, taps: Lynette Perry), see UNSUNGS1
Follies, The Complete Recording (Tony Roberts), see FOLLIES05
New York City Gay Men's Chorus/*Love Lives On*, see NEWYORKCITYGAY2

"That'll Show Him" from *A Funny Thing Happened on the Way to the Forum* (1962)
FTPVS c^1-g^2, FTVS b♭-f^2 [e♭^{2} optional]
A Funny Thing . . . Original Cast (Preshy Marker), see FUNNY01
A Funny Thing . . . London Cast (Isla Blair), see FUNNY02
A Funny Thing . . . Revival Cast (Jessica Boevers), see FUNNY05
Stephen Sondheim's A Funny Thing . . . Forum . . . In Jazz (The Trotter Trio), see FUNNY04
Shore, Dinah, Capitol 45rpm 4774, 1962

"Theme" from *Reds*, see "Goodbye for Now"

"Theme" from *Stavisky* (1974)
ASIV, SSFTS piano solo
Stavisky[1] (instrumental), see STAVISKY1
Sondheim (Book-of-the-Month) (instrumental), see SOND1
Jackie & Roy/*A Stephen Sondheim Collection*, see JACKIE&1

"There Is No Other Way" from *Pacific Overtures* (1976), [also known as "Tamate's Dance"]
ASIV, POPVS duet, e^1-g^2/e^1-b^1
Pacific Overtures Original Cast (Alvin Ing, Ricardo Tobia), see PACIFIC-OVER1
Sondheim (Book-of-the-Month) (instrumental), see SOND1
Pacific Overtures English National Opera (Edward Byles, Alan Woodrow), see PACIFICOVER2
New York City Opera Orchestra/*Broadway's Best* (instrumental), see NEWYORKCITYOP1

"There Won't Be Trumpets" cut from *Anyone Can Whistle* (1964)
ACWPVS g-c^2, ACWVS a-d^2
Anyone Can Whistle[1] Original Cast (Lee Remick), see ANYONE1
Side by Side by Sondheim (Millicent Martin, David Kernan, Julia McKenzie), see SIDEBYS1
Marry Me a Little (Suzanne Henry), see MARRYME1
Anyone Can Whistle Live at Carnegie Hall (Bernadette Peters), see ANYONE2

Sondheim: A Celebration (Joan Ryan), see SONDACEL2
Moving On (Company), see MOVINGON
Barr, John/*In Whatever Time We Have*, see BARRJ1
De Ferranti, Margie/*Margie De Ferranti*, see DEFERRANT1
Kostelanetz, Andre/*Andre Kostelanetz Plays Broadway's Greatest Hits: from Annie, I Love My Wife, Side by Side by Sondheim, The King and I*, Columbia PC 34864, 1977
New York City Gay Men's Chorus/*New York, New York, A Broadway Extravaganza*, see NEWYORKCITYGAY1
Patinkin, Mandy/*Oscar and Steve*, see PATINKIN4
Peters, Bernadette/*Sondheim, Etc.*, see PETERSB1
Streisand, Barbra/*Just for the Record*, Columbia C4K 44111/CK 48646, 1991
Turner, Geraldine/*Old Friends*, see TURNERG1 [in medley]
Upshaw, Dawn/*I Wish It So*, see UPSHAWD1
VerPlanck, Marlene/*A Breath of Fresh Air*, Audiophile ACD 109, 1993

"There's a Hole in the World," see "No Place Like London"

"There's a Parade in Town" from *Anyone Can Whistle* (1964)
ACWPVS g♭-b♭^{1} + chorus, ACWVS, ASI c♭^{1}-e♭^{2}
Anyone Can Whistle Original Cast[2] (Angela Lansbury, Ensemble), see ANYONE1
Sondheim: A Musical Tribute (Angela Lansbury), see SONDAMUST1
A Broadway Extravaganza (instrumental), see BROADWAYEX [in medley]
Anyone Can Whistle Live at Carnegie Hall (Madeline Kahn, Ensemble), see ANYONE2
Kaye, Judy/*Diva by Diva*, Varese Sarabande VSD-5589, 1995 [in medley]
Mendelssohn Choir/*Mendelssohn Sings Sondheim*, see MENDELSSOHN1
Turner, Geraldine/*Old Friends*, see TURNERG1 [in medley]

"There's Always a Woman" cut from *Anyone Can Whistle* (1964)
Unsung Sondheim[3] (Kaye Ballard, Sally Mayes), see UNSUNGS1
Anyone Can Whistle Live at Carnegie Hall (Madeline Kahn, Bernadette Peters), see ANYONE2

"There's Something About a War" cut from *A Funny Thing Happened on the Way to the Forum* (1962)
A Stephen Sondheim Evening[1] (Cris Groenendaal and Men), see STEPHENSE1

"They Ask Me Why I Believe in You" from *I Believe in You* (1956, unproduced)
ASIV d^1-g^2
Unsung Sondheim (Rebecca Luker), see UNSUNGS1

Color and Light: Jazz Sketches . . . (Herbie Hancock, Stephen Sondheim on piano), see COLOR1

"They Do an Awful Lot of Dancing, the Dead," see "Evoe for the Dead"

"They Hear Drums (Scene 3, Part III)" from *Passion* (1995)
PPVS e♯-c♯², PVS g♯-e²

"Thinking" from *Do I Hear a Waltz?* (1965), music by Richard Rodgers
DIHPVS duet b-d♯²/a♯-c♯²
Do I Hear a Waltz? Original Cast (Sergio Franchi, Elizabeth Allen), see DOIHEAR1
Do I Hear a Waltz? Pasadena Playhouse Production (Anthony Crivello, Alyson Reed), see DOIHEAR2

"Third Letter" from *Passion* (1995)
PPVS company number
Passion Original Cast (Marrin Mazzie, Jere Shea), see PASSION1
Passion London Concert (Helen Hobson, Michael Ball), see PASSION3

"This Is Nice, Isn't It?" see "Isn't It?"

"This Is Show Biz" for *Climb High* (1950–52, unproduced) [incomplete]

"This Turf Is Ours" cut from *West Side Story* (1957), music by Leonard Bernstein

"This Week, Americans" from *Do I Hear a Waltz?* (1965), music by Richard Rodgers
DIHPVS a-b♭¹
Do I Hear a Waltz? Original Cast (Carol Bruce), see DOIHEAR1
Do I Hear a Waltz? Pasadena Playhouse Production (Carol Lawrence), see DOIHEAR2

"This World (Candide's Lament)" added to 1974 production of *Candide*, music by Leonard Bernstein
CaPVS, CaVS b♭-e♭²
Candide Revival Cast (Mark Baker), see CANDIDE01
Mendelssohn Choir/*Mendelssohn Sings Sondheim*, see MENDELSSOHN1

"Three Wishes for Christmas" cut from *Gypsy* (1957), music by Jule Styne
Cabaret Noel: A Broadway Cares Christmas, Lockett-Palmer 932512, 1993
A Christmas Wish (Chris Groenendahl), Broadway Cares CDH041, 199?
Anderson, D.C./*All Is Calm, All Is Bright*, LML CD-136, 2001

"Tick-Tock" from *Company* (1970) [arranged by David Shire using themes from the show, cut in later productions]
CPVS instumental
Company Original Cast (Orchestra), see COMPANY01
Company Revival Cast (Orchestra), see COMPANY05

"Together Wherever We Go" from *Gypsy* (1959), music by Jule Styne
GPVS trio a-b^1 [1 voice goes up to d^2], GVS duet c^1-d^2 [both]
Gypsy Original Cast (Ethel Merman, Jack Klugman, Sandra Church), see GYPSY01
Herb Geller and His All-Stars Play Selections from "Gypsy" (Barbara Lang), see GELLERH
Gypsy Film (Rosalind Russell/Lisa Kirk, Natalie Wood), see GYPSY02
Gypsy London Cast (Angela Lansbury, Barry Ingham, Zan Charisse), see GYPSY03
Gypsy Revival Cast (Tyne Daly, Jonathan Hadary, Crista Moore), see GYPSY04
Gypsy TV Cast (Bette Midler, Peter Riegert, Cynthia Gibb), see GYPSY05
Selections from "Gypsy" and "Flower Drum Song" (Florence Henderson), see GYPSY08
Kay Medford in "Gypsy" (Kay Medford, Lorraine Smith, Jimmy Blackburn), see GYPSY09
Buffalo Bills/*Together*, Warner Bros. (S)WS-1520, 1963
Four Lads, Columbia 45rpm 4-41409, 1960
Four Lads/*Golden Dozen (Best of Jule Styne)*, Columbia CL-1462, 1960
Garland, Judy/*Judy Duets* (with Liza Minnelli), see GARLAND [in medley]
Garland, Judy/*Judy Duets* (with Ethel Merman), see GARLAND [in medley]
Garland, Judy & Ethel Merman, *The Judy Garland Show*, Broadcast Tributes BTRIB 00002, 1964; later issued as *The Greatest Duets*, Paragon 1001, and as *Great Garland Duets* [in medley]
Garland, Judy & Liza Minnelli/*Judy Garland and Liza Minnelli*, Capitol (S)SWBO-2295, 1966
Garland, Judy & Liza Minnelli/ . . . *"Live" at the London Palladium*, Capitol ST-11191, 1964
Harnar, Jeff/*Jeff Harnar Sings the 1959 Broadway Songbook*, see HARNARJ1
Harvey, Jane/*The Other Side of Sondheim*, see HARVEYJ1 [part of "Rose's Medley"]
Hayman, Dick/*After Six*, MGM (S)SE-3827, 1960
Hi-Lo's, The/*Broadway Playbill*, see HILOS
Jackie & Roy/*Double Take*, Columbia CL-1704, (S)CS-8504, 1962
Jackie & Roy/*A Stephen Sondheim Collection*, see JACKIE&1
Kirby Stone Four/*Things Are Swingin'*, Warner Bros. (S)WS-1540, 1965
Lee, Peggy/*Ole Ala Lee*, Capitol (S)ST-1475, 1960

Lewis, Monica/ . . . *Swings Jule Styne*, DRG 802, 1991

MacKenzie, Gisele/ . . . *In Person at the Empire Room of the Waldorf-Astoria*, Everest LPBR 5069, 1960 [in medley]

Marie, Rose/*Songs for Single Girls*, Kapp (S)KRS-4500, 1964

Merman, Ethel/*Mermania!*, see MERMANE1

Minnelli, Liza/*Liza*, Capitol (S)ST-2174, 1966

Parker, John/*Sound of Conversations in Music*, Medallion (S)MS-7504, 1960

Patty, Sandi & Kathy Troccoli/*Together*, Monarch Records, Mona 1022, 1999

Pringle, Anne & Mark Burnell/*Little Things We Do Together*, Spectrum SR003, [n.d.]

Rory/*Little Broadway—Showtunes for Kids*, Sony 7464-48697-2, 1992

Ross, Annie/*Gypsy*, see ROSSANNIE

Sherwood, Roberta/*Live Performance*, Decca (S)DL7-4100, 1961

Skinner, Emily/*Emily Skinner* (duet with Alice Ripley), Fynsworth Alley 302 062 102 2, 2000 [with "You'll Never Get Away from Me"]

Steve & Eydie/*We Got Us*, ABC-Paramount ABC-300, 196[?]

Styne, Jule/*My Name Is Jule*, see STYNEJ1

Sullivan, Maxine/*Together: Maxine Sullivan Sings the Music of Jule Styne*, Atlantic 7 81783-1, 1987

"Tomorrow's Mother's Day" cut from *Gypsy* (1959), music by Jule Styne

"Tonight (Balcony Scene)" from *West Side Story* (1957), music by Leonard Bernstein

BOB, WSSPVS duet b♭-a♭^{2} [both], SSS, WSSVS solo version a-e♭^{2}

West Side Story Original Cast (Larry Kert, Carol Lawrence), see WESTSIDE01

West Side Story Film (Jim Bryant, Marni Nixon), see WESTSIDE02

West Side Story Studio Cast (Kiri Te Kanawa, José Carreras), see WESTSIDE03

Bernstein On Broadway (Peter Hofmann, Debbie Sasson), see BERNSTEINON1

West Side Story Studio Cast London (Michael Ball, Barbara Bonney), see WESTSIDE04

West Side Story Studio Cast Leicester Haymarket (Paul Manuel, Tinuke Olafimihan), see WESTSIDE05

West Side Story, The Songs of (Kenny Loggins, Wynonna), see WESTSIDE06

West Side Story London Production (Don McKay, Marlys Watters), see WESTSIDE08

Showcase: The Musicals (Mary Carewe, Michael Dore), Carlton Sounds/ U.K. 30367 00672, 1995

Shakespeare on Broadway (Glory Crampton, Sal Viviano), Varese Sarabande VSD-5622, 1996

Leonard Bernstein's New York (Audra McDonald, Mandy Patinkin), see LEONARDB1

West Side Story, Dave Grusin presents (Gloria Estefan), see WESTSIDE07

West Side Story London Studio Cast (David Holliday, Jill Martin), see WESTSIDE09

Allen, Thomas & Valerie Masterson/*If I Loved You* (Love Duets from the Musicals), TER Limited, 1993 [reissued on JAY Records as CDJAY 1233, 1996]

Bassey, Shirley/*I Wish You Love*, MFP/EMI MFP 50330, 1965

Chakiris, George/*George Chakiris*, Capitol (S)ST-1750, 1962

Church, Charlotte/*Enchantment*, Columbia CK 89710, 2001

Cook, Barbara/*Barbara Cook Sings Mostly Sondheim* (sung by Malcolm Gets), see COOKB1 [with "Something's Coming"]

Crawford, Michael/*Songs from the Stage & Screen*, see CRAWFORDM1

Damone, Vic/*On the Street Where You Live*, see DAMONE1

Davis Jr., Sammy/*Sammy Davis Jr. at the Cocoanut Grove*, see DAVISS [part of *West Side Story* medley]

Domingo, Placido/*The Broadway I Love*, see DOMINGO1

Drake, Alfred/*Alfred Drake & Roberta Peters Sing the Popular Music of Leonard Bernstein*, see DRAKEA

Eckstine, Billy/*Broadway, Bongos and Mr. B.*, Mercury M6-20637, SR-60637, 1961

Fisher, [David] Du Du/*Over the Rainbow*, Helicon Records HL 8064, 1989 [in Hebrew]

Fisher, Eddie/*Tonight with Eddie Fisher*, Ramrod (S)ST-6002, 1962

Fisher, Eddie/ . . . *At the Wintergarden*, Ramrod Records RR1-2, Taragon TARCD-1054, 1962, 69 [with "Maria" and "Something's Coming"]

Four Aces/*Hits from Broadway*, Decca (S) DL7-8855, 1959

Franchi, Sergio/*Broadway, I Love You!*, RCA Victor LSC 2674, 1963

Garland, Judy/*Judy Duets* (with Vic Damone), see GARLAND [in *West Side Story* medley]

Guest, Rob/*Standing Ovation*, EMI Music (Australian Group) 7986212, 1991 [in medley]

Harnar, Jeff/*Jeff Harnar Sings the 1959 Broadway Songbook*, see HARNARJ1

Hooper, Jeff/*As Long as I'm Singing*, Silverword CDSMG0004, 2001

Jay and the Americans/*Other Girls*, United Artists 45rpm UAL-353, 1961

Lawrence, Carol/*Tonight at 8:30*, see LAWRENCEC

Lawrence, Steve/*Lawrence Goes Latin*, United Artists UAL-3114, (S) UAS-6114, 1961

McKenzie, Julia/*The Musicals Album*, see MCKENZIEJ1

Melis, Jose/*Jose Melis on Broadway*, Mercury MG-20610, (S) SR-6-610, 1960

Mendieter, Anna Maria/*Broadway Center Stage*, Sugo Music SR9674, 1996

Migenes Johnson, Julia/*In Love*, RCA ARL1-7034, 1985
Migenes, Julia/*Live at the Olympia*, see MIGENES1
Nicholson, Carla & Michael/*Just Duet*, see NICHOLSONC1 [with "I Feel Pretty" and "Somewhere"]
O'Brien, Joanne & Lee Lessack/*An Enchanted Evening: The Music of Broadway*, LML Music, LML CD-104, 1998 [with "Some Enchanted Evening"]
Paris, Jackie/*The Song Is Paris*, Impulse! MVCI-23054, n.d.
Pot Pourri/*Something Familiar, Something Peculiar*, Move MCD086, 2000
Prior, Marina/*Somewhere*, see PRIORM1
Roy Budd Trio/*Everything's Coming Up Roses: The Musical . . . Sondheim*, see ROYBUDD1
Sanders, Felicia/*Shall I Take My Heart and Go?*, Decca 45rpm 9-30798, 1959
Stapleton, Cyril/*Dancing Down Broadway*, London LL-3033, (S) PS-134, 1959
Suzuki, Pat/*Pat Suzuki's Broadway '59*, Victor (S) LSP-1965, 1959
Vaughn, Sarah/*Live in Japan*, Mainstream MFCD 2-844-1, 1973, 1975
Waring, Fred/*Broadway Cavalcade*, Capitol (S) SWBO-1079, 1959
Waring, Fred/*The Time, the Place, the Girl*, Capitol (S) ST-1298, [n.d.]
Winston, Vic, BTP 78rpm 3012, 1959

"Tonight (Quintet)" from *West Side Story* (1957), music by Leonard Bernstein
WSSPVS quintet or company number
West Side Story Original Cast (Larry Kert, Carol Lawrence, Chita Rivera, Ken Le Roy, Mickey Calin, Ensemble), see WESTSIDE01
West Side Story Film (Jim Bryant, Marni Nixon, Betty Wand, The Jets, The Sharks), see WESTSIDE02
West Side Story Studio Cast (Kurt Ollmann, Richard Harrell, Sharks, Jets, Tatiana Troyanos, José Carreras, Kiri Te Kanawa), see WESTSIDE03 [also included on *Showstoppers from Broadway*, JAY Records, CDJAY 1266, 199?]
West Side Story Studio Cast London (Michael Ball, Barbara Bonney, La Verne Williams, Christopher Howard, Ensemble), see WESTSIDE04
West Side Story Studio Cast Leicester Haymarket (Nicholas Warnford, Jets, Nick Ferranti, Sharks, Paul Manuel, Caroline O'Connor, Tinuke Olafimihan), see WESTSIDE05
A Gala Concert for Hal Prince (Teri Bibb, Dave Willetts, Company), see GALA1

"Too Many Mornings" from *Follies* (1971)
ASIV solo version $c^{\sharp 1}$-a$\flat^2$, FLVS, FVS solo version $c^{\sharp 1}$-f^2, FPVS duet b-e^2/c^1-f$^{\sharp 2}$
Follies Original Cast (John McMartin, Dorothy Collins), see FOLLIES01
Sondheim: A Musical Tribute (Dorothy Collins, John McMartin), see SONDAMUST1 [sung with "Pleasant Little Kingdom"]

Side by Side by Sondheim[1] (Julia McKenzie, David Kernan), see SIDEBYS1
Sondheim (Book-of-the-Month) (Cris Groenendaal, Betsy Joslyn), see SOND1
Follies in Concert (George Hearn, Barbara Cook), see FOLLIES02
Follies London Cast (Daniel Massey, Julia McKenzie), see FOLLIES03
Follies/Themes from the Legendary Musical (The Trotter Trio), see FOLLIES04
Celebrating Sondheim (Claire Moore, Michael Ball), see CELEBRATSON
Follies, The Complete Recording (Laurence Guittard, Donna McKechnie), see FOLLIES05
Clary, Robert/*Louis Lebeau Remembers . . . Stephen Sondheim . . .*, see CLARYR1
Jahana, Raishel/*Sondheim Songs*, see JAHANA1
Patinkin, Mandy/*Oscar and Steve*, see PATINKIN4 (duet with Judy Blazer) [sung with "Pleasant Little Kingdom"]
Roy, William/*When I Sing Alone*, Audiophile (D)AP-213, 1986; ACD-213, 1996
Wilk, Oystein/*Too Many Mornings*, see WILKO1
Wilson, Julie/*Julie Wilson Sings the Stephen Sondheim Songbook*, see WILSONJ2

"Toreadorables" from *Gypsy* (1959), music by Jule Styne
GPVS g^1-g^2 company number

"The Tower of Bray" from *Sweeney Todd* (1979), [see "Parlor Songs" for recordings]
STPVS trio d^1-e^3 [f^2 alternate]/d^1-d^3 [f^2 alternate]/d^1-f^2

"Transition(s)" from *Passion* (1995)
PPVS company numbers
Passion Original Cast (Various), see PASSION1
Stephen Sondheim's Passion . . . In Jazz (The Trotter Trio), see PASSION2
Passion London Concert (Company), see PASSION3

"Transition(s)," see "Merrily We Roll Along" from *Merrily We Roll Along*

"Traveling Music" from *The Frogs* (1975)
The Frogs/Evening Primrose Studio Recording (Nathan Lane, Brian Stokes Mitchell & Male Chorus), see FROGS1

"Trio (Scene Seven)" from *Passion* (1995)
PPVS trio
Passion Original Cast (Donna Murphy, Jere Shea, Marrin Mazzie), see PASSION1
Passion London Concert (Maria Friedman, Michael Ball, Helen Hobson), see PASSION3

"Trotsky at Saint-Palais" from *Stavisky* (1974)
Stavisky (instrumental), see STAVISKY1

"Truly Content" from *Passionella* (1962) [part of *The World of Jules Feiffer*]
ASIII g-c²
Unsung Sondheim (Judy Kaye), see UNSUNGS1
Malmberg, Myrra/*What Can You Lose?*, see MALMBERG1

"Two by Two" cut from *Do I Hear a Waltz?* (1965), music by Richard Rodgers
Bennett, Tony/*If I Ruled the World—Tony Bennett Songs for the Jet Set*, Columbia CL- 2343, (S)CS-9143, 1965, CBS/Sony CD 25DP-5320, 199[?]

"Two Fairy Tales" cut from *A Little Night Music* (1973)
ASIII b-f²/a#-f#5²
Sondheim: A Musical Tribute (Mark Lambert, Victoria Mallory), see SOND-
AMUST1
*Marry Me a Little*¹ (Suzanne Henry, Craig Lucas), see MARRYME1

"The Two of You" for *Kukla, Fran and Ollie* (1952)
ASIV b♭-e♭²
Unsung Sondheim (Christa Moore), see UNSUNGS1

"Unworthy of Your Love" from *Assassins* (1991)
APVS, ASIV, AVS duet b-f#²/a-d²
Assassins Original Cast (Greg Germann, Annie Golden), see ASSASSINS1

"Uptown, Downtown" cut from *Follies* (1971)
ASII a-c#²
*Marry Me a Little*¹ (Craig Lucas), see MARRYME1
Songs of New York (Judy Kaye), Book-of-the-Month Records 11-7500, 1984
Sondheim—A Celebration (Millicent Martin) see SONDACEL1
Follies, The Complete Recording (Dee Hoty, Ensemble), see FOLLIES05
Bennett, Richard Rodney/*A Different Side of Sondheim*, see BENNETTR1

"Variations on a Theme (Katie Malone)" (1947)
Sondheim Tonight (Dominic John, pianist), see SONDTON1

"A Very Nice Prince" from *Into the Woods* (1987)
ITWPVS duet a♭-c²/e♭¹-a♭¹, (Reprise) a-c#²/[dialogue]
Into the Woods Original Cast (Kim Crosby, Joanna Gleason) see INTOTHE1
Into the Woods London Cast (Jacqueline Dankworth, Imelda Staunton),
see INTOTHE2
Into the Woods Revival Cast (Laura Benanti, Kerry O'Malley), see INTOTHE3

"A Very Short Violin Sonata" (1951)
  Sondheim Tonight (Christina Sunnerstam, violinist), see SONDTON1

"Vincent and Vanessa," see "Bolero d'Amour"

"Wait" from *Sweeney Todd* (1979)
  ASIII, STVS c^1-f^2, STPVS b♭-e♭^{2}
  Sweeney Todd Original Cast (Angela Lansbury), see SWEENEYT1
  Sweeney Todd Barcelona Cast (Vicky Pena), see SWEENEYT3
  Sweeney Todd Live at the NYP (Patti LuPone), see SWEENEYT4
  The MUSICality of Sondheim[4] (Judy Kaye), JAY Records CDJAZ 9006, 2002
  Gay Men's Chorus of Los Angeles/*Simply Sondheim*, see GAYMENSCLA1 [in medley]

"Waiting for the Girls Upstairs" from *Follies* (1971)
  FPVS, SCCH octet, FLVS, FVS solo version b♭-c^2
  Follies Original Cast (Gene Nelson, John McMartin, Dorothy Collins, Alexis Smith, Harvey Evans, Kurt Peterson, Virginia Sandifur, Marti Rolph), see FOLLIES01
  Side by Side . . . Australian Cast (Jill Perryman, Bartholomew John), see SIDEBYS2
  Follies in Concert (Jim Walton, Howard McGillin, Mandy Patinkin, George Hearn, Lee Remick, Barbara Cook, Liz Callaway, Daisy Prince), see FOLLIES02
  Follies London Cast (Diana Rigg, Julia McKenzie, Daniel Massey, David Healy, Gillian Bevan, Deborah Poplett, Simon Green, Evan Pappas), see FOLLIES03
  Sondheim: A Celebration at Carnegie Hall (George Lee Andrews, Michael Jeter, James Naughton), see SONDACELATC1
  Follies/Themes from the Legendary Musical (The Trotter Trio), see FOLLIES04
  Follies, The Complete Recording (Tony Roberts, Laurence Guittard, Dee Hoty, Donna McKechnie, Billy Hartung, Michael Gruber, Meredith Patterson, Danette Holden), see FOLLIES05

"Wallflowers' Waltz" from *By George* (1946)

"Waltz" from *Climb High* (1950–52, unproduced)

"Water Under the Bridge" for *Singing Out Loud* (1992–93, unproduced)
  SCCH, SSFTS a-e^2, sheet music published as Warner Bros. VS6208
  Sondheim: A Celebration at Carnegie Hall (Liza Minnelli, Billy Stritch), see SONDACELATC1

Unsung Sondheim (Debbie Shapiro Gravitte), see UNSUNGS1
Out On Broadway (Eddie Webb), see OUTONB1
Moving On (Company), see MOVINGON

"We Do Not Belong Together" from *Sunday in the Park with George* (1984)
BSBB [incorporated into "Move On"], SPGPVS duet g-d^2/a-e^2
Sunday in the Park . . . Original Cast (Bernadette Peters, Mandy Patinkin), see SUNDAYIN1

"We Float" cut from *Pacific Overtures* (1976) [related to "The Advantages of Floating in the Middle of the Sea"]

"The Wedding Is Off" cut from *Company* (1970)

"Wedding Sequence" from *All That Glitters* (1949)

"A Weekend in the Country" from *A Little Night Music* (1973)
LNMPVS, SCCH sextet and vocal quintet
A Little Night Music Original Cast^2 (Company), see LITTLEN01
A Little Night Music London Cast^1 (Company), see LITTLEN02
A Little Night Music Film (Company), see LITTLEN03
A Little Sondheim Music (Janet Smith, Michael Gallup, Ensemble), see LITTLES1
A Little Night Music Studio Cast (Company), see LITTLEN04
Sondheim: A Celebration at Carnegie Hall (Kevin Anderson, George Lee Andrews, Mark Jacoby, Beverly Lambert, Maureen Moore, Susan Terry, Quintet), see SONDACELATC1
A Little Night Music Royal National Theatre (Company), see LITTLEN05
Celebrating the Musicals . . . (Ensemble), see CELEBRATTHEM
A Little Night Music Barcelona Cast (Company), see LITTLEN06 [and reprise by Quintet]

"Welcome to Kanagawa" from *Pacific Overtures* (1976)
POPVS c^1-e^2 & chorus
Pacific Overtures^1 Original Cast (Ernest Harada, Timm Fujii, Patrick Kinser-Lau, Gedde Watanabe, Leslie Watanabe, Mako), see PACIFICOVER1
Pacific Overtures English National Opera (Terry Jenkins, Gordon Christie, Michael Sadler, John Cashmore, Leon Berger, Richard Angas), see PACIFICOVER2

"We're Bringing Back Style to the White House," see "Bobby and Jackie and Jack"

"We're Gonna Be All Right" from *Do I Hear a Waltz?* (1965), music by Richard Rodgers
DIHPVS duet a-e♭^{2}/a-d^2
Do I Hear a Waltz? Original Cast^2 (Stuart Damon, Julienne Marie), see DOIHEAR1
Sondheim: A Musical Tribute (Laurence Guittard, Teri Ralston), see SONDAMUST1
Side by Side by Sondheim (Millicent Martin, David Kernan), see SIDEBYS1
Side by Side . . . Australian Cast (Bartholomew John, Geraldene Morrow), see SIDEBYS2
Do I Hear a Waltz? Pasadena Playhouse Production (Benjamin Sprunger, Annie Wersching), see DOIHEAR2
Singers Unlimited/*A Little Light Music* (Beryl Korman, Julia Meadows), see SINGERSUN1

"We're Gonna Have a Meeting" from *Phinney's Rainbow* (1948)

"What a Day," see "Auto da fé"

"What Can You Lose?" from *Dick Tracy* (1990)
ASIV, SSFTS b-f♯^{2}, DTVS c^1-g^2
Color and Light: Jazz Sketches . . . (Jim Hall, guitar), see COLOR1
Unsung Sondheim (Judy Kuhn), see UNSUNGS1
Sondheim at the Movies^3 (Guy Haines), see SONDATTHEM1
Sondheim: A Celebration (Billy Porter), see SONDACEL2 [with "Not a Day Goes By"]
Songs Without Words/A Windham Hill Collections (Stephen Sondheim), Windham Hill 01934-11212-2, 1997 [piano solo]
Out On Broadway (Quenten Schumacher), see OUTONB1
Madonna/I'm Breathless, (Madonna, Mandy Patinkin), see MADONNA1
Malmberg, Myrra/*What Can You Lose?*, see MALMBERG1
Prior, Marina/*Somewhere*, see PRIORM1
Turner, Geraldine/*Old Friends*, see TURNERG1 [with "Love I Hear"; added to 1997 reissue]
Wilk, Oystein/*Too Many Mornings*, see WILKO1 [duet with Guri Schanke]

"What Do We Do? We Fly!" from *Do I Hear a Waltz?* (1965), music by Richard Rodgers
DIHPVS quintet c^1-a♭^{2} [all]
Do I Hear a Waltz? Original Cast (Madelaine Sherwood, Jack Manning, Elizabeth Allen, Julienne Marie, Stuart Damon), see DOIHEAR1
Do I Hear a Waltz? Pasadena Playhouse Production (Elmarie Wendel, Jack Riley, Annie Wersching, Benjamin Sprunger), see DOIHEAR2

"What Do You Do with a Woman?" (incomplete) for *A Funny Thing Happened on the Way to the Forum* (1962)

"What More Do I Need?" from *Saturday Night* (1954)
ASII, SNVS b♭-e♭²
A Stephen Sondheim Evening[1] (Liz Callaway), see STEPHENSE1
Saturday Night Bridewell Cast (Anna Francolini, Sam Newman, Company), see SATURDAYN1
Saturday Night Original New York Cast (David Campbell, Lauren Ward, Company), see SATURDAYN2
Moving On (Company), see MOVINGON [with "Who Wants to Live in New York?"
Brightman, Sarah/*Encore*, Decca Broadway/Really Useful [n.n.], 2002
Harvey, Jane/*The Other Side of Sondheim*, see HARVEYJ1
O'Donnell, Kerryn/*What More Do I Need?*, [n.l., n.n.], 2001, [Australian]
Turner, Geraldine/ . . . *Sings the Stephen Sondheim Songbook, Vol. 2*, see TURNERG2
Upshaw, Dawn/*I Wish It So*, see UPSHAWD1
Woodfield, Ann/*Shades of Reflection*, Guild Music Ltd/Zah Zah ZZCD 9805, 1998

"What to Do at George School" from *By George* (1946)

"What Would We Do Without You?" from *Company* (1970) [usually considered a part of "Side by Side by Side"]
Putting It Together (Company [with lyric changes by Sondheim]), see PUTTINGIT1
Boston Pops Orchestra/*Songs of the '60s* (instrumental), see BOSTON1

"What's Next" written for *Gold!* (forthcoming)

"When?" from *Evening Primrose* (1966)
SSFTS duet b♭-f²/a♯-e²
Sondheim at the Movies (Liz Callaway, Gary Beach), see SONDATTHEM1
The Frogs/Evening Primrose Studio Recording (Neil Patrick Harris, Theresa McCarthy), see FROGS1
Patinkin, Mandy/*Dress Casual* (Mandy Patinkin, Bernadette Peters), see PATINKIN2

"When I Get Famous" from *Climb High* (1950–52, unproduced)

"When I See You" from *All That Glitters* (1949)
ATGVS b♭-e♭²

"Where Do I Belong?" from *Climb High* (1950–52, unproduced)

"Who Could Be Blue?" cut from *Follies* (1971) [usually paired with "Lit-tle White House"; music used for "Salon at Claridge #2" in *Stavisky*]
ASII duet d♭^{1}-g♭^{2}/b♭-g♭5^2 [with "Little White House"]
Marry Me a Little[1] (Craig Lucas), see MARRYME1
Follies, The Complete Recording (Laurence Guittard), see FOLLIES05
The Stephen Sondheim Album (Norm Lewis), see STEPHENSA1 [with "With So Little to Be Sure of"]

"Who Knows?/I Know" from *Hot Spot* (1963), music with Mary Rodgers, lyric with Martin Charnin, new lyrics by Mark Waldrop
hey, love (Faith Prince, Mark Waldrop, Jason Workman), see HEYLOVE1

"Who Needs Him?" cut from *Gypsy* (1959), music by Jule Styne

"Who Wants to Live in New York?" from *Merrily We Roll Along* (1981) [usually found as a section of "Opening Doors"]
Moving On (Company), see MOVINGON [with "What More Do I Need?"]

"Who's That Woman?" from *Follies* (1971)
FPVS e-f♯^{2} + chorus, FLVS, FVS b♭-g♭^{2} + chorus
Follies Original Cast (Mary McCarty, Company), see FOLLIES01
Follies in Concert (Phyllis Newman, Women, Chorus, Dancers), see FOLLIES02
Follies London Cast (Lynda Baron, Women), see FOLLIES03
Sondheim: A Celebration (Susan Johnson), see SONDACEL2
Follies/Themes from the Legendary Musical (The Trotter Trio), see FOL-LIES04
Follies, The Complete Recording (Phyllis Newman, "The Weismann Girls"), see FOLLIES05

"Wigmaker Sequence" from *Sweeney Todd* (1979)
STPVS duet B♭-d^1/c♯^{1}-d^2 + quintet
Sweeney Todd Original Cast (Len Cariou, Victor Garber), see SWEENEYT1
Sweeney Todd Barcelona Cast (Constantino Romero, Pep Molina), see SWEENEYT3
Sweeney Todd Live at the NYP (George Hearn, Davis Gaines), see SWEENEYT4

"Window Across the Way" cut from *A Funny Thing Happened on the Way to the Forum* (1962)

"Wise Guys" written for *Gold!* (forthcoming)

"Witch's Lament" from *Into the Woods* (1987)
ITWPVS a-d^2
Into the Woods Original Cast (Bernadette Peters), see INTOTHE1
Into the Woods London Cast (Julia McKenzie), see INTOTHE2
Into the Woods Revival Cast (Vanessa Williams), see INTOTHE3

"With So Little to Be Sure of" from *Anyone Can Whistle* (1964)
ACWPVS duet a-c$\sharp^2$/b-e^2, ACWVS, ASIV, SCCH solo version b-e^2
Anyone Can Whistle Original Cast^2 (Lee Remick, Harry Guardino), see
ANYONE1
Sondheim (Book-of-the-Month) (Chamber ensemble), see SOND1
A Little Sondheim Music (Darlene Romano, Paul Johnson), see LITTLES1
A Stephen Sondheim Evening (Victoria Mallory, Geoge Hearn), see
STEPHENSE1
Everyone's a Love Song, see EVERYONE1
Sondheim: A Celebration at Carnegie Hall (Jerry Hadley, Carolann Page),
see SONDACELATC1
Anyone Can Whistle Live at Carnegie Hall (Scott Bakula, Bernadette Pe-
ters), see ANYONE2
The Stephen Sondheim Album (Norm Lewis), see STEPHENSA1 [with "Who
Could Be Blue?"]
Moving On (Company), see MOVINGON [with "Our Time"]
Bennett, Richard Rodney/*A Different Side of Sondheim*, see BENNETTR1
Breach, Joyce/*This Moment*, Audiophile ACD-293, 1996
Ford, Anne Kerry/*Something Wonderful*, see FORDA1
Harvey, Jane/*The Other Side of Sondheim*, see HARVEYJ1
Intimate Broadway/*My Favorite Things*, Intersound 8311, 1996
Jiear, Alison/*Simply Alison Jiear*, Dress Circle DAD 007/1, 1995
Jobson, Mark deVille/*My House*, see JOBSON1
Lawrence, Steve/*Steve Lawrence Sings*, Columbia CL-2540, (S)CS-9340,
1967
Stage 3/*True Colors*, DINK [n.n.], 1998
Turner, Geraldine/*Old Friends*, see TURNERG1
Whyte, Ronny/*All in a Night's Work*, Audiophile ACD-247, 1989 [re-
issued]
Wilk, Oystein/*Too Many Mornings*, see WILKO1 [duet with Guri Schanke]
Wilson, Julie/*Julie Wilson Sings the Stephen Sondheim Songbook*, see
WILSONJ2

"With So Little to be Sure of" (first version) cut from *Anyone Can Whistle*
(1964)

"A Woman's Place Is in the Home," see "Simple"

"Women and Death" from *Stavisky* (1974)
   Stavisky (instrumental), see STAVISKY1

"Women Were Born to Wait" cut from *A Little Night Music* (1973) [related
   to "In Praise of Women"]

"The World's Full of Girls/ . . . Boys" cut from *Follies* (1971) [music used
   as "Operetta" in *Stavisky*]
   ASIV group number with solos

"The Worst Pies in London" from *Sweeney Todd* (1979)
   STPVS b-e♭²
   Sweeney Todd Original Cast (Angela Lansbury), see SWEENEYT1
   Sondheim (Book-of-the-Month) (Joyce Castle), see SOND1
   Sweeney Todd Barcelona Cast (Vicky Pena), see SWEENEYT3
   Sweeney Todd Live at the NYP (Patti LuPone), see SWEENEYT4

"The Year of the . . ." cut from *The Race to Urga* (1968, unproduced), music
   by Leonard Bernstein

"Yes" for *The Jet-Propelled Couch* (1958, unproduced) [music became "Salon at the Claridge #1" in *Stavisky*]

"Yoo-hoo!" from *Climb High* (1950–52, unproduced)

"Yoo-hoo!" cut from *Sunday in the Park with George* (1984) [portions can
   still be heard in the score]

"You" written for *Gold!* (forthcoming)

"You Can't Judge a Book by Its Cover," see "Simple"

"You [I] Could Drive a Person Crazy" from *Company* (1970)
   CPVS trio [voices range from b-a², CVS, HTSS, SCCH trio d¹-d² [one
   voice rises to a g²], CVS2 trio [voices range from a-g²]
   Company Original Cast (Donna McKechnie, Susan Browning, Pamela
   Myers), see COMPANY01
   Sondheim: A Musical Tribute (Donna McKechnie, Susan Browning,
   Pamela Myers), see SONDAMUST1
   Side by Side by Sondheim (Millicent Martin, David Kernan, Julia McKen-
   zie), see SIDEBYS1
   Side by Side . . . Australian Cast (Jill Perryman, Bartholomew John, Ger-
   aldene Morrow), see SIDEBYS2

Songs of Sondheim Irish Cast (Company), see SONGSOFSOND1

Sondheim: A Celebration at Carnegie Hall (Dorothy Loudon), see SOND-ACELATC1 [in medley]

Putting It Together (Christopher Durang), see PUTTINGIT1

Stephen Sondheim's Company . . . In Jazz (The Trotter Trio), see COMPANY03

Company Revival Cast (La Chanze, Charlotte d'Amboise, Jane Krakowski), see COMPANY05

Company London Revival Cast (Hannah James, Kiran Hocking, Anna Francolini), see COMPANY04

Sondheim: A Celebration[3] (David Cassidy, Patrick Cassidy, Shaun Cassidy), see SONDACEL2

Hey, Mr. Producer! (Maria Friedman, Ruthie Henshall, Millicent Martin, Lea Salonga), see HEYMRP

Celebrating Sondheim (Claire Moore, Rosemary Ashe, Mary Carewe), see CELEBRATSON

The 3 Divas (Judi Connelli, Suzanne Johnston, Jennifer McGregor), CDP 2000/DIVA003-1, 2000

Company Brazilian Cast (Doriana Mendes, Sabrina Korgut, Patricia Levy), see COMPANY06

Clary, Robert/*Robert Clary Sings at the Jazz Bakery in Los Angeles*, Original Cast Records 9799, 1997 [with "Not While I'm Around," and "Losing My Mind"]

Cook, Barbara/*Barbara Cook Sings Mostly Sondheim*, see COOKB1

East West Players/*East West Overtures* (Cindy Cheung, Jennifer Fujii, MaryAnn Hu), see EASTWEST1

Gillan, James/*James Gillan*, [n.l., n.n.], 2001

Laine, Cleo/*Cleo Sings Sondheim*, see LAINEC2

McKechnie, Donna/*Inside the Music*, see MCKECHNIED1

Peters, Bernadette/*Sondheim, Etc.*, see PETERSB1

Prior, Marina/*Somewhere*, see PRIORM1

"You Don't Want Me to Go" written for *Gold!* (forthcoming)

"You Gotta Have a Gimmick" from Gypsy (1959), music by Jule Styne GPVS trio g-d^2/b♭-d^2/b♭-d^2, HTSS solo version g-d^2

Gypsy Original Cast[2] (Faith Dane, Chotzi Foley, Maria Karnilova), see GYPSY01

Gypsy Film (Roxanne Arlen, Faith Dane, Betty Bruce), see GYPSY02

Gypsy London Cast (Kelly Wilson, Judy Cannon, Valerie Walsh), see GYPSY03

Jerome Robbins Broadway (Debbie Shapiro, Faith Prince, Susann Fletcher), see JEROMER1

Gypsy Revival Cast (Jana Robbins, Anna McNeely, Barbara Erwin), see GYPSY04

Gypsy TV Cast (Linda Hart, Anna McNeely, Christine Ebersole), see GYPSY05

Hey, Mr. Producer! (Ruthie Henshall, Julia McKenzie, Bernadette Peters, Michael Ball, Judi Dench, Maria Friedman, David Kernan, Millicent Martin, Lea Salonga), see HEYMRP

Gypsy German Cast (Pascale Camele, Janet Calvert, Michelle Becker), see GYPSY07

Kay Medford in "Gypsy" (Janet Webb, Janette Gale, Betty Winsett), see GYPSY09

"You Must Meet My Wife" from *A Little Night Music* (1973)
ASI, LNMVS, SSS solo version d♭^{1}-f^2, LNMPVS duet c^1-e^2
A Little Night Music Original Cast^2 (Len Cariou, Glynis Johns), see LITTLEN01
Side by Side by Sondheim (Millicent Martin, David Kernan), see SIDEBYS1
Side by Side . . . Australian Cast (Jill Perryman, Bartholomew John), see SIDEBYS2
A Little Night Music London Cast (Joss Ackland, Jean Simmons), see LITTLEN02
A Little Night Music Film (Len Cariou, Elizabeth Taylor), see LITTLEN03
Sondheim (Book-of-the-Month) (Chamber ensemble), see SOND1
A Little Night Music Studio Cast (Eric Flynn, Sian Phillips), see LITTLEN04
A Little Night Music Royal National Theatre (Judi Dench, Laurence Guittard), see LITTLEN05
Celebrating the Musicals . . . (Stephen Hill, Anita Dobson), see CELEBRATTHEM
A Little Night Music Barcelona Cast (Vicky Pena, Constantino Romero), see LITTLEN06 [and reprise by Alberto Demestres]
Bennett, Richard Rodney/*A Different Side of Sondheim* (piano solo), see BENNETTR1
Heller, Marc/*Take Me to the World: Songs by Stephen Sondheim*, see HELLERM1
Trotter, Terry/*Stephen Sondheim's A Little Night Music*, see TROTTERT1 [piano solo]

"You Would Love My Wife" incomplete for *Follies* (1971)

"You'll Never Get Away from Me" from *Gypsy* (1959), music by Jule Styne [same music as "I'm in Pursuit of Happiness" from *Ruggles of Red Gap*, lyric by Leo Robin, and "Why Did You Have to Wait So Long?" for *Pink Tights*, unfinished lyric by Sammy Cahn]
GPVS duet f♯-c^2/b-g♯^{1}, GVS solo version a-e♭^{2}
Gypsy Original Cast (Ethel Merman, Jack Klugman), see GYPSY01
Gypsy Film (Rosalind Russell), see GYPSY02

Gypsy London Cast (Angela Lansbury, Barrie Ingham), see GYPSY03
Gypsy Revival Cast (Tyne Daly, Jonathan Hadary), see GYPSY04
Gypsy TV Cast (Bette Midler, Peter Riegert), see GYPSY05
Gypsy German Cast (Angelika Milster, Cusch Jung), see GYPSY07
Selections from "Gypsy" and "Flower Drum Song" (Florence Henderson), see GYPSY08
Kay Medford in "Gypsy" (Kay Medford, Jimmy Blackburn), see GYPSY09
Bennett, Tony, Columbia 45rpm 4-41381, 1960
Bennett, Tony/*More Tony's Greatest Hits*, Columbia CL-1535, (S)CS8335, 1960
Bennett, Tony/*Mr. Broadway*, Columbia CL-1763, (S)CS-8563, 1962
Betts/Harry O. & Brown Singers/*Now Playing*, AVA (S)AS-23, 1963
Davis Jr., Sammy, Decca 45rpm 9-30898, 1960
Dijon, Coby, Epic 45rpm 5-9347, 1960
Feinstein, Michael/*Michael Feinstein Sings the Jule Styne Songbook*, see FEINSTEIN1
Harvey, Jane/*The Other Side of Sondheim*, see HARVEYJ1 [part of "Rose's Medley"]
Harnar, Jeff/*Jeff Harnar Sings the 1959 Broadway Songbook*, see HARNARJ1
Henderson, Bill, GM 45rpm K13155, 1964
Hi-Lo's, The/*Broadway Playbill*, see HILOS
Kuhn, Judy/*Just in Time—Judy Kuhn Sings Jule Styne*[3], Varese Sarabande VSD-5472, 1995
Lawrence, Carol/*Tonight at 8:30*, see LAWRENCEC
Merman, Ethel/*Mermania!*, see MERMANE1
Ross, Annie/*Gypsy*, see ROSSANNIE
Sherwood, Roberta/*Live Performance*, Decca (S)DL7-4100, 1961
Skinner, Emily/*Emily Skinner* (duet with Alice Ripley), Fynsworth Alley 302 062 102 2, 2000 [with "Together Wherever We Go"]
Smith, Ethel/*Ethel On Broadway*, Decca (S)DL7-8993, 1960
Styne, Jule/*My Name Is Jule*, see STYNEJ1
Turrentine, Stanley/*Never Let Me Go*, BLN (S)BST8-4129, 1964

"Your Eyes Are Blue" cut from *A Funny Thing Happened on the Way to the Forum* (1962), [see also "Love Story"]
Sondheim: A Musical Tribute (Harvey Evans, Pamela Hall), see SONDAMUST1
Marry Me a Little[1] (Craig Lucas, Suzanne Henry), see MARRYME1
Stephen Sondheim's A Funny Thing . . . Forum . . . In Jazz (The Trotter Trio) see FUNNY04
Mayes, Sally/*Boys and Girls Like You and Me* (with Brent Barrett), see MAYESS1 [with "All Things Bright and Beautiful"]

"Your Fault" from *Into the Woods* (1987)
ITWPVS vocal quintet
Into the Woods Original Cast (Chip Zien, Ben Wright, Danielle Ferland, Bernadette Peters, Kim Crosby), see INTOTHE1
Into the Woods London Cast (Ian Bartholomew, Richard Dempsey, Tessa Burbridge, Julia McKenzie, Jacqueline Dankworth), see INTOTHE2
Into the Woods Revival Cast (Stephen DeRosa, Molly Ephraim, Vanessa Williams, Laura Benanti), see INTOTHE3

"You're Gonna Love Tomorrow" from *Follies* (1971) [double duet with "Love Will See Us Through"]
FPVS double duet $c\sharp^1$-$g\flat^2$/$c\flat^1$-e^2/$d\flat^1$-$g\flat^2$/$e\flat^1$-$g\flat^2$
Follies Original Cast (Kurt Peterson, Virginia Sandifur), see FOLLIES01
Follies in Concert (Howard McGillin, Daisy Prince), see FOLLIES02
A Stephen Sondheim Evening[1] (Cris Groenendaal, Judy Kaye), see STEPHENSE1 [not on cd, available on *A Collector's Sondheim*]
Follies London Cast (Simon Green, Gillian Bevan), see FOLLIES03
Follies, The Complete Recording (Michael Gruber, Meredith Patterson), see FOLLIES05
Out On Broadway (Keith Thompson, Chris Brenner, Quenten Schumacher, Tracy Collins), see OUTONB1
The Stephen Sondheim Album (Christiane Noll), see STEPHENSA1 [with "Not a Day Goes By"]

"You've Broken My Heart" from *All That Glitters* (1949)

PRIMARY SONDHEIM RECORDINGS

ALEXR1: Roberta Alexander/*With You* (1996[?])
Et'Cetera
CD: KTC 1190
Songs: "Can That Boy Foxtrot!," "Good Thing Going," "I Remember"

ANYONE1: *Anyone Can Whistle* Original Broadway Cast Recording (1964)
Columbia Records
LP: KOL-6080 (M)/KOS-2480 (S)
S-32608 (S); reissue
AS-32608 (S) [Columbia Special Products]
CD: CK-02480
Cassette: JST-02480
Songs: "Anyone Can Whistle," "Come Play Wiz Me," "The Cookie Chase," "Everybody Says Don't," "I've Got You to Lean On," "Me and My Town," "Miracle Song," "A Parade in Town," "Prelude," "See What It Gets You," "Simple," "There Won't Be Trumpets," "With So Little to Be Sure of"

ANYONE2: *Anyone Can Whistle* Live at Carnegie Hall (1995)
Columbia
CD: CK 67224
Songs: "Anyone Can Whistle," "Come Play Wiz Me," "Cookie Chase," "Everybody Says Don't," "I'm Like the Bluebird," [included in "Miracle Introduction"] "I've Got You to Lean On," "Me and My Town," "Miracle Song," "A Parade in Town," "Prelude," [listed as "Overture"] "See What It Gets You," "Simple," "There Won't Be Trumpets," "There's Always a Woman," "With So Little to Be Sure of"

ANYONE3: *Anyone Can Whistle* Studio Cast Recording (ca. 2002, unreleased)
JAY Records
CD: TBD; 2-disc set

ASSASSINS1: *Assassins* Original Cast Recording (1991)
RCA Records
CD: 60737-2-RC [DDD]
Cassette: 60737-4-RC
Songs: "Another National Anthem," "The Ballad of Booth," "The Ballad of Czolgosz," "The Ballad of Guiteau," "Everybody's Got the Right," "Gun Song," "How I Saved Roosevelt," "Unworthy of Your Love"

BALLM1: Michael Ball/*The Musicals* (1996)
Polygram TV
CD: 533892-2
Songs: "Losing My Mind," "Loving You," "Something's Coming"

BARNETTEARLY1: Peter Barnett and Julia Early/*In So Many Words* (1996)
A Barnett Early Production
CD: PBJECD001
Songs: "The Boy From . . .," "Live Alone and Like It," "Marry Me a Little," "Take Me to the World"

BARRJ1: John Barr/*In Whatever Time We Have* (1998)
Dress Circle
CD: MBJBTDM2
Songs: "Multitudes of Amys," "Not While I'm Around," "One Hand, One Heart," "There Won't Be Trumpets"

BARROWMAN1: John Barrowman/*Reflections from Broadway* (2000)
JAY Records
CD: CDJAY 1333
Songs: "Anyone Can Whistle," "Being Alive," "Good Thing Going," "Not While I'm Around"

BEECHMAN1: Laurie Beechman/*No One Is Alone* (1996)
Varese Sarabande
CD: VSD-5623
Songs: "Being Alive," "No One Is Alone," "One Hand, One Heart"

BENNETTR1: Richard Rodney Bennett/*A Different Side of Sondheim* (1979)
DRG Records
LP: SL 5182
Cassette: SLC-5182
CD: 5182 (issued on cd in 1995)
Songs: "Anyone Can Whistle," "Barcelona," "I Do Like You," "I Remember," "Night Waltz (I)," "Salon at the Claridge #1," "So Many People," "Take Me to the World," "Uptown, Downtown," "With So Little to Be Sure of," "You Must Meet My Wife"

BERNSTEINON1: *Bernstein On Broadway*/Peter Hofmann & Debbie Sasson (1985)
Horzu/CBS [German release]
LP: FM 39535/CB 321
CBS [American release]
LP: 7464-39535-1
Songs: "Cool," "I Feel Pretty," "Maria," "One Hand, One Heart," "Prologue," "Something's Coming," "Somewhere," "Tonight"

BIRDCAGE: *The birdcage* Motion Picture Soundtrack (1996)
United Artists/e.a.r.
CD: 0029782EDL
Songs: "Can That Boy Foxtrot!," "Little Dream," "Love Is in the Air"

BLACKWELL1: Harolyn Blackwell/*A Simple Song: Blackwell Sings Bernstein* (1996)
RCAVictor
CD: 09026-68321-2
Songs: "America," "A Boy Like That," "I Have a Love," "Somewhere"

BLAINEV1: Vivian Blaine/*For You* (1983)
AEI Records
LP: AEI 1145
CD: AEI-CD 604 [1999 reissued under the title *Vivian Blaine Live in Hollywood*]
Songs: "Broadway Baby," "Everything's Coming Up Roses," "The Ladies Who Lunch"

BOSTON1: Boston Pops Orchestra/*Songs of the '60s* (1981) [instrumental]
   Time-Life
   STLF-0022
   Songs: "Another Hundred People," "Being Alive," "Company," "The Ladies Who Lunch," "Poor Baby," "Side by Side by Side," "Someone Is Waiting," "What Would We Do Without You?"

BOSTON2: [Boston] Pops on Broadway/*Music of the Night* 1990
   Sony Classical
   CD: SK 45567
   Songs: "Comedy Tonight," "No One Is Alone," "Send in the Clowns"

BROADWAYCEL: *A Broadway Celebration* (1989) [Lainie Nelson, Susan Watson, George Ball]
   "A Broadway Celebration"
   CD: [n.n.]
   Cassette: [n.n.]
   Songs: "Pretty Women," "Send in the Clowns," "Some People"

BROADWAYEX: *A Broadway Extravaganza* (1987) [instrumental]
   MCA Classics
   CD: MCAD-6219
   Songs: "Another Hundred People," "Anyone Can Whistle," "A Parade in Town"

BROADWAYTHEAT1: Broadway Theater Chorus/*Fiddler on the Roof; Gypsy* (1983)
   Stage and Screen Productions
   Cassette: XSSC 704
   Songs: "All I Need Is the Girl"

BRUSSELL1: Barbara Brussell/*patterns* (1998)
   LML Music
   CD: LML-CD 111
   Songs: "Buddy's Blues," "Everybody Says Don't," "Marry Me a Little," "Move On"

BUCKLEYB1: Betty Buckley/*Children Will Listen* (1993)
   Sterling
   CD: S1001-2
   Cassette: S1001-4
   Songs: "Children and Art," "Children Will Listen," "I Remember," "No One Is Alone," "Not a Day Goes By," "Not While I'm Around," "Sorry-Grateful," "Stay with Me"

BUCKLEYB2: Betty Buckley/*The London Concert* (1995)
Sterling (BBC)
CD: S1010-2Cassette: S1010-4
Songs: "Finishing the Hat," "Marry Me a Little," "Old Friends," "Rose's Turn," "Send in the Clowns"

BUCKLEYB3: Betty Buckley/*An Evening at Carnegie Hall* (1996)
Sterling
CD: S1012-2
Cassette: S1012-4
Songs: "Every Day a Little Death," "Now You Know," "Rose's Turn," "Something's Coming"

BYRNED1: Debra Byrne/*New Ways to Dream* (1997)
Polydor
CD: 537 324-2
Songs: "Being Alive," "Children Will Listen," "No One Is Alone"

CALLAWAYA&l: Ann Hampton Callaway & Liz Callaway/*Sibling Revelry* (1996)
Varese Sarabande
CD: VSD-5622
Songs: "A Boy Like That," "Every Day a Little Death," "If Momma Was Married," "Our Time"

CANDIDE01: Candide Revival Cast Recording (1974)
Columbia Records
LP: S2X 32923; 2-record set
Songs: "Auto da fé (What a Day)," "Life Is Happiness Indeed," "Sheep's Song," "This World"

CANDIDE02: Candide New York City Opera Cast Recording (1986)
New World Records
LP: NW 340/341
CD: NW 340/341-2
Songs: "Life Is Happiness Indeed," "Sheep's Song"

CANDIDE03: Candide/Scottish Opera Cast Recording (1988)
TER Classics
CD: CDTER 1156
Cassette: ZCTER 1156

CANDIDE04: *Candide*, Leonard Bernstein Conducts (1991)
Deutsche Grammophon
CD: 429734-2; 431328-2 (highlights only)

Cassette: 429734-4; 437328-4 (highlights only)
Songs: "Life Is Happiness Indeed"

CANDIDE05: *Candide* New Broadway Cast (1997)
RCAVictor
CD: 09026-68835-2
Songs: "Auto da fé (What a Day)," "Life Is Happiness Indeed," "Old Lady's False Entrance/Old Lady's Second False Entrance," "Sheep's Song"

CANDIDE06: *Candide* The 1999 Royal National Theatre Recording (2000) [recording does not make clear which lyrics are by Sondheim]
First Night Records
CD: Cast CD 75
Songs: "Auto da fé (What a Day)," "Life Is Happiness Indeed"

CANTD1: Donald Cant/*Donald Cant* (n.d.)
New Market Music
CD: 87-91
Songs: "Johanna," "Losing My Mind," "No One Is Alone," "Not While I'm Around," "Somewhere"

CELEBRATGYP: *Celebrating Gypsy, Funny Girl, Gentlemen Prefer Blondes: A Tribute to Jule Styne* (1998)
BBC Radio 2
CD: WMEU 0019-2
Songs: "All I Need Is the Girl," "Everything's Coming Up Roses," "Let Me Entertain You," "Rose's Turn," "Small World," "Some People"

CELEBRATSON: *Celebrating Sondheim (Follies, Sweeney Todd, Sunday in the Park with George* (1998)
BBC Radio 2
CD: WMEU 0018-2
Songs: "Being Alive," "Buddy's Blues," "Comedy Tonight," "Everybody Loves Louis," "Franklin Shepard, Inc.," "I Remember," "In Buddy's Eyes," "Johanna," "Me and My Town," "Move On," "Not While I'm Around," "Old Friends," "Our Time," "Overture to *Merrily We Roll Along*," "Sunday in the Park with George," "Too Many Mornings," "You Could Drive a Person Crazy"

CELEBRATTHEM: *Celebrating the Musicals Kismet, Guys and Dolls, A Little Night Music* (1998)
BBC Radio 2
CD: WMEU 0020-2

Songs: "Send in the Clowns," "A Weekend in the Country," "You Must Meet My Wife"

CLARKP1: Petula Clark/*here for you* (1998)
Varese Sarabande
CD: VSD-5978
Songs: "Children Will Listen," "I Never Do Anything Twice," "Losing My Mind," "Not a Day Goes By"

CLARYR1: Clary, Robert/*Louis Lebeau Remembers Cole Porter, Not Stephen Sondheim (But Sings Their Songs Anyway)* (2000)
Original Cast Records
CD: OC-2101
Songs: "Anyone Can Whistle," "Beautiful Girls," "I Remember," "I'm Calm," "Live, Laugh, Love," "Love, I Hear," "Marry Me a Little," "Old Friends," "Pretty Women," "Too Many Mornings"

COLOR1: *Color and Light: Jazz Sketches on Sondheim* (1995)
Sony Classical
CD: SK 66566
Songs: "Anyone Can Whistle," "Children and Art," "Color and Light," "Every Day a Little Death," "Losing My Mind," "Loving You," "One More Kiss," "Poems," "Pretty Women," "They Ask Me Why I Believe in You," "What Can You Lose?"

COMPANY01: *Company* Original Broadway Cast Recording (1970)
Columbia Records
LP: OS-3530 (S)/SQ-30993 (Q)
CD: CK-03550
Cassette: JST-03550
Sony Classical/Columbia/Legacy [1998 reissue, remastered w/bonus track]
CD: SK 65283
Songs: "Another Hundred People," "Barcelona," "Being Alive," "Bobby-Baby," "Company," "Getting Married Today," "Have I Got a Girl for You," "The Ladies Who Lunch," "The Little Things You Do To-gether," "Poor Baby," "Side by Side by Side," "Someone Is Waiting," "Sorry-Grateful," "Tick-Tock," "You Could Drive a Person Crazy"

COMPANY02: *Company* London Cast Recording [This is the same recording as the Original Broadway Cast Recording except for an all-new recording of "Barcelona" and Larry Kert tracking in all of Dean Jones's vocals] (1971)
E/CBS Records
LP: 70108 (S)

CD: SMK 53496 [reissue on Sony West End]
Songs: see COMPANY01 and note above

COMPANY03: *(Stephen Sondheim's) Company . . . In Jazz* (The Trotter Trio) (1995)
Varese Sarabande
CD: VSD-5673
Songs: "Another Hundred People," "Barcelona," "Being Alive," "Company," "The Ladies Who Lunch," "Side by Side by Side," "Someone Is Waiting," "Sorry-Grateful," "You Could Drive a Person Crazy"

COMPANY04: *Company* London Revival Cast Recording (1996)
RCAVictor/BMG Classics
CD: 09026-68589-2
Songs: "Another Hundred People," "Barcelona," "Being Alive," "Bobby-Baby," "Company," "Getting Married Today," "Have I Got a Girl for You," "The Ladies Who Lunch," "The Little Things You Do Together," "Poor Baby," "Marry Me a Little," "Side by Side by Side," "Someone Is Waiting," "Sorry-Grateful," "You Could Drive a Person Crazy"

COMPANY05: *Company* Revival Cast Recording (1996)
Angel
CD: 55608
Songs: "Another Hundred People," "Barcelona," "Being Alive," "Bobby-Baby," "Company," "Getting Married Today," "Have I Got a Girl for You," "The Ladies Who Lunch," "The Little Things You Do Together," "Marry Me a Little," "Poor Baby," "Side by Side by Side," "Someone Is Waiting," "Sorry-Grateful," "Tick-Tock," "You Could Drive a Person Crazy"

COMPANY06: *Company* Brazilian Cast Recording (2001)
[The label name is unclear, though information on the CD includes "cod. VSCD0001" and barcode number "7 897999 300555". In addition, the following website address is given: "www.showguide.com.br/company"]
Songs: "Another Hundred People," "Barcelona," "Being Alive," "Bobby-Baby," "Company," "Getting Married Today," "Have I Got a Girl for You," "The Ladies Who Lunch," "The Little Things You Do Together," "Marry Me a Little," "Poor Baby," "Side by Side by Side," "Someone Is Waiting," "Sorry-Grateful," "Tick-Tock," "You Could Drive a Person Crazy"

COMPANY07: *Company* German Cast Recording (2001)
[No label name or number, though the CD is apparently based on a production at the Prinzregententheater, Beyerische Theaterakademie.

The recording includes eight numbers from *Company* with the lyrics translated into German, followed by four songs from other shows sung in English]
Songs: "Barcelona," "Being Alive," "Bobby-Baby," "Company," "Could I Leave You," "Getting Married Today," "Have I Got a Girl for You," "The Ladies Who Lunch," "The Miller's Son," "Move On," "Not a Day Goes By," "Side by Side by Side"

CONNELLI1: Judi Connelli/*On My Way To You* (1997)
"I Hear Voices" Entertainment
CD: IHV 001
Songs: "Losing My Mind," "Move On" (includes uncredited portion of "We Do Not Belong Together"), "Stay With Me"

CONNELLI2: Judi Connelli/*Live in London* (1998)
Dress Circle
CD: DG CD 1
Songs: "Being Alive," "In Buddy's Eyes," "Move On" (includes uncredited portion of "We Do Not Belong Together"), "Something's Coming," "Stay With Me"

CONNELLI3: Judi Connelli and Suzanne Johnston/*Perfect Strangers* (1999)
ABC
CD: 465068-0
Songs: "Do I Hear a Waltz?," "Everybody Says Don't," "Johanna," "Our Time," "Pretty Women"

COOKB1: Barbara Cook/*Barbara Cook Sings Mostly Sondheim* (2001)
DRG Records
CD: 91464; 2-disc set
Songs: "Another Hundred People," "Anyone Can Whistle," "Everybody Says Don't," "Giants in the Sky," "Happiness," "Into the Woods," "Losing My Mind," "Loving You," "Move On," "Not a Day Goes By," "Not While I'm Around," "Send in the Clowns," "So Many People," "Something's Coming," "Tonight," "You Could Drive a Person Crazy"

CRAWFORDM1: *Michael Crawford Songs from the Stage and Screen* (199[?])
Atlantic Records
CD: 82472-2
Songs: "Not a Day Goes By," "Somewhere," "Tonight"

DAMONE1: Vic Damone/*On the Street Where You Live* (1964)
Capitol Records

LP: (S)ST-2133
Songs: "Maria," "Something's Coming," "Tonight"

DARIN1: Bobby Darin/*West Side Story* (1962)
Atco Records
LP: (S)141
Songs: "America," "Somewhere"

DAVIS5: *Sammy Davis Jr. at the Cocoanut Grove* (1961?)
Reprise Records
LP: 2R-6063
[*West Side Story* medley included in 4 cd box set: *Yes I Can/The Sammy Davis Jr. Story*, on Warner Archives/Reprise R2 75972/Rhino, 1999]
Songs, in medley: "America," "Cool," "Gee, Officer Krupke," "Jet Song," "Something's Coming," "Tonight"

DAYC1: Courtenay Day/*Courtenay Day Live at Don't Tell Mama* (2000)
Green Street Dance
CD: 0713
Songs: "Every Day a Little Death," "I've Got You to Lean On," "The Little Things You Do Together," "Pretty Women"

DEFERRANT1: Margie De Ferranti/*Margie De Ferranti, Live in New York, Live at '88's* (1999[?])
[No label name, Australian]
CD: [n.n.]
Songs: "Being Alive," "No One Is Alone," "There Won't Be Trumpets"

DELARIA1: Dea DeLaria/*Play It Cool* (2001)
Warner Bros. Jazz
CD: 9 47993-2
Songs: "The Ballad of Sweeney Todd," "Cool," "Losing My Mind"

DELORENZ1: Brian De Lorenzo/*Found Treasures* (1999)
Cabaret Classics
CD: CC9901
Songs: "Do I Hear a Waltz?," "Giants in the Sky," "No One Has Ever Loved Me"

DOIHEAR1: *Do I Hear a Waltz?* Original Broadway Cast Recording (1965)
Columbia Records
LP: KOL-6370 (M)/KOS-2770 (S)

AKOS-2770 (S); reissue Columbia Special Products
Sony Broadway (reissue 1992)
CD: SK-48206 [ADD]
Cassette: ST-48206
Songs: "Bargaining," "Do I Hear a Waltz?," "Here We Are Again,"
"Moon in My Window," "No Understand," "Perfectly Lovely Couple,"
"Someone Like You," "Someone Woke Up," "Stay," "Take the Mo-
ment," "Thank You So Much," "Thinking," "This Week, Americans,"
"We're Gonna Be All Right," "What Do We Do? We Fly!"

DOIHEAR2: *Do I Hear a Waltz?* Pasadena Playhouse Production (2001)
Fynsworth Alley
CD: 302 062 126 2
Songs: "Do I Hear a Waltz?," "Everybody Loves Leona," "Here We Are
Again," "Last Week Americans," "Moon in My Window," "No Under-
stand," "Perfectly Lovely Couple," "Someone Like You," "Someone
Woke Up," "Stay," "Take the Moment," "Thank You So Much/Finale,"
"Thinking," "This Week, Americans," "We're Gonna Be All Right,"
"What Do We Do? We Fly!"

DOMINGO1: Placido Domingo/*The Broadway I Love* (1991)
Atlantic Records
CD: 7 82350-2
Songs: "Send in the Clowns," "Somewhere," "Tonight"

DOWJ1: Judith Dow/*Regards to Broadway* (1981)
Centerline Records
LP: CPI8002
Songs: "All Things Bright and Beautiful," "Being Alive," "Do I Hear a
Waltz?," "Night Waltz," "Send in the Clowns"

DRAKEA: *Alfred Drake & Roberta Peters Sing the Popular Music of Leonard
Bernstein* (1963)
Command Records
LP: RS 855D
reissued as: *Show Time/Carousel (Complete)/West Side Story/On the Town/
Candide* (1973)
Command Records
LP: RSSD 982-2 (2-record set)
Songs: "Gee, Officer Krupke," "I Feel Pretty," "Somewhere," "Tonight"

Early, Julia, see BARNETTEARLY1: Peter Barnett & Julia Early/*In So Many
Words*

EASTWEST1: East West Players/*East West Overtures* (1996-97)
EWP [there is no label name, number or date]
CD: [n.n.]
Songs: "The Advantages of Floating in the Middle of the Sea," "Agony," "Another Hundred People," "The Ballad of Sweeney Todd," "Barcelona," "Giants in the Sky," "Good Thing Going," "Green Finch and Linnet Bird," "Into the Woods," "My Friends," "Next," "Not a Day Goes By," "Our Time," "Pretty Lady," "You Could Drive a Person Crazy"

Evening Primrose, see FROGS1: *The Frogs/Evening Primrose* (2001)
Evening Primrose, see PATINKIN2: Mandy Patinkin/*Dress Casual* (1990)
Evening Primrose, see SONDATTHEM1: *Sondheim at the Movies* (1997)

EVERYONE1: *Everyone's A Love Song* (1979)
Silver Flutes Productions
LP: JACW7779
Songs: "Being Alive," "Not a Day Goes By," "Send in the Clowns," "With So Little to Be Sure of"

FEINSTEIN1: *Michael Feinstein Sings The Jule Styne Songbook* with Jule Styne, piano (1991)
Elektra Nonesuch
CD: 79274-2
Cassette: 79274-4
Songs: "All I Need Is the Girl," "Everything's Coming Up Roses," "Home Is the Place," "Nice She Ain't," "Small World," "You'll Never Get Away from Me"

FERRERI1: Michael Ferreri/*Sweet Dreams* (2000)
Lumiere Musique
CD: FR293585
Songs: "Every Day a Little Death," "Move On," "Marry Me a Little"

FLORIDA1: Florida Symphonic Pops (John Cacavas)/*The Phantom of the Opera* (1989) [instrumental]
ProArte
CD: D475
or Rochester Pops Orchestra and Florida Symphonic Pops Orchestra/ *Opening Night* (1990)
ProArte
CD: S 528, 1990
Songs: "Broadway Baby," "Comedy Tonight," "Send in the Clowns"

FOLLIES01: *Follies* Original Broadway Cast Recording (1971)
Capitol Records
LP: SO-761 (S)
CD: CDP7 920942, 1989
Broadway Angel
CD: ZDM-64666
Cassette: EG-64666
Songs: "Ah, Paris!," "Beautiful Girls," "Broadway Baby," "Buddy's Blues," "Could I Leave You?," "Don't Look at Me," "Finale-Chaos," "I'm Still Here," "In Buddy's Eyes," "Live Laugh Love," "Losing My Mind," "Love Will See Us Through," "One More Kiss," "Overture," "The Right Girl," "The Road You Didn't Take," "The Story of Lucy and Jessie," "Too Many Mornings," "Waiting for the Girls Upstairs," "Who's That Woman?," "You're Gonna Love Tomorrow"

FOLLIES02: *Follies* in Concert (1985)
RCA Records
LP: HBC2-7128
CD: RCD2-7128; 2-disc set [includes the soundtrack to *Stavisky*]
Cassette: HBE2-7128
Songs: "Ah, Paris!," "Beautiful Girls," "Broadway Baby," "Buddy's Blues," "Could I Leave You?," "Don't Look at Me," "Finale-Chaos," "I'm Still Here," "In Buddy's Eyes," "Live Laugh Love," "Losing My Mind," "Love Will See Us Through," "Loveland," "One More Kiss," "Overture," "Rain on the Roof," "The Right Girl," "The Road You Didn't Take," "The Story of Lucy and Jessie," "Too Many Mornings," "Waiting for the Girls Upstairs," "Who's That Woman?," "You're Gonna Love Tomorrow"

FOLLIES03: *Follies* Original London Cast Recording (1987)
First Night Records
CD: Encore CD 2; (FIR-CD-3 [DDD])
Songs: "Ah, But Underneath . . .," "Ah, Paris!," "Beautiful Girls," "Broadway Baby," "Buddy's Blues," "Could I Leave You?," "Country House," "Don't Look at Me," "I'm Still Here," "In Buddy's Eyes," "Losing My Mind," "Love Will See Us Through," "Loveland [2]," "Make the Most of Your Music,""One More Kiss," "Rain on the Roof," "The Right Girl," "The Road You Didn't Take," "Social Dancing," "Too Many Mornings," "Waiting for the Girls Upstairs," "Who's That Woman?," "You're Gonna Love Tomorrow"

FOLLIES04: *(Stephen Sondheim's) Follies*/Themes from the Legendary Musical (The Trotter Trio) (1998)
Varese Sarabande

CD: VSD-5934

Songs: "Broadway Baby," "Buddy's Blues," "Could I Leave You?," "I'm Still Here," "In Buddy's Eyes," "Live Laugh Love," "Losing My Mind," "Loveland," "Opening [Overture]," "Too Many Mornings," "Waiting for the Girls Upstairs," "Who's That Woman?"

FOLLIES05: *Follies*, The Complete Recording (1998)

TVT Records/TVT Soundtrax

CD: TVT 1030-2; 2-disc set [includes appendix of cut songs]

Songs: "Ah, But Underneath . . .," "Ah, Paris!," "All Things Bright and Beautiful," "Beautiful Girls," "Beautiful Girls (Bring On the Girls)," "Bolero d'Amour," "Broadway Baby," "Buddy's Blues," "Can That Boy Fox-Trot!," "Could I Leave You?," "Don't Look at Me," "Finale-Chaos," "I'm Still Here," "In Buddy's Eyes," "Little White House," "Live Laugh Love," "Losing My Mind," "Love Will See Us Through," "Loveland," "One More Kiss," "Overture," "Pleasant Little Kingdom," "Prologue," "Rain on the Roof," "The Right Girl," "The Road You Didn't Take," "The Story of Lucy and Jessie," "That Old Piano Roll," "Too Many Mornings," "Uptown, Downtown," "Waiting for the Girls Upstairs," "Who's That Woman?," "You're Gonna Love Tomorrow"

FORDA1: Anne Kerry Ford/*Something Wonderful (Songs of Oscar Hammerstein and Stephen Sondheim)* (1998)

LML Music

CD: LML CD-109

Songs: "Being Alive," "Goodbye for Now," "The Miller's Son," "Not a Day Goes By," "Something's Coming," "With So Little to Be Sure of"

FROGS1: *The Frogs/Evening Primrose* (2001)

Nonesuch

CD: 79638-2

Songs: "Evoe for the Dead," "Exodos: The Sound of Poets," "Fanfare," "Fear No More," "Hymnos: Evoe!," "I Remember," "If You Can Find Me I'm Here," "Invocation to the Muses," "Parabasis: It's Only a Play," "Parados: The Frogs," "Prologos: Invocation and Instructions to the Audience," "Take Me to the World," "Traveling Music," "When"

FULLERM1: Mark Fuller/*Songs About Adam* (1996 or 97)

Pride Music

CD: PRIDE010LPD

Songs: "Can That Boy Foxtrot!," "Losing My Mind," "Not a Day Goes By"

FUNNY01: *A Funny Thing Happened on the Way to the Forum* Original Broadway Cast Recording (1962)
Capitol Records
LP: WAO (M)/SWAO (S)-1717; reissue W (M)/SW (S)-1717
Bay Cities (1990, reissue)
CD: BCD: 3002
Songs: "Bring Me My Bride," "Comedy Tonight," "Everybody Ought to Have a Maid," "Free," "Funeral Sequence," "I'm Calm," "Impossible," "Love, I Hear," "Lovely," "Lovely (Reprise)," "Overture," "Pretty Little Picture," "That Dirty Old Man," "That'll Show Him"

FUNNY02: *A Funny Thing Happened on the Way to the Forum* Original London Cast Recording (1963)
His Master's Voice/EMI Records (England)
LP: CLP: 1685 (M)/CSD 1518 (s)
DRG Records (reissue)
LP: Stet DS-15028 (S)
Cassette: STET DSC-15028
First Night Records (England; reissue)
LP: OCR 3, Cassette: OCR C3
Angel EMI (reissue)
CD: 7 89060 2
Songs: "Bring Me My Bride," "Comedy Tonight," "Everybody Ought to Have a Maid," "Free," "Funeral Sequence," "I'm Calm," "Impossible," "Love, I Hear," "Lovely," "Lovely (Reprise)," "Overture," "Pretty Little Picture," "That Dirty Old Man," "That'll Show Him"

FUNNY03: *A Funny Thing Happened on the Way to the Forum* Motion Picture Soundtrack Recording (1966) [incidental music by Ken Thorne]
United Artists Records
LP: UAL-4144 (M)/UAS-5144 (S); reissue UA-LA284-G (S)
Cassette: UA-EA284-H
RYCO
CD: RCD 10727 [1998 reissue]
Songs: "[Bring Me] My Bride," "The Chase," "Comedy Tonight," "The Dirge [Funeral Sequence]," "Everybody Ought to Have a Maid," "Lovely," "Lovely (Reprise)," "Riot at the Funeral"

FUNNY04: *(Stephen Sondheim's) A Funny Thing Happened on the Way to the Forum . . . In Jazz* (The Trotter Trio) (1996)
Varese Sarabande
CD: VSD-5707
Songs: "Comedy Tonight," "Everybody Ought to Have a Maid," "Free," "I'm Calm," "Impossible," "Love, I Hear," "Lovely," "That Dirty Old Man," "That'll Show Him," "Your Eyes Are Blue"

FUNNY05: *A Funny Thing Happened on the Way to the Forum* Revival Cast (1996)
Broadway Angel Records
CD: 52223
Songs: "Bring Me My Bride," "Comedy Tonight," "Everybody Ought to Have a Maid," "Free," "Funeral Sequence," "The House of Marcus Lycus," "I'm Calm," "Impossible," "Love, I Hear," "Lovely," "Lovely (Reprise)," "Overture," "Pretty Little Picture," "That Dirty Old Man," "That'll Show Him"

FUNNY06: *Amor al Reves es Roma [A Funny Thing . . .]* Mexican Cast Recording (n.d.)
CBS/Columbia
45rpm: EPC 274
"Comedy Tonight," "Love, I Hear," "Lovely," "Pretty Little Picture"

GALA1: *A Gala Concert for Hal Prince* (1996)
First Night Records/TriStar
CD: DOCRCD 2; 2-disc set
Songs: "The Advantages of Floating in the Middle of the Sea," "The Ballad of Sweeney Todd," "Beautiful Girls," "Broadway Baby," "Comedy Tonight," "Losing My Mind," "March to the Treaty House," "Next," "Night Waltz," "Not While I'm Around," "Side by Side by Side," "Tonight (Quintet)"

GARLAND: Judy Garland/*Judy Duets* (The Platinum Judy Garland in Commemoration of her 75th Birthday) (1998)
Wiley Entertainment, Ltd.
CD: 96883 67442
Songs: "Maria," "Something's Coming," "Somewhere," "Together Wherever We Go" (2), "Tonight"

GAYMENSCLA1: Gay Men's Chorus of Los Angeles/*Simply Sondheim* (2001)
Gay Men's Chorus of Los Angeles
CD: GMCLA09
Songs: "Could I Leave You?," "Good Thing Going," "Goodbye for Now," "I Remember," "The Little Things You Do Together," "Loving You," "Merrily We Roll Along," "No One Is Alone," "Old Friends," "Our Time," "Pleasant Little Kingdom," "Send in the Clowns," "Sunday," "*Sweeney Todd* Rhapsody": "The Ballad of Sweeney Todd," "Green Finch and Linnet Bird," "Johanna," "My Friends," "Not While I'm Around," "Pretty Women," "Wait"

GELLERH: Herb Geller/*Herb Geller and his all-stars play selections from "Gypsy"*
Atco Records

LP: Atco 33-109
Songs: "Everything's Coming Up Roses," "Momma's Talkin' Soft," "Small World," "Together Wherever We Go" [These songs, with vocals by Barbara Lang, are the only ones included in the body of the discography]

GYPSY01: *Gypsy* Original Broadway Cast Recording (1959)
Columbia Records
LP: OL-5420 (M)/OS-2017 (S)
S-32607 (reissue, 1973)
CD: CK 32607
Cassette: JST-3260K
CD: SK 60848 [1999 reissue, includes Bonus Tracks of previously unreleased material, and alternate or re-edited takes]
Songs: "All I Need Is the Girl," "Dainty June and Her Farmboys," "Everything's Coming Up Roses," "Gypsy Strip Routine," "If Momma Was Married," "Little Lamb," "Mr. Goldstone," "Momma's Talkin' Soft" [1999 reissue only], "Nice She Ain't" [1999 reissue only], "Rose's Turn," "Small World," "Some People," "Together Wherever We Go," "You Gotta Have a Gimmick," "You'll Never Get Away from Me"

GYPSY02: *Gypsy* Motion Picture Cast Recording (1962)
Warner Bros. Records
LP: B (M)-1480/BS (S)-1480
Songs: "All I Need Is the Girl," "Everything's Coming Up Roses," "Gypsy Strip Routine," "Mr. Goldstone," "Rose's Turn," "Small World," "Some People," "Together Wherever We Go," "You Gotta Have a Gimmick," "You'll Never Get Away from Me"

GYPSY03: *Gypsy* Original London Cast Recording (1974)
RCA Records
LP: SER-5686 (S)
LP: LBL 1-500 [American release]
CD: 60571-2-RG
Songs: "All I Need Is the Girl," "Dainty June and Her Farmboys," "Everything's Coming Up Roses," "Gypsy Strip Routine," "If Momma Was Married," "Little Lamb," "Mr. Goldstone," "Rose's Turn," "Small World," "Some People," "Together Wherever We Go," "You Gotta Have a Gimmick," "You'll Never Get Away from Me"

GYPSY04: *Gypsy* Revival Cast Recording (1990)
Elektra Nonesuch
LP: 79239-1

CD: 79239-2

Cassette: 79239-4

Songs: "All I Need Is the Girl," "Baby June and Her Newsboys," "Dainty June and Her Farmboys," "Everything's Coming Up Roses," "Gypsy Strip Routine," "If Momma Was Married," "Little Lamb," "Mr. Goldstone," "Rose's Turn," "Small World," "Some People," "Together Wherever We Go," "You Gotta Have a Gimmick," "You'll Never Get Away from Me"

GYPSY05: *Gypsy* TV Cast Recording (1993)

    Atlantic Records

    CD: 82551-2

    Cassette: 82551-4

Songs: "All I Need Is the Girl," "Baby June and Her Newsboys," "Dainty June and Her Farmboys," "Everything's Coming Up Roses," "Gypsy Strip Routine," "If Momma Was Married," "Little Lamb," "May We Entertain You," "Mr. Goldstone," "Rose's Turn," "Small World," "Some People," "Together Wherever We Go," "You Gotta Have a Gimmick," "You'll Never Get Away from Me"

GYPSY06: *Gypsy* Mexican Cast Recording (1998)[?]

    [no label name]

    CD: 11460503

[The contents of this recording are not listed in the body of the discography, because the lyrics are based on, but not a translation of, Sondheim's. The leads are played by Silvia Pinal and Alejandra Guzman.]

GYPSY07: *Gypsy* German Cast Recording (1998)[?]

    Theater Des Westens/Pallas Group Worldwide

    CD: LC 6377

Songs: "Everything's Coming Up Roses," "Gypsy Strip Routine," "If Momma Was Married," "Some People," "You Gotta Have a Gimmick," "You'll Never Get Away from Me"

GYPSY08: *Selections from "Gypsy" and "Flower Drum Song"* / (Florence Henderson) (1959)

    RCA Camden

    LP: CAS 560

Songs: "Everything's Coming Up Roses," "Small World," "Some People," "Together Wherever We Go," "You'll Never Get Away from Me"

GYPSY09: *Kay Medford in "Gypsy"* (1969)

    mfp (Music For Pleasure)

LP: MFP 50090

Songs: "All I Need Is the Girl," "Everything's Coming Up Roses," "If Momma Was Married," "Let Me Entertain You," "Mr. Goldstone," "Overture," "Rose's Turn," "Small World," "Some People," "Together Wherever We Go," "You Gotta Have a Gimmick," "You'll Never Get Away from Me"

Gypsy, see also CELEBRATGYP: *Celebrating "Gypsy," "Funny Girl," "Gentlemen Prefer Blondes: A Tribute to Jule Styne"* (1998)

Gypsy, see also FEINSTEIN1: *Michael Feinstein Sings The Jule Styne Songbook*

Gypsy, see also GELLERH: Herb Geller/*Herb Geller and His All-Stars Play Selections from "Gypsy"*

Gypsy, see also HARNARJ1: *Jeff Harnar Sings the 1959 Broadway Songbook*

Gypsy, see also HILOS: The Hi-Lo's/*Broadway Playbill* (1960)

Gypsy, see also MERMANE1: Ethel Merman/*Mermania!* (volume 1)

Gypsy, see also ROSSANNIE: Annie Ross/*Gypsy* (1959, 1960)

Gypsy, see also STYNEJ1: Jule Styne/*My Name Is Jule* (1966)

HARNARJ1: *Jeff Harnar Sings the 1959 Broadway Songbook* (1991)
    Original Cast Records
        CD: OC 916
Songs: "All I Need Is the Girl," "Everything's Coming Up Roses," "Let Me Entertain You," "One Hand, One Heart," "Tonight," "You'll Never Get Away from Me"

HARVEYJ1: Jane Harvey/*The Other Side of Sondheim* (1988)
    Atlantic Records
        LP: 81833-1
        CD: 81833-2
        Cassette: 81833-4
Songs: "Could I Leave You?," "Everybody Says Don't," "Everything's Coming Up Roses," "Good Thing Going," "I'm Still Here," "In Buddy's Eyes," "It Wasn't Meant to Happen," "The Ladies Who Lunch," "Losing My Mind," "Not a Day Goes By," "Not While I'm Around," "Old Friends," "Pretty Women," "Together Wherever We Go," "What More Do I Need?," "With So Little to Be Sure of," "You'll Never Get Away from Me"

HELLERM1: Marc Heller/*Take Me to the World: Songs by Stephen Sondheim* (1996)
    Etcetera Records Company B.V. the Netherlands
        CD: KTC 1185

Songs: "Another Hundred People," "Anyone Can Whistle," "Being Alive," "Comedy Tonight," "Everybody Says Don't," "Good Thing Going," "Green Finch and Linnet Bird," "The Hills of Tomorrow," "Johanna," "Later," "Losing My Mind," "Love, I Hear," "Loving You," "Not While I'm Around," "One More Kiss," "Pretty Women," "Send in the Clowns," "Silly People," "Sunday," "Take Me to the World," "You Must Meet My Wife"

HEYLOVE1: *hey, love: The Songs of Mary Rodgers* (1997)
 Varese Sarabande
 CD: VSD-5772
Songs: "The Boy From . . .," "Once I Had a Friend," "Show Me," "Who Knows?/I Know"

HEYMRP: *Hey, Mr. Producer! (The Musical World of Cameron Mackintosh)* (1998)
 First Night Records/Phillips
 CD: 314 538 030-2; 2-disc set
Songs: "Being Alive," "Broadway Baby," "Dueling Pianos," "Losing My Mind," "Send in the Clowns," "Side by Side by Side," "You Could Drive a Person Crazy," "You Gotta Have a Gimmick"

HILOS: The Hi-Lo's/*Broadway Playbill* (1960)
 Columbia
 Record: CL1416, (S)CS8213
Songs: "Everything's Coming Up Roses," "Little Lamb," "Mr. Goldstone," "Small World," "Together Wherever We Go," "You'll Never Get Away from Me"

HOLLYWOODB1: Hollywood Bowl Orchestra/*The Great Waltz* (1993) [instrumental]
 Phillips
 CD: 438 685-2
Songs: "The Glamorous Life," "Night Waltz," "Remember," "Soon"

INTOTHE1: *Into the Woods* Original Broadway Cast Recording (1987)
 RCA Records
 CD: 6796-2-RC [DDD]
 DCC: 09026-56795-5
 Cassette: 6796-4-RC9
Songs: "Agony," "Any Moment," "Children Will Listen," "Cinderella at the Grave," "Ever After," "First Midnight," "Giants in the Sky," "Hello Little Girl," "I Guess This Is Goodbye," "I Know Things Now," "Into

the Woods," "It Takes Two," "Jack, Jack, Jack," "Last Midnight," "Maybe They're Magic," "Moments in the Woods," "No More," "No One Is Alone," "On the Steps of the Palace," "So Happy," "Stay with Me," "A Very Nice Prince," "Witch's Lament," "Your Fault"

INTOTHE2: *Into the Woods* Original London Cast Recording (1991)
RCA Records
CD: 60752-2-RC [DDD]
Cassette: 60752-4-RC
Songs: "Agony," "Any Moment," "Children Will Listen," "Cinderella at the Grave," "Ever After," "First Midnight," "Giants in the Sky," "Hello Little Girl," "I Guess This Is Goodbye," "I Know Things Now," "Into the Woods," "It Takes Two," "Jack, Jack, Jack," "Last Midnight," "Maybe They're Magic," "Moments in the Woods," "No More," "No One Is Alone," "On the Steps of the Palace," "Our Little World," "So Happy," "Stay with Me," "A Very Nice Prince," "Witch's Lament," "Your Fault"

INTOTHE3: *Into the Woods* Revival Cast Recording (2002)
Nonesuch
CD: 79686-2
Songs: "Agony," "Any Moment," "Children Will Listen," "Cinderella at the Grave," "Ever After," "First Midnight," "Giants in the Sky," "Hello, Little Girl," "I Guess This Is Goodbye," "I Know Things Now," "Into the Woods," "It Takes Two," "Jack, Jack, Jack," "Lament," "Last Midnight," "Maybe They're Magic," "Moments in the Woods," "No More," "No One Is Alone," "On the Steps of the Palace," "Our Little World," "So Happy," "Stay with Me," "A Very Nice Prince," "Your Fault"

JACKIE&1: Jackie & Roy/*A Stephen Sondheim Collection* (1982)
Finesse Records
LP: FW 38324 (S)
Cassette: FWT 38324
DRG Records (1990, reissue)
CD: DSCD 25102
Cassette: DSC 25102
Red Baron (reissued as *Sondheim*)
CD: JK 57338
Songs: "Anyone Can Whistle," "Barcelona," "Buddy's Blues," "Comedy Tonight," "Everybody Says Don't," "I Do Like You," "I Remember," "Johanna," "The Little Things You Do Together," "Love Is in the Air," "Merrily We Roll Along," "Not a Day Goes By," "Send in the Clowns," "Side by Side by Side," "So Many People," "Theme" from *Stavisky*, "Together Wherever We Go"

JAHANA1: Raishel Jahana/*Sondheim Songs* (2000)
Cab-Art
CD: Cab-Art 3377
Songs: "Being Alive," "Broadway Baby," "Children Will Listen," "Everybody Says Don't," "Move On," "No More," "No One Is Alone," "Not a Day Goes By," "Too Many Mornings"

JEROMER1: *Jerome Robbins Broadway* Original Broadway Cast Recording (1989)
RCA Records
CD: 60150-2-RC; 2-disc set
Songs: "America," "Comedy Tonight," "Cool," "Somewhere," "You Gotta Have a Gimmick"

JOBSON1: Mark deVille Jobson/*My House* (1998)
Musical Journeys of the Heart
CD: MJOTHCD002
Songs: "The Hills of Tomorrow," "Move On, "No One Is Alone," "Not a Day Goes By," "Take Me to the World," "With So Little to Be Sure of"

Johnston, Suzanne see CONNELLI3: Judi Connelli and Suzanne Johnston/ *Perfect Strangers*

LAINEC1: *Cleo Laine Return to Carnegie* (1977)
RCA Records
LP: APL1-2407
Cassette: APK1-2407
Songs: "Being Alive," "Broadway Baby," "Company," "The Miller's Son"

LAINEC2: *Cleo Sings Sondheim*/Cleo Laine (1988)
RCA Records
LP: 7702-1-RC
CD: 7702-2-RC
Cassette: 7702-4-RC
Songs: "Ah, But Underneath," "Anyone Can Whistle," "Everybody Says Don't," "I Remember," "I'm Calm," "I'm Still Here," "The Ladies Who Lunch," "Liaisons," "The Little Things You Do Together," "Losing My Mind," "The Miller's Son," "No One Is Alone," "Not a Day Goes By," "Not While I'm Around," "Send in the Clowns," "You Could Drive a Person Crazy"

LAWRENCEC: Carol Lawrence/*Tonight at 8:30* (1962)
Chancellor Records
LP: (S)CHLS-5015

Songs: "Something's Coming," "Tonight," "You'll Never Get Away from Me"

LEARE1: *Evelyn Lear Sings Sondheim and Bernstein* (1981)
  Mercury Records Golden Imports
  LP: MR 75136
  Cassette: MRI 75136
  Songs: "Could I Leave You?," "Green Finch and Linnet Bird," "I Remember," "Losing My Mind," "Send in the Clowns"

LEMPER1: Ute Lemper/*City of Strangers* (1995)
  London
  CD: 444 400-2
  Songs: "Another Hundred People," "Being Alive," "The Ladies Who Lunch," "Losing My Mind"

LEONARDB1: *Leonard Bernstein's New York* (1996)
  Nonesuch
  CD: 79400-2
  Songs: "One Hand, One Heart," "Somewhere," "Tonight"

LITTLEL1: *A Little Light Music* (1996)
  Upbeat/Showbiz/U.K
  CD: URCD123
  Songs: "Anyone Can Whistle," "Can That Boy Foxtrot!," "Old Friends," "Send in the Clowns"

LITTLEN01: *A Little Night Music* Original Broadway Cast Recording (1973)
  Columbia Records
  LP: KS (S)/SQ (Q)-32265
  Cassette: ST 32265
  CD: CK 32265
  Sony Classical/Columbia/Legacy [1998 reissue, remastered w/bonus tracks]
  CD: SK 65284 (1998)
  Songs: "Every Day a Little Death," "The Glamorous Life," "The Glamorous Life (The Letter Song)" [1998 reissue only], "In Praise of Women," "It Would Have Been Wonderful," "Later," "Liaisons," "The Miller's Son," "Night Waltz," "Night Waltz II (The Sun Sits Low)" [1998 reissue only], "Now," "Overture," "Perpetual Anticipation," "Remember," "Send in the Clowns," "Send in the Clowns (Reprise)," "Soon," "A Weekend in the Country," "You Must Meet My Wife"

LITTLEN02: *A Little Night Music* Original London Cast Recording (1975)
RCA Records
LP: LRL1-5090 (S)
Cassette: CRK1-5090; reissue 5090-4-RG
CD: RCD1-5090; reissue 5090-2-RG
Songs: "Every Day a Little Death," "The Glamorous Life," "In Praise of Women," "It Would Have Been Wonderful," "Later," "Liaisons," "The Miller's Son," "Night Waltz," "Now," "Overture," "Perpetual Anticipation," "Remember," "Send in the Clowns," "Send in the Clowns (Reprise)," "Soon," "A Weekend in the Country," "You Must Meet My Wife"

LITTLEN03: *A Little Night Music* Motion Picture Soundtrack Recording (1978)
Columbia Records
LP: JS 35333 (S)
Cassette: JST 3533
Songs: "Every Day a Little Death," "The Glamorous Life (The Letter Song)," "It Would Have Been Wonderful," "Later," "Love Takes Time," "Night Waltz" [instrumental only], "Now," "Overture," "Send in the Clowns," "Send in the Clowns (Reprise)," "Soon," "A Weekend in the Country," "You Must Meet My Wife"

LITTLEN04: *A Little Night Music* Studio Cast Recording (1990)
TER - That's Entertainment Records (England)
Cassette: ZCTER 1179
CD: CDTER 1179
Songs: "Every Day a Little Death," "The Glamorous Life," "In Praise of Women," "It Would Have Been Wonderful," "Later," "Liaisons," "The Miller's Son," "Night Waltz," "Night Waltz II (The Sun Sits Low)," "Now," "Overture," "Perpetual Anticipation," "Remember," "Send in the Clowns," "Send in the Clowns (Reprise)," "Soon," "A Weekend in the Country," "You Must Meet My Wife"

LITTLEN05: *A Little Night Music* Royal National Theatre's Cast Recording (1996)
Tring
CD: TRING001
Songs: "Dinner Table Scene," "Every Day a Little Death," "The Glamorous Life," "The Glamorous Life (The Letter Song)," "In Praise of Women," "It Would Have Been Wonderful," "Later," "Liaisons," "The Miller's Son," "My Husband the Pig," "Night Waltz," "Night Waltz II (The Sun Sits Low)," "Now," "Overture," "Perpetual Anticipation," "Remember," "Send in the Clowns," "Send in the Clowns (Reprise)," "Soon," "A Weekend in the Country," "You Must Meet My Wife"

LITTLEN06: *A Little Night Music [musica per a una nit d'estiu]* Barcelona Cast (2001) [translated into Catalonian]
  K Industria Cultural
    CD: KO26CD
  Songs: "Every Day a Little Death," "The Glamorous Life," "In Praise of Women," "It Would Have Been Wonderful," "Later," "Liaisons," "The Miller's Son," "Night Waltz," "Night Waltz II (The Sun Sits Low)," "Now," "Overture," "Perpetual Anticipation," "Remember," "Send in the Clowns," "Send in the Clowns (Reprise)," "Soon," "A Weekend in the Country," "You Must Meet My Wife"

A Little Night Music see also TROTTERT1: Terry Trotter/*Stephen Sondheim's A Little Night Music* (1997)

LITTLES1: *A Little Sondheim Music*/Los Angeles Vocal Arts Ensemble (1984)
  EMI/Angel Records
    LP: EMI DS-37347 (S)
    Cassette: EMI 4DS-3747
  Songs: "All Things Bright and Beautiful," "The Ballad of Sweeney Todd," "By the Sea," "Cora's Chase" [listed as "Waltz I"], Green Finch and Linnet Bird," "The Hills of Tomorrow," "In Praise of Women," "Night Waltz," "Night Waltz II (The Sun Sits Low)," "Not a Day Goes By," "Not While I'm Around," "Overture" from *A Little Night Music*, "Pretty Lady," "Pretty Women," "Send in the Clowns," "A Weekend in the Country," "With So Little to Be Sure of"

MADONNA1: Madonna/*I'm Breathless* (1990)
  Sire/Warner Bros. Records
    CD: 9 26209-2
    Cassette: 26209-4
  Songs: "More," "Sooner or Later," "What Can You Lose?"

MAGICOF1: *The Magic of the Musicals* (1992)
  Quality Television (Great Britain)
    CD: QTVCD 013
  Songs: "Losing My Mind," "Not While I'm Around," "Send in the Clowns"

MALMBERG1: Malmberg, Myrra/*What Can You Lose?* (1995)
  Arietta Discs
    CD: ADCD1
  Songs: "Could I Leave You?," "Everybody Loves Louis," "The Glamorous Life (The Letter Song)," "I Remember," "Isn't It?," "Like It Was,"

"Marry Me a Little," "No One Is Alone," "So Many People," "Take Me to the World," "Truly Content," "What Can You Lose?"

MARKEY1: Enda Markey/*Another Place and Time* (2001)
Middle Eight Music
CD: EMCD01
Songs: "Anyone Can Whistle," "Broadway Baby," "Good Thing Going," "Losing My Mind," "Not a Day Goes By"

MARRYME1: *Marry Me a Little* (1981)
RCA Records
LP: ABL1-4159 (S)
Cassette: ABK1-4159; reissue 7142-4-RG
CD: 7142-2-RG
Songs: "All Things Bright and Beautiful," "Bang!," "Can That Boy Fox trot!," "The Girls of Summer," "Happily Ever After," "It Wasn't Meant to Happen," "Little White House," "Marry Me a Little," "A Moment with You," "Pour le sport," "Saturday Night," "Silly People," "So Many People," "There Won't Be Trumpets," "Two Fairy Tales," "Uptown, Downtown," "Who Could Be Blue?," "Your Eyes Are Blue"

MARSS1: Susannah Mars/*Take Me to the World* (1998)
LML Music
CD: LML CD-106
Songs: "Gun Song," "Loving You," "Not a Day Goes By," "Take Me to the World"

MAYESS1: Sally Mayes/*Boys and Girls Like You and Me* (2000)
Bayview Recording Company
CD: RNBW007
Songs: "All Things Bright and Beautiful," "Nice She Ain't," "Your Eyes Are Blue"

MCDERMOTTS1: Sean McDermott/*My Broadway* (1999)
JAY Records
CD: CDJAY 1316
Songs: "Being Alive," "Good Thing Going," "Loving You," "Maria," "Something's Coming"

MCKECHNIED1: Donna McKechnie/*Inside the Music* (2002)
Fynsworth Alley
CD: FA2124
Songs: "All I Need Is the Girl," "Everybody Says Don't," "In Buddy's Eyes," "Lovely," "You Could Drive a Person Crazy"

MCKENZIEJ1: Julia McKenzie/*The Musicals Album* (1992)
Telstar
CD: TCD 2612
Songs: "The Boy From . . .," "Losing My Mind," "Send in the Clowns," "Somewhere," "Tonight"

MCKENZIER1: Rita McKenzie/*Ethel Merman's Broadway* (1995)
Varese Sarabande
CD: VSD-5665
Songs: "Everything's Coming Up Roses," "Small World," "Some People"

MCLAREN1: Morag McLaren/*i never do anything twice* (1998)
Dress Circle
CD: MM777
Songs: "Every Day a Little Death," "I Never Do Anything Twice," "Make the Most of Your Music"

MENDELSSOHN1: The Mendelssohn Choir of Pittsburgh/*Mendelssohn Sings Sondheim* (1994)
atr digital
Casette: 26187
Songs: "Anyone Can Whistle," "The Ballad of Booth," "Being Alive," "Comedy Tonight," "Do I Hear a Waltz?," "I Remember," "Johanna," "The Ladies Who Lunch," "Let Me Entertain You," "The Little Things You Do Together," "Losing My Mind," "No One Is Alone," "Not a Day Goes By," "Not While I'm Around," "Old Friends," "Our Time," "Pretty Lady," "See What It Gets You," "Send in the Clowns," "There's a Parade in Town," "This World"

MERMANE1: Ethel Merman/*Mermania!* (Vol. 1) (1999)
Harbinger Records
CD: HCD 1711
Songs: "Everything's Coming Up Roses," "Little Lamb," "Mr. Goldstone," "Rose's Turn," "Small World," "Together Wherever We Go," "You'll Never Get Away from Me"

MERRILY1: *Merrily We Roll Along* Original Broadway Cast Recording (1982)
RCA Records
LP: CBL1-4197 (S)
CD: RCD1-5840
Cassette: CBK1-4197
Songs: "Bobby and Jackie and Jack," "Franklin Shepard, Inc.," "Good Thing Going," "The Hills of Tomorrow," "It's a Hit!," "Like It Was," "Merrily We Roll Along," "Not a Day Goes By," "Not a Day Goes By,

part II," "Now You Know," "Old Friends," "Opening Doors," "Our Time," "Overture," "Rich and Happy"

MERRILY2: *Merrily We Roll Along* Revival Cast Recording (1994)
Varese Sarabande
CD: VSD-5548
Songs: "Act Two Opening," "The Blob," "Bobby and Jackie and Jack," "Franklin Shepard, Inc.," "Good Thing Going," "Growing Up," "It's a Hit!," "Like It Was," "Merrily We Roll Along," "Not a Day Goes By," "Not a Day Goes By, part II," "Now You Know," "Old Friends," "Opening Doors," "Our Time," "Overture," "That Frank"

MERRILY3: *Merrily We Roll Along* London Cast Recording (1994, 1997)
TER—That's Entertainment Records (England)
CD: CDTER 1225
JAY Records (England)
CD: CDJAY2 1245, 2-disc set
Songs: "Act Two Opening," "The Blob," "Bobby and Jackie and Jack," "Franklin Shepard, Inc.," "Good Thing Going," "Growing Up," "It's a Hit!," "Like It Was," "Merrily We Roll Along," "Not a Day Goes By," "Not a Day Goes By, part II," "Now You Know," "Old Friends," "Opening Doors," "Our Time," "Overture," "That Frank"

MIGENES1: Julia Migenes/*Live at the Olympia* (1989)
Milan
CD: GH 503
Songs: "One Hand, One Heart," "Something's Coming," "Tonight"

MOREWEST: *More West End The Concert* (1999)
JAY Records
CD: [n.n.]
Songs: "Comedy Tonight," "Company," "Send in the Clowns"

MOVINGON: *Moving On (A 70th Birthday Celebration of Stephen Sondheim)* (2000)
Goldcrest Films International
CD: GF1001CD
[Note: Devised by David Kernan for the Bridewell Theatre London. Performers: Geoffrey Abbott, Linzi Hately, Belinda Land, Robert Meadmore, Angela Richards; not listed by cut]
Songs: "Ah, But Underneath . . .," "Another Hundred People," "Broadway Baby," "Everybody Says Don't," "Goodbye for Now," "I Do Like You," "I Know Things Now," "I Wish I Could Forget You," "In Buddy's Eyes," "Johanna," "Loving You," "Me and My Town," "The Miller's

Son," "Move On," "Multitudes of Amys," "No, Mary Ann," "Not a Day Goes By," "Opening Doors," "Old Friends," "Our Time," "Pretty Women," "Side by Side by Side," "So Many People," "Someone Is Waiting," "Take Me to the World," "There Won't Be Trumpets," "Water Under the Bridge," "What More Do I Need?," "Who Wants to Live in New York?," "With So Little to Be Sure of"

NEWYORKCITYGAY1: New York City Gay Men's Chorus/*New York, New York A Broadway Extravaganza* (1984, 1987)
    ProArte Records
    CD: CDG-3198; CDD-594
    Cassette: PCD-5995
    Songs: "All Things Bright and Beautiful," "Not While I'm Around," "Our Time," "Silly People," "Take Me to the World," "There Won't Be Trumpets"

NEWYORKCITYGAY2: New York City Gay Men's Chorus/*Love Lives On* (1991)
    Virgin Records America, Inc.
    CD: 2-91647
    Cassette: 91647-4
    Songs: "Another Hundred People," "No One Is Alone," "Not a Day Goes By," "That Old Piano Roll"

NEWYORKCITYOP1: New York City Opera Orchestra/*Broadway's Best* (1993) [instrumental]
    MusicMasters Classics
    CD: 01612-67099-2
    Songs: "The Advantages of Floating in the Middle of the Sea," "March to the Treaty House," "Night Waltz," "Tamate's Dance (There Is No Other Way)"

NICHOLSONC1: Carla and Michael Nicholson/*Just Duet* (2001)
    Duophon
    CD: [n.n.]
    Songs: "I Feel Pretty," "Send in the Clowns," "Somewhere," "Tonight"

NOONEIS1: *No One Is Alone . . . the Modern Sondheim* (1995 or 96)
    [Cast album of an Australian revue. There is no label name or number]
    CD: [n.n.]
    Songs: "Agony," "Another National Anthem," "Any Moment," "The Ballad of Booth," "The Ballad of Sweeney Todd," "Beautiful," "Children Will Listen," "Color and Light," "Everybody's Got the Right," "Finishing the Hat," "Good Thing Going," "Gossip Sequence," "Gun Song," "Hello, Lit-

tle Girl," "I Know Things Now," "Live, Laugh, Love," "Moments in the Woods," "My Friends," "No One Is Alone," "Not a Day Goes By," "On the Steps of the Palace," "Sunday," "Sunday in the Park with George"

ORCHESTRAMAN1: Orchestra Manhattan (Byron Olson)/*Digital Broadway* (1986) [instrumental]
   Manhattan
   CD: P-7-46288-2
   Songs: "Johanna," "Losing My Mind," "Pretty Women," "Putting It Together," "Send in the Clowns"

OUTONB1: *Out On Broadway* (2000)
   Original Cast
   CD: OC2015
   Songs: "Not a Day Goes By," "Our Time," " Sooner or Later," "Water Under the Bridge," "What Can You Lose?," "You're Gonna Love Tomorrow"

PACIFICOVER1: *Pacific Overtures* Original Broadway Cast Recording (1976)
   RCA Records
   LP: ARL1-1367 (S)
   CD: RCD1-4407
   Cassette: ARK1-4407
   Songs: "The Advantages of Floating in the Middle of the Sea," "A Bowler Hat," "Chrysanthemum Tea," "Four Black Dragons," "Next," "Please Hello," "Poems," "Pretty Lady," "Someone in a Tree," "Tamate's Dance (There Is No Other Way)," "Welcome to Kanagawa"

PACIFICOVER2: *Pacific Overtures* English National Opera (1988)
   TER Records
   CD: CDTER 1151
   Cassette: ZCTED 1151
   RCA Records
   CD: 7995-2-RC (highlights only)
   Cassette: 7995-4-RC (highlights only)
   Songs: "The Advantages of Floating in the Middle of the Sea," "A Bowler Hat," "Chrysanthemum Tea," "Four Black Dragons," "Next," "Please Hello," "Poems," "Pretty Lady," "Someone in a Tree," "Tamate's Dance (There Is No Other Way)," "Welcome to Kanagawa"

PASSION1: *Passion* Original Broadway Cast Recording (1994)
   Angel Records
   CD: CDQ 7243 5 55251 23
   Cassette: 4DQ 7243 5 55251 47

Songs: "Farewell Letter," "Finale," "First Letter," "Flashback," "Forty Days," "Fourth Letter," "Garden Sequence," "Happiness," "I Read," "I Wish I Could Forget You," "Is This What You Call Love?," "Loving You," "No One Has Ever Loved Me," "Second Letter," "Soldier's Gossip," "Sunrise Letter," "Third Letter," "Transition(s)," "Trio"

PASSION2: *(Stephen Sondheim's) Passion . . . in Jazz* (The Trotter Trio) (1994)
Varese Sarabande
CD: VSD-5556
Songs: "Fourth Letter," "Happiness," "I Wish I Could Forget You," "Love Like Ours," "Loving You," "No One Has Ever Loved Me," "Transition(s)"

PASSION3: *Passion* London Concert (1997)
First Night Records
CD: CAST CD61
Songs: "Farewell Letter," "Finale," "First Letter," "Flashback," "Forty Days," "Fourth Letter," "Garden Sequence," "Happiness," "I Read," "I Wish I Could Forget You," "Is This What You Call Love?," "Love Like Ours," "Loving You," "No One Has Ever Loved Me," "Second Letter," "Soldier's Gossip," "Sunrise Letter," "Third Letter," "Transition(s)," "Trio"

PATINKIN1: Mandy Patinkin/*Mandy Patinkin* (1989)
CBS Records
CD: MK44943 [DDD]
Cassette: FMT-44943
Songs: "Anyone Can Whistle," "No More," "No One Is Alone," "Pretty Lady"

PATINKIN2: Mandy Patinkin/*Dress Casual* (1990)
CBS Records
CD: MK45998
Cassette: FMT-45998
Songs: "Being Alive," "Giants in the Sky," "I Remember," "If You Can Find Me I'm Here," "Sorry-Grateful," "Take Me to the World," "When?"

PATINKIN3: Mandy Patinkin/*Experiment* (1994)
Elektra Nonesuch
CD: 79330-2
Cassette: FMT-79330-4
Songs: "Good Thing Going," "Multitudes of Amys," "The Road You Didn't Take," "So Many People," "Someone Is Waiting," "Something's Coming"

PATINKIN4: Mandy Patinkin/*Oscar and Steve* (1995)
Nonesuch
CD: 79392-2
Cassette: 79392-4
Songs: "Children Will Listen," "I Wish I Could Forget You," "Loving You," "Not a Day Goes By," "Pleasant Little Kingdom," "Poems," "Remember," "There Won't Be Trumpets," "Too Many Mornings"

PATINKIN5: Mandy Patinkin/*Mandy Patinkin Sings Sondheim* (2002)
Nonesuch
CD: 79690; 2-disc set
[The information on this recording came too late for the individual songs to be included in the body of the songlisting.]
Songs: "All Things Bright and Beautiful," "Another Hundred People," "Beautiful," "Broadway Baby," "Company," "Everybody Says Don't," "Finishing the Hat," "Free," "Green Finch and Linnet Bird," "If You Can Find Me, I'm Here," "In Someone's Eyes," "It Takes Two," "Johanna," "Lesson #8," "Liaisons," "Live Alone and Like It," "Losing My Mind," "Not While I'm Around," "Our Time," "Pleasant Little Kingdom," "Pretty Women," "Rich and Happy," "Send in the Clowns," "Someone Is Waiting," "Sunday," "Take the Moment," "Too Many Mornings," "Uptown, Downtown," "Waiting for the Girls Upstairs," "When?," "You Could Drive a Person Crazy"

PETERSB1: Bernadette Peters/*Sondheim, Etc. (Live at Carnegie Hall)* (1997)
Angel
CD: 55870
Songs: "Any Moment," "Being Alive," "Broadway Baby," "Happiness," "Hello, Little Girl," "Johanna," "Move On," "No One Is Alone," "Not a Day Goes By," "Some People," "Sooner or Later," "There Won't Be Trumpets," "You Could Drive a Person Crazy"

Peters, Roberta, see also DRAKEA: *Alfred Drake & Roberta Peters Sing the Popular Music of Leonard Bernstein*

PRIORM1: Marina Prior/*Somewhere* (1994)
Columbia Records
CD: 478068 2
Songs: "The Boy from . . .," "A Boy Like That," "Green Finch and Linnet Bird," "I Have a Love," "Move On," "Not While I'm Around," "One Hand, One Heart," "Send in the Clowns," "Somewhere," "Sooner or Later," "Tonight," "What Can You Lose?," "You Could Drive a Person Crazy"

PUTTINGIT1: *Putting It Together* Original Cast Recording (1993)
RCA Records
CD: 09026-61729-2
Cassette: 09026-61729-4
Songs: "Ah, But Underneath . . .," "Back in Business," "Bang!," "Being Alive," "Could I Leave You?," "Country House," "Every Day a Little Death," "Everybody Ought to Have a Maid," "Getting Married Today," "Gun Song," "Have I Got a Girl for You," "Hello, Little Girl," "I'm Calm," "Impossible," "In Praise of Women," "Invocation and Instructions to the Audience," "Like It Was," "A Little Priest," "Live Alone and Like It," "Love Takes Time," "Lovely," "Marry Me a Little," "Merrily We Roll Along," "The Miller's Son," "My Husband the Pig," "Now," "Perpetual Anticipation," "Pretty Women," "Putting It Together," "Remember," "Rich and Happy," "Sooner or Later," "Sorry-Grateful," "Sweet Polly Plunkett," "What Would We Do Without You?," "You Could Drive a Person Crazy"

REDS1: *Reds* (Original Soundtrack) (1981) [music for some cuts by Dave Grusin]
Columbia Records
LP: BJS 37690
Razor & Tie Entertainment
CD: 7940182203-2 [1999 reissue]
Songs: "Goodbye for Now"

ROCHESTERP1: Rochester Pops Orchestra (Erich Kunzel)/*Opening Night* (1990) [instrumental]
ProArte
CD: CDS 528
Songs: "Broadway Baby," "Comedy Tonight," "Send in the Clowns"

ROCHESTER POPS, see also FLORIDA1: Florida Symphonic Pops (John Cacavas)/*The Phantom of the Opera*

ROSSANNIE: Annie Ross/*Gypsy* (1959, 1960)
World Pacific Records
LP: (S)ST-1276, WP-1028
Pacific Jazz (1995 reissue)
CD: CDP 7243 8 33574 2 0
Songs: "All I Need Is the Boy," "Everything's Coming Up Roses," "Let Me Entertain You," "Small World," "Some People," "Together Wherever We Go," "You'll Never Get Away from Me"

ROYBUDD1: The Roy Budd Trio/*Everything's Coming Up Roses: The Musical World of Stephen Sondheim* (1976)
Pye Records
LP: NSPL 18494

Songs: "All I Need Is the Girl," "Another Hundred People," "Anyone Can Whistle," "Beautiful Girls," "Do I Hear a Waltz?," "Everything's Coming Up Roses," "The God-Why-Don't-You-Love-Me Blues," "Send in the Clowns," "Small World," "Take Me to the World," "Tonight"

RUBANOC1: Craig Rubano/*Finishing the Act* (1999)
AF Records
CD: HR 13680
Songs: "Now You Know," "Sunday," "Take the Moment"

SALONGAL1: Lea Salonga/*The Broadway Concert* (2002)
BMG
CD: [n.n.]
Songs: "Being Alive," "Together Wherever We Go," "You'll Never Get Away from Me"

SANDFORD1: Luke Sandford/*Shimmer* (2000) [piano solo]
Luke Sandford
CD: 11357 60082
Songs: "Giants in the Sky," "Night Waltz," "Salon at the Claridge #2"

SATURDAYN1: *Saturday Night* Bridewell Cast Recording (1998)
First Night Records
CD: CAST CD65
Songs: "All for You," "Class," "Exhibit 'A'," "I Remember That," "In the Movies," "Isn't It?," "Love's a Bond," "A Moment with You," "One Wonderful Day," "Saturday Night," "Saturday Night (reprise)," "So Many People," "That Kind of a Neighborhood," "What More Do I Need?"

SATURDAYN2: *Saturday Night* Original New York Cast (2000)
Nonesuch
CD: 79809-2
Songs: "All for You," "Class," "Delighted, I'm Sure," "Exhibit 'A'," "Gracious Living Fantasy," "I Remember That," "In the Movies," "Isn't It?," "Love's a Bond," "Love's a Bond (Blues)," "A Moment with You," "One Wonderful Day," "One Wonderful Day (Finale)," "Overture," "Saturday Night," "Saturday Night (Reprise) [2 versions]," "So Many People," "That Kind of a Neighborhood," "What More Do I Need?"

Satuday Night see also UNSUNGS1: *Unsung Sondheim* (1993)

SAXEE1: Emily Saxe/*Broadway & All That Jazz* (2000)
Orchard
CD: [n.n.]
Songs: "Losing My Mind," "Old Friends," "Send in the Clowns"

SHORTB1: Bobby Short/*Live at the Cafe Carlyle* (1974)
Atlantic Records
LP: SD 2-609; 2-record set
Songs: "Losing My Mind," "Send in the Clowns," "Sorry-Grateful"

SIDEBYS2: *Side by Side by Sondheim* Original Australian cast recording (1977)
RCA Red Seal (Australia)
LP: VRL2-0156; 2-record set
Cassette: VRK2-0156; 2-tape set
Songs: "Ah, Paris!," "Another Hundred People," "Anyone Can Whistle," "Barcelona," "Beautiful Girls," "The Boy From . . .," "Broadway Baby," "Buddy's Blues," "Can That Boy Foxtrot!," "Comedy Tonight," "Company," "Could I Leave You?," "Everybody Ought to Have a Maid," "Everybody Says Don't," "Getting Married Today," "I Never Do Anything Twice," "I Remember," "If Momma Was Married," "I'm Still Here," "The Little Things You Do Together," "Losing My Mind," "Love Is in the Air," "Marry Me a Little," "Pretty Lady," "Send in the Clowns," "Side by Side by Side," "Waiting for the Girls Upstairs," "We're Gonna Be All Right," "You Could Drive a Person Crazy," "You Must Meet My Wife"

Side By Side By Sondheim see also SONGSOFSOND1: *Songs of Sondheim* Original Irish Cast

SINGERSUN1: Singers Unlimited (Beryl Korman, Julia Meadows, Jennifer Partridge)/*A Little Light Music* (1996)
Upbeat Recordings
CD: URCD123
Songs: "Ah, Paris!," "Anyone Can Whistle," "A Boy Like That," "Broadway Baby," "Can That Boy Foxtrot!," "Losing My Mind," "Old Friends," "Send in the Clowns," "We're Gonna Be All Right"

SOND1: *Sondheim* (1985)
Book-of-the-Month Records
LP: 81-7515 (S); 3-record set
CD: 11-7517; 2-disc set (71-7016)
Cassette: 91-7516; 2-tape set
Songs: "The Advantages of Floating in the Middle of the Sea," "Anyone Can Whistle," "Buddy's Blues," "Comedy Tonight," "Everybody Says Don't," "Fear No More," "Finishing the Hat," "The Glamorous Life (The Letter Song)," "Good Thing Going," "Goodbye for Now," "Honey," "I Do Like You," "In Buddy's Eyes," "It's a Hit!," "Johanna," "Liaisons," "Like It Was," "A Little Priest," "The Little Things You Do Together," "Losing My Mind," "March to the Treaty House," "Me and

My Town," "Next," "Not While I'm Around," "Old Friends," "Pretty Lady," "Send in the Clowns," "Someone in a Tree," "Sorry-Grateful," "Take Me to the World," "Tamate's Dance (There Is No Other Way)," "Theme" from Stavisky, "Too Many Mornings," "With So Little to Be Sure Of," "The Worst Pies in London," "You Must Meet My Wife"

SONDACEL1: *Sondheim—A Celebration* (1997)
    Carlton Sounds
    CD: 30362 00382
Songs: "Back in Business," "Being Alive," "Buddy's Blues," "By the Sea," "Comedy Tonight," "Could I Leave You?," "In Buddy's Eyes," "It Takes Two," "The Ladies Who Lunch," "Liaisons," "Not While I'm Around," "Old Friends," "Side by Side by Side," "Uptown, Downtown"

SONDACEL2: *Sondheim: A Celebration* (1997)
    Varese Sarabande
    CD: VSD2-5820; 2-disc set
Songs: "The Ballad of Booth," "The Ballad of Sweeney Todd," "Barcelona," "Can That Boy Foxtrot!," "Children Will Listen," "Everybody Loves Louis," "Everybody Ought to Have a Maid," "Everybody's Got the Right," "Franklin Shepard, Inc.," "Getting Married Today," "Good Thing Going," "Invocation and Instructions to the Audience," "Losing My Mind," "Loving You," "The Miller's Son," "More," "Move On," "Multitudes of Amys," "No More," "Not a Day Goes By," "Not While I'm Around," "Our Time," "Send in the Clowns," "Side by Side by Side," "Someone in a Tree," "Sooner or Later," "Sorry-Grateful," "Sunday," "There Won't Be Trumpets," "What Can You Lose?," "Who's That Woman?," "You Could Drive a Person Crazy"

SONDACELATC1: *Sondheim: A Celebration at Carnegie Hall* (1993)
    RCA Records
    CD: 09026-61484-2 [DDD]; 2-disc set
    Cassette: 09026-6184-4
    CD: 09026-61516-2 (highlights only)
    Cassette: 09026-61516-4 (highlights only)
Songs: "Anyone Can Whistle," "Back in Business," "The Ballad of Booth," "The Ballad of Sweeney Todd," "Barcelona," "Being Alive," "Broadway Baby," "Children Will Listen," "Comedy Tonight," "Company," "Getting Married Today," "Good Thing Going," "Green Finch and Linnet Bird," "I Never Do Anything Twice," "Johanna," "Live Alone and Like It," "Losing My Mind," "Love, I Hear," "Loveland," "Not a Day Goes By," "Old Friends," "Our Time," "Pretty Lady," "Pretty Women," "Remember," "Send in the Clowns," "Someone Is

Waiting," "Sooner or Later," "Sunday," "Waiting for the Girls Upstairs," "Water Under the Bridge," "A Weekend in the Country," "With So Little to Be Sure of," "You Could Drive a Person Crazy"

SONDAMUST1: *Sondheim: A Musical Tribute* (1973) [also known as the "Scrabble Album"]
    Warner Bros. Records
    LP: 2WS 2705 (S); 2-record set
    RCA Records (1990, reissue)
    Cassette: 60515-4-RC
    CD: 60515-2-RC
Songs: "America," "Another Hundred People," "Anyone Can Whistle," "Beautiful Girls," "Being Alive," "Broadway Baby," "Buddy's Blues," "Could I Leave You," "Do I Hear a Waltz?," "Getting Married Today," "Happily Ever After," "I Remember," "If Momma Was Married," "I'm Still Here," "The Little Things You Do Together," "Losing My Mind," "Love Is in the Air," "Me and My Town," "One More Kiss," "Pleasant Little Kingdom," "Side by Side by Side," "Silly People," "So Many People," "Take Me to the World," "There's a Parade in Town," "Too Many Mornings," "Two Fairy Tales," "We're Gonna Be All Right," "You Could Drive a Person Crazy," "Your Eyes Are Blue"

SONDATTHEM1: *Sondheim at the Movies* (1997)
    Varese Sarabande
    CD: VSD-5895
Songs: "Back in Business," "Dawn," "The Glamorous Life (The Letter Song)," "Goodbye for Now," "I Remember," "If You Can Find Me I'm Here," "It Takes All Kinds," "Little Dream," "More," "Sand," "Sooner or Later," "Stavisky Suite" [in 3 parts], "Take Me to the World," "What Can You Lose?," "When?"

SONDTON1: *Sondheim Tonight* (Live from the Barbican Centre, London) (1999)
    JAY Records
    CD: CDJAY2 1313; 2-disc set
Songs: "Another Hundred People," "The Ballad of Sweeney Todd," "Barcelona," "Beautiful Girls," "Being Alive," "Broadway Baby," "Comedy Tonight," "Company," "Good Thing Going," "Green Finch and Linnet Bird," "I Never Do Anything Twice," "I Remember," "The Ladies Who Lunch," "Losing My Mind," "Loving You," "March to the Treaty House," "More," "Next," "Night Waltz," "Not a Day Goes By," "Not While I'm Around," "Send in the Clowns," "Side by Side by Side," "*Stavisky* Suite," "Sunday in the Park with George," "Variations on a Theme (Katie Malone)," "A Very Short Violin Sonata"

SONGSOFSOND1: *Songs of Sondheim* Original Irish cast recording of *Side by Side by Sondheim* (1977)
  RAM Records
  LP: RMLP 1026
  Cassette: RMCS 1026
Songs: "Anyone Can Whistle," "Barcelona," "The Boy From . . .," "Broadway Baby," "Comedy Tonight," "Could I Leave You?," "I Never Do Anything Twice," "I'm Still Here," "The Little Things You Do Together," "Love Is in the Air," "Pretty Lady," "Send in the Clowns," "Side by Side by Side," "You Could Drive a Person Crazy"

SONGSOFSTEP1: *Songs of Stephen Sondheim*/You Sing the Hits (1991) [Side A has complete tracks; Side B has background tracks without vocals]
  MMO Music Group
  Cassette: PS 198
Songs: "Being Alive," "Could I Leave You?," "I'm Still Here," "Losing My Mind," "Send in the Clowns"

STAROBIND1: David Starobin/*New Music with Guitar, Volume 3*; "Sunday Set" [Patrick Mason, baritone] (1985)
  Bridge
  LP: BDG-2006
  CD: BCD-9009; reissued on *New Music with Guitar*, a compilation from volumes 1-3 (1988)
Songs: "Color and Light," "Finishing the Hat," "Lesson #8," "Putting It Together"

STAVISKY1: *Stavisky* (1975) [CD recording on *Follies in Concert*—FolIC]
  RCA Records
  LP: ARL1-0952
Songs: "Airport at Biarritz," "Arlette and Stavisky," "Arlette by Day," "Arlette by Night," "Auto Show," "Distant Past," "Easy Life," "Erna," "Erna Remembered," "The Future," "Goodbye Arlette," "Hideout Chamonix," "Montalvo at Biarritz," "Old House," "Operetta (C'est moi)," "Recent Past," "Salon at the Claridge #1," "Salon at the Claridge #2," "Secret of Night," "Suite at the Claridge," "Theme" from *Stavisky*, "Trotsky at Saint-Palais," "Women and Death"

STEPHENSA1: *The Stephen Sondheim Album* (2000)
  Fynsworth Alley
  CD: FA-2101-SE

Songs: "Another Hundred People," "Anyone Can Whistle," "Broad-way Baby," "Children Will Listen," "Everybody Says Don't," "Getting Married Today" [on special edition only], "Giants in the Sky," "I Must Be Dreaming," "I'm Still Here," "It Wasn't Meant to Happen," "Losing My Mind," "Make the Most of Your Music," "A Moment with You," "Not a Day Goes By," "So Many People," "Sorry-Grateful," "Who Could Be Blue?," "With So Little to Be Sure of," "You're Gonna Love Tomorrow"

STEPHENSE1: *A Stephen Sondheim Evening* (1983)
   RCA Records
   LP: CBL2-4745 (S); 2-record set
   Cassette: CBK2-4745; 2-tape set
   CD: 09026-61174-2 (reissue) ["Fear No More" and "You're Gonna Love Tomorrow" were not included on the CD reissue]
   Songs: "Another Hundred People," "Anyone Can Whistle," "Broadway Baby," "Children Will Listen," "Everybody Says Don't," "Getting Married Today," "Giants in the Sky," "I Must Be Dreaming," "I'm Still Here," "It Wasn't Meant to Happen," "Losing My Mind," "Make the Most of Your Music," "A Moment with You," "Not a Day Goes By," "So Many People," "Sorry-Grateful," "Who Could Be Blue?," "With So Little to Be Sure of," "You're Gonna Love Tomorrow"

STEPHENSS1: *Stephen Sondheim Songs* (2002) [instrumental accompaniments without vocals]
   MMO Music Group/Pocket Songs
   CD: JTG 068
   Songs: "Anyone Can Whistle," "Being Alive," "Broadway Baby," "Children Will Listen," "Comedy Tonight," "Could I Leave You?," "Do I Hear a Waltz?," "Everybody Ought to Have a Maid," "Everybody Says Don't," "I'm Still Here," "The Ladies Who Lunch," "Losing My Mind," "Loving You," "Not While I'm Around," "Putting It Together," "Sooner or Later"

STREISAND1: Barbra Stresiand/*The Broadway Album* (1985)
   Columbia Records
   LP: OC 40092
   CD: CK 40092
   Cassette: OCT 40092
   Minidisc: CM 40092
   Songs: "Being Alive," "The Ladies Who Lunch," "Not While I'm Around," "Pretty Women," "Putting It Together," "Send in the Clowns," "Something's Coming," "Somewhere"

STREISAND2: Barbra Streisand/*Back to Broadway* (1993)
Columbia Records
CD: CK 44189
Cassette: CT 44189
Minidisc: CM 44189
Songs: "Children Will Listen," "Everybody Says Don't," "I Have a Love," "Move On," "One Hand, One Heart"

STREISAND3: Barbra Streisand/*Timeless—Live in Concert* (2000)
Columbia
CD: C2K 63778; 2-disc set
Songs: "Being Alive," "Putting It Together," "Send in the Clowns," "Something's Coming," "Somewhere"

STRITCHE1: Elaine Stritch/*Elaine Stritch at Liberty* (2002)
DRG Records
CD: DRG-12994
Songs: "Broadway Baby," "I'm Still Here," "The Ladies Who Lunch"

STYNEJ1: Jule Styne/*My Name Is Jule* (1966)
United Artists
LP: UAS-6469
Songs: "All I Need Is the Girl," "Everything's Coming Up Roses," "Let Me Entertain You," "Small World," "Some People," "Together Wherever We Go," "You'll Never Get Away from Me"

SUNDAYIN1: *Sunday in the Park with George* Original Broadway Cast Recording (1984)
RCA Records
LP: HBC1-5042 (S)
Cassette: HBE1-5042
CD: RCD1-5042
Songs: "Beautiful," "Children and Art," "Chromolume #7," "Color and Light," "The Day Off," "Everybody Loves Louis," "Finishing the Hat," "Gossip Sequence," "It's Hot Up Here," "Lesson #8," "Move On," "No Life," "Putting It Together," "Sunday," "Sunday in the Park with George," "We Do Not Belong Together"

Sunday in the Park with George, see also STAROBIND1: David Starobin/*New Music with Guitar, Volume 3;* "Sunday Set"

SWEENEYT1: *Sweeney Todd* Original Broadway Cast Recording (1979)
RCA Records

LP: CBL2-3379 (S); 2-record set
Cassette: CBK2-3379; 2-tape set
CD: 3379-2-RC; 2-disc set
CD: RCD1-5033 (highlights only)
Songs: "Ah, Miss," "The Ballad of Sweeney Todd," "The Barber and His Wife," "By the Sea," "City on Fire," "The Contest," "Epiphany," "Final Scene," "Fogg's Asylum/Fogg's Passacaglia," "God, That's Good!," "Green Finch and Linnet Bird," "Johanna," "Johanna (Act 2)," "Johanna (Judge Turpin)," "Kiss Me," "Ladies in Their Sensitivities," "The Letter," "A Little Priest," "My Friends," "No Place Like London," "Not While I'm Around," "Parlor Songs," "Pirelli's Miracle Elixir," "Poor Thing," "Prelude," "Pretty Women," "Searching," "Wait," "Wigmaker Sequence," "The Worst Pies in London"

SWEENEYT2: *(Stephen Sondheim's) Sweeney Todd . . . In Jazz* (The Trotter Trio) (1995)
Varese Sarabande
CD: VSD-5603
Songs: "The Ballad of Sweeney Todd," "By the Sea," "The Contest," "Finale [Final Scene]," "Green Finch and Linnet Bird," "Johanna," "Johanna (Judge Turpin)" [included in "Finale"], "Kiss Me," "A Little Priest," "Not While I'm Around," "Parlor Songs," "Pretty Women"

SWEENEYT3: *Sweeney Todd* Barcelona Cast (1995) [translated into Catalonian]
Horus [E.M. Horus, S.A.]
CD: CD-25002; 2-disc set
Songs: "Ah, Miss," "The Ballad of Sweeney Todd," "The Barber and His Wife," "By the Sea," "City on Fire," "The Contest," "Epiphany," "Final Scene," "Fogg's Asylum/Fogg's Passacaglia," "God, That's Good!," "Green Finch and Linnet Bird," "Johanna," "Johanna (Act 2)," "Johanna (Judge Turpin)," "Kiss Me," "Ladies in Their Sensitivities," "The Letter," "A Little Priest," "My Friends," "No Place Like London," "Not While I'm Around," "Parlor Songs," "Pirelli's Death," "Pirelli's Miracle Elixir," "Poor Thing," "Pretty Women," "Searching," "Wait," "Wigmaker Sequence," "The Worst Pies in London"

SWEENEYT4: *Sweeney Todd* Live at the New York Philharmonic (2000)
New York Philharmonic Special Editions
CD: NYP 2001/2002 (19054-1855-2); 2 disc set
Songs: "Ah, Miss," "The Ballad of Sweeney Todd," "The Barber and His Wife," "[Beggar Woman's] Lullaby" [included in "City on Fire" sequence], "By the Sea," "City on Fire," "The Contest," "Epiphany," "Final Scene," "Fogg's Asylum/Fogg's Passacaglia," "God, That's Good!," "Green Finch and Linnet Bird," "Johanna," "Johanna (Act 2)," "Johanna (Judge Turpin)," "The Judge's Return," "Kiss Me," "Ladies

in Their Sensitivities," "The Letter," "A Little Priest," "My Friends," "No Place Like London," "Not While I'm Around," "Parlor Songs," "Pirelli's Death," "Pirelli's Miracle Elixir," "Poor Thing," "Prelude," "Pretty Women," "Wait," "Wigmaker Sequence," "The Worst Pies in London"

SYMPHONICSON1: *Symphonic Sondheim*/Don Sebesky Conducts The London Symphony Orchestra (1990)
    WEA Records (London)
        LP: 9031-72 119-1
        Cassette: 9031-72 119-4
        CD: 9031-72 119-2
    EMI Classics (1991 reissue)
        CD: CDC 7 54285 2
    Songs: "Barcelona," "Comedy Tonight," "Finishing the Hat," "Into the Woods Suite," "Losing My Mind," "Multitudes of Amys," "Not a Day Goes By," "Pretty Lady," "Send in the Clowns," "Side by Side by Side," "Sweeney Todd Suite"

TROTTERT1: Terry Trotter/*Stephen Sondheim's A Little Night Music* (1997) [piano solo]
    Varese Sarabande
        CD: VSD-5819
    Songs: "Every Day a Little Death," "The Glamorous Life," "The Glamorous Life (The Letter Song)," "Later," "Night Waltz," "Night Waltz-II (The Sun Sits Low)," "Now," "Remember," "Send in the Clowns," "Soon," "You Must Meet My Wife"

Trotter Trio, see COMPANY03: *(Stephen Sondheim's) Company . . . In Jazz* (The Trotter Trio)
Trotter Trio, see FOLLIES04: *(Stephen Sondheim's) Follies*/Themes from the Legendary Musical (The Trotter Trio)
Trotter Trio, see FUNNY04: *(Stephen Sondheim's) A Funny Thing Happened on the Way to the Forum . . . in Jazz* (The Trotter Trio)
Trotter Trio, see PASSION2: *(Stephen Sondheim's) Passion . . . In Jazz* (The Trotter Trio)
Trotter Trio, see SWEENEYT2: *(Stephen Sondheim's) Sweeney Todd . . . In Jazz* (The Trotter Trio)

Turned-On Broadway 2/*Standing Room Only* (1982) [contains 10 Sondheim songs as instrumentals within medleys, usually very foreshortened; individual titles are not included in the previous song listing]
    RCA Records
        LP: AFL1-4512

TURNERG1: Geraldine Turner/*Old Friends* [*Geraldine Turner Sings the Songs of Stephen Sondheim*] (1986)
Larrikin Records (Australia)
LP: LRF-169
Cassette: TC-LRF-169
Silva Screen Records (London) [under the title *The Stephen Sondheim Songbook*]
LP: Song 001
CD: Song CD001
Cassette: Song C001
[1997 reissue with additional cuts]
CD: Silvad 3011
Songs: "Another Hundred People," "Anyone Can Whistle," "Being Alive," "Buddy's Blues," "Could I Leave You?," "Goodbye for Now," "I Remember," "I Wish I Could Forget You," "Like It Was," "Losing My Mind," "Love, I Hear," "The Miller's Son," "Not While I'm Around," "Old Friends," "There Won't Be Trumpets," "There's a Parade in Town," "What Can You Lose?," "With So Little to Be Sure of"

TURNERG2: Geraldine Turner/ . . . *Sings the Stephen Sondheim Songbook, Vol.2* (2002)
Bayview Records
CD: RNBW016
Songs: "Can That Boy Foxtrot!," "I Never Do Anything Twice," "I'm Still Here," "The Little Things You Do Together," "Loving You," "Moments in the Woods," "No More," "Not a Day Goes By," "Pretty Little Picture," "Rose's Turn," "Send in the Clowns," "So Many People," "Take Me to the World," "What More Do I Need?"

UNSUNGS1: *Unsung Sondheim* (1993)
Varese Sarabande
CD: VSD-5433
Cassette: VSC-5433
Songs: "All for You," "Goodbye for Now," "In the Movies," "Incidental Music" from *Invitation to a March*, "Incidental Music" from *The Enclave*, "Love's a Bond," "Multitudes of Amys," "No, Mary Ann," "Saturday Night," "That Old Piano Roll," "There's Always a Woman," "They Ask Me Why I Believe in You," "Truly Content," "The Two of You," "Water Under the Bridge," "What Can You Lose?"

UPSHAWD1: Dawn Upshaw/*I Wish It So* (1994)
Elektra Nonesuch
CD: 79345-2
Cassette: 79345-4

Songs: "The Girls of Summer," "I Feel Pretty," "Like It Was," "Take Me to the World," "There Won't Be Trumpets," "What More Do I Need?"

WESTSIDE01: *West Side Story* Original Broadway Cast Recording (1957)
    Columbia Records
    LP: JS 32603
    CD: CK 32603
    Cassette: JST-32603
Songs: "America," "A Boy Like That," "Cool," "Gee, Officer Krupke," "I Feel Pretty," "I Have a Love," "Jet Song," "Maria," "One Hand, One Heart," "Something's Coming," "Somewhere," "Tonight (Balcony Scene)," "Tonight (Quintet)"

WESTSIDE02: *West Side Story* Film (1963)
    Columbia Records
    LP: OS 2070
    CD: SK-48211 [ADD] [includes previously unreleased material, all instrumental]
    Cassette: ST-48211
Songs: "America," "A Boy Like That," "Cool," "Gee, Officer Krupke," "I Feel Pretty," "I Have a Love," "Jet Song," "Maria," "One Hand, One Heart," "Something's Coming," "Somewhere," "Tonight (Balcony Scene)," "Tonight (Quintet)"

WESTSIDE03: *West Side Story* Studio Cast (1985)
    Deutsche Grammophon
    LP: 415 253-1[GH2]; 2-record set
    CD: 289 457 199-2
Songs: "America," "A Boy Like That," "Cool," "Gee, Officer Krupke," "I Feel Pretty," "I Have a Love," "Jet Song," "Maria," "One Hand, One Heart," "Something's Coming," "Somewhere," "Tonight (Balcony Scene)," "Tonight (Quintet)"

WESTSIDE04: *West Side Story* London Studio Cast (1993)
    IMG Records
    CD: IMGCD 1801
Songs: "America," "A Boy Like That," "Cool," "Gee, Officer Krupke," "I Feel Pretty," "I Have a Love," "Jet Song," "Maria," "One Hand, One Heart," "Something's Coming," "Somewhere," "Tonight (Balcony Scene)," "Tonight (Quintet)"

WESTSIDE05: *West Side Story* London Studio Cast (based on Leicester Haymarket Theatre Production) (1993) [includes multiple versions of some songs in both their stage and film versions]

TER Classics
 CD: CDTER2 1197
 Cassette: ZCTED 1197
Songs: "America," "A Boy Like That," "Cool," "Gee, Officer Krupke,"
"I Feel Pretty," "I Have a Love," "Jet Song," "Maria," "One Hand, One
Heart," "Something's Coming," "Somewhere," "Tonight (Balcony
Scene)," "Tonight (Quintet)"

WESTSIDE06: *West Side Story*, The Songs of (1996)
 RCAVictor/BMG
  CD: 09026-63707-2
  Cassette: 09026-62707-4
Songs: "America," "A Boy Like That," "Cool," "Gee, Officer Krupke,"
"I Feel Pretty," "I Have a Love," "Jet Song," "Maria," "One Hand, One
Heart," "Something's Coming," "Somewhere," "Tonight (Balcony
Scene)"

WESTSIDE07: *West Side Story*, Dave Grusin presents (1997)
 N2K Encoded Music
  CD: N2K-10021
Songs: "America," "Somewhere," "Tonight (Balcony Scene)"

WESTSIDE08: *West Side Story* London Production (1959)
 E.M.I. Records/His Master's Voice
  45rpm: 7EG/8429
Songs: "I Feel Pretty," "Maria," "One Hand, One Heart," "Tonight"

WESTSIDE09: *West Side Story* London Studio Cast (1966)
 MFP (Music For Pleasure)
  LP: MFP 50363 [previously released as MFP 1256]
Songs: "America," "A Boy Like That," "Cool," "Gee, Officer Krupke,"
"I Feel Pretty," "I Have a Love," "Jet Song," "Maria," "One Hand, One
Heart," "Something's Coming," "Tonight"

West Side Story [inaccurately described as "Original London Cast"; indi-
vidual song listings not included in body of discography as there is no
casting or other information]
 La Brea
  LP: L 8003
Songs: "America," "A Boy Like That," "The Dance at the Gym," "Gee,
Officer Krupke," "I Feel Pretty," "Jet Song," "Maria," "One Hand, One
Heart," "Tonight"

West Side Story [individual song listings not included in body of discography as there is no casting or other information] (1962)

Pickwick International/Design
LP: DLP-167
Songs: "Finale," "I Feel Pretty," "I Have a Love," "Maria," "Tonight"

West Side Story [described in one version as "Original English Cast"; individual song listings not included in body of discography]
SAGA
10" LP: STL 9100
LP: ERO 8106
FORUM
LP: SF 9045
Songs: "A Boy Like That," "Cool," "I Feel Pretty," "I Have a Love," "Maria," "One Hand, One Heart," "The Rumble," "Something's Coming," "Somewhere," "Tonight"

West Side Story, see also BERNSTEIN1: *Bernstein On Broadway*
West Side Story, see also DAVISS: *Sammy Davis Jr. at the Cocoanut Grove*
West Side Story, see also DRAKEA: *Alfred Drake & Roberta Peters Sing the Popular Music of Leonard Bernstein*
West Side Story, see also GARLAND: Judy Garland/*Judy Duets*

WILKO1: Oystein Wilk/*"Too Many Mornings" Songs by Sondheim* (1991)
Minos
CD: MCD 0000004
Songs: "Another Hundred People," "Anyone Can Whistle," "Finishing the Hat," "Good Thing Going," "I Remember," "Johanna," "Losing My Mind," "No One Is Alone," "Not a Day Goes By," "Not While I'm Around," "Pretty Women," "Send in the Clowns," "Someone Is Waiting," "Sooner or Later," "Too Many Mornings," "What Can You Lose?," "With So Little to Be Sure of"

WILSONJ1: *Julie Wilson at Brothers & Sisters* Volume Two (1975)
Arden
LP: B&S2
Songs: "Beautiful Girls," "Could I Leave You?," "The Ladies Who Lunch," "Losing My Mind," "The Story of Lucy and Jessie"

WILSONJ2: *Julie Wilson Sings the Stephen Sondheim Songbook* (1988)
DRG Records
LP: SL 5206
CD: CDSL 5206
Cassette: SLC 5206
Songs: "Beautiful Girls," "Can That Boy Foxtrot!," "Could I Leave You?," "Good Thing Going," "I Do Like You," "I Never Do Anything Twice," "I'm Still Here," "The Ladies Who Lunch," "Losing My Mind,"

"Love, I Hear," "Not a Day Goes By," "Not While I'm Around," "Send in the Clowns," "The Story of Lucy and Jessie," "Too Many Mornings," "With So Little to Be Sure of"

WILSONL1: Lambert Wilson/*Musicals* (1989)
EMI Records
CD: C 7 49792 2
Songs: "Finishing the Hat," "Johanna," "Maria," "Silly People"

WRIGHTB1: Bill Wright/*It Takes Two* (1994)
Wright/Marshall
CD: GVCD 9416
Songs: "It Takes Two" [2 versions], "The Little Things You Do To-gether," "Live Alone and Like It," "Old Friends," "Sorry-Grateful"

YORKJ1: Joe York/*My Favorite Year* (1998)
[No label name]
CD: [no number]
Songs: "Anyone Can Whistle," "No One Is Alone," "Not While I'm Around"

The following collections contain previously issued recordings:

A Collector's Sondheim (1985) [tracks with a superscript [1] are included in this collection]
RCA Records
LP: CRL4-5359 (S); 4-record set
Cassette: CRK4-5359; 4-tape set
CD: RCD3-5480; 3-disc set
Songs: "Ah, Paree!," "All Things Bright and Beautiful," " Auto Show," "The Ballad of Sweeney Todd," "Bang!," "Beautiful Girls," "Being Alive," "Broadway Baby," "Buddy's Blues," "Can That Boy Foxtrot!," "Children and Art," "Comedy Tonight," "Could I Leave You?," "Epiphany," "Fear No More," "The Glamorous Life," "The Glamorous Life (Letter Song)," "Happily Ever After," "The House of Marcus Ly-cus," "I Never Do Anything Twice," "I Remember," "I'm Still Here," "In Praise of Women," "Invocation and Instructions to the Audience," "It Wasn't Meant to Happen," "It's a Hit!," "Liaisons," "A Little Priest," "Little White House," "Losing My Mind," "Love Is in the Air," "Love Will See Us Through," "Marry Me a Little," "The Miller's Son," "Move On," "Night Waltz," "Night Waltz II," "Not a Day Goes By," "Old Friends," "Our Time," "Please Hello," "Pour le Sport," "Pretty Little Picture," "Pretty Women," "Salon at the Claridge #2," "Send in the Clowns," "Silly People," "So Many People," "Someone in a Tree,"

"Theme from *Stavisky*," "There Won't Be Trumpets," "There's Something About a War," "Too Many Mornings," "Two Fairy Tales," "Uptown, Downtown," "A Weekend in the Country," "Welcome to Kanagawa," "What More Do I Need?," "Who Could Be Blue?," "Your Eyes Are Blue," "You're Gonna Love Tomorrow"

Stephen Sondheim [includes original Broadway cast albums of *A Funny Thing Happened on the Way to the Forum*; *Company*; and *A Little Night Music*]
Time-Life Records "American Musicals" series
LP: STL-AM12
Cassette: 4TL-AM12

The Stephen Sondheim Songbook (1993) [tracks with a superscript [2] are included in this collection]
Sony Broadway
CD: SK-48201 [ADD]
Cassette: ST-48201
Songs: "Anyone Can Whistle, "Barcelona," "Being Alive," "The Boy From . . .," "Every Day a Little Death," "Gee, Officer Krupke," "The Ladies Who Lunch," "Liaisons," "The Little Things You Do Together," "Moon in My Window," "A Parade in Town," "Send in the Clowns," "Some People," "Something's Coming," "A Weekend in the Country," "We're Gonna Be All Right," "With So Little to Be Sure Of," "You Gotta Have a Gimmick," "You Must Meet My Wife"

The Sondheim Collection (1999) [tracks with a superscript [3] are included in this collection]
Varese Sarabande
CD: VSD-6012
Songs: "By the Sea," "Children Will Listen," "Every Day a Little Death," "Goodbye for Now," "I Remember," "Loving You," "Mama's Talkin' Soft," "Marry Me a Little," "More," "No One Is Alone," "Old Friends Part II," "Opening from *Follies*," "Send in the Clowns," "Sooner or Later," "That Old Piano Roll," "There's Always a Woman," "What Can You Lose?," "You Could Drive a Person Crazy," "You'll Never Get Away from Me"

The MUSICality of Sondheim (2002) [tracks with a superscript [4] are included in this collection]
JAY Records
CD: CDJAZ 9006
Songs: "Anyone Can Whistle," "Being Alive," "Broadway Baby," "Honey," "I Remember," "Liaisons," "Lion Dance," "Lovely," "Loving You," "Sooner or Later," "Stay with Me," "Wait," ["Honey," "Lovely," and "Wait" are new recordings]

The following are (predominantly) instrumental albums of Sondheim lyric-only scores

Do I Hear a Waltz?
    Percy Faith/*Do I Hear a Waltz?*, Columbia CL 2317, 1965
    The Ralph Sharon Trio/*Do I Hear a Waltz?*, Columbia CL 2321/CS 9121, [n.d.]

Gypsy
    Herb Geller and His all-stars play selections from Jule Styne and Stephen Sondheim's Music for "Gypsy", ATCO 33-109, [n.d.]
    Teddy Wilson and His Trio/*Gypsy in Jazz*, Columbia CL 1353, [n.d.]
    The Jack Sterling Quintet/*Music from Gypsy*, Columbia HL 7210, [n.d.]
    Tony Scott/*Tony Scott Plays "Gypsy"*, Signature SM6001, [n.d.]
    Urbie Green His Trombone and Rhythm, The Best of New Broadway Show Hits, RCA Victor LPM-1969, 1959 ["Small World" and "You'll Never Get Away from Me"]

West Side Story
    Stan Kenton/*Kenton's "West Side Story"*, Capitol T 1609, [n.d.]
    Manny Alban and His Jazz Greats/*Manny Alban and His Jazz Greats Play Music from the Broadway Musical "West Side Story"*, Coral CRL 57207, [n.d.]
    Bill Barron Orchestra/*West Side Story Bossa Nova*, Dauntless DS 6312, mono DM 4312, stereo DLP 25673, 1963
    Cal Tjader/*West Side Story*, Fantasy 3310, [n.d.]
    Oscar Peterson Trio/*West Side Story*, Verve V-8454, 1962

Music Acknowledgments

Music Acknowledgments

Passion (includes: "Clara/Giorgio," "Happiness," "4th Letter/Fosca's Ent," "Fosca" "I Wish I Could Forget You," "Soldiers," "Train," "Train Song, Sc. 11/Loving You," "Emperor Waltz," "Transition"
By: Stephen Sondheim

Sunday in the Park with George (includes: "George (painting)," "Move On," "Sunday in the Park/It's Hot," "Finishing the Hat/Putting It Together," "Act 1 Opening Prelude," "Alternate Pointilism " from "Color and Light," "Colors Are Talking" from "Color and Light," "Sunday," "Progression Up," "Miscellaneous," "Opening (George)"
By: Stephen Sondheim

Sweeney Todd (includes: "Johanna, Pt. II," "Home/There's No Place Like London," "Epiphany/Stravinsky Motif," "The Worst Pies in London," "My Friends," "Green Finch and Linnet Bird," "Final Scene," "Johanna (Judge Turpin)," "City on Fire," "Not Whole I'm Around," "Wait," "Prayer"
By: Stephen Sondheim

Index

About the Author

Mark Horowitz is a senior music specialist in the music division at the Library of Congress. He has been the archivist for the Library's Jerome Kern, Vincent Youmans, Cole Porter, Vernon Duke, Richard Rodgers, David Merrick, Frederick Loewe, and Leonard Bernstein Collections. He coproduced the Library's 70th Birthday Concert for Stephen Sondheim in 2000, and in 2002 presented the lecture series "Six by Sondheim," a joint presentation of the Library and the Smithsonian Resident Associates Program. While at the Library, he also taught "The History of the Musical on Stage and Screen" at Georgetown University; presented the lecture series "Masters of the Musical" for the Smithsonian; and has written articles and reviews for *The Sondheim Review* and the *Kurt Weill Quarterly*.

Prior to working at the Library, Horowitz worked at Arena Stage in Washington, D.C., for eleven years. Among the shows he worked on there were *Merrily We Roll Along, Tomfoolery, Animal Crackers,* and *God Bless You Mr. Rosewater,* the last directed by Howard Ashman. He is a graduate of Clark University in Worcester, Massachusetts and studied musical composition privately with Asher Zlotnick.